WORST
OF THE WORST
WORST

Other World Peace Foundation Books
by Robert I. Rotberg

Building a New Afghanistan
(2007)

Battling Terrorism in the Horn of Africa
(2005)

State Failure and State Weakness in a Time of Terror
(2003)

Ending Autocracy, Enabling Democracy:
The Tribulations of Southern Africa 1960–2000
(2002)

Peacekeeping and Peace Enforcement in Africa:
Methods of Conflict Prevention
(2000)

Creating Peace in Sri Lanka: Civil War and Reconciliation
(1999)

Burma: Prospects for a Democratic Future
(1998)

War and Peace in Southern Africa: Crimes, Drugs, Armies, Trade
(1998)

Haiti Renewed: Political and Economic Prospects
(1997)

Vigilance and Vengeance:
NGOs Preventing Ethnic Conflict in Divided Societies
(1996)

From Massacres to Genocide:
The Media, Public Policy, and Humanitarian Crises
(1996)

WORST
OF THE WORST
DEALING WITH REPRESSIVE AND ROGUE NATIONS

ROBERT I. ROTBERG

Editor

WORLD PEACE FOUNDATION
Cambridge, Massachusetts

BROOKINGS INSTITUTION PRESS
Washington, D.C.

Copyright © 2007
WORLD PEACE FOUNDATION
P.O. Box 382144
Cambridge, Massachusetts 02238

Worst of the Worst: Dealing with Repressive and Rogue Nations may be ordered from:
Brookings Institution Press
1775 Massachusetts Avenue, N.W.
Washington, D.C. 20036
Telephone: 1-800/537-5487 or 410/516-6956
E-mail: hfscustserv@press.jhu.edu;
www.brookings.edu

Library of Congress Cataloging-in-Publication data
Worst of the worst : dealing with repressive and rogue nations / Robert I. Rotberg, editor.
    p.   cm.
Summary: "Identifies and characterizes the most repressive states and singles out which are
aggressive. Defines the actions constituting repression and proposes a method of measuring
human rights violations, presenting an index of nation-state repressiveness. Offers a way to
decide which repressive and rogue states are most deserving of strong policy attention"—
Provided by publisher.
  Includes bibliographical references and index.
  ISBN-13: 978-0-8157-7566-9 (cloth : alk. paper)
  ISBN-10: 0-8157-7566-0 (cloth : alk. paper)
  ISBN-13: 978-0-8157-7567-6 (pbk. : alk. paper)
  ISBN-10: 0-8157-7567-9 (pbk. : alk. paper)
  1. Political persecution. 2. Human rights. 3. Despotism. 4. World politics—1989–
I. Rotberg, Robert I. II. World Peace Foundation. III. Title.
JC571.W8893 2007
323.4'9—dc22   2007023899

9 8 7 6 5 4 3 2 1

The paper used in this publication meets minimum requirements of the
American National Standard for Information Sciences—Permanence of Paper
for Printed Library Materials: ANSI Z39.48-1992.

Typeset in Minion and Univers Condensed

Composition by R. Lynn Rivenbark
Macon, Georgia

Printed by R. R. Donnelley
Harrisonburg, Virginia

Contents

Preface

A fair proportion—much too large—of the planet's people live day to day unfree, as helots in a modern world that is supposed to be enlightened and to permit, even enshrine, the individual pursuit of liberty and happiness. These unfortunates deserve better but are subject to tyrannies and tyrants that terrorize them, oppress them, and compel conformity to authoritarian whims and brutally anachronistic exactions. Some of the despotic rulers are sadists. Some are merely venal. All are kleptocrats. But whatever their personal styles, they repress their subjects both for the sheer pleasure of demonstrating omnipotence and for fear of losing power to rivals. Either motive leads to the steady ratcheting up of mechanisms of control: heavy policing, physical attacks, collective punishment, torture, arrest and imprisonment without fair trial, censorship, indoctrination, rigged elections, travel prohibitions, forced relocations, coerced labor, compulsory cultivation of cash crops, and more. Everything is forbidden unless it is expressly permitted. Capriciousness substitutes for reason; unpredictability for logic. All an inhabitant of such a stultifying regime receives is the security and stability of being repressed. Syrian President Hafiz al-Asad claimed that he and his subjects had concluded such a Faustian bargain—exchanging the loss of freedom for stability. But no subject ever knowingly acquiesces in such a bargain, for only the ruler and the state win.

Are there varieties of nation-state repression and tyranny? If so, what are they and how best can they be categorized? Is it possible to generalize, to typify repression, to differentiate among and between repressive regimes? Best of all, is it possible to discriminate—to measure the distinctive degrees of repression and rank order the repressive nation-states?

Those and similar questions are at the heart of this inquiry. Additionally, this book characterizes "rogue" nations—special examples of tyranny that are not only repressive but also aggressive. Those are the real "rogues," as distinguished from the casual foreign policy declamation and declaration of roguedom.

This book includes chapters on gross repressors, on high repressors, and on aggressive repressors or rogues. It indicates how a nation-state falls into one of those three odious categories and what happens in such nation-states. It does not propose remedies, nor does it offer the obvious panacea of democracy's spread.

Under the auspices of the Kennedy School of Government's Program on Intrastate Conflict and Conflict Resolution and the World Peace Foundation, the participants of three meetings held in 2004 sought to understand the nature of roguishness, state repression, and state aggressiveness in the current state of world disorder. The academic, diplomatic, and practitioner participants at these meetings grappled with what these terms meant in practice, on the ground, and how the terms were deployed for policy purposes. Ultimately, spirited discussion and disagreement culminated in the writing of case studies, most of which are now contained in heavily revised form in this book and in the formulation of a number of theoretical constructs. The contents of this book grew out of that dialogue, and the conclusions presented here in more mature form have been subject to serious reconsideration and reconceptualization.

This book follows and is conceptually related to two books on the nature of nation-state failure and a report and an article on the meaning of governance in global politics. The books and, primarily, the report and article focus on methods of assessing governance and distinguishing strong, weak, failing, and collapsed states. In particular, the report and the article advocate objective measurements, explicit rankings, and the construction of indexes, and offer specific indicators and subindicators.[1] This volume is also about how best to provide accurate measures of repression and rogueness in nation-states.

Some of the country cases in this volume are moving targets. As this book moved through production, some of the gross repressors and the high repressors exerted even heavier exactions on their subjects, and a few backpedaled. Civil wars occurred. A few despots aged rapidly or otherwise appeared to come to the end of their power. Others are at the beginning of their reigns, and one provided direct testimony to one of our authors. This book reflects the situation in nearly every country through March 2007. In a few cases, changes have been made in proofs at an even later stage.

Analyzing repressors, aggressors, and rogues entails major conceptual as well as temporal challenges. As editor, I am enormously grateful to the contributors to this book, many of whom are close observers or intimately involved in the affairs of their country cases. Each contributor cheerfully responded to several calls for revision and to questions of fact and interpretation. Debbie West helped superbly to keep the project together and to edit the volume. Marisa Bassett and Heather Jensen provided timely and critical research assistance. Elisa Pepe organized the original conferences with panache. Among the gifted conferees, aside from the chapter authors, Barbara Bodine, Ashton T. Carter, Chester Crocker, Rust Deming, Richard Jones, Theodore Khattouf, Robert Legvold, and Monica D. Toft were strong and persuasive participants. I greatly appreciate their significant contributions as well the affirmative support of Philip Khoury, chair, and the other trustees of the World Peace Foundation, and Graham Allison, the director of the Belfer Center on Science and International Affairs in the Kennedy School.

ROBERT I. ROTBERG
May 2007

Note

1. Robert I. Rotberg (ed.), *State Failure and State Weakness in a Time of Terror* (Washington, D.C., 2003); Rotberg (ed.), *When States Fail: Causes and Consequences* (Princeton, 2004); Robert I. Rotberg and Deborah L. West, "The Good Governance Problem: Doing Something about It," WPF Report 39 (Cambridge, Mass., 2004); Rotberg, "Strengthening Governance: Ranking Countries Would Help," *Washington Quarterly*, XXVIII (2004).

one

Repressive, Aggressive, and Rogue Nation-States: How Odious, How Dangerous?

Robert I. Rotberg

In the post–cold war era, some of the greatest threats to global stability come not from powerful hegemonic powers battling each other but from smaller, much less intrinsically powerful polities refusing to abide by the common principles of reciprocity and civility that guide world order. Many of these weak, outlaw nations attack their own people; they are seriously repressive, showing no respect for human rights and disdaining basic freedoms and democratic values. These heavy repressors breach official international conventions and covenants (such as the International Covenant on Economic, Social, and Cultural Rights and the International Covenant on Civil and Political Rights), and offend against unofficial global human rights norms. A handful of these internally abusive nation-states also behave in a provocative, pugnacious manner regionally; they are aggressive to their neighbors and serial offenders against world order. It is the actions and postures of these two kinds of nation-states—the gross repressors and the hostile, aggressive repressors—not rivalries among the big powers, that are currently the causes of conflict and the main perils to the peace of the world.

This book attempts, in the first decade of the twenty-first century, to specify attributes common to those of the world's nation-states that behave odiously and in a truly troubling manner—those that operate beyond the international normative pale. From a human rights perspective—and presuming its value in an orderly world—those states are the worst of the worst. They breach a variety of "civilized" norms. They undermine regional and global stability.

This book seeks a common understanding of what constitutes gross repression by nation-states. It defines the kinds of actions that constitute repression and proposes a method of measuring repressiveness (human rights violations by nation-states). It further advances the possibility of creating a scale capable of distinguishing among the repressors according to the quality of their predatory rapaciousness. By thus formulating the basis of an index of nation-state repressiveness, with a rank ordering of miscreants and malefactors among countries, we create a valuable diagnostic tool capable of guiding the United Nations and big powers as they seek to mitigate manifest injustice and curb tyranny in the developing world. Such an index would also identify and target gross offenders of the "responsibility to protect" norm, which the UN is pledged to enforce.[1] In this book, each of the regimes discussed is repressive toward its own citizens. North Korea, Turkmenistan, Burma, Zimbabwe, and Equatorial Guinea are much more repressive than the others, and are designated here as gross repressors. The remaining countries—Belarus, Uzbekistan, Syria, Togo, and Tunisia—are deemed somewhat less nasty to their own citizens but are still highly repressive internally.

This book also seeks to characterize and measure aggressiveness among repressors, and to single out as a category for separate study those nation-states that rank high on both the repressive and aggressive axes of a carefully delineated representation of nation-state behavior. Although many scholars and policymakers tend loosely to label both the most heavily repressive states and the aggressive repressors as rogue states, this book seeks to reserve that pejorative designation primarily for the handful of national repressors that are also aggressive. Analytically, the term "rogue state" should be reserved for the North Koreas and Irans of the world—those nation-states that both immiserate their own citizens and also act belligerently and in a destabilizing manner toward the rest of the world. Of the cases discussed in this book, only North Korea, Belarus, and Syria are true rogues because they marry high levels of internal repression with aggressive behavior to their neighbors and beyond.[2] North Korea spreads weapons of mass destruction (WMD), Belarus exports arms and drugs (as does North Korea), and Syria sponsors terrorism.[3]

The Nature of Repression

All repressive states, by definition, greatly abuse their own citizens. They prey on them. They deny all or virtually all fundamental human rights and civil liberties; eschew or make mockery of democracy; use the mailed fist to compel obedience and achieve compliance with the demands (even whims) of their rulers or ruling juntas; obliterate the rule of law and instead follow the law of the jungle; assassinate opponents and take political prisoners; favor collective punishment of families, groups, and lineages; often are capricious in their policies and actions; totally command their economies; inhibit individual prosperity; are seriously corrupt; operate patrimonially, with fawning clients; build a personality cult while otherwise minimizing ideology; and often manage over many years to create a culture of dependency and conformity. In some cases, these repressive regimes even starve their followers, withholding food rations from most citizens while their rulers live luxuriously.

The essence of such state-enforced terror is its unpredictable arbitrariness, the absence of explanation, the lack of any means whereby wrongs can, even theoretically, be redressed, and the inculcation of a widespread feeling of mental impotence and lethargy. Dictators and authoritarian regimes intimidate their citizens by whimsical, quixotic, bizarrely idiosyncratic behaviors (as each of the cases in this book exemplifies) and by seductive forms of co-optation—all well mixed together with mindless brutalities. Malevolent rulers are clever enough to manipulate their subjects and simultaneously to keep them supinely in thrall. The sinister François (Papa Doc) Duvalier, dictator of Haiti in the 1950s and 1960s, provides an instructive example of how such regimes suppress individuality and enforce obedience. "Haiti," a contemporary report concluded, "is the paralytic fear of a capricious dictatorial regime of unusual malevolence; none but the most secure Haitians are immune from the stabbing anxiety which afflicts all [of their] days and nights. . . . The dominant feature of the dictatorship is its arbitrariness: the blue-serge-suited Al Capone-like figures who live in the white rococo presidential palace have never thought twice about drawing a revolver from their shoulder holsters and mutilating someone suspected of antagonism, disobedience, or mere idiosyncratic behavior." Nothing of any moment "happens without [Duvalier's] specific approval."[4]

Using the criteria set out above and additional indicators, it is possible to rank nation-states according to their levels of depravity—according to the extent to which each preys mercilessly on its own people. Rather than differentiating impressionistically between repressive and not so repressive states, and in order to distinguish more precisely the worst of the worst from the merely unpleasant, one can assign objective numerical scores to each aspect of a state's repressiveness. One state holds more political prisoners annually and across time than another. A second assassinates opponents, and the number and frequency of those mysterious deaths can be counted. The denial of basic freedoms can be documented and assessed, and given a score based on an objective set of measurements. The absence of any rule of law would be compared to other polities with diminished legal provisions. A state's command of its economy would be noted and evaluated. Food scarcities would be documented. Degrees of corruption would be approximated using existing measurement techniques.

Overall, it is possible both theoretically and practically to measure the repressiveness of individual states, using many more, and more refined, indicators and subindicators than those employed in the construction of the otherwise worthy index proposed by Caprioli and Trumbore in chapter 2. Such a new, comprehensive system, ranking repressors and human rights violators more clearly and more objectively (that is, not by the employment of opinions and survey data) than existing methods (including the tripartite "free," "partly free," and "unfree" parsings of Freedom House), would separate—even gradate—those states that qualify as grossly repressive or very highly repressive from those that fall below such thresholds. Of the cases in this book, for example, North Korea obviously represses its people with a greater fervor and ferocity than does Tunisia. But Tunisia is still sufficiently repressive, by our criteria, to qualify as highly repressive, and the proposed ranking system would display that behavioral pattern quantitatively.

The availability of such a carefully researched and classified catalogue of repressive regimes would enable international and national policymakers to focus appropriately on such extreme offenders of established or emerging behavioral norms. Instead of responding to ad hoc claims or impressionistic reports, defenders of world order and the UN conventions on human rights and against genocide—as well as the new responsibility to protect norm—would then be equipped to craft effective responses, knowing that accusations of regime misbehavior were concretely based on methods of collecting and arraying data that themselves possessed the virtues of transparency and comparison.

Fortunately, the proposition that human rights and other violations can be measured follows and is derived from the proposal that governance is itself measurable, using proxy indicators and subindicators, and that repressive states are fundamentally nation-states that deliver the least good governance to their peoples. This measurement paradigm, explored at length elsewhere, assumes that nation-states exist to deliver political goods such as security, rule of law, political freedom, economic opportunity, education, health, and a functional infrastructure. Repressive states provide little of those goods, except

Table 1-1. Indicators of Repression: A Checklist[a]

Outputs	Inputs
Political prisoners	Number of police per head
House arrestees	Number of security forces per head
Abuses of prisoners	Interference with privacy
Secret Incarcerations	Restrictions on religious freedom
Assassinations or attempted murders of political opponents	Travel restrictions
Disappearances	Restrictions on press and speech
Torture cases	Restrictions on freedom of assembly and association
Collective punishment	Rule of law abuses
Conformity imposition	Judicial independence
Pretrial detention duration	Denial of basic rights to food
Violence against women	State-sponsored corruption (Transparency International rankings)
Forced abortions	Personality cult (for example, existence of "Little Green Book")
Child labor incidence	
Trafficking of women and children	Internet harassment and restrictions
Trafficking of small arms	Discrimination against minorities
Trafficking of narcotics	

a. The higher the value per capita of population per year, the more repressive the regime.

for security (the reverse twist of denial and oppression), so they can be scored according to already developed criteria.[5] In addition, to assess a repressive state's true character more finely, additional indicators of repression can be used as measurement tools and appropriate numbers developed. Table 1-1 lists the different repressive practices that are capable of being quantified.

That explained, it is important heuristically to understand the value and possibility of measuring repressiveness—of arraying human rights violators according to sets of objective criteria—even though in practice it can sometimes prove exceedingly difficult to measure the actual performance of the worst of the worst in a strictly quantitative manner. A fundamental problem is the paucity of good data. Those nation-states that deserve scrutiny and qualify for it on anecdotal or impressionistic grounds have the most to hide. They rarely provide or publish accurate statistics. Numbers of assassinations and prisoners as well as violations of human rights must be gathered clandestinely or estimated from credible rumors. Repressive regimes themselves will not offer up infractions for outside inspection or admit to wrongdoing. The necessary data must be gathered from fugitive sources, making quantification questionable and precision impossible.[6] Nevertheless, it is critical—as the chapters that follow explain—to provide the basis of a framework for measuring repressiveness within and among states. Without it, throwing up pejorative designations like "very highly repressive" or "rogue" has little analytical meaning or utilitarian value. Too easily, a nation-state is now said in quasi-diplomatic parlance to exhibit roguish behavior merely whenever a big power such as the United States becomes displeased.

Aggressiveness and Repression

Among the worst states in the world are a number that behave excessively badly toward their own people; they oppress and repress them systematically, and over long periods. But not all of those miserable human rights performers endanger other nation-states, even their neighbors. Only a few nation-states at any one time are both significantly repressive on one scale and, on the other scale, decidedly aggressive in their neighborhood or exporters of danger beyond their borders. It is the intersection of the two scales that describes "aggressive repressors." In order to qualify, a nation-state must demonstrate disdain for the rights and liberties of its own citizens and disdain for world order norms by behaving aggressively beyond its borders.

Many more nation-states are repressive than are aggressive. That is, not all repressive states, despite a predilection to aggression and danger, flout the procedures of world order. (Caprioli and Trumbore suggest otherwise.)[7] To do so as outlaws, as disturbers of the global system in the sense that former secretary of state Madeleine Albright described, they have to possess or be working to develop WMD, sponsor or give support to terrorists, or traffic in fissile material, WMD components, long-range or short-range delivery systems, small arms, or narcotics. (WMD includes chemical and biological warfare as well as nuclear warfare capability.) Additionally, even if they do not engage in these activities, such countries still may be considered aggressive if, within their neighborhood or region, they foment trouble or destabilize their own areas. Libya certainly was dangerous in that last sense, as well as in some of the aforementioned ways. Liberia and Burkina Faso also sought to undermine their neighbors in West Africa, succeeding for a time. Belarus and North Korea are state suppliers of small arms. They also traffic in narcotics, and North Korea has gained infamy and foreign exchange by counterfeiting currency. But some of the more odiously internally repressive states, like Equatorial Guinea or Zimbabwe, have not been accused of trafficking violations or of deliberately attempting to destabilize their regions.

Measuring most forms of aggression or dangerousness is obviously both easy—the International Atomic Energy Agency tries to monitor WMD violations, as do the big powers; the U.S. State Department names sponsors of terror; and suppliers of arms and drugs are generally listed—and elusive, since most of the alleged activity is illicit and covert. (Measuring nuclear capability is easier than discovering chemical and biological warfare capability, as the inspections of prewar Iraq amply demonstrate.) Even so, more precision is necessary to separate the unquestionably aggressive states from those whose infractions of international codes of behavior are serious but less threatening or destabilizing to the global system. Greater objectivity is desperately needed if high levels of aggressiveness, together with gross repressiveness, are going to qualify a nation-state for rogue status. Thus a method of quantifying levels of aggression or dangerousness is here proposed. It scores countries depending on the level of their trafficking of small arms, narcotics, and fissile material; backing, funding, and export of terror; possession of or attempted possession of WMD; and number and extent of cross-border attacks within a recent five-year period. (See figure 1-1 and table 1-2.)

Using those numbers permits answers to questions such as, is Iran more or less dangerous to international order than North Korea—or Pakistan? Responses to such questions hitherto have been based on impressionistic or ad hoc criteria. One of the purposes of this book is to offer more specific methods of answering such questions and to provide transparent ways of deciding which among the grossly repressive states are the real rogues and deserving of greater policy attention.

Qualifying as a Rogue State

Those nation-states in today's world that are both highly repressive internally and highly aggressive externally can be classified as rogues. (See table 1-2.) Depending on their externally oriented activities, even straightforward repressive states may qualify for rogue status and thus for strong policy attention.

Regardless of whether the rogue label makes sense analytically, the term remains in public discourse. As a shorthand expression of particular opprobrium, it became popular in the 1990s. After the "evil empire" was dispatched and America's global power ascendance was assured, world order was still disturbed by jumped-up nation-states that breached international norms of behavior, outrageously and always egregiously. From Washington's perspective, those were the nation-states that played by no known rules of world order, pursuing at best idiosyncratic designs. They disregarded Washington's predominant military might and followed autarkic rather than collegial, consensual, or respectful policy trajectories. First in the Clinton administration

Figure 1-1. Repression and Aggression: A Display

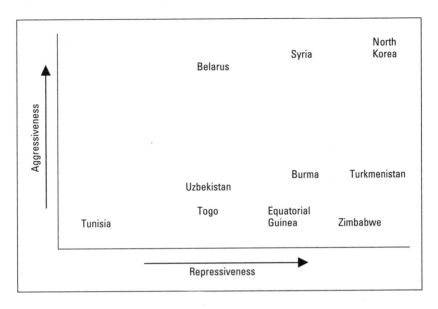

and then in the George W. Bush administration, Washington began calling these outlaw, anomic, unsavory, and troublesome places "rogues."

A rogue is an outlier, an elephant pushed out of the herd. Horses that misbehave or shirk are rogues. Worse, animals are rogues when they are vicious and destructive. For humans, *rogue* once referred to criminals, tramps, or scoundrels. It still carries those definitions but also connotes a dishonest or worthless person. Rogues are caddish, disreputable, and unsavory, with questionable antecedents and impure intentions. Etymologically derived from *rogare* (Latin, to ask and to beg), the word slipped into *roger* in mid-sixteenth century English (a begging vagabond pretending to be a poor scholar from Oxford or Cambridge). That usage possibly led to the use of *rogue* to describe a class of vagrants and unprincipled persons.[8] Whatever the precise etymological origin of the word, it was always employed pejoratively. Likewise, by the late twentieth century, there could be little uncertainty about the meaning of Washington's labels. Rogues simply did not belong to the family of nations. Their bizarre, unprincipled, cantankerous methods of operating in the global arena set them outside its bounds.

In 1996, President Clinton called Iran and Iraq rogue states. He spoke in 1997 and 1998 of the vulnerability of the United States to the "reckless acts of

Table 1-2. Characteristics of Countries in the Sample[a]

Country	Repressiveness and aggressiveness	True rogue
Belarus	Highly repressive and aggressive	Yes
Burma	Grossly repressive	No
Equatorial Guinea	Grossly repressive	No
North Korea	Grossly repressive and aggressive	Yes
Syria	Highly repressive and aggressive	Yes
Togo	Highly repressive	No
Tunisia	Highly repressive	No
Turkmenistan	Grossly repressive	No
Uzbekistan	Highly repressive	No
Zimbabwe	Grossly repressive	No

Source: Author's calculations.

a. Based on a scale that depends on the level of their trafficking of small arms, narcotics, and fissile material; backing, funding, and export of terror; possession of or attempted possession of WMD; and number and extent of cross-border attacks within a recent five-year period.

rogue states" and to "an unholy axis of terrorists, drug traffickers, and international criminals." They were the "twenty-first century predators." As Hoyt shows so well, the Clinton administration's thirty-six leading policy articulators condemned rogue or pariah states more than 150 times throughout the 1990s.[9]

Anthony Lake, former president Clinton's national security adviser, identified nation-states "on the wrong side of history" because they failed to respect basic international values such as democracy, the market economy, collective security, and the peaceful settlement of disputes. "Our policy," wrote Lake, "must face the reality of recalcitrant and outlaw states that not only choose to remain outside the family but also assault its basic values." Lake named Cuba, North Korea, Iran, Iraq, and Libya as "backlash" states. "Their behavior is often aggressive and defiant." They suppressed human rights and had embarked on costly military programs to produce weapons of mass destruction. They had exhibited siege mentalities.[10]

Then secretary of state Albright said that dealing with "rogue states" was one of the "great challenges of our time" because rogues' "sole purpose" was destroying "the system." The very essence of "rogue states," said Albright, involved being outside the international system and "throwing, literally, hand grenades inside in order to destroy it."[11] Albright much later decided for tactical reasons to refer to this class of adversary—supporters of terrorism, developers of missiles, and disrupters of international order—as "states of concern." Those states, whether of concern or as rogues, desired to disrupt the international system.[12] Rogue states, in other words, were the primary policy worry of the post–cold war era; rogues collectively and individually replaced the Soviet Union as the repositories of evil.

The second Bush administration's National Missile Defense system and reports emanating from the Pentagon were predicated on countering rogue states. Even before the destruction of the World Trade Center's twin towers on September 11, 2001, Secretary of State Colin L. Powell declared that the United States required a missile defense shield for protection against rogue states. "We believe," he said, "that it was Washington's responsibility to protect against rogue states."[13] President Bush conflated rogue behavior with evil behavior. In today's dangerous world, he worried about the world's least responsible states—nation-states for whom "terror and blackmail" were a way of life. The "axis of evil" was composed of roguish states.[14]

Commentators and scholars, both present and past, employed the appellation "rogue" to describe those polities that opposed the dominant powers in the international system (especially the United States), showed aggressiveness, operated in a manner that troubled world order, were human rights violators, or otherwise flouted international law. Possessors of WMD and sponsors of terrorism obviously were rogues because they refrained from obeying international standards. Rogues were "crazy" states.

Henriksen's rogue states are those that exhibit contempt for international norms, as per Albright's model.[15] Klare's definition echoes Lake: his rogues are those "hostile (or seemingly hostile) Third World state[s] . . . with large military forces and nascent WMD capabilities . . . bent on sabotaging the prevailing world order." They oppose the spread of democracy and harbor aggressive intentions toward less powerful neighbors.[16] The actions of such states are unpredictable and hence roguish.

Calling a nation a rogue state admittedly inhibits dispute and conflict resolution. Yet policymakers are going to continue to decry annoying or difficult states as rogues. It is a form of Washingtonian shorthand and will not easily be replaced. At a series of meetings that preceded the writing of this book, participants initially decided that the word "rogue" should be banished because it lacked precise and uncontested analytical content. Later, after lengthy discussion, the participants concluded reluctantly that the word would continue to be used by politicians, regardless of what analysts preferred. Therefore, it was important to attempt to give the essence of rogueness in international relations meaningful content. In their chapter, Caprioli and Trumbore also argue that providing a specific designation for "states that systematically violate international norms [and] are . . . dangerous to international society is valuable[,] . . . [calling on] us to think seriously about the . . . factors that lead states toward . . . dangerous international behavior."[17]

Rather than simply drop the word *rogue* from the analytical vocabulary, it is more productive to define precisely how and when a nation-state becomes classified as a rogue. Before the end of the cold war, the term *rogue* was used much more narrowly by a limited coterie of scholars to describe a nasty nation-state that refused to treat its inhabitants decently—that is, in accord with the provisions of the Universal Declaration of Human Rights. In one of their several pathbreaking articles, Caprioli and Trumbore argue that for the term *rogue* to possess analytical utility, its usage should be restricted to "domestic characteristics of state repression and domestic inequality." They wanted the designation to be used only for those states that "systematically allow domestic discrimination and inequality on the basis of ethnicity and gender, and perpetrate systematic repression against their own citizens." However, Caprioli and Trumbore went on to contend that such discriminators and repressors would always exhibit aggression and violence internationally.[18]

This volume offers a fuller, measurable, and more comprehensive definition. Rogues, to repeat, are only those few nation-states that exhibit grossly repressive and unquestionably aggressive tendencies. The existing policy and academic usages are too imprecise, too ad hoc, and too rhetorical by design to give the quality of being a rogue state sufficient meaning and analytical utility. Despite the attractiveness of the Caprioli and Trumbore index, and their detailed argument that repressiveness predisposes a nation-state to behave in a "roguish" manner, I prefer to classify nation-states according to the degrees of their repressiveness internally and aggression externally. Such a system of ranking is capable of distinguishing the world's worst states from those that abuse their own citizens or behave badly but—compared to the truly atrocious examples—merely constitute international embarrassments. It is possible, in other words, to compare and parse distinctions in practice between, say, North Korea and Cambodia, or Equatorial Guinea and Gabon.

At the core of this search for the common characteristics of the world's most unsavory and dangerous nation-states is the quest to develop satisfactory ways of measuring and assessing the nature and extent of a nation-state's repression.[19] In their chapter for this book, Caprioli and Trumbore suggest that rogue states can be identified by measuring a specific, limited set of human rights violations. Persistent violators among states pose both conventional and unconventional threats to international security. They are the states that refuse to protect against human rights attacks within their own borders. They discriminate on grounds of ethnicity, religion, language, and gender. Moreover, the same attitude that favors abuses of human rights can express itself in a state's international as well as its other domestic behavior. Nation-states that prey upon their own people are illegitimate both internally and externally.

Caprioli and Trumbore construct a rogue state index to classify "human rights rogues."[20] The index represents political and economic discrimination on the basis of gender and ethnicity, and violent attacks on political opponents. This method codes for public policies that have affected or are affecting a group's political status, exclusion, or other restriction vis-à-vis other groups within the same society. The authors are consequently able to affix scores to the performance of a country, based on state discrimination against out-groups. They can do the same for discrimination against and relative economic and social opportunities afforded to women. Their repression measure includes the prevalence of political imprisonment, torture, disappearances, and so on. They provide a table listing average index scores by country for 1980–2001; Sweden is the least repressive state; Iran, the most repressive.

Additionally, Caprioli and Trumbore show that highly repressive rogues (by their definition) are more aggressive externally and more apt to sponsor terrorism. They also have been more likely to pursue or possess WMD.

Caprioli and Trumbore, effectively in the vanguard of scientific studies of the rogue phenomenon among states, have been inventive and innovative, not least in their chapter for this book. But, as helpful as their carefully calibrated methodological proposal may be, it narrows the range of potential measures of repression, and it also relies on data gathered by others for different purposes. A fuller repertoire of possible indicators and subindicators of repression would provide more points of comparison and more complex ways to distinguish venal from somewhat less venal nation-states. The goal is to be able to aggregate any nation-state's human rights and analogous failings, using quantifiable measurements that are not derived primarily from compilations by others of subjectively obtained data.

Repressive nation-states endanger their own citizens and consequently are serious threats to national, regional, and international order. State-sponsored repression, often directed at ethnic, linguistic, religious, or other minorities or majorities, leads to civil wars and carnage. Sometimes war and carnage infect a broader region, as in West Africa. Even if repression within a state remains confined, the suffering of target populations constitutes a grave threat to world order. Repressive states thus are "dangerous" globally on that account alone. But they attain full status as "rogues" if, additionally, they are aggressive—if they seek confrontationally to destabilize world order.

The Cases

The sample of country cases in this book was chosen to provide a range of nation-state examples of repression and aggression, or both. Even before the chapters were written and this book prepared, these countries were suspect as serious human rights violators and, in some cases, as notorious WMD proliferators. Obviously, these were normative presumptions, but those preconceptions had yet to be tested. Moreover, the gradations among the nation-states accused of repressive tendencies could only have been guessed at, a priori. How the cases would be arrayed and sorted was not known. Only much later did it become clear, as it is now, that there is a set of grossly repressive polities and another set of highly (but not grossly) repressive states. Furthermore, the true rogue states are both grossly repressive and highly aggressive; they lie at the intersection between the repressive and aggressive axes.[21] Of the arguably most repressive nation-states among our selected cases—North Korea, Burma, Turkmenistan, Zimbabwe, and Equatorial Guinea—only the first is truly dangerous and therefore an outstanding rogue. If Iran may be considered (and measured) as less repressive than the members of the first group, it still has aggressive tendencies as a wannabe WMD proliferator and serial sponsor of terrorism. Its designation as a rogue thus ultimately depends on its double ranking along the two axes.

Many of the worst of the worst country examples are gathered in this volume, but not all. Most of our sample is drawn from the ranks of developing nations. Many repressors are small in terms of population numbers, but a few exhibit average demographic densities. Not all are low-income countries. Some are wealthy from oil or gas extraction, on an average per capita basis, and a few are growing rapidly, again because of petroleum. But among the wealthy, unequal distribution is the norm, with remarkably skewed Gini coefficients. Tables 1-3 and 1-4 array salient demographic, human development, educational, and economic characteristics of the country cases in this book, and several others, for easy comparison.

Adding to and expanding upon these tables, Yi Feng and Saumik Paul have examined available quantitative data from standard sources for our sample (and for Cuba, Iran, Saudi Arabia, and the Sudan) of highly repressive states, assessing both the quality of the data and their meaning.[22] Their findings enable us to sort our countries according to their degrees of political freedom, political stability, rule of law, control of corruption, and amount of accountability. Feng and Paul supplement the array of economic statistics

Table 1-3. The Worst of the Worst: Comparative Profiles, 2005
Units as indicated

Countries	Human Development Index (HDI) rank (177 = least developed)[a]	GDP per capita (in U.S.$)[b]	Population, 2003 (millions)	Literacy rate (percent) Male	Literacy rate (percent) Female	Life expectancy at birth (years)	Infant mortality rate (per 1,000 live births)[c]
Rogues							
Belarus	67	2,299	9.9	99.8	99.4	68.1	13.37
Burma (Myanmar)	129	n.a.	49.5	93.7	86.2	60.2	63.56
Equatorial Guinea	121	6,393	0.5	92.1	76.4	43.3	91.16
North Korea[i]	n.a.	n.a.	22.9	99.0	99.0	71.4	24.04
Syria	106	1,301	18.1	91.0	74.2	73.3	29.53
Togo	143	415	5.8	68.5	38.3	54.3	62.20
Tunisia	89	2,815	9.9	83.4	65.3	73.3	24.77
Turkmenistan	97	1,251	4.7	99.3	98.3	62.4	73.08
Uzbekistan	111	461	25.8	99.6	98.9	66.5	71.10
Zimbabwe	145	1,350	12.9	93.8	86.3	36.9	52.34
Comparisons							
Azerbaijan	101	1,029	8.3	99.5	98.2	66.9	81.74
Iran	99	2,431	68.2	83.5	70.4	70.4	41.58
Saudi Arabia	77	10,793	23.3	87.1	69.3	71.8	13.24

Source: Except where noted, all data are from UN Development Programme, *Human Development Report 2005* (September 7, 2005), hdr.undp.org/reports/global/2005/.

a. Interestingly, none of the rogue states fall in the "Low Human Development" category. All of them qualify as "Medium Human Development" states, and some are actually quite close to the top of that categorization (most notably, Belarus).

b. GDP per capita calculated using World Bank, "Quick References Tables," web.worldbank.org.

c. CIA, *The World Factbook* (April 2005).

d. For comparison, the high-HDI country average is 2.1 percent of 2003 GDP. (Some high spenders include the United States, at 3.8 percent, and Israel, at 9.1 percent. Data for several significant states, such as Taiwan and Cuba, are missing.) The average for medium-HDI countries is 2.5 percent. (Some states' data are missing, but in the "medium" category, these are generally small states that probably spend little.)

e. Transparency International, "2005 Corruption Perceptions Index," www.transparency.org/policy_research/surveys_indices/cpi/2005. Note that in some cases, states are tied in their rankings in this index.

f. Heritage Foundation, "2005 Index of Economic Freedom," www.heritage.org/research/features/index/countries.cfm. Note that in some cases, states are tied in their rankings in this index.

shown in tables 1-3 and 1-4, using GNI rather than per capita GDP and for slightly different years. They show foreign direct investment amounts as well as foreign assistance per capita. Feng and Paul enhance the social numbers in the tables, adding an important gender dimension. (Caprioli and Trumbore's index also emphasizes gender.) They import official figures for the degree of religious freedom in the sample countries. Finally, the authors construct and analyze composite indexes. Their findings indicate a strong correlation

Telecommunications density (per 1,000 population)		Total armed forces	Military expenditure percentage (of 2003 GDP)[d]	Develop- ment aid received (millions of U.S.$)	Corruption rank (158 = most corrupt)[e]	Economic freedom rank (155 = most repressed)[f]	Freedom House ranking[g]
Telephone lines	Internet users						
311	141	73,000	1.3[h]	31.9	107	143	Not free
7	1	378,000	3.4[i]	125.8	155	154	Not free
18	n.a.	1,000	n.a.	21.3	152	118	Not free
48	n.a.[k]	1,000,000	33.9[l]	m	Not ranked	155	Not free
n.a.	35	297,000	7.1	160.3	70	139	Not free
12	42	9,000	1.6	44.8	Not ranked	Not ranked	Not free
118	64	35,000	0.9	305.5	43	83	Not free
77	n.a.	26,000	n.a.	27.2	155	151	Not free
67	19	14,000	0.5	194.4	137	147	Not free
n.a.	n.a.	29,000	2.1	186.4	107	151	Not free
114	n.a.	67,000	1.9	296.7	137	103	Not free
220	72	540,000	3.8	133.1	88	148	Not free
155	67	200,000	8.7	21.9	70	72	Not free

g. Freedom House, "Freedom in the World 2005: Comparative Measures of Freedom," www.freedomhouse.org/research/freeworld/2005/table2005.pdf. Countries are ranked either "free," "partly free," or "not free."

h. Russia pays for some of it.

i. 1990 value; has presumably increased as forces have nearly doubled.

j. Unless otherwise noted, data on North Korea are from CIA, *World Factbook* (2005), www.cia.gov/cia/publications/factbook/geos/kn.html.

k. Presumed little to none.

l. Estimate. Figure from NationMaster, "Military Statistics. Expenditures: Percent of GDP by Country" (2007), www.nationmaster.com/graph-T/mil_exp_per_of_gdp. According to the CIA *World Factbook*, North Korea is estimated to spend approximately $5.2 billion on its military annually.

m. Food aid provided to North Korea since 1995 valued at approximately $1.5 billion. UN World Food Programme, "World Hunger–Korea (DPR)" (2005), www.wfp.org/country_brief/indexcountry.asp?region=5&section=9&sub_section=5&country=408.

between their political and economic indexes, but only moderate correlation between the political index and the social index.

If a citizen had to live in one of these repressive societies, they show how to choose among them depending on whether political, economic, or social standards were the main criterion. Unfortunately, however, even the analysis of fundamental data by Feng and Paul cannot fully provide more than a rough approximation of repressiveness in the world's worst states.

Table 1-4. The Worst of the Worst: Comparative Profiles, 2006
Units as indicated

Countries	Human Development Index rank, 2006 (177 = least developed)	GNI per capita, 2006 (in U.S.$)[a]	Population, 2004 (millions)	Literacy rate, 2004 (percent)		Life expectancy at birth, 2004 (years)	Infant mortality rate, 2004 (per 1,000 live births)[b]
				Male	Female		
Rogues							
Belarus	67	2,760	9.8	99.8	99.4	68.2	13.00
Burma (Myanmar)	130	n.a.	50.0	93.9	86.4	60.5	61.85
Equatorial Guinea	120	n.a.	0.5	93.4	80.5	42.8	89.21
North Korea[g]	n.a.	n.a.	23.1	99.0	99.0	71.7	23.29
Syria	107	1,380	18.6	86.0	73.6	73.6	28.61
Togo	147	350	6.0	68.7	38.5	54.5	60.63
Tunisia	87	2,890	10.0	83.4	65.3	73.5	23.84
Turkmenistan	105	n.a.	4.8	99.3	98.3	62.5	72.56
Uzbekistan	113	510	26.2	n.a.	n.a.	66.6	69.99
Zimbabwe	151	340	12.9	93.8	86.3	36.6	51.71
Comparisons							
Azerbaijan	99	1,240	8.4	99.5	98.2	67.0	79.00
Iran	96	2,770	68.8	83.5	70.4	70.7	40.30
Saudi Arabia	76	11,770	24.0	87.1	69.3	72.0	12.81

Source: Except where noted, all data are from UN Development Programme, *Human Development Report 2006* (November 2006), hdr.undp.org/hdr2006/.
a. GNI per capita calculated using World Bank, "Quick References Tables," web.worldbank.org.
b. CIA, *The World Factbook* (2006).
c. See table 1-3, note d.
d. Transparency International, "2006 Corruption Perceptions Index," www.transparency.org/policy_research/surveys_indices/cpi/2006. Note that in some cases, states are tied in their rankings in this index.

All failed states are by definition repressive, but not all repressive states have failed. Indeed, several of the most repressive states in this book's sample are hollow states—failed but for the excessive security that prevents the state in question from being characterized as "failed."[23] No collapsed state—the analytical designation beyond "failed"—can be repressive because the apparatus of repression is by definition lacking. But repressive states are often "weak"—the analytical position between "strong" and "failed"—possibly harboring the ingredients of failure once their vaunted security apparatuses are challenged. None is a "strong" state, for none delivers political goods in quality and quantity as defined in earlier studies. A few, wealthy and secure, nevertheless deliver little in terms of rule of law, political freedom, and economic opportunity to most citizens. Those latter examples also supply little in terms of educational or health services. Repressive regimes,

Telecommunications density, 2004 (per 1,000 population)		Total armed forces, 2006	Military expenditure (percentage of 2004 GDP)c	Development aid received, 2004 (millions of U.S.$)	Corruption rank, 2006 (163 = most corrupt)d	Economic freedom rank, 2007 (157 = most repressed)e	Freedom House ranking, 2006f
Telephone lines	Internet users						
329	163	73,000	1.4	46.2	151	145	Not free
8	1	376,000	n.a.	121.1	160	153	Not free
n.a.	10	1,000	n.a.	29.7	151	128	Not free
h	n.a.	n.a.	n.a.	118	Not ranked	157	Not free
143	43	308,000	6.6	110.2	93	142	Not free
n.a.	37	9,000	1.6	61.4	130	139	Not free
121	84	35,000	1.5	327.7	51	69	Not free
n.a.	8	26,000	n.a.	37.2	142	152	Not free
n.a.	34	55,000	n.a.	245.5	151	132	Not free
25	63	29,000	n.a.	186.5	130	154	Not free
118	49	67,000	1.8	175.6	130	107	Not free
n.a.	82	545,000	4.5	189.4	105	150	Not free
154	66	200,000	8.3	32.3	70	85	Not free

e. Heritage Foundation, "2007 Index of Economic Freedom,"www.heritage.org/research/features/index/countries.cfm. Note that in some cases, states are tied in their rankings in this index.

f. Freedom House, "Freedom in the World 2006: Comparative Measures of Freedom," http://freedomhouse.org/template.cfm?page=15. Countries are ranked either "free," "partly free," or "not free."

g. Unless otherwise noted, data on North Korea are from CIA, *The World Factbook* (2005), www.cia.gov/cia/publications/factbook/geos/kn.html.

h. 980,000 total.

focused as they are on bolstering and protecting heavy-handed rule and the extraction of riches from a subservient population, usually pay little attention, almost by definition, to delivering political goods beyond the political good of security.

This volume includes a careful dissection of Belarus, Burma (Myanmar), Equatorial Guinea, North Korea, Syria, Togo, Turkmenistan, Tunisia, Uzbekistan, and Zimbabwe. We would have liked to have included chapters on Cuba, Iran, Libya, Pakistan, Saudi Arabia, and the Sudan to round out more fully the A list of repressive and threatening nation-states. The absence of such chapters testifies more to contributor failures than to selection bias, however, and also includes an element of accident. Additionally, this book excludes—largely on account of space—the discussion of a bevy of smaller despotisms and near-despotisms, such as Azerbaijan, Cambodia, Eritrea, and monarchical Swaziland.

China deserves to be assessed as a sometime repressor and potentially aggressive rogue, but no study of China is included; it is a big power and thus cannot be defined as a rogue. Likewise, Russia represses some of its many peoples and may be considered aggressive. Some readers may regard the United States and Russia as rogues for ideological reasons, but neither fits the criterion of acting against world order as set out here. All three big powers, in fact, define world order by virtue of possessing a veto in the UN Security Council.

In any event, our collection of potential rogues is intended to be suggestive, not inclusive. All the cases discussed are abusers of human rights and abridgers of civil liberties. How much is too much? How high on the scale of repression does a nation-state have to reach to merit international attention and condemnation? Using our scale, it is possible analytically to compare, say, Uzbekistan and Turkmenistan and contrast Togo and Tunisia to Equatorial Guinea and Zimbabwe, and thus to formulate proportionate and consistent policies.

The Gross Repressors

North Korea and Niyazov's Turkmenistan (until the end of 2006) are the nation-states among our cases that exceed the others in their respective slavish devotion to semidivine, all-powerful, rulership. In both cases, post-Soviet rulers acted idiosyncratically, without even a minor genuflection to the welfare of the ordinary inhabitants of their Potemkin-like countries. Styling himself Turkmenbashi (chief of all Turkmen), Saparmurad Niyazov in Turkmenistan exceeded the tyrannical outbursts of his neighbors by removing physicians and other health care professionals, banning higher education, and providing ideologies of his own devising. Kim Jong-il, in North Korea, presided over a decade-long confiscation of his people's food supplies, starving about 1 million of his citizens as an afterthought. Neither all-powerful despot pretended to be participatory. Neither pretended to respect human rights or grant the usual civil liberties. Each respected no laws other than those of his own devising. Although Turkmenistan should be comparatively prosperous thanks to abundant supplies of natural gas (it is the tenth largest producer in the world), petroleum wells, and a small population of 5 million, Turkmenbashi confiscated the wealth of his country no less than Kim Jong-il in his much poorer domain.[24] Global Witness, a judicious investigative British nongovernmental organization (NGO), accused Niyazov of siphoning off most of his country's estimated $2 billion a year in gas revenues and concealing them in offshore accounts.[25] About half of the population of Turkmenistan still lives below the regional and national poverty level, and per capita GDP is estimated at $640. In 2006, virtually all pensions were cancelled, and sickness and maternity benefits were abrogated. All business activity depended upon government approval and patronage. Moreover, the public health system was in shambles, infant mortality rates were high, and life expectancy levels were low (for ex-Soviet satrapies). By 2006, most hospitals outside the capital had been shut down. The remaining clinics offered only rudimentary care, "condemning thousands to death from common, treatable illnesses such as tuberculosis."[26] Niyazov also banned the import of pharmaceutical supplies from Russia, leading to severe shortages of common medicines and drugs. Gurbanguly Berdymukhammedov, his self-appointed successor, promised—in the first weeks after his "election" as president in February 2007—to redress some of the unfortunate excesses of Turkmenbashi's reign while, simultaneously, ruling with a similarly heavy, autocratic hand.

Both North Korea and Turkmenistan are and were tyrannies for tyranny's sake. At least, few outsiders could discern any rationales and little rational behavior on the part of the two despots and their arrays of acolytes. Kim Jong-il and his associates are much more paranoid than Turkmenbashi was, perhaps with reason, but neither Asian leader ever evinced concern for fellow countrymen. Those poor, downtrodden Koreans and Turkmen existed, from the rulers' points of view, strictly to be preyed upon and terrorized. Sovereigns in most of the hereditary monarchies of yore were obliged, at various levels, to deliver political goods to their followers, else their followers would leave the kingdom or otherwise defect; however, North Korea and Turkmenistan have bolted shut their borders and have refused so far to deliver political goods that are not relevant to the regime's control or the regime's economy. It is obvious that there is no freedom of movement or expression in either country. As Marcus Noland writes in his chapter, North Korea is "hermetically sealed."[27] Even the Russian media have been eliminated in Turkmenistan, but that may now change. Freedom of religion is curtailed if not abolished in North Korea. Freedom from want has obviously been honored in the breach in North Korea and, to some extent, in Turkmenistan.

The regimes in both North Korea and Turkmenistan, as well as in so many of the other remarkable cases in this book, have long ago compelled conformity among their peoples. The deification of North Korea's dynastic leadership has been accomplished through intense political socialization, emphasizing ideological and "personal devotion of religious intensity." Freely voicing impure or antiregime thoughts in public is impossible; speaking one's mind within the confines of one's home, to family members or trusted friends, is unwise. "Any sign of political deviance, from listening to radio broadcasts to singing South Korean songs to sitting on a newspaper containing the photograph of Kim Il-sung is subject to punishment," reports Noland.

The regime in Turkmenistan has been unable since 1991 to acculturate its people to the same extent, but Turkmenbashi certainly tried. As president for life, he produced his own two-volume "little green book"—the *Ruhnama*—of spiritual teachings and revisionist history, erected expensive monuments to himself throughout the country, constructed gold-domed palaces and huge mosques, changed the names of months to remind citizens of him and his mother, and named towns, mountains, libraries, and schools in his honor.[28] Turkmenbashi even altered the Turkmen word for bread, giving that staple his mother's name. He tightened the vise on independent talk, closed most libraries outside the capital, and restricted educational opportunities by ending public secondary schooling beyond the ninth grade. Moreover, Russian-language instruction was cut back severely, and a rigid affirmative action policy meant the dismissal of thousands of non-Turkmen (defined as being descended from three generations of Turkmen) teachers. Niyazov refused to recognize foreign university degrees obtained after 2005, and his home-grown higher education system was in shambles at his death. In 2006, the rector of a regional teachers' college in Turkmenabad burned 500,000 Russian-language volumes since there was no need to house books printed in a foreign language.

In Turkmenistan, criticism or dissent was defined (as it is in so many of our cases) as treason. Such offenses were and may still be punishable by long prison terms, confinement to psychiatric hospitals (as the Soviets were wont to do), and internal banishment to arid salt flats along the Caspian Sea. Private conversations were monitored by informers, telephones and e-mails were tapped, and Internet access was severely limited.

The imposition of collective punishment on families and groups (up to three generations in a family for one person's offense in North Korea, with similar instances being reported in Turkmenistan), the arbitrary and random (and thus terroristic) practice of coercion, and a blanket imposition of an atmosphere of fear across all levels of society are but three ways in which these quintessentially despotic regimes control and repress those who have the misfortune to reside there. Their prisons are full of inmates, their indigenous dissidents are deeply underground or in exile, and torture is widespread. Forced abortions and infanticide are said to occur in North Korea. The external critics of both regimes are at risk, even well outside national borders.

Assassinations occur. Accountability does not exist. Everything that is not specifically permitted (as in Duvalier's Haiti) is forbidden. Effectively, there is no independent press or judiciary, and virtually no civil society.

The U.S. State Department's 2006 summary of Turkmenistan's human rights record under Niyazov concluded that "the government continued to commit serious abuses . . . [and] severely restricted political and civil liberties." Torture, prolonged detention without trial, abuse of religious minorities, collective punishment, denial of fair trials, arbitrary interference with privacy, a blacklist preventing travel, and violence against women were among the charges. But there was less evidence in 2006 of child labor during the cotton harvest.[29]

For North Korea, the same report said that the regime "continued to commit numerous serious abuses," subjecting its citizens to rigid controls. It said that there were reports of extrajudicial killings, disappearances, and arbitrary detention. Prison conditions remained harsh and life threatening. Torture was common. Pregnant female prisoners were compelled to undergo abortions. Babies born in prison were killed at birth. There were widespread reports of trafficking in women and girls among refugees and workers crossing the border into China.[30]

As the authors of the respective chapters on those two cases rightly suggest, precise measurement of the depths of each nation's depravity is impossible and conceivably pointless. There are no reliable data. Nevertheless, North Korea is the world's most militarized society, with a massive share of the country's population under arms and a preponderance of GDP devoted to the military. Noland believes that North Korea's network of camps for political prisoners holds 200,000 or more inmates, but that is a crude estimate. Enforcement squads would be able to testify about assassinations perpetrated or incarcerations arranged. Spies and thought police would be able to offer comments on conformity and successful self-censorship. A tour of the prisons and reeducation centers would provide specific human instances of deprivation and state attack, and there are fugitive memoirs of occasional prison camp survivors. Even a postconflict truth commission would find it difficult to specify every example of repression, however, and to add them up. At the same time, mere impressionistic summations will not do.

Turkmenistan in 1997 decreed that all economic statistics were state secrets. So are all other numbers. Turkmenbashi doled out what figures he pleased. In his chapter, Gregory Gleason says that this sole ruler practiced the "big lie," exaggerating national progress and pillorying those who would say otherwise. Naturally, officially there are no political prisoners and no violations of the rights of Turkmen citizens. Gleason's chapter includes a postscript examining the beginnings of the post-Niyazov era.

Data to demonstrate the depth of tyranny in Burma (Myanmar) are no more abundant than they are for North Korea and Turkmenistan.[31] There are few reliable statistics, not even for Burma's population. GDP numbers are wild estimates, with $225 per capita in 2004 being employed by outsiders for want of anything better. The amount of corruption in Burma is not exactly known either, although Transparency International ranks Burma second to last on its index.[32] Precise numbers of political prisoners are not available. Nevertheless, since 1962 the military rulers of the once wealthy and food-sufficient country have compelled conformity through brutal means; eviscerated its agricultural, economic, medical, and educational infrastructures; prevented freely elected members of parliament from taking their seats and forming a democratic government (in 1990); and removed political freedoms and eliminated human rights with no less efficiency and just as much deadening impact as in North Korea and Turkmenistan. The rulers of Burma absolutely shun debate of any kind and assert that democracy is a foreign notion to be combated at all costs.

General Ne Win ruled Burma, almost single-handedly, in an idiosyncratic, xenophobic, kleptocratic manner from 1968 to 1988. Thereafter, military juntas that first called themselves the State Law and Order Restoration Council and then the State Peace and Development Committee exercised power in Burma through a decisionmaking apparatus that was at least nominally collective. Since a purge in 2004, however, General Than Shwe, the senior officer in the collective, has emerged as its leading figure, with dominant authority. All of the members of the junta are required to sleep every night at military headquarters, obviously to prevent dissent and defection. In 2005, Than Shwe moved much of the ruling apparatus out of Rangoon (Yangon) to an obscure new national government center and mountain redoubt 200 miles north. Overtures to Aung San Suu Kyi, the Nobel Prize–winning opposition leader who remains under house arrest, largely ceased in 2005.

A very large army, as in North Korea, maintains a tight grip on the country. It enforces Than Shwe's orders and, along with the police, operates an elaborately detailed spying system, exercises autarkic economic influence, creates social norms, imposes conformity, prevents mobility, and, to Burmese, presents a mailed fist, never a velvet glove. No more than five people are allowed to gather in public without official permission. For decades, the army has imposed compulsory labor requirements on rural inhabitants, taken political prisoners, destroyed unfriendly villages, employed torture and "elimination," raped widely, and prevented all free expression and nearly all Internet usage. The State Department said that Burma's human rights record worsened during 2006: students were detained, ethnic minority villagers were attacked, and there were notable extrajudicial killings, disappearances, rapes, and torture. Villagers were compelled to relocate. Children were recruited forcibly for labor brigades; women and children were trafficked.[33] The army has practiced forced removal, arbitrarily dumping large numbers of urban dwellers in rural areas, sometimes into "model villages." Telephones and electronic equipment must be "authorized" by the regime. In her chapter, Priscilla Clapp reports that the Burmese army has laid waste to large areas, along the Thai border for example, leaving tens of thousands homeless. But it has not needed to massacre opponents, Buddhist monks, and protesting civilians on the scale employed to suppress the 1988 uprising.

Robert Gabriel Mugabe has issued no "little green book" of sayings to be memorized. Nor is he referred to as "Dear Leader," as in North Korea—but then neither was Pol Pot of Cambodia nor Ne Win of Burma, both of whom Mugabe tends despotically to resemble. His unprovoked, seemingly mindless destruction of periurban shanty towns and informal business premises near Harare in 2005 left at least 700,000 and up to 1.2 million Zimbabweans without shelter, livelihood, or the accumulated furnishings of homes and businesses.[34] At the same time, throughout 2005 and 2006 and well into 2007, millions of Zimbabweans went hungry, some starving, because Mugabe and his henchmen used access to dwindling food supplies as a direct political weapon. Ruthlessly, Mugabe has systematically been punishing urban dwellers and other supporters of the Movement for Democratic Change (MDC), Zimbabwe's opposition, for their impudence in contesting elections (and winning many seats) against himself and his dominant party in 2000, 2002, and 2005. In March 2007, Mugabe also unleashed a brutal assault on the leaders and key operatives of the MDC, killing a few and maiming at least 200 others.

The 2000, 2002, and 2005 elections were rigged and the results falsified. Mugabe has nevertheless waved away criticism and rebuffed diplomatic intervention from African neighbors, Britain, the European Union, South Africa, and the United States. Meanwhile, he has tightened economic and political screws within the country, kept tight media bans and deported all foreign journalists, subverted the once independent supreme court and high court, used police and informal militia to inhibit opposition political rallies and all citizen protest, employed the tools of assassination and political imprisonment where necessary, and attempted to sell sections of Zimbabwe for personal profit to concessionaires from China, Libya, Malaysia, and South Africa.

Mugabe's regime routinely brutalizes both its opponents and persons or groups critical of the policies and procedures of the government—as the events of March 2007 clearly demonstrated. There is no coerced labor, on the Burmese model, and until 2005, there were no compulsory removals of populations. But arbitrary arrests, detentions without trial, sexual assaults, torture, political killings, and generalized mayhem are all tools used by the Mugabe machine—to repress and terrorize Zimbabweans.

Seventeen of the then fifty-three MDC members of parliament were arrested during 2003, some more than once, and held for varying lengths of time. Supreme Court Justice Benjamin Paradza was arrested in his court chambers for "hostile rulings" against the government. One of those hostile rulings was an order releasing MDC mayor Elias Mudzuri from police custody; Mugabe had demanded Mudzuri's arrest and removal from office on trumped-up charges.[35] The leader of the opposition party was tried for treason, on fake charges and with falsified testimony. In 2005 and 2006, there was a wave of arrests for hoarding food, withholding foreign exchange, manipulating the currency, and being disrespectful economically and politically to Mugabe and his regime. In 2007, MDC leader Morgan Tsvangirai, after suffering a concussion at the hands of Mugabe's enforcers, was arrested along with dozens of his key supporters.

Mugabe has successfully eradicated civil society, just as he has destroyed the free press, neutered the independent judiciary, muted foreign criticism, emasculated the opposition, curtailed local protest by the meting out of exemplary punishments, and deflected external African criticism via a vigorous nationalistic propaganda campaign. Equally, the Mugabe regime has denied the existence of widespread hunger and starvation. He has effectively channeled internationally supplied food assistance to cities and rural areas dominated by his political party, hoarding available rations for his own favorites in order to influence political results in 2005.[36] As Roman Catholic archbishop Pius Ncube has oft complained, Mugabe uses maize rations to "reward supporters and punish dissidents."[37] In 2007, Ncube urged fellow Zimbabweans to use civil disobedience to resist the regime.

Although there are no gulags, a combination of Central Intelligence Organization, military, and police operations successfully intimidates Zimbabwe's people. Their actions make MDC members and supporters miserable, successfully spread terror throughout the nation-state, force innocent and apolitical citizens to run for the lives, and destroy the educational and health services. Demoralizing and disheartening, too, widespread corruption under

Mugabe has sapped the country of its entrepreneurial vitality and poured sand on the wheels of national progress.

Equatorial Guinea, never a paragon of political and social advancement, is Africa's other odious tyranny. A tiny (population 500,000), oil-rich, former Spanish colony on the western edge of Gabon, it rivals Mugabe for oppressive excesses. Never a democracy and never well run (unlike Zimbabwe in earlier times), and always without the sparkling human resource capacities of Zimbabwe, Equatorial Guinea has equally abused human rights and indigenous aspirations without the steep fall from attainment and grace that Zimbabweans have endured since 1998. In its 2007 report, the Department of State listed a concatenation of state-sponsored abuse: torture; beatings; abuse of prisoners; harsh and life-threatening prison conditions; arbitrary arrest; harassment of foreigners; judicial corruption; severe restrictions on freedom of speech, press, and assembly; violence against women; trafficking in persons; and forced child labor.[38] John Heilbrunn argues that Equatorial Guinea's long entrenched practices of violence against opponents, nepotism, collusion, and wholesale corruption deny its rulers, the Mongomo-Nguema clan, any possibility of liberalization. They "cannot permit meaningful reforms since decades of human rights abuses . . . have intensified demands for revenge and retribution."[39]

President Theodore Obiang Nguema came to power through violence—killing his uncle—and has perpetuated his dominance only through the persecution of opponents and potential future adversaries, and by denying the entire populace of his country any freedoms whatsoever. Indeed, Nguema has even refused them an opportunity to participate in Equatorial Guinea's remarkable recent economic returns from petroleum discoveries. Like most dictators, he keeps those proceeds for himself and his family.

Nguema is a Weberian "sultan," exercising power without restraint and unencumbered by any rules or any commitment to an ideological or any other set of values. Unrestrained greed and unrestrained power, together with meaningful paranoia, necessarily drive his regime. Discoveries of offshore petroleum obviously played into and strengthened existing acquisitive tendencies. Like Mugabe, Nguema and his family have confiscated desirable land and ousted groups with preexisting tenure in order to lease territory to foreign enterprises and to monopolize resources of timber on the mainland. Zimbabwe and Equatorial Guinea are criminal states; so are nearly all of the examples discussed in this chapter and elaborated upon throughout the book.

Equatorial Guinea has never known more than a rudimentary rule of law. Nor has it known anything that would resemble fair play. Routine violence, reports Heilbrunn, "shapes everyday life." Amnesty International lists beatings, disappearances, and arbitrary incarcerations. Detention, harassment, intimidation, and loss of property occur without the possibility of redress or adjudication. Macías Nguema, Obiang Nguema's equally destructive predecessor, reputedly killed 50,000 of his own people (a tenth of the total national population) between 1969 and 1979. In Zimbabwe, Mugabe massacred a mere 30,000 between 1982 and 1984.

Nor does today's President Nguema redeem himself by spending oil wealth for the welfare of his subjects. In 2002, barely more than 1 percent of government expenditure was devoted to health, with slightly more being allocated to education. Much of the rest of the budget is spent on security. Paying soldiers and police well is a requirement for despotic regimes. Without the enforcers, an absolute state risks losing control and encouraging coups from among the ranks of the disgruntled legions bearing arms.

The High Repressors

Alexander Lukashenko, Europe's lone tyrant and president of Belarus, resembles Mugabe much more than Nguema in his postures and actions. As Margarita Balmaceda suggests in her chapter on Belarus, the Lukashenko regime poses a serious threat both to its own citizens and to Europe's still fragile security system.[40] Moreover, even if Lukashenko has fewer political prisoners than other repressive regimes and has not starved his people in the North Korean, Cambodian, and Zimbabwean manner, his regime has institutionalized a strategy of repression with such force that contemporary Belarus closely resembles many aspects of the atrocious nation-state exemplars of despotism already discussed.

Balmaceda characterizes Belarus as moderately high on a scale of repression. That is, Belarus no longer routinely imprisons or assassinates hosts of opponents. Instead, thugs (possibly police in mufti) working for the state systematically beat up opposition figures and sympathizers—even presidential candidates in 2006—thus successfully sowing fear. These same political nonconformers are subjected to serial arrest, release, and rearrest—and prison conditions are harsh. In addition, the state harasses anyone with views antithetical to Lukashenko, often hounding them out of private jobs. Since 2004, officers of the state have been permitted to enter any home for any reason. The state severely limits freedom of expression, restricts access to independent thinking and education, and dramatically restricts the activities of international and local NGOs (as Burma and Zimbabwe also do). Self-censorship is ubiquitous. Judicial decisions are controlled by Lukashenko. Elections are rigged. The state limits permits for most kinds of economic activity and, through its control of commercial real estate, inhibits any kind of independent initiative. Formal local political institutions exist, but Lukashenko manipulates them, and his subordinates, as if they were marionettes. As in most of the "worst of the worst" cases discussed in this book, the requests and criticisms of international organizations and the world's big powers are largely ignored, thanks in this case to slavish backing (at least until the natural gas controversy of early 2007) from Russia. The regime's harsh actions together create an atmosphere of repression that permeates "all aspects of life" in Belarus. Balmaceda concludes that in Belarus, "repression is a way of life."

For each of our examples of repression, we must ask how the national despot—in this modern, globalized age—manages to stay in power. Obviously, each of the all-powerful leaders and presidents for life, even the leader of the Burmese junta, survives by being ruthless, by creating an effective apparatus of intimidation, and by socializing his people to accept a massive degree of implicit coercion and conformity. That is more the North Korean, Turkmen, and Burmese model, where informing and spying have been developed to a fine art. However, Zimbabweans are too sophisticated to become willing conformists. Instead, in Zimbabwe and Equatorial Guinea, as well as in the more effectively conformist countries, naked force is employed to cow a potentially restive population and impose subservience.

Like Mugabe in Zimbabwe, Lukashenko in Belarus has advanced the arts of soft and hard repression by terrorizing his own deputies and cabinet ministers, moving all government employees to short-term contracts, and blackmailing senior and junior officials. As in all authoritarian states, patronage is also essential in Belarus, for Lukashenko, like Mugabe, has made all major political and economic actors dependent on his own patrimonial largesse. There are no nonexecutive sources of autonomous economic power; gainful employment opportunities are in state hands, giving the regime and Lukashenko immense leverage on what remains a tightly regulated post-Soviet economy. Furthermore, Lukashenko has successfully managed the flow of information to Belarus's formidable nonurban population; they know little about the progressive economic reforms and rapid growth in neighboring former Soviet countries. Lukashenko also regularly empties state coffers for the purposes of regime maintenance.

Lukashenko, like Niyazov and Kim Jong-il, believes in ideological indoctrination. Belarus has its handbook of authorized ideas and aphorisms. At private and public workplaces, and in the schools, the workers and students of Belarus are exposed to such instruction. A youth brigade, to which all students must belong, helps to enforce the instruction, and, since 2004, students at all universities in Belarus have had to pass an ideological foundations course based on the handbook. Moreover, each school and workplace has— in the Soviet manner—an ideological controller.

Most of the country cases of repression examined in this book are comparatively impoverished, in some cases (Burma, North Korea, Turkmenistan, and Zimbabwe) as a direct result of human agency. Belarus, almost despite the initiatives and methods of Lukashenko, is comparatively well off, ranking relatively high (sixty-seventh) in the UN Development Programme's Human Development Report listings for 2006 thanks to high levels of literacy and low levels of infant mortality. The per capita GDP for 2006 was $1,868, putting Belarus at a disadvantaged place in Europe but at a higher position relative to the benighted polities in our sample.[41] Only Tunisia and Equatorial Guinea, because of recent oil production, rank higher.

The citizens of Belarus, despite their ruler's attempt to impose a blanket of conformity, appear to have a degree of personal space greater than that enjoyed by comparable citizens of North Korea and Turkmenistan. They can exercise somewhat more freedom of movement and thought, if never to excess. Syrians, amid the reign of Bashar al-Asad (from 2000), the son of the founding despot, were gaining such personal space before 2006, amid the verbal battering that their country and their rulers received from the UN, the United States and France, and their fellow members of the Arab League. As David Lesch notes in his chapter, under Hafiz al-Asad—the current president's father and the architect of Syria's special form of harsh authoritarian rule—a Faustian bargain was struck between the regime and the country's people: in return for stability and security, and doses of economic progress, freedom was banished.[42] Under Asad the son, there was at first some mild relaxation of restrictions. But in 2006, especially after the battles of the latest war in Lebanon and Syria's earlier compelled withdrawal from Lebanon subsequent to its complicity in the murder of a key Lebanese leader, the regime's harsh internal control of dissent and political opportunity was largely restored.

Asad the father came to power in 1970 and forcibly eliminated and filled prisons with opponents, eradicated free expression, massacred 20,000 supporters of the Muslim Brotherhood in Hama in 1982, and constructed a tough apparatus of repression comparable to those in Turkmenistan, Uzbekistan, and Belarus. In early 2006, with Syria in transition, there were fewer political prisoners, somewhat more space than before for nongovernmental organizations and civil society, and limited new openings for the media.

By early 2007, however, Syria, coming in from the cold, remained a repressive state. The security forces, under the ruler's brother-in-law, were still powerful. A discussion of Asef al-Shawkat's pervasive national influence as head of military intelligence, and his methods, was suggested by a Syrian television newscaster who subsequently fled the country: "The fascination of such people is that we all know that in one moment they could give you everything that you wish for, or they could kick you into an iron box." He continued, "They have fists of steel and ropes of silk."[43]

The UN Human Rights Committee and Human Rights Watch in 2005 reminded the international community that Asad's Syria continued to be governed under emergency legislation promulgated in 1963. The regime greatly limits rights to freedom of opinion and expression, curbs the right of peaceful assembly, and ignores the right to freedom of association (and trade unions). It routinely practices torture, provisions of the national constitution to the contrary. Seven political prisoners allegedly died of torture in 2004; despite more recent releases of hundreds of fellow political prisoners, thousands more still languished in Syrian prisons in 2005, and there were new arrests. Others simply "disappeared" during the 1990s and into this century.[44]

Amnesty International in 2005 reported the continued harassment of human rights defenders. They are put under constant surveillance, banned from traveling, tortured, imprisoned after rigged trials in special military courts, and smeared in the official media as "traitors." In Human Rights Watch's words, "Syria has a long record of arbitrary arrests, systematic torture, prolonged detention of suspects, and grossly unfair trials."[45] Preventive arrests are common.

Widespread internal spying is the norm, with public or private expressions of discontent still discouraged and forcibly curtailed. Opposition websites have routinely been shut down. The regime's channeling of economic privilege and opportunity to relatives of the ruler, and its wholesale nepotism and corruption, remains with little change. Likewise, families close to the Asads still receive favored access to educational and employment opportunities. Syria continued through 2007 to be a bifurcated state, with the Alawi minority and cronies of the Asad family still in ascendance and other Syrians— Sunni, Turkmen, Christian, and Kurdish (2 million, or 10 percent of the national population)—treated as inferiors.

According to the U.S. State Department's 2006 country report on terrorism, Syria's aggressiveness is exemplified by its political and material support
for Hezbollah, the radical Shiite terror group in Lebanon, and for several
Palestinian terrorist organizations. Damascus shelters the leaders of these
organizations. As Imad Moustapha, Syria's ambassador to Washington, said
in 2006, "I . . . now occupy the unique position of being the only ambassador
of a rogue state in the United States." He continued, "That's a joke. We are not
a rogue state, but no other 'quote-unquote' rogue state has an ambassador
here."[46]

Uzbekistan is a toughly run, heavily repressive, ex-Soviet state being scru-
tinized in 2007 by the arbiters of world order as thoroughly as Syria (and
North Korea), but for different reasons. Uzbekistan had been an ally of the
United States in the war against the Taliban in neighboring Afghanistan,
despite the antidemocratic actions and human rights abuses of its regime,
until Islam Karimov, its longtime president, perpetrated one brutal massacre
too many in 2005. That year the Andijan atrocities brought the regime's
excesses sharply before international viewers, truncated relations with the
United States and the EU, and intensified scrutiny of Uzbekistan's highly
repressive tendencies.

Karimov extended his presidential term to 2007 by means of a controlled
referendum in 2002. But, like so much in hypercentralized Uzbekistan, that
show of participatory rule fooled no one. Karimov is the supreme ruler of his
country in this era, as he was as a regional super apparatchik in Soviet times.
Yet he is more modern and more sophisticated than Niyazov or Kim Jong-il,
and has not instituted a cult of personality. Nor has he transformed Uzbekistan into an autarky, as Ne Win did in Burma and Niyazov did in Turkmenistan. Even so, the International Crisis Group maintained that Uzbekistan was "well down the path of self-destruction followed by such countries
as Burma, Zimbabwe, and North Korea."[47] Karimov is no more and no less
than a straightforward authoritarian determined to maintain a firm grip on
power and on the corrupt distribution of wealth within his cotton-growing
country.

There are no significant countervailing institutions. The legislature is a rubber stamp, and cabinet members exist to do the president's bidding. However,
Karimov and the regime owe their survival in good times and bad to the backing of the Ministry of Internal Affairs and the State Committee on Security,
complementary if competitive focuses of intrigue and strife. Additionally, Karimov, unlike the much more totalitarian despots in this book's sample, draws
support from and to some extent depends upon the acquiescence of local-level

elites much more than contemporary tyrants in Turkmenistan or Zimbabwe. In that sense, he is even more precariously perched as a ruler than Asad in Syria. His citizens are also much more connected to the globalized world than those in North Korea and Turkmenistan, adding to his vulnerability.

No human rights or civil liberties are respected. Free expression is banished, and sources of information are tightly controlled. Islamists, especially those who belong to Hizb ut-Tahrir, have been hounded and imprisoned. Thousands of religious extremists have been arrested and their movements banned. In her chapter, Martha Olcott estimates that Uzbekistan holds several thousand political prisoners.[48] The security forces routinely compel confessions, employ instruments of torture, and curb redress to even a rudimentary rule of law. Journalists are also beaten for "defaming the nation," and evidence is planted on suspects. The judicial system, as in all of the cases in this volume, is a sham. Ordinary Uzbeks remain wary of arousing security suspicions, but there is less private self-censorship than in several other of our country cases.

Togo is an African version of Uzbekistan. For twenty-seven years under Etienne Gnassingbé Eyadéma, Togo was the home of Africa's most enduring dictatorship. He and his associates, from the country's north, persecuted southerners. Then the despot died of a heart attack in 2005. His security forces rallied around Eyadéma's son, killed hundreds and attacked many more of his potential opponents, and made sure that Faure Gnassingbé, the son, won an election with about 60 percent of the votes cast. The son's regime took up in terms of repression where the father left off, and (like Bashar al-Asad) kept family members and other cronies in positions of authority and influence.

Gnassingbé's government employs terror to prevent competition and dissent, and to compel obedience. There is routine intimidation, despite Togo being packed between two democratic African states, Ghana and Benin. The ruling regime also colludes, as Eyadéma did, with Togo's commercial sector. It binds them and others to the state by restricting opportunities for corrupt gain to a favored few, most often relatives. As in nearly all of our other cases, the ruler hardly can thrive without being patrimonial. He must provide opportunities for enrichment to a flock of retainers while keeping most of his citizens in poverty. (Togo's per capita GDP in 2005 was about $415.)[49] Eyadéma's nationalization of the country's most important resource—its phosphate mines—helped to reward a small group well. In such an atmosphere, the security forces have to receive special privileges and, to succeed, the president must play client against client, occasionally throwing some to the wolves.

Gnassingbé's father, according to international human rights NGOs, was a merciless despot. His security forces in 1998 supposedly captured opponents, bound them, and tossed them out of airplanes, in the manner of Argentina's armed forces; bodies were found on beaches along the Gulf of Guinea. Togolese were kept poor, illiterate, and insufficiently educated. Togo's people also suffer from other human development deficiencies, as the annual UN Development Programme Report and Index show so well. Infant mortality is high (62.2 per 1,000), life expectancy is low (54.3 years), and more than half of the population lacks consistent access to clean water.[50]

Despite having a new, younger ruler, Togo, like Syria, suffers from decades of authoritarian leadership. Human rights and civil liberties are absent. Censorship is standard. Spying is fundamental. The security forces control individuals just as they do, say, in Burma—but with less determination and ferocity. The death of Eyadéma and the election of Faure Gnassingbé have made little difference to the ways in which the peoples of Togo are unable to pursue life, liberty, and happiness. As Heilbrunn shows in his chapter, hardly anything has changed since the death of Eyadéma.[51]

Although participants in the conferences that preceded the development of this volume initially expressed surprise at the inclusion of Tunisia, our last example, a close inspection reveals that this country is no longer (if it ever was) a progressive North African nation-state. Under Habib Bourguiba, Tunisia's founding president, the impress of authoritarian rule was somehow softened by the ruler's legitimacy and by the absence of overt avarice. Tunisia became an oasis of peace in a turbulent region consumed by strife. Its comparatively high levels of development also testified to Bourguiba's deft leadership. Moreover, compared to their neighbors and the peoples of much of the rest of the Middle East and Africa, Tunisians complained less about the oppression of their government. Yet another difference between then and now in Tunisia is that times, and external expectations, have changed.

Tunisian perceptions of the effective governance of their rulers and, objectively, the manner in which their government performed (and delivered political goods) altered for the worse when President Zine El Abidine Ben Ali pushed the aging Bourguiba out of office in 1987. A critical period of "cleansing" followed in 1991–1992, when the Ben Ali regime eliminated Islamists. Subsequently, Ben Ali and his family have arrogated and aggregated perquisites of dominance, extirpated rivals, and put a tight lid on potential dissent and dissenters. A recent U.S. Department of State report said that official Tunisia remained "intolerant of public criticism and used physical abuse, criminal investigations, the [military] court system, arbitrary arrests, residential restrictions, and travel controls . . . to discourage criticism. . . . The Government restricted freedom of assembly and association."[52] All media are "asphyxiated," and self-censorship is common. The Internet is closely monitored. The Tunisian security forces, like those in Uzbekistan and elsewhere, use physical abuse and beatings against those considered threats. Ben Ali also employs a paramilitary group of thugs to intimidate his antagonists. Furthermore, the Ben Ali regime utilizes torture in many forms and treats political prisoners harshly. Some Islamists and other opponents of Ben Ali have died in prison or shortly after being released. The Department of State's report for 2006 stressed how intolerant of criticism the Ben Ali government continued to be, how corrupt it was, and how it continued to commit heinous human rights abuses.[53]

Like all of the other examples in this book, and several outside its pages, Tunisia—despite its reputation and wealth—is a police state. According to Clement Henry, there are 150,000 police in a country of 10 million, a proportionally higher number than in Britain, France, or Germany.[54] Yet, although Ben Ali's men routinely torture opponents, Henry suggests that Tunisia is less repressive than many, if not all, of the case studies contained in this book. Compared to other places, political prisoners are fewer, and the denial of liberties and rights is more limited. Ben Ali, across some dimensions, may also have begun his reign using less draconian methods of rule than had Bourguiba. But Ben Ali's presidency in the 1990s soon consumed the other ministries, dominated the ruling party, morphed into a cult of personality without much of a guiding personality, ramped up his family's intervention in and accumulation of sources of significant state wealth, and ran roughshod over the judicial and legal institutions of the state. Ben Ali's Tunisia is a corrupt as well as a repressive state, now obligated institutionally to serve the ruling family and the Ben Ali regime and not, as in earlier times, some kind of postcolonial national destiny.

In the new Tunisia, as in the old, elections and their results are manipulated. Indeed, the fact that many of the countries represented in this book hold elections constitutes no claim against their nondemocratic repressiveness. In all of the cases, elections are cosmetic. In a few less hypocritical examples, elections are no longer held because the supreme ruler has been designated "for life," or because the regimes do not believe that the democratic practice of elections suits their needs. Ben Ali's regime is in the first camp, where elections are conducted to appease international public opinion and in order to provide a justification, domestically, for continued repression.

Likewise, even Tunisia, arguably the least venally repressive of our sample of nation-states, permits no public free expression. Thus accountability is limited, and civil society has no significant voice. Self-censorship exists in Tunisia, also, but in contrast to other cases, its practice may be less consistent. And the French connection, especially Tunisia's proximity geographically and intellectually to France, serves (along with a thriving and outspoken diaspora) to limit the oppressive character of Tunisia's official censorship. Unlike the successful spying and surveillance operations of Syria or Turkmenistan, Ben Ali cannot so easily control what Tunisians say in private to each other. Nor, as in Bourguiba's Tunisia, can the long, sinister arm of the regime reach into Europe to assassinate and intimidate opponents.

By 2006–2007, Tunisia was also a target of Salafist terrorists linked to al Qaeda. From their bases in neighboring Algeria, militants attempted to place bombs in Tunis and thus to disrupt Tunisia's thriving tourist industry. Better governance as well as tighter surveillance were the presumed antidotes to the effective spread of terror.

Methods of Repression and Policy Responses

The recipe for effective state repression is clear. Construct a large, powerful, and omnipotent security force apparatus. Use it to terrorize your own people, employing a variety of techniques to impose conformity and isolate potential dissidents. Spy on everyone; tap telephones and interfere with the Internet. Employ a network of informers; pay well for information from concierges, barkeepers, street sweepers, and so on. Encourage eavesdropping. Eliminate free expression in the press or in other media. Control clerics. Construct a lavish cult of personality around the ruler. Create a bogus philosophy to undergird and provide justification and apologetics for the foundations of the repressive regime. Distribute compendiums of "glorious thoughts." Manipulate all of the levers of economic opportunity so that the prosperity of individuals and families depends on the ruler and his or her close associates. Wrap the ruler and a vast array of associates in a web of corruption, the better to distort priorities and control all lucrative avenues of wealth and patrimony. Close the national borders. Prevent travel. Crack down on protests and protesters. Beat people almost at random. Arrest ordinary people as well as suspects arbitrarily; interrogate them mercilessly. Torture them. Incarcerate dastardly miscreants, or persons with independent ideas, after show trials in fake courts. Assassinate some, and subject others to mysterious accidents. Meddle in the national diaspora, even to the extent of attacking opponents overseas. At home, impose collective punishment for the acts of a few, or even of a single person, on whole families or clans. In special cases, in order to demonstrate the power of the ruling regime, use food deprivation as a weapon, or send soldiers to wipe out whole villages and cities, massacre civilians, or perpetrate genocide. Most of all, rulers and ruling regimes must never flinch. Even when international bodies or international NGOs bleat, deny all accusations, avoid exploratory visits by international rapporteurs, and complain mightily about infringements of national sovereignty.

Each of these steps down the nefarious road of gross repressiveness can be documented and measured, either directly or by using proxies. Even a rough ranking permits good and appropriate policy to be made toward countries sharing the same kinds of repressive pursuits rather than doing so episodically and ad hoc. It also encourages intelligent policymaking well before (not after) willful nation-states impose insuperable restraints on their own peoples or lash out aggressively at neighbors and the international order. By having a publicly available method of identifying repressive states clearly and measuring the magnitude of their repressiveness, Washington and other capitals will be unable to ignore the harmful quality of nation-states with whom they might need or wish to share strategic or economic interests. They will have to confront the realities of repression and will find it uncomfortable to embrace nations that fundamentally prey on their own people.

Likewise, because it is only among the highly repressive states that the real rogues—the aggressive and dangerous rogues—will be found, policy actions can and should be crafted to encourage those outlaw states to adhere more strictly to global basic values. Incentives can be provided by the big powers and international order to elicit behavioral reforms. If not, the international system and the United Nations will have a transparent foundation on which to base a campaign of sanctions, possibly leading to forceful initiatives under chapter VII of the UN Charter.[55]

The proliferation of nuclear arms, chemical or biological capabilities, and light weapons is dangerous and destabilizing, as is regime support of transborder terrorism. Of equal concern as a threat to stability and normative behavior is internal repression. In order to achieve a more peaceful, prosperous world, it behooves the UN and big powers to act consistently against the repressors. Only by their so doing will widespread deprivations of human rights and the immiseration of whole peoples over long periods of time be reduced. State-sponsored oppression is just as dangerous in terms of lives lost and opportunities forfeited as state-sponsored terrorism. Explicitly measuring and labeling highly repressive states, and showing how they attack their own citizens, is the first step toward reform and the improved well-being of millions of the poorest and most abused peoples of the world.

Notes

1. See Kofi Annan, "In Larger Freedom: Towards Development, Security and Human Rights for All. Report of the Secretary-General" (New York, March 21, 2005), www.un.org/largerfreedom/contents.htm.

2. Mary Caprioli and Peter Trumbore prefer a much broader definition of "rogue." Their data show that all gross repressors are rogues because such human rights violators inevitably breach world order norms. See chapter 2 in this volume.

3. Syria may also possess WMD in the form of biological and chemical weapons. See David Lesch, chapter 11 in this volume.

4. Robert I. Rotberg, *Haiti: The Politics of Squalor* (Boston, 1971), 2, 227.

5. See Robert I. Rotberg, *When States Fail: Causes and Consequences* (Princeton, 2004), 3–5; Robert I. Rotberg and Deborah West, *The Good Governance Problem: Doing Something about It* (Cambridge, Mass., 2004); Robert I. Rotberg, "Strengthening Governance: Ranking Countries Would Help," *Washington Quarterly*, XXVIII (2004), 71–81.

6. See Patrick Ball, Herbert F. Spirer, and Louise Spirer (eds.), *Making the Case: Investigating Large-Scale Human Rights Violations Using Information Systems and Data Analysis* (New York, 2000).

7. See their analysis in chapter 2.

8. *The Oxford Dictionary of English Etymology* (Oxford, 1966), 773.

9. Quoted in Paul D. Hoyt, "'Rogue' States and International Relations," paper presented at the 1999 annual meeting of the International Studies Association (Washington, D.C., February 16–20).

10. Anthony Lake, "Confronting Backlash States," *Foreign Affairs*, LXXIII (March-April 1994), 45–46.

11. Madeleine Albright, "Address and Question and Answer Session before the Council on Foreign Relations" (September 30, 1997), www.ciaonet.org/conf/alm01/; Albright, "Remarks at Tennessee State University" (February 19, 1998), secretary.state. gov/www/statements/1998/980219b.html.

12. Office of the Spokesman, U.S. Department of State, "Secretary of State Madeleine K. Albright, Interview on the Diane Rehm Show—WAMU-FM" (Washington, D.C., June 19, 2000), permanent.access.gpo.gov/lps11558/secretary.state.gov/ www/statements/2000/000619.html.

13. Colin Powell, "U.S. Has No Problem with European Force, Says Powell," *Guardian* (February 28, 2001).

14. President Bush, "Remarks by the President to Students and Faculty at the National Defense University" (May 1, 2001), www.whitehouse.gov/news/releases/ 2001/05/20010501-10.html; Bush, "President Delivers State of the Union Address" (January 29, 2002), www.whitehouse.gov/news/releases/2002/01/20020129-11.html.

15. Thomas H. Henriksen, "The Rise and Decline of Rogue States," *Journal of International Affairs*, LIV (2001), 349.

16. Michael Klare, *Rogue States and Nuclear Outlaws: America's Search for a New Foreign Policy* (New York, 1995), 26. See chapter 2 in this book for a good discussion on the earlier use of "rogue" to describe human rights infringers.

17. See chapter 2.

18. Mary Caprioli and Peter Trumbore, "Identifying 'Rogue' States and Testing Their Interstate Conflict Behavior," *European Journal of International Relations*, IX (2003), 378–381.

19. Michael Ignatieff and Kate Desormeau weigh the normative and practical reasons why such measurement is long overdue, especially for the human rights community. See their essay, "Measurement and Human Rights: Introduction," in Carr Center for Human Rights Policy, *Measurement and Human Rights: Tracking Progress, Assessing Impact* (Cambridge, Mass., 2005), 1–8. The remainder of this report demonstrates how little is being done in this field and also criticizes existing data arrays.

20. See chapter 2.

21. Ambassador Richard Jones, now the envoy of the United States to Israel, suggested this formulation at a meeting of the Kennedy School's Rogue States Project in October, 2004.

22. See chapter 3 in this volume for Feng and Paul's methodology and analysis.

23. For an elaboration of these concepts and distinctions, see Rotberg, *When States Fail*, 20–30.

24. Most observers believe that Turkmenistan has been losing, not gaining, population, but Niyazov insisted that his nation-state must grow, so in 2006 the Turkmenistan National Institute of Statistics reported a growth rate of nearly 3 percent and a total population of nearly 7 million. No census, however, has been taken since the early 1990s. See "The Overview of the Social and Economic Development of Turkmenistan in January–March 2006" (April 17, 2006), www.turkmenistan.gov.tm/ekonom/ek_stat/170406_eng.htm.

25. See *Economist* (May 27, 2006).

26. Ibid.

27. For this and other quotes on North Korea, see Marcus Noland, chapter 4 in this volume.

28. For a full exploration of Turkmenistan under the Niyazov regime, see Gregory Gleason, chapter 5 in this volume.

29. U.S. Department of State, "Turkmenistan," in *2006 Country Reports on Human Rights Practices* (March 6, 2007), www.state.gov/g/drl/rls/hrrpt/2006/78845.htm.

30. U.S. Department of State, "Democratic People's Republic of Korea," in *2006 Country Reports on Human Rights Practices* (March 6, 2007), www.state.gov/g/drl/rls/hrrpt/2006/78777.htm.

31. See Priscilla Clapp, chapter 6 in this volume.

32. Burma (Myanmar) ranks 160 of 163 on the 2006 Corruption Perceptions Index. (The state shares its place with Guinea and Iraq, making its rank fall second from the

bottom of the index.) See Transparency International, "Corruption Perceptions Index 2006" (2006), www.transparency.org/policy_research/surveys_indices/cpi/2006.

33. See U.S. Department of State, "Burma," in *2006 Country Reports on Human Rights Practices* (March 6, 2007), www.state.gov/g/drl/rls/hrrpt/2006/78768.htm.

34. For a full description of Zimbabwe under Mugabe, see Robert Rotberg, chapter 7 in this volume.

35. Paradza was eventually found guilty in late 2005, fleeing to Britain in early 2006 to avoid a possible ten-year sentence by the High Court. See UN High Commissioner for Refugees, *Country of Origin Information Report: Zimbabwe* (Geneva, April 2006).

36. The party referred to is the Zimbabwe African National Union–Patriotic Front (ZANU-PF).

37. *New York Times* (August 28, 2004).

38. U.S. Department of State, "Equatorial Guinea," in *2006 Country Reports on Human Rights Practices* (March 6, 2007), www.state.gov/g/drl/rls/hrrpt/2006/78732.htm.

39. See John Heilbrunn, chapter 9, in this volume, for a discussion of Equatorial Guinea and further references.

40. See chapter 8 in this volume.

41. UN Development Programme, "Statistics in the Human Development Report," in *Human Development Report 2006* (November 2006), hdr.undp.org/hdr2006/statistics; see also www.worldbank.org.

42. See chapter 11 in this volume.

43. Quoted in Michael Slackman and Katherine Zoepf, "A Syrian Tale: Passion, Power, Assassination," *New York Times* (November 3, 2005), A10.

44. For details, see Human Rights Watch, "Human Rights Overview: Syria" (January 2005), hrw.org/english/docs/2006/01/18/syria12231.htm, and "Country Summary: Syria" (January 2007), hrw/org/wr2k7/pdfs/Syria.pdf; Amnesty International, "Syria," web.amnesty.org/web/web.nsf.

45. Human Rights Watch, "Syria," in *World Report 2005* (January 2005), hrw.org/english/docs/2005/01/13/syria9812.htm. See also U.S. State Department, "Syria," in *2003 Country Reports on Human Rights Practices* (February 25, 2004), www.state.gov/g/drl/rls/hrrpt/2003/27938.htm; Amnesty International, www.amnestyusa.org/countries/syria/document.do?id.

46. U. S. Department of State, "Country Reports on Terrorism" (April 28, 2006), www.state.gov/s/ct/rls/crt/2005; Thom Shanker, "For Syria's Voice in the U. S., Isolation but Not Silence," *New York Times* (July 29, 2006).

47. International Crisis Group, "Uzbekistan: In for the Long Haul" (February 16, 2006), www.crisisgroup.org/home/index.cfm?id=3952.

48. See chapter 10 in this volume.

49. World Bank, "World Development Indicators," www.worldbank.org.

50. UN Development Programme, *Human Development Report 2005* (New York, September 8, 2005); Central Intelligence Agency, *The World Factbook 2005* (Washington, D.C., 2005).

51. See chapter 9.

52. U.S. State Department, "Tunisia," in *2003 Country Reports on Human Rights Practices* (February 25, 2004), www.state.gov/g/drl/rls/hrrpt/2003/27939.htm.

53. U.S. Department of State, "Tunisia," in *2006 Country Reports on Human Rights Practices* (March 6, 2007), www.state.gov/g/drl/rls/hrrpt/2006/78864.htm.

54. For Clement Henry's discussion of repression in Tunisia, see chapter 12 in this volume.

55. For the language of this chapter, see United Nations, "Chapter VII: Action with Respect to Threats to the Peace, Breaches of the Peace, and Acts of Aggression" (January 2007), www.un.org/aboutun/charter/chapter7.htm.

two
Human Rights Rogues:
Aggressive, Dangerous, or Both?

Mary Caprioli and Peter F. Trumbore

Are rogue states more violent or dangerous than other international actors, and can they be identified on the basis of objective criteria? The concept of the rogue state, which became a prominent part of American foreign policy discourse and planning with the end of the cold war, is based upon the premise that states that consistently violate important international norms of behavior represent particular dangers to the international order. In a 1998 speech, then secretary of state Madeleine Albright characterized rogue states as lurking outside the international system, countries "whose very being involves being outside of it and throwing, literally, hand grenades inside in order to destroy it."[1] Yet the question of which countries warrant the rogue state label has been controversial.

Beginning in the 1980s, American policymakers seized upon a formula for identifying rogue states that focused on a narrow set of external behaviors, namely, support for international terrorism and illicit pursuit of weapons of mass destruction (WMDs). While rogue states were often described as despotic dictatorships, dictatorship itself was never a sufficient condition to

This chapter summarizes and expands on conceptual and theoretical arguments first published in Mary Caprioli and Peter F. Trumbore, "Identifying Rogue States and Testing Their Interstate Conflict Behavior," *European Journal of International Relations*, IX (2003), 377–406. The data analyses presented here, covering the period 1980–2001, have been done specifically for this chapter.

qualify a state for rogue status.[2] As critics have long noted, however, far more states engaged in rogue behavior than were ever branded rogues by the U.S. government. Studies of American foreign policy rhetoric and policy planning documents have shown that from the late 1980s onward, only five states—Cuba, Iran, Iraq, Libya, and North Korea—have been consistently branded rogues by American decisionmakers; yet the behaviors that were said to qualify a state for rogue status have been engaged in by dozens of states, including long-standing and more recent American allies such as South Korea, Israel, Taiwan, Pakistan, and Egypt, which were never tarred with the rogue brush.[3] It is no surprise, then, that academic critics have rejected policymakers' singling out of these actors as little more than a political exercise by the United States to isolate or confront countries that it does not like.[4] As evidence, they point to the fact that Cuba remains a charter member of the rogues' club, despite the lack of credible evidence of Cuban WMD programs, while Syria, a perennial sponsor of terrorism with long-standing ambitions to acquire WMDs, has rarely been characterized as a rogue.[5]

In this chapter, a method for identifying rogue states is developed using objective measures of state observance of internationally recognized human rights norms. We then demonstrate that the states thus characterized as human rights rogues present both conventional and unconventional threats to international security. One of the most frustrating problems for the international human rights community has been the difficulty of convincing foreign policy practitioners of the relevance of human rights to international security. As Forsythe noted, "A fundamental challenge is how to reduce the enormous gap between the liberal legal framework on human rights that most states have formally endorsed, and the realist principles that they often follow in their foreign policies."[6] This chapter intends to narrow that gap by showing that persistent violators of human rights—in short, human rights rogues—present specific threats to international security through their involvement in the troubling behaviors that American foreign policymakers came to focus on after the end of the cold war.

What Makes a Rogue State?

Academics' general rejection of the rogue label—more precisely, rejection of the standard criteria for rogue status and its application by American policymakers—has resulted in a paucity of systematic research on the phenomenon of rogue states. Yet the idea that there are in fact rogue states, however defined, is an attractive notion. The premise that states that systematically violate international norms are also particularly dangerous to international society is valuable in that it forces us to think seriously about the characteristics or factors that lead states toward violent or otherwise dangerous international behavior. It also affirms the idea that the international system is a society of states with accepted norms of behavior and that violations of those norms have critical implications for the stability and security of the system as a whole.[7]

While policymakers have focused on a specific set of norms related to external conduct, there is an earlier understanding of international rogue or pariah status that predates by more than a decade the emergence of the rogue doctrine currently favored in U.S. foreign policy circles. This conception, popular in academic circles and among some policy analysts in the 1970s, emphasized human rights observance as the key to membership in or exclusion from the society of states.

In adopting the label "human rights rogues" to characterize states whose violent norms drive them toward roguish international conduct, we return to this earlier conception of rogue or pariah status, one rooted in the liberal tradition of political thought and enshrined in what Donnelly has called the "Universal Declaration model" of international human rights.[8] For much of the 1970s, the label of "international pariah" was applied to those states whose egregious treatment of their own populations placed them outside the boundaries of polite international society. Countries such as Chile during the Pinochet era, Cambodia under the Khmer Rouge, and white minority–ruled South Africa and Rhodesia were all at one time or another considered pariah states, diplomatically isolated from much of the rest of the international community because of their domestic conduct.[9] While these earlier studies employed general criteria of repressiveness to identify pariah states, a more specific set of criteria is developed here. States are classified as human rights rogues based on those recognized norms of international human rights that Frost has described as among the settled norms of contemporary international society.[10]

In important ways, American policymakers' focus on rogue states was unanticipated by leading academic security theorists as they sought to sketch out the dimensions of the post–cold war international environment and to speculate about its future. A central expectation shared by many of these theorists was that a new great-power rival would inevitably emerge from East Asia or Europe to balance the power of the United States.[11] In such a setting, where there are few immediate threats to American security, the United States enjoys great latitude to determine where and how it will become engaged internationally. Thus, as Waltz argues, choice, not necessity, dictates foreign policy, which may be driven more by internal political pressures and national ambitions than by external security threats.[12] This analysis fits nicely with that of critics who have linked the emergence of the rogue concept to the Pentagon's quest for a post–cold war mission that would justify maintaining as much as possible of its cold war–era force levels and budgets.[13] The American fixation on rogue states may therefore be understandable not as a reaction to genuine security interests but to political pressures emanating from an entrenched national defense and foreign policy establishment trying to stay relevant in a drastically altered international environment.

While compelling, the Waltz framework is likely not the entire explanation. It can also be argued that the foreign policy focus on rogue states after the cold war was driven by a strategy of preponderance of power, the requirement of what Mastanduno called "preserving the unipolar moment."[14] Such a strategy requires the dominant power to respond seriously to challenges to its power and authority, wherever they arise, if it is to retain its position of primacy. One consequence of the close of the cold war has been that developing world states have both greater freedom and increasingly greater capacity to threaten the interests of the United States, even militarily.[15] Thus the focus on rogue states that came to dominate American foreign and defense policies in the 1990s may be a matter of both choice and necessity.

This strategy would make sense if the countries that were being singled out as rogues really were the aggressive threats that American policymakers assumed them to be. A central component of the rogue doctrine that had emerged by the early 1990s was the belief that rogue states were outwardly aggressive, posing conventional military threats to their neighbors and the vital regional interests of the United States. This image was captured in a *Washington Post* front page news analysis not long after Iraq's invasion of Kuwait: "Saddam also revealed the perilous fragility of the 'post postwar' epoch, as [James] Baker called it. . . . For pessimists, Iraq's adventure may be the first in a sequence of heavily armed rogue states bullying their neighbors without the restraints once imposed by a U.S.-Soviet rivalry."[16] With this vision in mind, the Defense Department's 1993 "bottom-up" review of national security priorities and strategies called for the United States to be ready to fight and defeat rogue states "set on regional domination through military aggression while simultaneously pursuing nuclear, biological, and chemical weapons capabilities."[17]

There is a problem with this framework, however. Our own prior research has shown that as a group, neither the five countries publicly singled out as rogues by American policymakers, nor the roughly two dozen or so that fit policymakers' rogue criteria of supporting terrorism or pursuing illicit WMDs, evidence any difference in their international conflict behavior compared to other states.[18] We find that as a group, rogue states as defined by American policymakers are no more likely to become involved in interstate disputes in any given year, are no more likely to initiate militarized disputes, and are no more likely to use force first when disputes turn violent. In short, a central component of the rogue doctrine, that these states are aggressive military threats, fails to hold up.

Yet, in a fundamental way, we agree with the central premise of the rogue state concept, that there are states whose violations of recognized international norms of behavior are indicators of their aggressive character. Where we part company with the policy community, however, is on the question of which norms matter for identifying potentially aggressive or dangerous states. While the conventional definition of a rogue state is anchored to a narrow pair of norms governing unacceptable external conduct, we contend that the norms that matter are those of the international human rights regime governing states' treatment of their own citizens. In earlier studies we showed that states with identifiable domestic patterns of systematic discrimination on the basis of gender and ethnicity and general political repressiveness— states we label "human rights rogues" to distinguish them from the policy-oriented definition—are more likely than other states to engage in violence when involved in interstate disputes and are more likely than their opponents to resort to violence first.[19]

This chapter expands upon those findings and explores other indicators of aggressive and dangerous international behavior. Specifically, it goes beyond indicators of conventional military aggressiveness to ask whether there is a relationship between human rights rogue status and such dangerous external behaviors as the illicit pursuit of weapons of mass destruction and support for international terrorism.

By examining these other dangerous behaviors, we bring our conception of rogue states back toward the flawed construction employed by American policymakers since the early 1990s. The key difference, however, is that for policymakers the rogue behavior was the essence of the rogue identity. Rarely, if ever, did policymakers ponder underlying commonalities that might lead states to engage in such roguish conduct. What we show is that internal characteristics, specifically a systematic failure to observe internationally recognized human rights norms, are the common thread linking rogue states to the aggressive and dangerous external behavior that is of concern to policymakers.

Violent Norms, Violent Actions

In linking internal and external characteristics and behaviors, we are guided by the work of those who beginning in the late 1960s sought to demonstrate that democracies were more peaceful than other types of regimes.[20] This research failed to find compelling evidence of a general trend toward democratic pacifism. However, its central premise—that states duplicate patterns of domestic politics in the international arena and apply the same norms of conflict resolution in both domestic and international settings—has found a place in the canon of international relations scholarship as the centerpiece of the normative explanation for the democratic peace, which holds that democratic states do not go to war with each other.[21] This literature's focus has been on the pacifying effect of benign norms, leading Russett, one of the most prominent advocates of the democratic peace thesis, to call for the reconstruction of the international system from the bottom up, "that is, norms and rules of behavior internationally can become extensions of the norms and rules of domestic political behavior."[22] But if norms drive state behavior internationally, Russett's prescription becomes a double-edged sword when the norms in question are violent rather than pacific—particularly given democratic peace advocates' own admission that the anarchic nature of the international system facilitates the expression of violent norms as violent international action.[23]

It is at the intersection of violent norms and violent behaviors that our alternative conception of rogue states comes into focus. Our understanding of this relationship is informed by Galtung's concept of structural violence and by feminist critiques of traditional state-centered conceptions of security.[24] For Galtung violence is understood as a process that transcends the relationship of actor to subject, perpetrator to victim. Rather than conceiving of violence as a purely physical and intentional act of harm connecting one individual to another, Galtung points to the diminished life expectancy that results from unequal social and economic structures. In short, social injustice itself represents a form of violence.

Feminist international relations scholars build upon this foundation to construct a more inclusive understanding of security than the state-centric model that dominates the traditional international relations field. This alternative conception begins not with the state but with individuals and groups, asserting that violence—both physical and structural—at all levels of human society is interrelated, a dynamic overlooked by purely state-centric analyses. A considerable body of scholarship demonstrates that norms of violence are inherent in hierarchical social structures, and while states have the power to undermine structural hierarchies through policies that seek to minimize domestic inequalities, discrimination, and repression, some instead choose either to ignore or actually to exacerbate these inequalities and power hierarchies.[25] This approach recognizes that "where a state refuses to intervene to protect against human right[s] violations, to investigate charges, to prosecute and punish perpetrators of harmful acts, it does, in effect, condone those acts."[26] We brand such states human rights rogues.

Our approach to the question of rogue states and the intersection of domestic characteristics and international conduct adopts the causal logic inherent in the normative explanation of the democratic peace: that the same norms influence both domestic and international behavior. For states where those prevailing norms and values are violent, one would expect to see violent conduct both internally and externally. Guided by Galtung and the emphasis of feminist security analysis on the interrelated nature of violence, we look to systematic violation of internationally recognized human rights norms for evidence of the presence of the violent norms and values that affect states' international behavior.

Therefore human rights rogues are those states whose behavior runs afoul of these accepted international standards. Consistent with the Universal Declaration model's emphasis on the rights of individuals to equal concern and respect, and the responsibility of sovereign states for implementing those rights, we propose that human rights rogues are any states that systematically allow or facilitate domestic discrimination on the basis of ethnicity and gender, and violate individual rights to personal integrity. Furthermore, we argue that such internal violations of human rights reflect prevailing social norms and values of violence that will also manifest themselves in more violent international behavior on the part of human rights rogues.

Identifying Human Rights Rogues: The Rogue State Index

To identify states classified as human rights rogues, we have created a rogue state index (RSI), a composite indicator of state observance of international human rights norms, particularly as regards political and economic discrimination on the basis of gender and ethnicity, and violent repression of political opponents. These individual elements of the RSI are designed to capture the key components of the Universal Declaration model of human rights: first, the right of individuals to equal concern and respect, values enshrined in the International Covenant on Economic, Social and Cultural Rights and reflected in the International Covenant on Civil and Political Rights; and second, the individual right to personal integrity reflected in the International Covenant on Civil and Political Rights, which includes rights to life, liberty, and security of person, and protection against arbitrary arrest and imprisonment.

Rather than treat each of these components separately, we have created the index for three essential reasons: first, we believe that a single indicator simply cannot adequately represent such complex concepts as those of prevailing social norms and values; second, the components that make up the index are the best indicators we have found of the violent norms that are at the center of our research; and, finally, our approach is consistent with the understanding that within the Universal Declaration model, internationally recognized human rights are "treated as an interdependent and indivisible whole, rather than as a menu from which one may freely select (or choose not to select)."[27] Therefore, focusing on only one of these indicators would have the effect of emphasizing the observance or protection of that particular right over the others rather than demonstrating the interdependent nature of all rights.

The RSI is an eight-point scale representing a continuum of human rights observance. The individual components of the index are described below.

Ethnic Dimension

The ethnic discrimination component of the RSI comprises indicators of political and economic discrimination faced by ethnic minorities relative to other groups in society. These indicators are based on data from the Minorities at Risk project, which tracks the political, economic, and cultural status and characteristics of more than 200 politically active ethnic groups worldwide since 1945, and identifies whether group members are or have been deliberately restricted in their access to economic resources or political participation and influence in comparison to other social groups.[28] As such, the very existence of an at-risk minority group within a state indicates an underlying condition of ethnic social inequality.

For both economic and political discrimination, we code the highest level of discrimination recorded for any group within the state during each calendar year, thus capturing the upper limit of the types of policies and practices supported by societal norms. Both the political and economic indicators follow the Minorities at Risk five-point scale: 0, no political or economic discrimination; 1, public policies designed to protect or improve groups' political status; 2, historical neglect with no social practice of exclusion, protective, or remedial public policies; 3, social practice of exclusion, with any existing formal public policies neutral or inadequate to offset discrimination; 4, public policies, formal exclusion or recurring repression, or both, that substantially restrict the group's political and economic participation in comparison with other groups. A single ethnic component of the RSI is created from these separate indicators by averaging and rounding to the highest integer the political and economic discrimination scores conforming to the five-point scale.

For example, for 1997 Iran receives an ethnic discrimination index score of 4, reflecting substantial political and economic discrimination against minority groups. According to the Minorities at Risk project, of the eight at-risk minority groups in Iran, the Baha'i community remains the most persecuted, as they were in 1997.[29] The observance of their faith is prohibited by the Iranian constitution, as is the celebration of their holidays. Politically, organizations promoting Baha'i culture are banned, their political organization is restricted, and their rights during judicial proceedings are limited compared to the majority population. Economically, Baha'is have been subject to confiscation of their homes by government officials, seizure of personal property, and denial of access to education and employment. In addition to discrimination, the Baha'i community has also been victimized by explicit policies of group repression leading to arrests and detentions, show trials, and monitoring by domestic security agencies.

Gender Dimension

The gender component of the rogue state index captures norms of discrimination as measured by female political, economic, and social inequality.[30] Three separate indicators are combined to produce a single measure of gender-based discrimination: the percentage of women in the lower house of parliament, the percentage of women in the paid labor force, and the fertility rate. These indicators are each transformed into five-point scales and then combined.

Beyond nominal political equality obtained through suffrage, women obtain formal political power by serving as members of government. The exclusion of women from politics is thus a function of discrimination on the basis of gender stereotypes and is the strongest indicator of gender inequality available. Percent women in the legislature (lower house) is available from the Inter-Parliamentary Union. In our coding system, a value of 0 indicates at least 30 percent women in parliament, in keeping with the UN Commission on the Status of Women's identification of 30 percent as a threshold in order for women to influence key decisions and be taken seriously.[31] The remaining values are assigned by creating four equal categories: 4, up to 7.5 percent women in parliament; 3, from 7.51 to 15 percent; 2, from 15.01 to 21.5 percent; and 1, from 21.51 percent up to but not including 30 percent women in parliament.

The extent of economic opportunity available to women is captured by measuring the percentage of women in the paid labor force. Economic parity by gender results in greater equality in men's and women's power and prestige more generally.[32] The World Bank collects data on percent women in the paid labor force.[33] To match the ethnic component of the RSI, these data are recoded into an ordinal scale, with the value of 0 indicating that at least 40 percent of the paid labor force is made up of women. The remaining categories are divided equally: 4, 0 to 9.999 percent of the paid labor force is made up of women; 3, 10 to 19.999 percent; 2, 20 to 29.999 percent; and 1, 30 to 39.999 percent.

A direct measure of gender equality and an indirect measure of gender discrimination in education, employment, healthcare, and social standing are provided by the fertility rate.[34] Fertility rates are available from the World Bank.[35] An average fertility rate of three children per woman or fewer is a rough indicator of gender equality, as this reflects both the current average global fertility rate (2.7) and the necessary fertility rate (2.1) to ensure population replacement.[36] This fertility rate is assigned a value of 0. The remaining categories are divided equally: 4, an average fertility rate of nine or more children per woman; 3, an average rate of 7 to 8.99; 2, an average rate of 5 to 6.99; and 1, an average rate of more than three but less than five.

The gender component of the RSI is ultimately created by averaging and rounding to the highest integer the three individual measures of gender equality and discrimination, resulting in a possible range from 0 to 4.

As an illustration, consider the case of Pakistan, which for 1999 had an indexed gender score of 2. During this year women made up 40 percent of Pakistan's paid labor force, while the average fertility rate for Pakistani women was 4.77. Finally, women constituted less than 2 percent of the members of the Pakistani parliament. Compare this figure with that of Iran in 1997, which scored a gender index of 3. In that year, women made up only 25 percent of the paid labor force, but the fertility rate was a relatively modest 2.8. Yet in 1997 women constituted only about 3 percent of the members of the Iranian legislature.

Repression Dimension

The political repression component of the RSI accounts for violations of the individual right to personal integrity. Specifically, the data measure the prevalence of political imprisonment, torture, killings, or disappearances. Measures of state repression are adopted from Gibney's political terror scale (PTS) to capture the extent of personal integrity violations.[37] The PTS offers two measures of political repression, one based on annual human rights reports from the Department of State and the other based on Amnesty International's annual country reports. We use the Amnesty-based scores to avoid any potential political bias embedded in the State Department reports. While the rights violations included in this component of the RSI are more narrowly focused than the broad social practices and government policies represented by the discrimination components, it has been argued that violations of personal integrity rights are considered the most egregious and severe crimes against humanity and among the most easily avoided.[38] At the same time, it has been recognized that these represent core rights that must be fulfilled in order for the provision of other rights to be meaningful.[39]

The repression component of the RSI adopts the PTS coding:

—0, countries with a secure rule of law; people are not imprisoned for their views, torture is rare or exceptional, and political murders are extraordinarily rare.

—1, limited amount of imprisonment for nonviolent political activity with few affected; torture and beatings are exceptional, and political murder is rare.

— 2, extensive political imprisonment, or a recent history of such imprisonment with execution or other political murders; brutality may be common; and unlimited detention for political views, with or without a trial, is accepted.

—3, the practices described at level 2 are applied to more people such that murders, disappearances, and torture are a common part of life, primarily affecting those who interest themselves in politics or ideas.

— 4, the violence of level 3 has been extended to the whole population, with the leaders of these societies placing no limits on the means or thoroughness with which they pursue personal or ideological goals.

To illustrate, Iran receives a repression score of 3 for 1997, indicating extensive political imprisonment, extrajudicial killings, disappearances, and use of torture against significant proportions of the population, especially those who involve themselves in politics. For example, in its report on human rights conditions inside Iran for 1997, Amnesty International pointed to hundreds of political prisoners being held, many detained without charge or trial.[40] Among those arrested were Grand Ayatollah Hossein Ali Montazeri and other religious leaders critical of the government; many of these clerics' followers were also detained. Leaders of opposition political organizations, such as Ebrahim Yazdi of the Iran Freedom Movement, were also arrested and imprisoned, as were writers and publishers. Disappearance and extrajudicial killings were also used to silence media critics of the Iranian government. Finally, Amnesty International reported that various methods of torture, including beatings, severe burns, electric shocks, and sleep deprivation were employed by security forces against political detainees.

Index Formulation and Results

The rogue state index is created by combining the composite measures of gender and ethnic discrimination with the PTS scale. The RSI is weighted to correct problems associated with a statistical correlation among index variables. In this case, both the ethnic discrimination and repression variables are each assigned half the weight of the gender discrimination component, resulting in an RSI index scaled from 0 to 8 in increments of 0.5. Tukey's test for nonadditivity with the weighted components is significant; thus we can reasonably conclude that no interaction among index components is biasing the index and that we can be confident in applying it.

The average RSI score for all states from 1980 to 2001 is 4.18 (see figure 2-1)—a score that highlights the grim state of gender and ethnic discrimination and inequality, and the amount of repression in the world.[41]

During the twenty-two years for which data were available, the highest human rights rogue score recorded was 7.5, reached during various years by Algeria, Argentina, Colombia, El Salvador, Guatemala, Iran, Pakistan, Saudi Arabia, the Sudan, and Uganda. The lowest RSI score recorded, a 0.5, was obtained by Denmark, Finland, Iceland, Norway, and Sweden during various years. Average RSI scores for this twenty-two year period indicate that 25 percent of the states score 3.1 or lower on the RSI scale, 50 percent score 4.2 or lower, and 75 percent score 5.4 or lower. Stated differently, 25 percent of states score above 5.4 on the RSI scale. Table 2-1 provides a comprehensive list of states with their average RSI scores from 1980 to 2001.

Human Rights Rogues as Conventional Security Threats

The RSI can be used to assess rogue states as conventional threats to international security. We test whether states scoring higher on the RSI—those that are characterized by higher levels of discrimination and repression—are more likely to initiate interstate conflicts, become involved in violent conflicts, and use force first during interstate disputes.

The first model tests whether a higher RSI score is associated with an increased likelihood of conflict initiation, a binary variable taken from the Militarized Interstate Disputes (MIDs) data set.[42] The dispute initiator is

Figure 2-1. Rogue State Distribution: Average RSI Score, 1980–2001[a]

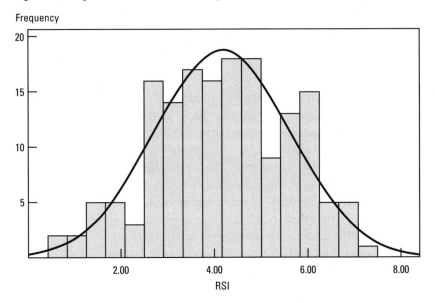

Source: Authors' calculations.
a. Number of countries in sample = 161; mean index score - 4.18; standard deviation = 1.45.

defined as the first state to take any form of militarized action, including the threat to use force or the display of force as well as the actual use of violence. In the first model, dispute initiators are coded as 1, with all others assigned a value of 0.

The second model examines the likelihood that human rights rogues will become involved in violent interstate conflict in any given year. Violent conflict involvement is a binary variable also coded from the MIDs data set. A score of 1 indicates that the state was involved in at least one violent militarized interstate dispute for that year whereas a score of 0 indicates that the state was not involved in any violent MIDs that year. A violent dispute is one that obtains a MID score of either 4, the use of force, or 5, war, on the hostility scale.

The third model assesses the likelihood that human rights rogues will use force first when involved in violent interstate disputes. First use of violent force is a binary variable coded as the first state to use military *violence* in an interstate dispute.[43] Testing for first use of force helps to isolate more directly the security risk posed by states that score high on the RSI and provides

Table 2-1. Average RSI Scores, 1980–2001

Country	RSI	Country	RSI	Country	RSI
Iran	7.1	Nicaragua	4.9	Slovakia	3.5
Guatemala	7.0	Yugoslavia	4.9	Ukraine	3.5
Saudi Arabia	6.8	Cameroon	4.8	Comoros	3.4
Sudan	6.8	Mali	4.8	Malawi	3.4
Afghanistan	6.7	Yemen Arab Republic	4.8	Suriname	3.4
Iraq	6.7	Argentina	4.7	United States	3.4
Pakistan	6.6	Cambodia	4.7	Uzbekistan	3.4
Ecuador	6.4	Senegal	4.7	Belarus	3.3
Sri Lanka	6.4	Fiji	4.6	Belize	3.3
Uganda	6.4	Malaysia	4.6	Czech Republic	3.3
Colombia	6.2	France	4.5	Latvia	3.3
Peru	6.2	Laos	4.5	Maldives Islands	3.2
Nigeria	6.1	Namibia	4.5	Benin	3.1
Somalia	6.1	Panama	4.5	Moldova	3.1
Honduras	6.0	Syria	4.5	Uruguay	3.1
Lebanon	6.0	China	4.4	Brunei	3.0
Paraguay	6.0	Italy	4.4	Gabon	3.0
Turkey	6.0	Japan	4.4	Gambia	3.0
Angola	5.9	Macedonia	4.4	Guinea-Bissau	3.0
Bhutan	5.9	Thailand	4.4	Kyrgyz Republic	3.0
Democratic Republic		Czechoslovakia	4.3	New Zealand	3.0
of Congo	5.9	Guyana	4.3	Armenia	2.9
El Salvador	5.9	Oman	4.3	Australia	2.9
India	5.9	Togo	4.3	Costa Rica	2.9
Indonesia	5.9	Bulgaria	4.2	Germany	2.9
Myanmar	5.8	Singapore	4.2	Canada	2.7
Venezuela	5.8	Spain	4.2	Estonia	2.7
Bahrain	5.7	Switzerland	4.2	Cape Verde	2.6
Ethiopia	5.7	Ghana	4.1	Ireland	2.6
Bangladesh	5.6	South Korea	4.1	Turkmenistan	2.6
Brazil	5.6	Tunisia	4.1	Belgium	2.5
Rwanda	5.6	Botswana	4.0	Cuba	2.5
South Africa	5.6	Eritrea	4.0	Hungary	2.5
Azerbaijan	5.5	Kazakhstan	4.0	Jamaica	2.5
Croatia	5.5	Lesotho	4.0	Malta	2.5
Dominican Republic	5.5	Nepal	4.0	Sao Tome-Principe	2.5
Niger	5.5	Romania	4.0	Solomon Islands	2.5
Sierra Leone	5.5	Albania	3.9	Barbados	2.3
Burundi	5.4	Guinea	3.9	Luxembourg	2.3
Congo	5.4	United Arab Emirates	3.9	Mongolia	2.2
Israel	5.4	Yemen	3.9	Bahamas	2.0
Bolivia	5.3	Haiti	3.8	Poland	2.0
Mauritania	5.3	Kuwait	3.8	Portugal	2.0
Chad	5.2	Burkina Faso	3.7	Trinidad	2.0
Kenya	5.1	Equatorial Guinea	3.7	Netherlands	1.7
Mexico	5.1	Malagasy Republic	3.7	Austria	1.5
Zimbabwe	5.1	Federal Republic		Iceland	1.5
Egypt	5.0	of Germany	3.6	Seychelles	1.5
Georgia	5.0	Swaziland	3.6	Slovenia	1.5
Morocco	5.0	United Kingdom	3.6	Vanuatu	1.5
Papua New Guinea	5.0	USSR-Russia	3.6	Denmark	0.9
Philippines	5.0	Libya	3.5	Finland	0.9
Chile	4.9	Mozambique	3.5	Norway	0.8
Greece	4.9	North Korea	3.5	Sweden	0.7
Côte d'Ivoire	4.9				

Source: Authors' calculations.

greater detail about the more general test of violent conflict involvement. Specifically, first use of violent force better captures aggressive actions perpetrated by the human rights rogue, given that such states might become embroiled in violent disputes as the targets rather than the perpetrators of interstate violence. The state to use force first during a MID is coded as 1; otherwise, the assigned value is 0.

Controls for other possible influences on state conflict behavior are added to the analysis, including the number of allies to control for the unpredictable impact of alliances on international conflict; number of neighbors as a control for conflict opportunity (states are considered contiguous if separated by up to 400 miles of water); major-power status, coded as 1, to control for the conflicting impact of major powers on international dispute behavior; and the cold war as a control for the bipolar period, with a score of 1 identifying the post–cold war era from 1990 to 2001.[44] Previous conflict is also included as a control for ongoing disputes, which may result in higher levels of domestic repression and discrimination, particularly related to the repression component of the RSI. Prior conflict, a binary variable, identifies whether or not the state experienced an MID in the past decade, with a score of 1 representing one or more MIDs in the preceding decade.

Stata statistical software was used to run logistic regression testing to determine whether states scoring higher on the RSI pose a conventional threat to international security as described above.[45] The models span the 1980–2001 time period, a function of data availability. Given this limited temporal domain, caution about the generalizability of the findings is warranted.

As shown in table 2-2, the higher a state scores on the rogue state index—that is, the greater the extent to which a state violates the norms of the international human rights regime—the more likely that state is to initiate militarized interstate disputes, become involved in violent militarized disputes, and be the first to use violence within an interstate dispute, even while controlling for other known causes of interstate conflict. Indeed, a state with the highest possible human rights rogue score of 8 will be more than nine times (9.44) more likely to initiate a militarized interstate dispute than a state that scores 0 on the RSI. In other words, each additional step on the RSI increases the likelihood that a state will initiate an interstate dispute by nearly 20 percent. Thus states exhibiting more rogue characteristics—those characterized by increasingly severe norms of violence—are more likely to start international conflicts.

Similarly, states scoring higher on the RSI are also more likely to find themselves embroiled in violent interstate disputes. A state with the highest

Table 2-2. Assessing Rogue States as Conventional Military Threats[a]

Variables and controls	Initiation	Violent conflict	First use of violent force
RSI	1.18* (0.045)	1.53* (0.065)	1.18* (0.074)
Major power	0.896 (0.161)	1.610* (0.308)	0.428* (0.115)
Number of allies	1.070* (0.026)	1.100* (0.029)	0.971 (0.030)
Number of neighbors	1.060* (0.014)	1.020 (0.015)	0.998 (0.019)
Prior conflict	0.854 (0.195)	2.000* (0.509)	1.070 (0.492)
Cold war	1.330* (0.147)	1.150 (0.134)	0.543* (0.088)
Summary statistic			
N	1,549	1,549	800
Model significance	$p > 0.0000$	$p > 0.0000$	$p > 0.0000$
Log likelihood	−1,042.58	−954.73	−511.01

Source: Authors' calculations using Stata software to run the logistic regression.
* Meets or exceeds the $p < 0.05$ standard of statistical significance.
a. The table includes odds ratio with standard errors in parentheses.

human rights rogue score of 8 will be more than twelve times (12.24) more likely to become involved in a violent militarized interstate dispute than a state scoring 0 on the RSI. In other words, each additional step on the RSI increases the likelihood of a state becoming involved in a violent interstate dispute by 53 percent.

Finally, human rights rogues are also more likely to use force first when involved in militarized interstate disputes. A state with the highest human rights rogue score of 8 will be more than nine times (9.44) more likely to use force first during militarized interstate disputes than a state scoring 0 on the RSI. In other words, each additional step on the index increases the likelihood of a state using force first during interstate disputes by nearly 20 percent.

The results of these tests clearly indicate that human rights rogues pose a conventional military threat to international security. This is in keeping with the conceptual framework laid out at the beginning of this chapter, which argues that the same norms and values drive state behavior both internally and externally and that violent norms will manifest themselves as violent actions. As the tests show, persistent human rights violators, whose failure to observe international human rights standards are a reflection of their violent social norms and values, are also much more likely to engage in violent actions internationally. As noted earlier, getting foreign policy practitioners to take human rights violations seriously has been a tremendous challenge for the international human rights community. The findings reported above, that human rights violators also represent significant international security threats, should help the human rights community make that case more compellingly. The importance of considering the security implications of human rights violations is reinforced when one looks beyond these conventional measures of international aggression to consider the extent to which human rights rogues also represent unconventional threats to international security.

Human Rights Rogues as Unconventional Security Threats

The post–cold war era is characterized as much by unconventional security risks—as the events of September 11, 2001, demonstrate—as by conventional military threats. Though human rights rogues should be considered conventional military threats, should the policy community consider such states as dual risks in also posing unconventional security threats? Our theoretical argument that domestic norms of violence are reliable predictors of violent international behavior led us to suspect and demonstrate a causal relation between human rights rogue status and aggression internationally. Similarly, we argue that state support for terrorism is an aspect of aggression and violence that can be predicted by human rights rogue status. In particular, those who study state-sponsored terrorism generally characterize it as a form of aggressive foreign policy behavior, "a cost-effective means of waging war covertly, through the use of surrogate warriors or 'guns for hire'—terrorists."[46]

To test whether human rights rogue status predicts support for terrorism, Stata software was used to run a logistic regression covering the years 1980–2001. Data on state sponsorship of terrorism are taken from terrorist group profiles and chronologies available through the Terrorism Knowledge Base.[47] Forms of support include direct sponsorship; provision of material, financial, or logistical assistance; or provision of safe havens. As with the tests for interstate dispute behavior discussed above, the limited temporal domain of the analysis limits the generalizability of the findings. In addition to our measure of state support for terrorism, the model includes a control for regime type, using the Polity2 variable from the Polity IV data.[48] This is introduced to control for the possibility that more democratic states might resort to supporting terrorism as a covert means of achieving unpopular foreign policy goals, as the United States sought to do by supporting various anti-Sandinista groups in Nicaragua during the 1980s.

Table 2-3. Assessing Human Rights Rogues and Support for Terrorism[a]

Variables	Terror support
RSI	1.66*
	(0.191)
Polity[b]	0.869*
	(0.019)
Summary statistic	
N	2,257
Model significance	$p > 0.0000$
Log likelihood	−315.78

Source: Authors' calculations using Stata software to run the logistic regression.
* Meets or exceeds the $p < 0.05$ standard of statistical significance.
a. The table includes odds ratio with standard errors in parentheses.
b. Polity 2 variable from the Polity IV data. See Marshall and Jaggers, "Polity IV Project, Dataset Users Manual," Center for International Development and Conflict Management (2002).

As hypothesized, human rights rogues—states that score highly on the rogue state index—are far more likely to support terrorism than states with lower RSI scores. Table 2-3 shows that with control for regime type, the greater the number of human rights rogue attributes a state has, the more likely that state is to support terrorism. A perfect human rights rogue—one scoring an 8 on the RSI scale—will be more than thirteen times more likely to support terrorism than a state scoring 0 on the RSI. A state scoring a 4 on the RSI, for instance, is more than six-and-a-half times more likely to support terrorism than a state scoring a 2. In other words, each additional step on the RSI increases the likelihood of a state supporting terrorism by 63 percent. Thus states exhibiting more rogue characteristics—those whose value systems are characterized by norms of violence—are more likely to be associated with terrorist activities, as our theoretical framework leads us to expect.

These findings show that rogue states—those states scoring higher on the RSI scale—are more aggressive, as evidenced by their conventional military behavior and by their greater likelihood of sponsoring terrorism. Thus the policy community should be particularly concerned if these aggressive states are also more likely to pursue weapons of mass destruction. Based on the evidence presented here, one cannot assume that rogue states would obtain WMDs for defensive purposes. Thus we provide a cross-tabulation between the RSI and the illicit pursuit of WMDs to further assess the security risk posed by human rights rogues. The intent is to discover whether states scoring higher on the RSI are more likely to engage in this behavior than are states with lower RSI scores. We do not necessarily argue that a causal relation exists between human rights rogue status and the pursuit of WMDs, as technological sophistication and material resources are necessary.

From 1980 to 2001, we find that rogue states were more likely illicitly to pursue or possess weapons of mass destruction—chemical, biological, or nuclear—as well as the means to deliver them.[49] It is important to note that the act of illicitly pursuing or possessing weapons of mass destruction cannot be used to identify rogue states; human rights rogue status accounts for only 23 percent of the variation for pursuit of WMDs. Thus we conclude that human rights rogues are more likely to pursue weapons of mass destruction, but this behavior by itself cannot be used to identify rogue states. In other words, the pursuit of WMDs, much as with the support for terrorism, should be considered an aggressive international behavior linked to violent domestic norms.

Pakistan and Iran: Exemplars of Human Rights Rogues

As shown earlier, both Pakistan and Iran fall squarely into the category of human rights rogues by virtue of their persistently high levels of political repression and discriminatory social and political structures and practices. They also have engaged in the kinds of roguish international behaviors that our model expects and that policymakers have feared. To illustrate, we offer brief summaries of Pakistan's and Iran's involvement in interstate disputes (see table 2-4) and descriptions of their domestic nuclear, chemical, and biological programs. It is also interesting to note that while both of these states fit the profile here for human rights rogues and have engaged in the same types of roguish international conduct, only Iran has been singled out as a rogue by U.S. policymakers; Pakistan enjoys the status of valued partner of the United States in its ongoing war on terrorism.

Pakistan

From 1980 to 2001, Pakistan was involved in sixteen militarized interstate disputes, clashing most frequently with its neighbors Afghanistan and India. In three of those disputes, Pakistan was the first state to take a militarized action. In other words, Pakistan was the first actor in the dispute to threaten, display, or use force. In each of those instances, when Pakistan initiated the militarized action, the first action taken was the actual use of military force rather than simple display or threat. One of these disputes reached a sufficiently high level of intensity to be considered an interstate war, as marked by an excess of 1,000 battlefield deaths sustained by all combatants in a single

Table 2-4. Pakistan and Iran Militarized Dispute Summary, 1980–2001

Units as indicated

Country	RSI average	Total number of disputes	Initiated action		Used force	
			Number of times	Percent of time	Number of times	Percent of time
Pakistan	6.6	16	3	18.75	11	68.75
Iran	7.1	100	49	49.00	71	71.00

Source: Authors' calculations.

year. Of the other thirteen disputes in which Pakistan was involved, it also resorted to military force in eight of them.

Just as its military conflict behavior marks Pakistan as a conventional risk to international security, Pakistan's activities involving weapons of mass destruction, particularly nuclear weapons development, and its record of sponsoring terrorist organizations marks it also as an unconventional security threat. The Federation of American Scientists (FAS) estimates that Pakistan began developing its nuclear weapons program in 1972, an effort that reached fruition with successful nuclear tests in 1998.[50] In addition to developing nuclear weapons, Pakistan has also acquired a considerable stockpile of chemical weapons and developed the capability to deliver them. Although Pakistan had been dependent on foreign sources for its chemical warfare technology, the FAS estimates that by 2000 Pakistan had the technical ability to produce its own chemical weapons. Not only is Pakistan stockpiling chemical weapons, but it also apparently has the will to use them; it is widely believed that Pakistan used chemical weapons against Indian troops in 1987. In addition to chemical weapons, Pakistan has a sound biotechnology infrastructure and is believed to have the ability to support a limited offensive biological warfare research and development effort.[51]

Finally, the government of Pakistan, through its external intelligence arm known as Inter-Services Intelligence, has been linked to a half-dozen terrorist organizations since the 1980s. Among them were the Taliban, which enjoyed Pakistani patronage as it rose to dominate Afghanistan in the late 1990s and ultimately to play host to al Qaeda. Likewise, several Kashmiri secessionist groups have received Pakistani support for campaigns of terrorism against Indian targets. One of these groups, Jaish-e-Mohammed, was responsible for a 2001 attack on the Indian Parliament in New Delhi in which fourteen people were killed, including the five attackers.[52]

Iran

From 1980 to 2001, Iran was involved in 100 militarized interstate disputes, most frequently with its neighbors Turkey and Iraq but also with the United States, Soviet Union–Russia, Saudi Arabia, and Kuwait. In 49 of those disputes, Iran was the first state to take a militarized action, and in 37 of those instances, Iran's first action was the actual use of military force. Of the 51 disputes in which Iran did not take the first militarized action, 35 cases involved the actual use of force. Thus Iran used force in a total of 71 militarized interstate disputes from 1980 to 2001, and one of these disputes, with Iraq, escalated to full-scale interstate war.

As with Pakistan, Iran began developing nuclear technology in the 1970s, but unlike Pakistan, as of early 2007 it had yet to test or deploy a nuclear weapon. However, beginning in the summer of 2005, there has been considerable tension between the Iranian government and the international community as Iran resumed uranium enrichment in defiance of the United States and the European Union, which called on Iran to abandon its nuclear programs. According to the FAS, Iran is believed to be pursuing nuclear weapons though there is little hard evidence, in part because Iran claims that its nuclear technology is aimed at energy production. The International Atomic Energy Agency continues to investigate concerns about Iran's compliance with the Nuclear Non-Proliferation Treaty, in part due to the discovery of blueprints for an advanced centrifuge design that Iran hid from nuclear inspectors.[53]

While there is some doubt about the intentions of the Iranian nuclear program, there is no doubt at all about the nature of its chemical weapons capability. Iran is able to employ chemical weapons on the battlefield, as it did during its eight-year war with Iraq, and has in the past supplied chemical warfare agents to other countries, specifically Libya in 1987. The FAS judges that Iran is close to having a large, self-supporting chemical weapons infrastructure and has boosted its chemical warfare capability by developing chemical warheads for its Scud missile systems.[54] Iran's offensive biological warfare research program is traced to the Iran-Iraq war and is now considered to be in the advanced research and development phase. It is considered likely that Iran has developed a small biological warfare arsenal that could be delivered by a variety of systems.

Like Pakistan, Iran has a long record of support for terrorist organizations. Since 1980 the Iranian government has been linked to ten different terrorist groups, several of them Palestinian groups opposed to Israel, including Palestinian Islamic Jihad and Hamas, as well as other anti-Israeli groups, especially Hezbollah. Iran's patronage of Hezbollah came under renewed scrutiny in the summer of 2006 when a raid by Hezbollah into northern Israel triggered the most intense Israeli military response since the 1982 invasion of Lebanon. As of the August 14, 2006, cease-fire, 791 Lebanese had been killed, and as many as a million Lebanese, roughly a quarter of the population, were displaced. Among Israelis, 154 died, about three quarters of them soldiers, either in combat or as the victims of Hezbollah rocket attacks.

Iran has also provided patronage for terrorist organizations targeting neighboring rival Turkey, including Turkish Islamic Jihad, the Kurdistan Workers' Party, and the Patriotic Union of Kurdistan. It has also acted as patron for terrorist groups active in Iraq, including the Organization of Islamic Action in Iraq, which opposed the Saddam regime, and the Mahdi Army and its various offshoots in the post-Saddam period.[55]

Both Pakistan and Iran clearly fit our human rights rogue profile. Both states, perennial human rights abusers, have consistently engaged in behavior that poses both conventional military threats to their neighbors and regions and unconventional threats to international security more generally. Both states have repeatedly engaged in military clashes, most often with their neighbors. Both states have advanced programs for WMDs, with Pakistan's including nuclear arms. Both states have long records of backing terrorism. That American policymakers have adopted such differential postures toward these rogue actors, embracing Pakistan while confronting and threatening Iran with military action, underscores the serious inadequacy of U.S. decisionmakers' conception of and approach to the security challenge posed by rogue states.

Conclusion

Rogue states are real, and they represent real threats to international security. But the criteria that American policymakers have adopted and unevenly applied to brand a limited set of actors as rogues fail to capture either the identity of the real rogues or the scope of the threat rogue states represent. When observance of international human rights norms is used as the standard against which to measure rogue state status, we find that states characterized by more severe violations of those standards are also more likely to engage in a host of aggressive and dangerous international behaviors than states with better performance on human rights. Human rights rogues represent conventional threats to international security through their greater likelihood to engage in aggressive interstate conflict. Furthermore, in comparison to states whose behavior is characterized by closer adherence to the standards of the international human rights regime, these human rights rogues are also more likely to pose unconventional threats to international security through a greater propensity to support international terrorism and to develop and acquire weapons of mass destruction. Thus, even in a world driven by the security priorities of "realist" foreign policies, the advance of human rights must be on the agenda.

Notes

1. Madeleine K. Albright, "Remarks at Tennessee State University" (February 19, 1998), secretary.state.gov/www/statements/1998/980219b.html.

2. For a good example of this phenomenon, see Raymond Tanter, *Rogue Regimes: Terrorism and Proliferation* (New York, 1995).

3. See Paul D. Hoyt, "Rogue States and International Relations," paper presented at the 1999 annual meeting of the International Studies Association (Washington, D.C., February 16–20); Mary Caprioli and Peter F. Trumbore, "Rhetoric vs. Reality: Rogue States in Interstate Conflict, 1980–2001," *Journal of Conflict Resolution*, XLIX (2005), 770–791.

4. For example, see Noam Chomsky, *Rogue States: The Rule of Force in World Affairs* (Cambridge, Mass., 2000); Robert S. Litwak, *Rogue States and U.S. Foreign Policy: Containment after the Cold War* (Washington, D.C., 2000); Robert S. Litwak, "What's in a Name? The Changing Foreign Policy Lexicon," *Journal of International Affairs*, LIV (2001), 375–392; Meghan L. O'Sullivan, "Les dilemmas de la politique américaine vis-à-vis des 'rogue states'," *Politique Etrangère*, I (2000), 67–80.

5. O'Sullivan, "Les dilemmas."

6. David P. Forsythe, *Human Rights in International Relations* (Cambridge, 2000), 139.

7. In Elizabeth Saunders, "Setting Boundaries: Can International Society Exclude 'Rogue States'?" *International Studies Review*, VIII (2006), 23–54, the concept of the rogue state is used to explore the issue of international society and how it is defined. While this is an interesting theoretical exercise, Saunders offers little insight into what we consider the critical questions about rogue states, their identity, and behavior.

8. Jack Donnelly, *Universal Human Rights in Theory and Practice*, 2nd ed. (Ithaca, N.Y., 2003).

9. For a general discussion of pariah states see Lewis A. Dunn, "Nuclear Grey Marketeering," *International Security*, I (1977), 107–118; Lawrence Freedman, "British Foreign Policy to 1985, IV: Britain and the Arms Trade," *International Affairs*, LIV (1978), 377–392; Litwak, *Rogue States*. For a representative discussion of specific pariah cases, see John C. Donnell, "Vietnam 1979: Year of Calamity," *Asian Survey*, XX (1980), 19–32; Kenneth W. Grundy, "Intermediary Power and Global Dependency: The Case

of South Africa," *International Studies Quarterly*, XX (1976), 553–580; Raimo Väyry-nen, "Economic and Military Position of the Regional Power Centers," *Journal of Peace Research*, XVI (1979), 349–369; Edward S. Milenky, "Latin America's Multilateral Diplomacy: Integration, Disintegration, and Interdependence," *International Affairs*, LIII (1977), 73–96.

10. Mervyn Frost, *Ethics in International Relations: A Constitutive Theory* (Cambridge, 1996).

11. See Robert J. Art, "Geopolitics Updated: The Strategy of Selective Engagement," *International Security*, XXIII (1998), 79–113; John J. Mearsheimer, "Back to the Future: Instability in Europe after the Cold War," *International Security*, XV (1990), 5–56; John J. Mearsheimer, "Why We Will Soon Miss the Cold War," *Atlantic Monthly*, CCLXVI (1990), 35–50; Kenneth N. Waltz, "Structural Realism after the Cold War," *International Security*, XXV (2000), 5–41.

12. Waltz, "Structural Realism," 20.

13. See Michael Klare, *Rogue States and Nuclear Outlaws: America's Search for a New Foreign Policy* (New York, 1995); Litwak, *Rogue States*.

14. Michael Mastanduno, "Preserving the Unipolar Moment: Realist Theories and U.S. Grand Strategy after the Cold War," *International Security*, XXI (1997), 49–88.

15. Regarding strategies of preponderance, see Christopher Layne, "From Preponderance to Offshore Balancing: America's Future Grand Strategy," *International Security*, XXII (1997), 86–124; Barry R. Posen and Andrew L. Ross, "Competing Visions for U.S. Grand Strategy," *International Security*, XXI (1997), 5–53. For a discussion on emerging third world challenges to American security interests, see Steven R. David, "Why the Third World Still Matters," *International Security*, XVII (1992), 127–159.

16. "Suddenly a Long Costly Crisis Looms," *Washington Post* (August 12, 1990).

17. U.S. Department of Defense, *Report on the Bottom-up Review* (Washington, D.C., October 1993), 19.

18. Caprioli and Trumbore, "Rhetoric."

19. Mary Caprioli and Peter F. Trumbore, "Identifying 'Rogue' States and Testing Their Interstate Conflict Behavior," *European Journal of International Relations*, IX (2003), 378–381; Mary Caprioli and Peter F. Trumbore, "Human Rights Rogues in Interstate Disputes, 1980–2001," *Journal of Peace Research*, XLIII (2006), 131–148.

20. In particular, see Rudolph J. Rummel, "Domestic Attributes and Foreign Conflict," in J. David Singer (ed.), *Quantitative International Politics* (New York, 1968); Melvin Small and J. David Singer, "The War-Proneness of Democratic Regimes," *Jerusalem Journal of International Relations*, I (1976), 50–69.

21. For an overview of this literature, see Michael E. Brown, Sean M. Lynn-Jones, and Steven E. Miller (eds.), *Debating the Democratic Peace* (Cambridge, Mass., 1996).

22. Bruce Russett, "Why Democratic Peace," in Brown, Lynn-Jones, and Miller (eds.), *Debating the Democratic Peace*, 114.

23. See Zeev Maoz and Bruce M. Russett, "Normative and Structural Causes of the Democratic Peace," *American Political Science Review*, LXXXVII (1993), 624–638.

24. On the theory of structural violence, see Johan Galtung, "Violence, Peace, and Peace Research," *Journal of Peace Research*, VI (1969), 167–191. For an overview of feminist approaches to understanding security and security analysis, see J. Ann Tickner, *Gender in International Relations* (New York, 1992); J. Ann Tickner, *Gendering World Politics* (New York, 2001). For a gendered analysis of security, see Mary Caprioli, "Democracy and Human Rights versus Women's Security: A Contradiction?" *Security Dialogue: Special Issue Gender and Security*, XXXV (2004), 411–428.

25. For example, see Charlotte Bunch and Roxanna Carrillo, "Global Violence against Women: The Challenge to Human Rights and Development," in Michael T. Klare and Yogesh Chandrani (eds.), *World Security* (New York, 1998), 229–248; Mary Caprioli, "Primed for Violence: The Role of Gender Equality in Predicting Internal Conflict," *International Studies Quarterly*, XLIX (2005), 161–178; Mary Caprioli, "Gender Equality and State Aggression: The Impact of Domestic Gender Equality on State First Use of Force," *International Interactions,* XXIX (2003), 195–214; Jean Bethke Elshtain, *Women and War* (New York, 1987); Judith Stiehm, *Women's Views of the Political World of Men* (New York, 1984); Bernard Yack, "The Myth of the Civic Nation," in Ronald Beiner (ed.), *Theorizing Nationalism* (Albany, N.Y., 1999), 103–118.

26. Pamela Goldberg, "Where in the World Is There Safety for Me? Women Fleeing Gender-Biased Persecution," in Julie Peters and Andrea Wolper (eds.), *Women's Rights, Human Rights: International Feminist Perspectives* (Oxford, 1995), 347.

27. Donnelly, *Universal*, 23.

28. Ted Robert Gurr, *Minorities at Risk: A Global View of Ethnopolitical Conflicts* (Washington, D.C., 2003).

29. Minorities at Risk, "Assessment for Baha'is in Iran" (2005), www.cidcm.umd.edu/inscr/mar/assessment.asp?groupId=63003.

30. For a thorough discussion of various measures of gender inequality and discrimination, see Caprioli, "Democracy."

31. Inter-Parliamentary Union, *Women in Parliaments 1945–1995: A World Statistical Survey* (Geneva, 1995); Inter-Parliamentary Union, *Women in Politics 1945–2000* (Geneva, 2000); United Nations Development Programme, *Human Development Report 1995* (New York, 1995), 108.

32. Joan Huber, "Macro-Micro Links in Gender Stratification," in Joan Huber (ed.), *Macro-Micro Linkages* (Newbury Park, Calif., 1991), 11–25.

33. World Bank, *World Development Indicators* (Washington, D.C., 2003).

34. Rae Lesser Blumberg, "Women and the Wealth and Well-Being of Nations: Macro-Micro Interrelationships," in Huber (ed.), *Macro-Micro Linkage*s, 121–140; Caprioli, "Gender Equality" and "Democracy."

35. Ibid.

36. Figures obtained from UNICEF, "Fertility and Contraceptive Use" (2003), childinfo.org/eddb/fertility/index.htm.

37. See Mark Gibney, "Political Terror Scale" (2004), www.unca.edu/politicalscience/DOCS/Gibney/Political%20Terror%20Scale%201980-2005.pdf, published yearly.

38. Steven C. Poe and C. Neal Tate, "Repression of Human Rights to Personal Integrity in the 1980s: A Global Analysis," *American Political Science Review*, LXXXVIII (1994), 853–872.

39. Linda Camp Keith, "The United Nations International Covenant on Civil and Political Rights: Does It Make a Difference in Human Rights Behavior?" *Journal of Peace Research*, XXXVIII (1999), 95–118.

40. Amnesty International, "Amnesty International 1998 Annual Report: Iran" (1998), www.amnesty.org/ailib/aireport/ar98/mde13.htm.

41. Due to missing data, no RSI was computed for Andorra, Antigua and Barbuda, Bosnia, Cyprus, Democratic Republic of Germany, Democratic Republic of Vietnam, Djibouti, Dominica, Federated States of Micronesia, Grenada, Liberia, Liechtenstein, Lithuania, Marshall Islands, Mauritius, Monaco, Palau, People's Democratic Republic of Yemen, Qatar, St. Kitts and Nevis, St. Lucia, St. Vincent and the Grenadines, San Marino, Taiwan, Tajikistan, Tanzania, Western Samoa, and Zambia.

42. Faten Ghosn and Glenn Palmer, "Codebook for the Militarized Interstate Dispute Data, Version 3.0" (2003), cow2.la.psu.edu, version 3.02.

43. Mary Caprioli and Peter F. Trumbore, "Special Data Feature: First Use of Violent Force in Militarized Interstate Disputes, 1980–2001," *Journal of Peace Research*, XLIII (2006), 765–773.

44. Zeev Maoz, "Alliances: The Street Gangs of World Politics—Their Origins, Management, and Consequences, 1816–1986," in John A. Vasquez (ed.), *What Do We Know about War?* (New York, 2000), 111–144; Stuart Bremer, "Dangerous Dyads: Conditions Affecting the Likelihood of Interstate War, 1816–1965," *Journal of Conflict Resolution*, XXXVI (1992), 309–341; John A. Vasquez, *The War Puzzle* (Cambridge, Mass., 1993); Daniel S. Geller, "Material Capabilities: Power and International Conflict," in Vasquez (ed.), *What Do We Know about War?* 259–277.

45. See Stata Statistical Software for Professionals, "Logistic Regression" (College Station, Texas, December 2006), www.stata.com/capabilities/logistic.html.

46. Bruce Hoffman, *Inside Terrorism* (New York, 1998), 187. See also Daniel Byman, *Deadly Connections: States That Sponsor Terrorism* (New York, 2005).

47. Memorial Institute for the Prevention of Terrorism, "Terrorism Knowledge Base" (December 2006), www.tkb.org.

48. Monty G. Marshall and Keith Jaggers, "Polity IV Project, Dataset Users Manual," Center for International Development and Conflict Management (2002), www.cidcm.umd.edu/polity/data/.

49. Pearson chi-square (14) 172.97, $p > 0.000$, $N = 2,432$, Cramer's V = 0.267. Data sources: Federation of American Scientists (FAS); U.S. Department of State, Bureau of Nonproliferation; Carnegie Endowment for International Peace; and the Stockholm International Peace Research Institute.

50. FAS, "Pakistan Special Weapons Guide" (2005), www.fas.org/nuke/guide/pakistan/index.html.

51. Ibid.

52. Institute for Conflict Management, South Asia Terrorism Portal, "Jaish-e-Mohammed" (2005), www.satp.org/satporgtp/countries/india/states/jandk/terrorist_outfits/jaish_e_mohammad_mujahideen_e_tanzeem.htm.

53. FAS, "Iran Special Weapons Guide: Nuclear Weapons" (2005), www.fas.org/nuke/guide/iran/nuke/index.html.

54. FAS, "Iran Special Weapons Guide: Chemical Weapons" (2006), www.fas.org/nuke/guide/iran/cw/index.html.

55. Memorial Institute, "Terrorism Knowledge Base."

three
Running the Numbers:
A Comparative Perspective

Yi Feng and Saumik Paul

This chapter compares fourteen countries characterized by poor human rights records. Four of them—Cuba, Iran, Saudi Arabia, and the Sudan—are referenced but not profiled in this book. The process of categorization and evaluation across political, social, and economic dimensions relies primarily on data published in 2004 and 2005. (See appendix 3A.) As an introduction, table 3-1 presents three or four key characteristics for each of these countries.

Political Dimensions

Freedom House scores nations on two separate seven-point scales that measure their levels of political rights and civil liberties.[1] The fourteen countries evaluated here ranked low on political rights and civil liberties according to the Freedom House data. (See table 3-2.)

In terms of political rights, countries rated 1 come closest to political democracy whereas a score of 7 indicates those with the least freedom. All fourteen countries had political rights scores of either 6 or 7, which classifies them as "unfree." Such states are likely to be ruled by a single party, military dictatorships, autocrats, or theocracies. The difference between "partly free" and "unfree" nations lies in the minimal freedoms that citizens in the former category possess, such as the right to organize national political parties and compete in national elections. The difference between countries designated 6 and 7 lies in whether local governments are elected competitively and

Table 3-1. Key Attributes of Fourteen Sample States

Countries by region	Attributes
East Asia and Pacific	
Burma	Rule of law practically nonexistent under the military regime
	State Law and Order Restoration Council, based on ethnic rebel groups; controls both administrative and religious affairs
	Trade unions, collective bargaining, and strikes illegal
	Recently forced to rewrite its constitution because of U.S. and EU threats to boycott Association of Southeast Asian Nations meeting
North Korea	Complete absence of democracy, autocratic regime since the 1950s
	Only state-sponsored candidates participate in elections
	Religious practices restricted to state-sponsored services
	Economic stagnation and resource misallocation for decades
Europe and Central Asia	
Belarus	Former Soviet republic
	Judicial branch highly influenced by President Lukashenko
	No freedom of press
Turkmenistan	Former Soviet republic and a communist state
	Economy based on agriculture and mineral resources
	Abject poverty, hyperinflation, and shortage of foodstuffs common through last decade
	Government controls and funds all electronic and print media
Uzbekistan	Former Soviet republic and one-party state dominated by communists
	Second largest cotton exporter in the world
	Most media activities controlled by the government
Latin America and Caribbean	
Cuba	One of the oldest communist governments; run by Fidel Castro
	Strict dichotomy between inefficient domestic sector and comparatively efficient export sector
	One of the highest per capita rates of imprisonment for political offenses
Middle East and North Africa	
Iran	World's first Islamic republic
	Oil export–based economy
	Persistent high inflation and unemployment rate in last two decades
	Discrimination against women in employment and legal sectors

(continued)

whether minorities have some political autonomy. In those countries that score a 7, even limited freedoms are nonexistent or their exercise may come at the risk of extreme political violence. Indonesia, for example, has been classified as unfree since 1990–1991, when the political rights score changed from 5 to 6, and then from 6 to 7 in 1993–1994.[2]

The civil liberties score also ranges from 1 to 7, with 7 representing the most unfree. The fourteen countries all earned a score of 6 or 7 except Togo and Tunisia, which each received a 5. Countries that receive a score of 6 have partial freedom in regard to religious beliefs and business activities (for example, Indonesia during 1993–1994). In nations receiving a score of 7,

Table 3-1. Key Attributes of Fourteen Sample States (*Continued*)

Countries by region	Attributes
Saudi Arabia	International human rights groups banned No election at any level; constitution governed by Islamic law World's largest exporter of petroleum Only electricity and telecommunications are under private control
Syria	Military-based regime; no opposition party against government permitted Kurdish community faces cultural and linguistic constraints Any union is controlled by government
Tunisia	Legal system based on French civic law and Islamic law Progressive social conditions for women largely unmatched in Arab region Domestic broadcast media tightly controlled by government; all foreign publications censored
Sub-Saharan Africa Equatorial Guinea	One of the world's most closed and repressed societies Freedom of religion but widespread evidence of violence against women Government permission needed to travel abroad and within country Any gathering against government with more than ten people is illegal
Sudan	Ethnic conflict and civil war common in the past decades Broadcast media entirely state controlled Women face extensive social discrimination and unequal treatment based on sharia (Islamic law)
Togo	Opposition has no impact in the parliament Prevalent ethnic discrimination Religious freedom constitutionally protected and generally allowed Discrimination against women despite constitutional provision Evidence of massive fraud in recent presidential election won by Gnassingbé
Zimbabwe	More than 60 percent of population below poverty line Extensive legal protection for women All broadcast media directly or indirectly government controlled

Sources: Central Intelligence Agency (CIA), *The World Factbook* (2006), www.cia.gov/cia/publications/factbook; *Democracy at Large: Building Democracy in Africa's Weak States*, I, no. 3 (2005); Adrian Karatnycky (ed.), *Freedom in the World 1997–98: The Annual Survey of Political Rights and Civil Liberties* (Piscataway, N.J., 1998).

however, even these partial freedoms are nonexistent (for example, China during 1989–1990, when students' pro-democracy demonstrations in Beijing ended in bloodshed). The countries that are ranked lowest in both political rights and civil liberties are Saudi Arabia (monarchy), Syria (authoritarian, military-dominated republic), Turkmenistan (authoritarian presidential rule), North Korea (communist), Cuba (communist), Burma (military rule), and the Sudan (authoritarian republic).[3]

Kaufmann, Kraay, and Mastruzzi developed a set of six governance indicators for 213 countries and territories for five time periods: 1996, 1998, 2000, 2002, and 2005 (and subsequently 2003 and 2004 in their 2006 report).[4] The

Table 3-2. Political Indicators, 2005

| | | Freedom ranking[a] | | |
		Political rights	Civil liberties	Status
Countries by region	*Government type*			
East Asia and Pacific				
Burma	Military junta	7	7	NF
North Korea	Communist state	7	7	NF
Europe and Central Asia				
Belarus	Dictatorship	7	6	NF
Turkmenistan	Republic, authoritarian presidential rule	7	7	NF
Uzbekistan	Republic, authoritarian presidential rule	7	6	NF
Latin America and Caribbean				
Cuba	Communist state	7	7	NF
Middle East and North Africa				
Iran	Theocratic republic	6	6	NF
Saudi Arabia	Monarchy	7	7	NF
Syria	Republic, under military regime	7	7	NF
Tunisia	Republic	6	5	NF
Sub-Saharan Africa				
Equatorial Guinea	Republic	7	6	NF
Sudan	Authoritarian regime	7	7	NF
Togo	Republic, under transition to multiparty democratic rule	6	5	NF
Zimbabwe	Parliamentary democracy	7	6	NF

Source: For government type, CIA, *The World Factbook*; for freedom ranking, Freedom House, "Table of Independent Countries" (2006), www.freedomhouse.org/uploads/WoW/2006/TableofIndependentCountries2006.pdf.

a. A score of 1, most free; score of 7, least free. See text for further description of scoring. Under status, NF indicates not free.

values were derived from several hundred individual variables, measuring perceptions of governance, drawn from thirty-one separate data sources by twenty-five different organizations.

These six dimensions of governance are voice and accountability, political stability, government effectiveness, regulatory quality, rule of law, and control of corruption. The first two indicators evaluate the process used to select political authority. Government effectiveness and regulatory quality portray government capacity and efficiency. Rule of law and control of corruption indicate citizen respect for the government that exercises lawful control over social interactions. For these measures, the world average is zero.

Table 3-3 shows the values of these six dimensions for the selected fourteen countries. They are also classified by income group according to the latest World Bank country classification (2006): six countries were in the low-income group (North Korea, Burma, the Sudan, Togo, Uzbekistan, and

Zimbabwe); six were in the lower-middle-income group (Belarus, Cuba, Iran, Syria, Tunisia, and Turkmenistan); one was in the upper-middle-income group (Equatorial Guinea); and one was in the high-income group (Saudi Arabia). Among these economies, Equatorial Guinea and Saudi Arabia are clearly outliers, being well endowed with oil. Tunisia may be another outlier: though it was classified as a lower-middle-income country, its economic growth rate has been respectable compared to that of sub-Saharan African countries.

Among the fourteen countries, Burma, Cuba, North Korea, the Sudan, and Turkmenistan ranked very low on voice and accountability; Tunisia and Togo rated the highest. With respect to political stability, the Sudan, Uzbekistan, and Zimbabwe ranked very low; Equatorial Guinea and Tunisia had the highest political stability. In terms of government effectiveness, the least competent governments were found in North Korea, Burma, Turkmenistan, Equatorial Guinea and Zimbabwe (tied), Togo, and the Sudan; the most effective governments were in Tunisia, Saudi Arabia, and Iran. All fourteen nations fell below the world average in regulatory quality, with the worst quality found in North Korea, Zimbabwe, Burma, and Turkmenistan. Saudi Arabia, Tunisia, and Togo had the highest regulatory quality among this group. Tunisia and Saudi Arabia were found to have better rule of the law than the others; rule of law was worst in Burma, the Sudan, and Zimbabwe. The most corrupt country in the group was Equatorial Guinea, followed by Burma and the Sudan; Tunisia and Saudi Arabia had the best control of corruption. Both of them had scores not only higher than their income group average but also than the world average.

When the six scores were averaged, they yielded the following ranking, from the least to the most politically desirable among this group of countries: North Korea, Zimbabwe, the Sudan, Uzbekistan, Burma, Turkmenistan, Equatorial Guinea, Togo, Belarus, Iran, Syria, Cuba, Saudi Arabia, and Tunisia.

Economic Dimensions

According to the *2005 Human Development Report* and the country classification from the *2006 World Development Indicators,* all of the countries studied or referenced in this chapter belonged to either low-income or lower-middle-income categories except Equatorial Guinea (upper middle income) and Saudi Arabia (high income).[5] Most of these countries have experienced persistent economic crises in the past decades. Economic stagnation resulting

Table 3-3. Governance Indicators, 2005

Countries	Income category	Accountability	Political stability	Government effectiveness	Regulatory quality	Rule of law	Control of corruption
Belarus	Lower middle	-1.68 (0.12)	0.01 (0.26)	-1.19 (0.16)	-1.53 (0.18)	-1.04 (0.16)	-0.90 (0.16)
Burma	Low	-2.16 (0.14)	-1.00 (0.23)	-1.61 (0.17)	-2.19 (0.18)	-1.56 (0.17)	-1.44 (0.20)
Cuba	Lower middle	-1.87 (0.14)	0.03 (0.23)	-0.94 (0.18)	-1.75 (0.18)	-1.14 (0.16)	-0.26 (0.18)
Equatorial Guinea	Upper middle	-1.71 (0.19)	0.21 (0.35)	-1.42 (0.22)	-1.31 (0.22)	-1.33 (0.20)	-1.79 (0.24)
Iran	Lower middle	-1.43 (0.12)	-1.14 (0.22)	-0.77 (0.17)	-1.49 (0.18)	-0.76 (0.14)	-0.47 (0.17)
North Korea	Low	-2.06 (0.14)	-0.12 (0.30)	-1.82 (0.20)	-2.31 (0.19)	-1.15 (0.18)	-1.32 (0.23)
Saudi Arabia	High	-1.72 (0.14)	-0.70 (0.22)	-0.38 (0.18)	-0.01 (0.18)	0.20 (0.15)	0.23 (0.17)
Sudan	Low	-1.84 (0.14)	-2.05 (0.23)	-1.30 (0.17)	-1.29 (0.17)	-1.48 (0.17)	-1.40 (0.18)
Syria	Lower middle	-1.67 (0.12)	-0.91 (0.23)	-1.23 (0.18)	-1.22 (0.18)	-0.42 (0.16)	-0.59 (0.18)
Togo	Low	-1.23 (0.15)	-1.22 (0.29)	-1.38 (0.19)	-0.81 (0.19)	-1.07 (0.19)	-0.70 (0.21)
Tunisia	Lower middle	-1.13 (0.12)	0.12 (0.22)	0.43 (0.16)	-0.07 (0.16)	0.21 (0.14)	0.13 (0.15)
Turkmenistan	Lower middle	-1.95 (0.12)	-0.34 (0.27)	-1.57 (0.16)	-1.95 (0.19)	-1.41 (0.15)	-1.30 (0.15)
Uzbekistan	Low	-1.76 (0.11)	-1.91 (0.24)	-1.20 (0.15)	-1.71 (0.17)	-1.31 (0.14)	-1.07 (0.13)
Zimbabwe	Low	-1.65 (0.14)	-1.58 (0.22)	-1.42 (0.15)	-2.20 (0.16)	-1.47 (0.14)	-1.24 (0.15)

Sources: Daniel Kaufmann, Aart Kraay, and Massimo Mastruzzi, "Governance Matters V: Governance Indicators for 1996–2005" (Washington, D.C., September, 2006); "Worldwide Governance Indicators Country Snapshot 2005," info.worldbank.org/governance/kkz2005/year_report.asp?yearid=1.
Note: Standard deviations are shown in parentheses.

from excessive government control was common in all of these countries. Some suffered from strict currency practices (Turkmenistan, Uzbekistan), some from overvalued exchange rates (Zimbabwe), and some from high inflation, unemployment, and trade deficits (Belarus, Syria).

To explore in detail whether economic problems are sui generis or are common to these politically repressive states, we analyzed some key economic data both at country-specific and respective region-specific levels to see how disproportionate their economic conditions were compared to their neighbors and the world. Table 3-4 sorts these countries according to income groups using the World Bank Atlas method and geographical locations.[6] The World Bank classifies these regional geographic groups based on location as well as on similar developmental experience. Equatorial Guinea was the only sub-Saharan upper-middle-income country in this group. The Middle East and North African states, also known as the "Arab world," had a relatively dispersed economic status. While Saudi Arabia belonged to the high-income group, Syria, Iran, and Tunisia were all in the lower-middle-income group. The two countries in the sample from the East Asia and Pacific region, North Korea and Burma, both belonged to the low-income category.

Table 3-5 uses a similar format to sort these countries with respect to their indebtedness and income groups. There was a strong correlation between low-income and severely indebted states. By the World Bank definition, most of the low-income states other than Uzbekistan and North Korea were severely indebted.[7] Almost all of the lower-middle-income category countries were moderately or less indebted, with Cuba, North Korea, and Saudi Arabia not classified by indebtedness.

In table 3-6, five of the major domestic economic indicators are used to evaluate domestic economic conditions. In 2005, world average per capita gross national income (GNI) stood at $6,988. When this measure is examined by region, sub-Saharan Africa's average per capita GNI was, unsurprisingly, much below any of the other regions. This region of the world has remained poor because of its deficient governance, oppressive political leadership, and inefficient domestic markets. From the available World Bank data on the Europe–Central Asia region, Uzbekistan's per capita GNI was much lower than the regional average and in comparison to two other countries from the region, Belarus and Turkmenistan.

In the Middle East–North Africa region, only Syria had a per capita GNI below average, with the lowest GDP growth rate (among these countries), at

Table 3-4. Country Classification by Geographic Region and Income Categories, 2005[a]

Geographic region	Income category			
	Low	*Lower middle*	*Upper middle*	*High*
East Asia and Pacific	Burma North Korea			
Europe and Central Asia	Uzbekistan	Belarus Turkmenistan		
Latin America and Caribbean		Cuba		
Middle East and North Africa		Iran Syria Tunisia		Saudi Arabia[b]
Sub-Saharan Africa	Sudan Togo Zimbabwe		Equatorial Guinea	

Source: World Bank, "Country Classification" (July 2006), www.worldbank.org/data/countryclass/class-groups.htm.

a. Geographic regions are based on similar development experience. Income categories are based on 2005 gross national income (GNI) per capita, using the World Bank Atlas method (see text). Low income, ≤ $875; lower middle income, $876 to $3,465; upper middle income, $3,466 to $10,725; high income, ≥ $10,726.

b. The geographic categories used here are based only on developing countries; Saudi Arabia does not fall into the developing country groups.

4.2. Both Iran and Tunisia recorded above average per capita GNI with an impressive 6 and 5 percent annual GDP growth, respectively.

Most of the sub-Saharan African states in the sample performed below their regional average. Togo had a per capita GNI of only $350, and Zimbabwe was not only below the low-income group average but also had a negative GDP growth rate in 2005 and 2006. Equatorial Guinea was the only country in this region that stood above the regional average in terms of per capita GNI, boasting an impressive 9.9 percent annual GDP growth. Overall, the available data showed that only three countries had a per capita GNI less than the low-income group average ($578); these were Togo ($350), Uzbekistan ($510), and Zimbabwe ($340).

The level of capital formation among these countries ranged from 10 to 40 percent of their GDP in 2005. Zimbabwe recorded the highest investment share of GDP at 38.3 percent. Both Saudi Arabia and Togo had an investment share that was less than 20 percent of their GDP. There was almost no positive trend between income level and investment share among these countries, which explains the inadequate infrastructure in most of these repressed states. Six of these states had an annual inflation rate (GDP deflator) somewhere between 10 to 20 percent. Cuba, Tunisia, Turkmenistan, and Togo

Table 3-5. Country Classification by Income Category and External Indebtedness, 2005[a]

| | Income category | | | |
Indebtedness category	Low	Lower middle	Upper middle	High
Severely indebted	Burma Sudan Togo Zimbabwe	Syria		
Moderately indebted	Uzbekistan	Tunisia Turkmenistan		
Less indebted		Belarus Iran	Equatorial Guinea	
Not classified by indebtedness	North Korea[b]	Cuba		Saudi Arabia

Sources: World Bank, "Country Classification." Indebtedness data from World Bank Debtor Reporting System. See World Bank List of Economies (July 2005), www.iscb.org/pdfs/WorldBankClassificationList2005.pdf.

Note: As of April 2006, the World Bank no longer classifies countries by indebtedness level.

a. Indebtedness categories are based on present value of debt service to GNI (a) and present value of debt service to exports (b). Severely indebted: (a) > 80 percent; (b) > 220 percent. Moderately indebted: (a) = 60–79 percent; (b) = 60–219 percent. Less indebted: (a) < 60 percent; (b) < 60 percent.

b. North Korea does not report to the World Bank Debtor Reporting System; therefore the following criteria are used to measure indebtedness: debt to GNI, debt to exports, debt service to exports, and interest to exports.

maintained an inflation rate of less than 5 percent. Equatorial Guinea was the only country that experienced deflation in 2005. Zimbabwe continued to have very high inflation, reaching over 1,000 percent in 2006 and reaching 1,700 percent in 2007, as a result of its persistent fiscal deficit and overvalued exchange rate.

Most of the countries in the Arab region are prime oil exporters, which explains their positive current account balance. In 2005, Saudi Arabia had a huge current account surplus of $90.73 billion. The other sample countries in the Arab world, except Tunisia, also showed a positive balance—of a smaller magnitude—on their current accounts. All of the sub-Saharan countries had negative current account balances except Equatorial Guinea, which also exports oil. Zimbabwe had an almost $519 million deficit in its current account with a negative annual GDP growth rate of around 7 percent. All the countries from Europe and Central Asia displayed a current account surplus in 2005.

As shown in table 3-7, in terms of exports as a share of GDP, most of these states performed above the low-income category average (19.6 percent of GDP). From the available data, except for the Sudan, the rest of the low-income-group countries shown in table 3-7 had an exports-to-GDP ratio much higher than 19.6 percent in 2005. Almost 33.7 percent of Togo's GDP

Table 3-6. Domestic Economic Performance, by Region, Country, and Income Level, 2005[a]

Units as indicated

Location and income level	Gross national income (GNI) per capita (current U.S. dollars)[b]	GDP growth per year (percent)	Gross capital formation (percent of GDP)	Current account balance (current billions of U.S. dollars)	Annual inflation rate, GDP deflator (percent)
World	6,988	3.5	22.5 (2004)	n.a.	4.8
East Asia and Pacific	1,627	8.7	38.8	n.a.	4.6
Burma	n.a.	5.0	15.0 (2001)	0.70	17.6
North Korea	n.a.	n.a.	n.a.	n.a.	n.a.
Europe and Central Asia	4,113	5.9	22.5	n.a.	6.5
Belarus	2,760	9.2	29.6	0.85	16.6
Turkmenistan	1,340 (2004)	17.0 (2004)	27.1 (2003)	0.24	2.6 (2004)
Uzbekistan	510	7.0	25.1	1.10	15.9
Latin America and Caribbean	4,007	4.4	20.2	n.a.	5.8
Cuba	n.a.	1.1 (2000)	9.74 (2000)	0.05	2.6 (2000)

Middle East and North Africa	2,241	4.6	25.6	n.a.	5.4
Iran	2,770	5.9	31.5	13.27	18.0
Saudi Arabia	11,770	6.6	16.2	90.73	16.0
Syria	1,380	4.2	22.9 (2004)	1.10	6.7
Tunisia	2,890	4.9	25.4	-0.36	1.8
Sub-Saharan Africa	745	5.3	19.7	n.a.	6.6
Equatorial Guinea	9,110 (2002)	9.9 (2004)	n.a.	0.26	-8.3 (2003)
Sudan	640	8.0	22.4	-3.01	12.1
Togo	350	2.8	17.6	-0.19	3.8
Zimbabwe	340	-7.1	38.3	-0.52	240.3
Income level					
Low income	578	7.5	22.2 (2003)	n.a.	7.9
Lower middle income	1,918	6.9	30.7	n.a.	5.2
Upper middle income	5,625	5.5	21.4	n.a.	4.9
Upper income (non-OECD)[c]	17,656	6.0	20.2	n.a.	n.a.

Sources: World Bank, "Key Development Data and Statistics" (2005), www.worldbank.org/data/countrydata/countrydata.html, and "World Development Indicators Database" (August 2006), devdata.worldbank.org/data-query/. Figures for current account balance are taken from CIA, *The World Factbook* (2006).

n.a. Not available.

a. Values are for 2005 except as otherwise noted. Regional averages are based on developing countries in each specific region, as categorized by the World Bank.

b. Based on World Bank Atlas method (see text).

c. OECD, Organization for Economic Cooperation and Development.

Table 3-7. External Economic Performance, by Region, Country, and Income Level, 2005[a]

Units as indicated

Location and income level	Exports of goods and services (percent of GDP)	Imports of goods and services (percent of GDP)	Reserves of foreign exchange and gold (current billions of U.S. dollars)	Foreign direct investment (current billions of U.S. dollars)[b]	Aid per capita (current U.S. dollars), 2003
World	24.7 (2004)	24.9 (2004)	n.a.	664.9	12.3
East Asia and Pacific	44.9	42.7 (2004)	n.a.	64.6	3.8
Burma	n.a.	n.a.	0.76	0.2	2.5
North Korea	n.a.	n.a.	n.a.	n.a.	7.4
Europe and Central Asia	38.6	38.1	n.a.	62.2	22.2
Belarus	61.4	60.4	1.22	0.2	3.2
Turkmenistan	70.1	58.9	2.96	n.a.	5.5
Uzbekistan	39.6	31.9	2.68	0.2	7.6
Latin America and Caribbean	25.9	23.2	n.a.	60.8	20.9
Cuba	15.7 (2000)	18.2 (2000)	2.62	n.a.	6.2

Middle East and North Africa	34.8	33.5	n.a.	5.3	26.3
Iran	31.9 (2000)	27.4	45.46	0.5	2.0
Saudi Arabia	60.7 (2003)	26.4	26.76	0	0.9
Syria	40.6 (2004)	33.4 (2004)	5.40	0.3	9.2
Tunisia	47.9	51.1	4.37	0.6	30.8
Sub-Saharan Africa	34.7	34.3	n.a.	11.3	34.3
Equatorial Guinea	n.a.	n.a.	2.11	1.6	43.1
Sudan	20.7	24.8	2.45	1.5	18.5
Togo	33.7	46.6	0.31	0.1	9.2
Zimbabwe	170.2	205.3	0.16	0.1	14.2
Income level					
Low income	19.6 (2004)	22.3 (2004)	n.a.	16.6	13.8
Lower middle income	33.4 (2004)	32.1 (2004)	n.a.	106.1	8.4
Upper middle income	33.9	33.5	n.a.	88.8	10.2
Upper income (non-OECD)	91.0	80.0	n.a.	54.0	n.a.

Source: World Bank, "Key Development Data and Statistics" (2005), and "World Development Indicators Database" (August 2006); UN Development Programme, "Human Development Report 2005" (2005), hdr.undp.org/reports/global/2005/. For data on reserves of foreign exchange and gold, see CIA, *The World Factbook*.

n.a. Not available.

a. Values are for 2005 except as otherwise noted. Regional averages are based on developing countries in each specific region.

b. Net inflows in reporting country. Regional and world figures are total debts received by all the countries under that category.

came from exporting primarily agricultural (cocoa, coffee, and cotton) products. The Middle Eastern regional states earned 35 percent of their GDP from exports, primarily oil. In the Europe–Central Asia region, agricultural and mineral economies such as Turkmenistan and Uzbekistan exported around 70 and 40 percent of their GDP, respectively.

Imports as a share of GDP ranged from 18 to 47 percent for most of the sample countries. The exceptions were Belarus (60.4 percent), Tunisia (51.1 percent), and Turkmenistan (58.9 percent), all having imports-to-GDP ratios above the lower-middle-income average of 32.1 percent. Zimbabwe is clearly an outlier here with an import share of 240.3 percent of GDP in 2005.

In 2005, total net foreign direct investment to the recipient countries worldwide amounted to $664.9 billion. Among the fourteen countries analyzed, Saudi Arabia was the only donor country, thus showing no net inflow of foreign aid. With the exception of North Korea, Turkmenistan, and Cuba, for which data are not available, the rest were recipient countries. In sub-Saharan Africa, Equatorial Guinea and the Sudan received more than $1.5 billion of foreign direct investment, whereas the rest recorded about $100 million.

In 2003, the average aid per capita in the East Asia–Pacific region ($3.8) was much lower than the world average ($12.3), the Europe–Central Asia region average ($22.2), and the Middle East–North Africa region average ($26.3)—mainly because of higher populations. In terms of aid per capita, only Tunisia in the Middle East–North Africa region and Equatorial Guinea in the sub-Saharan Africa region exceeded both the regional and world averages. The rest of the countries were below their respective regional averages (except North Korea), and most fell below the world average.

In the area of foreign exchange and gold reserves, Saudi Arabia and Iran recorded far higher amounts—in excess of $25 billion—than the other countries in the sample.

Overall, the economic performance of these fourteen countries was poor compared to the world and their neighbors within the same region, as defined by the World Bank. From the sample, only the economies in the Middle East–North Africa region, which mostly are based on oil exports, performed better than the average for their region.

Social Dimensions

Table 3-8 presents some of the important social indicators of these fourteen states. The East Asia–Pacific region had an average population density of

110 persons per square kilometer, the highest in the world. Among the sample countries, North Korea had the highest density, at almost 188 persons per square kilometer. Most of these countries are densely populated because of their small country size or high fertility rate, which partially explains their very low per capita gross national income. This theory holds for Equatorial Guinea in an opposite way: the country had around eighteen persons per square kilometer and an above average per capita GNI in the sub-Saharan region. Countries such as the Sudan and Turkmenistan had very low population densities and low per capita GNI.

Infant mortality was very high in the sub-Saharan region, mainly because of malnutrition and significantly large numbers of undernourished children. On average, 10 percent of total live births result in death in sub-Saharan Africa. Among the fourteen countries, Equatorial Guinea had the highest infant mortality rate, at 122.4 deaths per 1,000 live births. Furthermore, life expectancy at birth in sub-Saharan Africa is 46.2 years, much lower than both the world average of 67.3 and the low-income category average of 58.7. In Zimbabwe in 2004, life expectancy at birth was only 37.3 years. The countries in East Asia and the Pacific as well as in Europe and Central Asia had life expectancies hovering around the worldwide average of 67.3, whereas in Cuba and the Middle Eastern–North African countries, life expectancies exceeded 70 years.

Education is one of the prime indicators of the social condition of a country. In the economic literature, increases in education positively affect the prosperity of a country by creating and improving human capital. In 2004, the average literacy rate in the world was around 78 percent, more than 15 percent higher than the average literacy rate in low-income countries. Income always has a strong positive correlation with the literacy rate; as nations climb the ladder from low-income to upper-income, they attain higher literacy rates.

In the sample group, countries from the Europe–Central Asia region had a literacy rate of nearly 100 percent. Middle Eastern and North African countries showed on average more than a 72 percent literacy rate. Zimbabwe's literacy rate stood at more than 90 percent, despite its poor economic performance and unfree political environment.

A related consideration revolves around the question of how important the Internet is in today's society. Whatever the answer, there is an overwhelming consensus about the growing popularity and usefulness of the Internet to connect people all over the world. Oppressive leaders prefer to control the media; such control now includes the Internet and is a common

Table 3-8. Social Indicators, by Region, Country, and Income Level, Years as Indicated

Units as indicated

Location and income level	Population density (population per sq. km.), 2003	Infant mortality rate (deaths per 1,000 live births), 2004	Life expectancy at birth (years), 2004	Literacy: age ≥15 (percent that read or write), 2004	Internet users (per 1,000 persons), 2004	Female economic activity rate: age ≥15 (as percent of male), 2003
World	45.5	54.1	67.3	78.2	139.9	69
East Asia and Pacific	110.4	29.2	70.3	90.7	73.8	52
Burma	75.1	75.6	60.7	89.9	1.3	75
North Korea	187.8	42.0	60.6	99.0	n.a.	n.a.
Europe and Central Asia	19.5	28.5	68.7	97.1	137.9	81
Belarus	47.6	8.6	68.4	99.6	162.9	82
Turkmenistan	10.3	80.2	62.7	98.0	7.5	82
Uzbekistan	61.7	57.2	67.1	99.3	33.6	85
Latin America and Caribbean	25.1	26.5	72.2	90.2	114.8	52
Cuba	103.1	6.3	77.0	99.8	13.4	67
Middle East and North Africa	24.6	44.1	69.4	72.1	58.1	42
Iran	40.5	32.0	70.8	77.0	82.1	39
Saudi Arabia	10.4	21.4	72.3	79.4	66.3	29
Syria	94.5	15.0	73.6	79.6	43.1	38
Tunisia	63.6	21.0	73.3	74.3	84.1	48
Sub-Saharan Africa	27.0	101.0	46.2	59.6	19.4	73
Equatorial Guinea	17.6	122.4	42.7	86.9	10.2	52
Sudan	14.1	62.6	56.5	60.9	32.1	41
Togo	89.3	78.4	54.8	53.2	40.0	62
Zimbabwe	33.8	79.4	37.3	90.7	63.4	78
Income level						
Low income	69.6	79.5	58.7	61.5	24.4	62
Lower middle income	40.3	32.6	70.3	88.9	74.1	73
Upper middle income	43.3	23.2	69.2	93.6	161.5	73
Upper income (non-OECD)	113.2	n.a.	76.0	n.a.	345.0	n.a.

Source: World Bank, "World Development Indicators Database" (August 2006); UN Development Programme, "Human Development Report 2005"; CIA, *The World Factbook*.
n.a. Not available.

phenomenon in all of the countries discussed here. In 2004, the world average of Internet users per 1,000 persons was around 139.9. None of these fourteen states was close to reaching that level except Belarus, which was slightly above average with 162.9 Internet users per 1,000 persons. In Burma, this number was just over 1. People in these repressed countries do not have sufficient access to the Internet to reach people outside their borders.

Female economic activity is a direct measure of how advanced and balanced a society is in its economic development. In the countries under discussion, religious beliefs and practices largely determine the degree of female activity in a society. In most of the countries in the Middle East region, women lack equal rights and many of the opportunities that exist in most parts of the Western world. The last column in table 3-8 reveals this fact: in all of the countries from the Middle East–North Africa region, women had less than 50 percent of the economic activity of men. Even the most progressive state in the region, Tunisia, fell below that threshold for female economic activity, which was 48 percent of that of men.

Using data from the Center for Religious Freedom, table 3-9 ranks religious freedom according to predominant religious background; the rankings correspond to female economic activity.[8] Based on the data available for the sample countries, Iran, Saudi Arabia, the Sudan, Turkmenistan, and Uzbekistan—all Muslim nations—score either 6 or 7 and thus fall into the religiously unfree category. Burma and North Korea, primarily Buddhist countries, also received a score of 7. Cuba, a communist country that is ostensibly Catholic, ranks as religiously unfree with a score of 6. Only Zimbabwe, a primarily Protestant country, was found to be religiously free, with a score of 3.

In addition, there was a high correspondence between lower religious freedom and lower female economic participation among three of the Middle Eastern and North African Islamic countries. However, although the Muslim former Soviet republics had the same lack of religious freedom as the other Islamic countries, they had a much higher female economic participation rate—more than 80 percent.

Conclusion

To evaluate overall performance across political, economic, and social dimensions, we created three composite indexes for the fourteen target countries in order to rank them with respect to the group and to the world (see table 3-10).

For the composite political index, each of the six dimensions mentioned by Kaufmann, Kraay, and Mastruzzi was used to determine the relative position

Table 3-9. Religious Freedom and Female Economic Participation, Years as Indicated[a]

Units as indicated

Predominant religion and country	Religious freedom, 2000		Female economic participation (percent of male), 2003[b]
	Score	Classification	
Catholic			
Cuba	6	Unfree (lower degree)	67
Protestant			
Zimbabwe	3	Free (lower degree)	78
Buddhist and related			
Burma	7	Unfree (higher degree)	75
North Korea	7	Unfree (higher degree)	n.a.
Muslim			
Iran	7	Unfree (higher degree)	38
Saudi Arabia	7	Unfree (higher degree)	29
Sudan	7	Unfree (higher degree)	41
Turkmenistan	7	Unfree (higher degree)	82
Uzbekistan	6	Unfree (lower degree)	85

Source: Paul A. Marshall, *Religious Freedom in the World* (Washington, D.C., October 2000), figure 2.
n.a. Not available.
a. Profiles in *Religious Freedom in the World* describe, evaluate, and rate countries that together constitute more than 90 percent of the world's population, using a scale from 1 (highest religious freedom) to 7 (lowest). There is no documentation on religious freedom data for Belarus, Equatorial Guinea, Syria, Togo, and Tunisia.
b. See table 3-8.

of the fourteen sample countries by considering the highest and lowest score in each category.[9] The following is the range of lowest to highest scores for each of these categories:

—voice and accountability, –2.16 to –1.13;
—political stability, –2.05 to 0.21;
—government effectiveness, –1.82 to 0.43;
—regulatory quality, –2.31 to –0.01;
—rule of law, –1.56 to 0.21; and
—control of corruption, –1.79 to 0.23.

These category indexes were then averaged to construct a composite political index for each country.

The composite economic index was calculated from the GDP index reported in the Human Development Index (HDI) in the UN's *Human Development Report 2005.*[10] According to this report, the GDP index ranged from 0.26 to 1 from the total sample of 177 countries. The relative positions of the fourteen countries were evaluated using this scale. Among the countries in the sample, Equatorial Guinea had the highest GDP index score, despite the fact that Saudi Arabia was the only high-income country. The

Table 3-10. Composite Political, Economic, and Social Indexes

Country	Index Political	Economic	Social
Belarus	0.40	0.55	0.86
Cuba	0.44	0.54	0.90
Equatorial Guinea	0.31	0.93	0.53
Iran	0.43	0.59	0.73
Burma	0.22	0.18	0.60
North Korea	0.13	0.34	0.53
Saudi Arabia	0.73	0.74	0.74
Sudan	0.17	0.30	0.45
Syria	0.44	0.46	0.76
Togo	0.38	0.26	0.45
Tunisia	0.86	0.59	0.76
Turkmenistan	0.24	0.50	0.82
Uzbekistan	0.20	0.28	0.83
Zimbabwe	0.15	0.36	0.39

Source: Authors' calculations (see explanation in text).

GDP index is based on indirect methods such as regression to generate an estimated figure. This kind of approximation is often based on a single year, unless otherwise specified. Since figures on North Korea are not available in the 2005 Human Development Index, we used the low-income group average GDP index as a proxy for North Korea.

The composite social index was constructed as the average of life expectancy and educational indexes from the 2005 HDI. The same method discussed above was employed to find the relative positions of each of these fourteen countries within the ranges 0.13 to 0.94 and 0.16 to 0.99 for the life expectancy index and the educational index respectively (out of the total sample of 177 countries). Values for North Korea were derived using the same proxy method applied in constructing the composite economic index.

The correlation between the political composite index and the economic composite index (0.52) was fairly strong relative to that between the political composite index and the social composite index (0.43), but the correlation between the economic composite index and the social composite index was weak (0.29).

If anyone had to choose to live in one of the societies under review according to political standards, the choice would be Tunisia, Saudi Arabia, Cuba, Syria, Iran, Belarus, Togo, Equatorial Guinea, Turkmenistan, Burma, Uzbekistan, the Sudan, Zimbabwe, and North Korea—in that order. By the economic criterion, the ranking from most to least desirable would be Equatorial Guinea, Saudi Arabia, Iran and Tunisia, Belarus, Cuba, Turkmenistan, Syria,

Figure 3-1. Three-Dimensional Distribution of Sample Countries along Political, Economic, and Social Dimensions

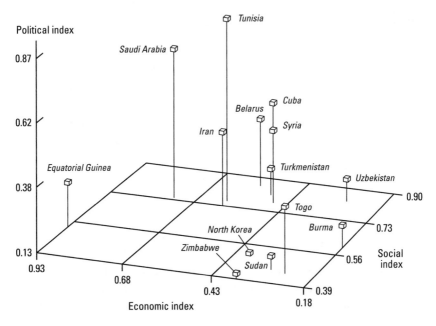

Source: Authors' calculations (see table 3-10).

Zimbabwe, North Korea, the Sudan, Uzbekistan, Togo, and Burma. Finally, based on social standards, the top to bottom ranking would be Cuba, Belarus, Uzbekistan, Turkmenistan, Syria and Tunisia, Saudi Arabia, Iran, Burma, Equatorial Guinea and North Korea, the Sudan and Togo, and Zimbabwe.

Figure 3-1 shows the three-dimensional distribution of the fourteen sample countries based on the three composite criteria. Combining the composite scores of the political, economic, and social indexes produces the following rank for the fourteen-country sample, from highest to lowest: Tunisia, Saudi Arabia, Cuba, Belarus, Equatorial Guinea, Iran, Syria, Turkmenistan, Uzbekistan, Togo, North Korea, Burma, the Sudan, and Zimbabwe.

Notes

1 . The following description is based on Freedom House, "Survey Methodology," *Freedom Review*, XXVIII (1997), 8–11.

2. Ibid.

3. Ibid.

4. Daniel Kaufmann, Art Kraay, and Massimo Mastruzzi, "Governance Matters V: Governance Indicators for 1996–2005" (Washington, D.C., September 15, 2006).

5. See UN Development Programme, "Human Development Report 2005" (2005), www.sd.undp.org/HDR/HDR05e.pdf; World Bank, "Country Classification" (July 2006), www.worldbank.org/data/countryclass/classgroups.htm.

6. According to the World Bank, "the purpose of the Atlas conversion factor is to reduce the impact of exchange rate fluctuations in the cross-country comparison of national incomes." For an explanation of this method, see World Bank, "Country Classification: World Bank Atlas Method," web.worldbank.org/WBSITE/EXTERNAL/DATASTATISTICS/0,,contentMDK:20452009~menuPK:64133156~pagePK:64133150~piPK:64133175~theSitePK:239419,00.html. The same classification is also used for governance indicators. See Kaufmann, Kraay, and Mastruzzi, "Governance Matters V."

7. The World Bank defines indebtedness on the basis of two key ratios, present value of debt service to gross national income and present value of debt service to exports. For the countries that do not report to the World Bank Debtor Reporting System, the World Bank considers two additional ratios: debt service to exports, and interest to exports. World Bank, "List of Economies" (July 2005), www.iscb.org/pdfs/WorldBankClassificationList2005.pdf.

8. Paul A. Marshall, *Religious Freedom in the World* (Washington, D.C., October 2000), figure 2.

9. See Kaufmann, Kraay, and Mastruzzi, "Governance Matters V."

10. The HDI focuses on three measurable dimensions of human development: living a long and healthy life, being educated, and having a decent standard of living. For methods of calculating the different indexes, see UN Development Programme, "Human Development Report 2005," 340.

Appendix 3A. Terminology

This study is descriptive; we compared fourteen countries on the basis of political, economic, and social indicators from the data sources available. These data sources use various measurements of the economic activity of a nation, namely gross domestic product (GDP), gross national income (GNI), and gross national product (GNP). For example, the World Bank classifies *income groups* of countries according to GNI, but development indexes used in the UN Development Programme's Human Development Report are measured in GDP per capita. We use these various measurements to indicate a country's present status or activity, but from an accounting point of view, they are not exactly the same. Any standard textbook provides the following relationship between GNI, GDP, and GNP:

GNI = Compensation of employees (wages) + net interest + rental income + profits + indirect business taxes.

GNP = GNI + statistical discrepancy + depreciation.

GDP = GNP + income paid to other countries – income received from other countries.

Source: William J. Baumol and Alan S. Blinder, *Macroeconomics, Principles and Policy*, 9th ed. (Mason, Ohio, 2004), 138.

four
North Korea:
The Tyranny of Deprivation

Marcus Noland

Using the definition employed in this volume, North Korea is a quintessential rogue state, combining systematic internal repression with aggressive and dangerous external behavior. Its oppression of its own people can be demonstrated amply: up to a million deaths in a famine during the 1990s, for which North Korea's political leadership bears considerable responsibility; the maintenance of a Soviet-style gulag that houses as many as 200,000 political prisoners; and a pervasive climate of fear and privation that has encouraged citizens, perhaps hundreds of thousands, to flee North Korea in favor of uncertain prospects in neighboring China. Emblematic of North Korea's external behavior has been its withdrawal from the Nuclear Non-Proliferation Treaty (the only country to have done so) followed by a nuclear test in October 2006, its lack of interest in joining the Missile Technology Control Regime, and state involvement in criminal activity, ranging from drug trafficking to counterfeiting and even to the smuggling of endangered animal parts in contravention of the Convention on International Trade in Endangered Species. By these criteria, North Korea is a model rogue state.

Yet, as objectionable as North Korea's behavior is, it may be worth keeping in mind that its ambitions appear to be limited to the Korean peninsula. North

I thank Paul Karner for research assistance. This chapter summarizes and updates arguments made in greater detail in Marcus Noland, *Korea after Kim Jong-il* (Washington, D.C., 2004).

Korea is not a revolutionary state actively attempting to overthrow dominant international norms and institutions; rather, it is an "alienated state"—one regarding itself as having no real stake in the existing international order. In its internal organization it hews to a Westphalian notion of sole and exclusive sovereignty over what occurs within its borders and does not recognize other parties as having any legitimate interests in this sphere. Externally, its behavior appears largely driven by two imperatives associated with regime survival: to address its military security concerns—as it sees them—and to make money. Its illicit activities appear to have no aims beyond revenue generation; likewise nuclear weapons development and missile trafficking seem to be motivated by the regime's perceptions of its security, not by any broader strategic aims. Of course, regardless of motive, the effect of this behavior is to undercut the aims and functioning of the existing order and its institutions.

The Nature of Tyranny

North Korea is a product—some would say a vestige—of the cold war. At the conclusion of World War II, the Japanese colony of Korea was partitioned into zones of U.S. and Soviet occupation. Various Korean factions were unable to agree on a formula for unification, and in 1948 the Republic of Korea was proclaimed in the zone of U.S. occupation in the south while the Democratic People's Republic of Korea (DPRK) was established under Soviet tutelage in the north. In June 1950, North Korea invaded South Korea. The initial success of the invading forces was reversed with the support of a U.S.-dominated United Nations contingent, driving China to enter the war in October to prevent North Korea's defeat. The conflict ended in 1953 with the original borders more or less reestablished, the notable exception being the Kaesong high ground, which was ceded to North Korea, arguably putting South Korea at a disadvantage by enabling Pyongyang to hold Seoul hostage militarily. The seesaw character of the war, involving armies from both sides traversing the peninsula, left both countries economically devastated and reliant on their respective patrons.

In this environment, North Korean founding leader Kim Il-sung succeeded in constructing arguably the strangest political culture extant, combining elements of Stalinism, corporatism, and Confucian dynastic practice. But the most important element was Korean nationalism, embodied in the form of the deified Great Leader and his heir the Dear Leader Kim Jong-il, and inculcated through a political socialization of the masses that emphasized an ideological and personal devotion of religious intensity.[1]

The regime classifies the population according to perceived political loyalty, and the share deemed reliable is relatively small, on the order of one-quarter of the population, with a core elite of perhaps 200,000, or roughly 1 percent of the population.[2] Some argue that the "spiritual" basis of regime legitimacy may buy it a certain margin of tolerance for its apparent inability to deliver the conventional benefits of material prosperity or political freedom, though the existence of the gulag suggests that the regime is not taking any chances.[3]

For the nondevout, the regime practices forced internal exile and maintains a network of political prison camps that holds 200,000 or more political prisoners.[4] Prisoners have been executed for ill-defined political crimes such as "ideological divergence," and until the 2004 revisions to the penal code, *any* unauthorized attempt to leave the country was a capital crime.[5] There are numerous eyewitness accounts of public executions, including cases of schoolchildren being forced to witness these killings.[6]

Any sign of political deviance, from listening to foreign radio broadcasts to singing South Korean songs to sitting on a newspaper containing the photograph of Kim Il-sung is subject to punishment.[7] Collective punishment is practiced, with up to three generations of a family interned for an individual's offense. Death rates in these camps are high, torture is practiced, and there have been unconfirmed reports of prisoners being used for chemical and biological weapons testing. How important these camps are to the functioning of the North Korean economy is unknown, though reportedly some export goods are produced in the camps.

A second network of smaller extrajudicial detention centers exists, many located near the Chinese border. They developed partly as an ad hoc response to famine-coping behavior, such as foraging, unauthorized internal movement, or crossing the border into China, by the populace during the 1990s. Death rates are high, torture is practiced, and there are extensive anecdotal reports of forced abortions and infanticide.[8] There are no firm estimates of the number of people detained in these facilities.[9]

In 2004 the Supreme People's Assembly passed revisions to the criminal code. The revisions could be interpreted as an attempt to bring the penal code in line with the changes that had occurred in North Korea over the previous decade, for example, by indicating what kinds of economic activity were legal and which were not. Sentencing was also revised, with the specified categories including "unlimited-term correctional labor," "limited-term correctional labor," and "labor training."[10]

The North Korean government denies the existence of any human rights problems, has refused entry to outside groups since an Amnesty International visit in 1996, and demonizes foreign critics. A special rapporteur of the Commission on Human Rights was appointed by the United Nations in 2004 but was denied permission to visit the country. The North Korean government did hold one meeting with a European Union delegation to discuss human rights in 2004, however.

By standard statistical measures, such as the share of the population under arms or the share of national income devoted to the military, North Korea is the world's most militarized society, with the bulk of its million-strong army deployed in an offensive posture along the demilitarized zone separating it from South Korea. Domestic propaganda incessantly proclaims the virtues of "military-first" politics, and given the regime's extreme preference for guns over butter, the North Korean economy does not produce enough output to sustain the population biologically. A famine in the late 1990s resulted in the deaths of perhaps 600,000 to 1 million people out of a prefamine population of roughly 22 million.[11] Population maintenance is aid dependent. As in the case of the UN special rapporteur for human rights, the UN's special rapporteur on the right to food has been denied entry to the DPRK five times, despite the fact that UN and other humanitarian assistance has been feeding roughly one-third of the populace since the mid-1990s.

International assistance is important to North Korea: from a balance of payments standpoint, it appears that in recent years North Korea has derived roughly one-third of its revenues from aid, roughly one-third from conventional exports, and roughly one-third from unconventional sources (in estimated order of significance, missile sales, drug trafficking, remittances, counterfeiting, and smuggling). Remittances come mostly from a community of pro-Pyongyang ethnic Koreans in Japan; contract laborers in Russia, Eastern Europe, and elsewhere; and increasingly from highly vulnerable refugees in China, who number possibly 100,000. The latter, in effect, have exchanged one prison for another.[12]

Isolation and Engagement

In the early 1990s, as it was entering a famine, North Korea was also stumbling into a nuclear confrontation with the United States. The two events became inextricably linked as the provision of aid was highly politicized, reflecting the interests of the main donors, and was often used to induce North Korean participation in diplomatic negotiations.[13] More than a decade into the food emergency, North Korean practices still fall far short of minimum standards with respect to transparency and nondiscrimination in providing access to relief.[14] Even so, North Korea subsequently emerged as the largest Asian recipient of U.S. aid in the 1990s, receiving more than $1 billion in food and energy assistance between 1995 and 2002.

Famine relief is one component of North Korea's three-pronged engagement with the outside world. Its nuclear weapons program is another, giving rise to the Agreed Framework and the Korean Peninsula Energy Development Organization. This organization was officially shuttered in 2006 in response to the DPRK's continued failure to fulfill commitments in its agreement with the organization. However, energy assistance has been renewed under the terms of the Six Party Talks joint statement of February 2007.

The third component of North Korea's engagement with the outside world has been the effective shift, over the 1990s, from reliance on Soviet patronage to a more diversified multilateral set of supporters. (Despite its national ideology of *juche*, or self-reliance, North Korea has been dependent on outside assistance throughout its entire history.) The most important enabler of this adjustment has been the ideological and strategic shift in South Korea, manifested in the 1997 and subsequent elections.

Nevertheless, this coping behavior proved inadequate to pull the country out of its decline, and in 2002 North Korea arguably attempted its first strategic reorientation in half a century toward a policy of peaceful coexistence built around a three-part strategy of deterrence, demobilization of conventional forces, and economic policy changes.

More than a decade of economic decline in North Korea in the face of South Korea's growing prosperity and alliance with the United States has rendered the dream of unification on Pyongyang's terms an anachronism. Under such circumstances, the North Koreans have two basic options: to play for time, hoping that the strategic environment changes favorably, or throw in the towel, recognizing that they are on the wrong side of history and redefining the strategic goals of the regime. In the second case, one such goal could be self-enrichment. The North Korean elite's one card is its control over the levers of power, which it can use to appropriate the lion's share of economic gains generated by economic reform.

From this perspective, an investment in weapons of mass destruction and delivery systems capable of striking targets beyond the Korean peninsula is probably warranted to maintain double-sided deterrence. However, once deterrence is secured, the mass deployment of conventional forces would be an impediment to its rapprochement with South Korea, a prospective provider of capital, technology, and commercial and diplomatic entrée around the world. If a nuclear-armed North Korea were to forswear aggression toward South

Korea, its huge conventional forces would then be redundant, and its million-man army, an albatross around the economy's neck, could be demobilized. North Korea signaled in 2002 that it was contemplating cutting the size of its armed forces by as many as 500,000 soldiers, which perhaps more than coincidentally would have reduced them to roughly the same size as South Korea's armed forces. This signal appears to have fallen on receptive ears, at least in South Korea, where a growing majority of the population, accustomed to living for decades in the shadow of North Korea's forward-deployed artillery, do not regard the DPRK as a serious threat. In a recent public opinion poll, more South Koreans identified the United States as the principal threat to peace than North Korea. The younger the respondent and the higher the level of educational attainment, the wider this gap is. Fifty-eight percent of respondents in their twenties and 52 percent of students and white-collar workers polled singled out the United States as the primary threat to peace.[15] Another survey found that more than three-quarters of South Korean students polled actually supported North Korea's development of nuclear weapons.[16]

The demobilization of conventional forces can work only if the troops have somewhere to go. North Korea has huge infrastructure needs that can be met using labor-intensive techniques. Its sectors of comparative advantage—apart from missiles—tend to be labor intensive, too. With economic reform, demobilization could yield a sizable peace dividend.[17]

It is pure speculation as to whether this shift is what the North Koreans actually had in mind. Nevertheless, the actions and statements that the North Koreans made in 2002 were consistent with such an interpretation. However, the October 2002 American claim of a second nuclear weapons program based on highly enriched uranium made this gambit diplomatically unsustainable, and the regime is now left with the legacy of the July 2002 economic reforms but without the politically derived complementary parts of the package.

Today, North Korea is less a revolutionary state than an "alienated state" with no stake in the status quo of international relations aside from exploiting the UN system for humanitarian relief. North Korea is the first (and only) country to withdraw from the Nuclear Non-Proliferation Treaty. It is the first (and only) country to be formally censured by the Convention on International Trade in Endangered Species for repeatedly using diplomatic pouches to smuggle endangered animal parts. North Korea has shown no interest in joining the International Labour Organization or adhering to that organization's prohibitions on the use of slave labor. North Korean state involvement in illegal drug trafficking has been documented extensively, though the U.S. government does not list North Korea as a major state drug trafficker. The

United States does list North Korea as a state sponsor of terrorism, though the last documented incident was seventeen years ago. However, the DPRK continues to harbor a few aging Japanese Red Army hijackers. The separate issue of abductees from Japan has yet to be completely resolved.

The North Korean case is intriguing on multiple levels: its strange and repressive internal political practices together with the ambiguous role of nationalism and, by extension, South Korea; the stresses placed on the regime by its anomalous position in the world system and its attempt at internal reforms; and the external threat posed by its development of weapons of mass destruction and their missile delivery systems. These characteristics generate an unusually broad set of possible transition paths and successor regimes.

Recent Policy Changes

After the Korean War, a thoroughly orthodox Soviet-type central planning model was adopted, distinguished only by the degree to which markets were thoroughly suppressed. As with many centralized planning systems, it achieved some early success in mobilizing resources, and the conventional wisdom is that per capita income in North Korea exceeded that in South Korea until the 1970s. However, by that time, opportunities to grow through "extensive" means of marshaling greater resources began to dwindle, and North Korea proved largely incapable of growing through the "intensive" means of raising the productivity of existing assets. Having borrowed extensively on international markets in the aftermath of the first oil shock, it defaulted on its loans and was effectively cut off from international capital markets, narrowing the regime's economic options and leaving it dependent on the Soviet bloc for support.

The economy began to experience significant difficulties at least as early as the mid-1980s. In 1987, frustrated by North Korea's unwillingness to repay accumulated debts, the Soviets withdrew support. The economy was hit by massive trade shocks beginning in 1990 as the Soviet Union disintegrated and the Soviet bloc collapsed. As North Korea's industrial economy collapsed, agricultural output plummeted, deprived of industrial inputs such as fertilizer, insecticides, electricity-driven irrigation, and fuel. As yields declined, hillsides were denuded to bring more and more marginal land into production. This practice contributed to soil erosion, river silting, and ultimately flooding.

China initially stepped into the breach, offsetting some of the fall in trade with the Soviet Union and emerging as North Korea's primary supplier of imported food, most of it reportedly on concessional terms. But in 1994 and 1995, a disillusioned China reduced its exports to North Korea. If there were a single proximate trigger for the North Korean famine, this reduction was it. The floods of 1995 and 1996, though a contributory factor, were not a primary cause of the famine.

In North Korea, the famine period of the 1990s is known as the "arduous march." North Korean fortunes began to improve in early 1998 with the inauguration of South Korean president Kim Dae-jung and initiation of his "sunshine policy" of expanded contact and assistance. In July 2002, possibly as part of an aborted strategic reorientation, the government of North Korea announced changes in economic policy that could be regarded as having four components: microeconomic policy changes, macroeconomic policy changes, special economic zones, and aid seeking.

In all likelihood, the microeconomic reforms have not delivered as hoped. The state has told the enterprises that they must cover costs, yet it continues to administer prices, and in the absence of any formal bankruptcy or other "exit" mechanism, there is no prescribed method for enterprises that cannot cover costs to cease operations. Nor, in the absence of a social safety net, is there any way to aid workers from closed enterprises. Anecdotal evidence suggests that North Korean enterprises are exhibiting a variety of responses: some have set up side businesses, either as a legitimate coping mechanism or as a dodge to shed unwanted labor; some have cut wages (despite the official wage increase); some have kept afloat by procuring loans from the central bank; and a few enterprises have closed.[18] It is likely that some enterprises will be kept in operation, supported by implicit subsidies, either through national or local government budgets.

The government has implemented a policy in the agricultural sector of increasing both the procurement prices of grains, to increase the volume of food entering the public distribution system (PDS), and the PDS prices for consumers, with the retail cost of grains rising dramatically from 40,000 to 60,000 percent in the space of six months in 2002.[19] Some have questioned the extent to which this price increase was a real policy change versus simply a ratification of a system fraying that had already occurred; there is considerable evidence that most food, for example, was already being distributed through markets, not the PDS.[20]

The increase in the price for grain was partly intended to counter the supply response of the farmers, who, in the face of derisory procurement prices, were diverting acreage away from grain to tobacco and using grain to produce liquor for sale. It is notable that despite these changes, as well as donations of fertilizer and other inputs, North Korean grain production remained below the 1990 level. Yet, during the fall of 2005, reports began filtering out of North Korea that the government had confiscated grain and had reneged on commitments to the farmers regarding the shares of output that they could retain for free disposal. Then, in September, buoyed by a good harvest and enhanced bilateral assistance from South Korea and China, the government announced that it was banning private trade in grain, resuscitating the PDS, and expelling the UN World Food Programme (WFP) and private nongovernmental organizations engaged in humanitarian assistance. The North Korean political gambit in effect worked: in March 2006 the WFP's executive board approved a proposal for a downsized assistance program, with virtually no monitoring permitted.

When China began its reforms in 1979, more than 70 percent of its population worked in the agricultural sector, as was also the case in Vietnam when it initiated reforms the following decade.[21] Debureaucratization of agriculture under these conditions permits rapid increases in productivity and the release of labor into the nascent non-state-owned manufacturing sector. The key is that change is likely to produce few losers: farmers' incomes go up as marginal and average value products in the agricultural sector increase; the incomes of those leaving the farms rise as they receive higher-wage jobs in the manufacturing sector; and urban workers in the state-owned heavy industry sector benefit as their real wages rise as a result of lower food prices associated with expanded supply. The efficiency gains in agriculture essentially finance an economywide Pareto improvement (that is, no one is made worse off). This dynamic was understood by Chinese policymakers, who used a combination of the dual price system (allowing the market to surround the plan, to use a Maoist metaphor) and side payments to state-owned enterprises, their associated government ministries, and allied local politicians to suppress political opposition to the reforms. The existence of a large, labor-intensive agricultural sector is one of the few robust explanations for relative success in the transition from central planning to a market economy.[22]

In contrast to China and Vietnam, North Korea has perhaps half that share of the population employed in agriculture. As a consequence, the absolute magnitude of the supply response is likely to be smaller, and the proportion of the population directly benefiting from the increase in producer prices for agricultural goods would be roughly half as large as that in China and Vietnam. Thus reform in North Korea is less likely to be Pareto improving than in the case of China or Vietnam. Instead, reform in North Korea is more likely to create losers and with them the possibility of unrest. The dynastic aspects of the North Korean regime further complicate its ability to implement reform compared to China and Vietnam.

With respect to the policy changes undertaken in 2005, the North Korean government may be able to operate the PDS on an expanded, if not universal, basis in the short run. However, having reneged on its commitments to the farmers, it would not be surprising if cultivators reverted to famine-era coping behavior such as preharvesting, hoarding, and diversion of effort—tending secret private plots to the detriment of observable cooperative farms—thereby setting the stage for an intensification of distress in subsequent years, absent some compensatory assistance by external donors. In 2006, the recorded harvest fell, though it is unclear what shares of this decline should be attributed to bad weather, a reduction of fertilizer and other inputs, or coping responses by the farmers.

At the same time that the government announced the marketization initiatives, on the macroeconomic front it also announced tremendous administered increases in wages and prices. To grasp the magnitude of these price changes, consider that when China raised the price of grains at the start of its reforms in 1979, the increase was on the order of 25 percent. In comparison, North Korea raised the prices of corn and rice in 2002 by more than 40,000 percent. In the absence of huge supply responses, the result was an enormous jump in the price level and ongoing inflation abetted by central bank loans to uncompetitive state-owned enterprises. Unfortunately, macroeconomic stability at the time that reforms are initiated is the second robust predictor of relative success in transitioning from a planned to a market economy.[23] High rates of inflation did not portend well for North Korea.

Under these conditions, access to foreign currency may act as insurance against inflation, and in fact, the black market value of the North Korean *won* has depreciated at an annualized rate of 130–140 percent since August 2002. Those with access to foreign exchange, such as senior party officials, are relatively insulated from the effects of inflation. Agricultural workers benefit from "automatic" pay increases as the price of grain rises, but salaried workers without access to foreign exchange fall behind. In other words, the process of marketization and inflation has exacerbated existing social differences in North Korea.

The third component of the North Korean economic policy change was the formation of various sorts of special economic zones.[24] In September 2002, the North Korean government announced the establishment of a special administrative region at Sinuiju that was to exist completely outside

North Korea's usual legal structures, having its own flag and issuing its own passports. To top it off, the special administrative region would not be run by a North Korean but instead by Yang Bin, a Chinese-born entrepreneur with Dutch citizenship. He was promptly arrested by Chinese authorities on fraud charges (and subsequently imprisoned).[25]

Ultimately, the industrial park at Kaesong, oriented toward South Korea, almost surely has had a greater impact. In the long run, South Korean small- and medium-sized enterprises are a natural source of investment and transfer of appropriate technology to North Korea. However, in the absence of physical or legal infrastructure, they are unlikely to invest. The signing of four economic cooperation agreements between North and South Korea on issues such as taxation and foreign exchange transactions could be regarded as providing the legal infrastructure for economic activity by small- and medium-sized enterprises of negligible political influence, and the South Korean government also provides fiscal incentives to its investors in the zone. Although the Kaesong Industrial Complex has encountered repeated setbacks in its establishment, as of 2006, roughly one dozen South Korean firms operated there, employing more than 6,000 North Korean workers. South Korea envisions firms in the industrial complex eventually hiring hundreds of thousands of North Koreans. However, labor conditions for North Korean workers within the enclave have become a source of contention given South Korea's request in free trade agreement negotiations with the United States that goods produced in the Kaesong industrial complex be granted extraterritorial duty-free treatment.[26]

The fourth component of the economic plan consists of passing the hat. In September 2002, during the first-ever meeting between the heads of government of Japan and North Korea, Chairman Kim managed to extract from Prime Minister Junichiro Koizumi a commitment to provide a large financial transfer to North Korea as part of the diplomatic normalization process to settle postcolonial claims (possibly on the order of $10 billion), despite the shaky state of Japanese public finances. However, Kim's bald admission that North Korean agents had indeed kidnapped twelve Japanese citizens and that most of the abductees were dead set off a political firestorm in Japan. This revelation, together with the 2003 admission that North Korea possessed a nuclear weapons program in contravention of multiple international agreements, put the diplomatic rapprochement on hold and with it the prospects of a large capital infusion from Japan. It also lessened the already dim prospects of admission to international financial institutions such as the

World Bank and Asian Development Bank. A second visit to Pyongyang by Koizumi in mid-2004 generated a resumption of Japanese aid. However, after the first tranche was delivered, the disclosure that the remains of one allegedly deceased Japanese abductee turned out not to be her bones (and were probably the remains of several individuals) created such a political backlash that the Japanese government suspended further aid deliveries, and its Diet passed legislation making it easier to impose economic sanctions on the DPRK.

North Korean economic policy changes have had the effect of exacerbating preexisting social inequality and creating a new group of food-insecure households among the urban nonelite. According to a World Food Programme survey, most urban households are food insecure, spending more than 80 percent of their incomes on food.[27] According to the Food and Agricultural Organization, for the period 1999–2001, 34 percent of North Korea's population was malnourished, though it is unclear on what basis the organization reached such a precise figure, especially in light of the problematic nature of the survey evidence.[28] Figures from the 1998 nutritional survey jointly conducted by the DPRK government and United Nations agencies imply that North Korean children are not only smaller than South Korean children but that they are smaller than Korean children at the advent of Japanese colonialism nearly a century ago.[29] The WFP declined to release comparable data from subsequent surveys.

Yet, even if one should be skeptical about the precise figures, there is less room to doubt the rupture of the traditional social compact, necessitating a reinterpretation of the North Korean doctrine of juche to legitimate the reforms and justify the departure from the country's socialist tradition. The response has been to intensify the military-first campaign, elevating the military above the proletariat in the North Korean political pantheon.[30] The effect has been to overturn traditional paths to power and status: captains and entrepreneurs have now replaced party cadres and bureaucrats as preferred sons-in-law. As the military waxes while the commitment to socialism wanes, North Korea appears to be evolving toward some kind of unique postcommunist totalitarian state—not the sort of classically fascist regime that its propaganda excoriates but rather a strange revival of dynastic feudalism in the form of a nonsocialist, patrimonial state with a more efficient state apparatus than, for example, Iraq under Saddam Hussein. The central issue is whether the regime can manage this internal change while confronting economic stress, the implicit legitimacy challenge posed by a prosperous and democratic South Korea, and diplomatic tensions emanating from its nuclear weapons programs.

Political Transition

These challenges, while daunting, may not signal the imminent demise of the regime. According to figures published by the Bank of Korea, North Korea experienced a decline in per capita GDP of approximately 25 percent over the twelve-year interval from 1990 to 2002, with the maximum decline of roughly 33 percent (implying a compounded rate of more than 5 percent a year) occurring between 1990 and 1998—before the economy began to stabilize.[31] In 1997, the North Koreans themselves presented data to a visiting informational mission from the International Monetary Fund indicating that GDP had fallen by nearly 50 percent between 1993 and 1996. There was no way to verify these figures, however, and there was some suspicion that the decline in income had been exaggerated in a bid to obtain more aid.[32]

Taken at face value, the Bank of Korea figures depict performance that is bad but certainly not unique by contemporary standards. According to World Bank data on national economic performance since 1960, not counting North Korea, forty-two countries have suffered declines of 25 percent or more in per capita income over a twelve-year period, with per capita income falling 50 percent or more in fourteen of these countries (table 4-1). Even applying the more rigorous standard of a 33 percent fall in eight years (that is, the worst single period of the North Korean experience), the DPRK is still not alone: twelve countries suffered per capita income declines of 50 percent or more, and including the DPRK, another seventeen endured declines of 33–50 percent, with Kuwait and Nicaragua experiencing two such episodes.

Yet another way of looking at the issue is to identify uninterrupted declines in per capita income of 33 percent or more, regardless of the duration of the downturn. Inclusive of the DPRK, there are thirty-three such episodes involving thirty-one countries (again Kuwait and Nicaragua experienced this twice). Around half are postcommunist transition countries, and a few more are oil exporters (although the decline in income in Iran may have as much to do with its revolution as with oil prices). Most of the remaining countries experienced civil wars or other forms of instability. As a general proposition, uninterrupted declines of per capita income of the magnitude experienced by North Korea in the 1990s do not appear to be associated with political durability.

Although North Korea's economic travails are not unique, in the face of such woeful performance, what about its political stability? Table 4-2 summarizes data on a number of economically challenged but long-lived political regimes, including two discussed in this volume (Syria and Togo); however,

Table 4-1. Economic Declines, 1960–2001[a]

Country	Per capita income declines ≥ 25 percent over 12 years	Per capita income declines ≥ 33 percent over 8 years	Uninterrupted per capita income declines ≥ 33 percent
North Korea	x	x	x
Albania	x	x	x
Angola		x	x
Armenia		x	✓
Azerbaijan			x
Bahamas		x	
Belarus			x
Brunei	x	x	
Burundi	x	x	
Cameroon	x	x	x
Central African Republic	x		
Congo, Democratic Republic of the	✓	✓	
Congo, Republic of	x		
Côte d'Ivoire	x		
Croatia			x
Cuba			x
Djibouti	x	x	x
El Salvador	x		x
Estonia	x		x
Gabon	✓	x	
Georgia	✓	✓	✓
Ghana	x		
Guyana	x		
Haiti	x		
Iran	x		x
Jamaica	x		
Kazakhstan		x	x
Kiribati	✓	✓	✓
Kuwait	✓	✓	✓
Kyrgyz Republic	x	x	✓

(continued)

none of them is as long lived as the Kim regime. In this regard, its combination of longevity and underperformance is unparalleled.

A second factor auguring against the collapse of the regime is the complete absence (with the possible exception of the Korean People's Army) of institutions capable of channeling mass discontent into effective political action. There is no Solidarity trade union, as in Poland, or Civic Forum, as in Czechoslovakia. Indeed, there are not even alternative sources of moral authority capable of legitimating dissent, as, for instance, the Roman Catholic church was in both the uprising against the martial law regime of Wojciech Jaruzelski in Poland and the "People Power" revolt against the dictatorship of Ferdinand Marcos in the Philippines. Any unauthorized gathering is considered a "collective disturbance" and subject to punishment. As an official once

Table 4-1. Economic Declines, 1960–2001[a] (*Continued*)

Country	Per capita income declines ≥ 25 percent over 12 years	Per capita income declines ≥ 33 percent over 8 years	Uninterrupted per capita income declines ≥ 33 percent
Latvia	x	x	x
Lebanon			x
Liberia	✓	✓	✓
Lithuania			x
Madagascar	x		
Moldova	✓	✓	✓
Mozambique			x
Nicaragua	✓	x	x
Niger	x	x	
Nigeria	x		
Peru	x		
Romania	x		x
Russian Federation	x	x	x
Rwanda	✓	✓	x
Saudi Arabia	x		x
Sierra Leone	✓	✓	
Suriname	x	x	x
Tajikistan	✓	✓	✓
Togo	x		
Turkmenistan	✓	✓	✓
Ukraine	✓	✓	✓
United Arab Emirates	✓	✓	
Venezuela	x		
Zambia	x		

Source: The source for North Korea is the Bank of Korea. Data for Cuba come from Alan Heston, Robert Summers, and Bettina Aten, *Penn World Table*, version 6.1 (Philadelphia, October 2002). Romanian data are from Angus Maddison, *The World Economy: Historical Statistics* (Paris, 2003). All other data are derived from the World Bank, *World Development Indicators* (Washington, D.C., various years).

a. General coverage is 1960–2001, though data availability varies widely; *N* = 178. A ✓ indicates declines greater than 50 percent. Blank cells indicate that the given decline did not occur.

explained to a group of prospective investors, "Our country is well organized. There are no riots, no strikes, no differences in opinion."[33]

Furthermore, Pyongyang accounts for about a quarter of the country's nonrural population, excluding the military, and the Kim family regime has assiduously catered to the needs of its residents. An additional though unknown share of the non-Pyongyang urban population should probably be classified as similarly privileged. Unlike the situation in Eastern Europe, where the educated urban population exhibited little loyalty when it became apparent that the Soviets would not use force to back their satellite regimes, the North Korean elite appears to be relatively coherent—many are either blood relatives or descendants of guerillas who fought with Kim Il-sung, and they recognize that as a class they would have no real role in a unified Korea.[34]

Table 4-2. Economic Downturns in Selected Long-Lived Regimes
Units as indicated

| Country | Regime characteristics | | Per capita income growth or decline | | Longest downturn during the regime[a] | Per capita income growth or decline | | Largest decline during the regime | Per capita income growth or decline | |
	Beginning	End	Duration (years)	Cumulative (percent)	Annualized rate (percent)	Duration (years)	Cumulative (percent)	Annualized rate (percent)	Duration (years)	Cumulative (percent)	Annualized rate (percent)
North Korea[b]	1948	Present	55	n.a.	n.a.	8	-33	-5	8	-33	-5
Cuba[c]	1959	Present	44	n.a.	n.a.	4	-28	-8	4	-28	-8
Romania	1965	1989	24	65	2	4	-3	-1	3	-7	-2
Syria[d]	1970	Present	33	106	2	3	-11	-4	1	-12	-12
Haiti[e]	1957	1986	29	-6	0	2	-8	-4	2	-8	-4
Kenya[f]	1963	2002	39	61	1	4	-7	-2	1	-8	-8
Togo[g]	1967	Present	36	-11	0	4	-26	-7	4	-26	-7
Zambia	1972	1991	19	-36	-2	6	-17	-3	6	-17	-3

Source: The source for North Korea is the Bank of Korea. Data for Cuba come from Alan Heston, Robert Summers, and Bettina Aten, *Penn World Table*, version 6.1 (Philadelphia, October 2002). Romanian data are from Angus Maddison, *The World Economy: Historical Statistics* (Paris, 2003). All other data are from the World Bank, *World Development Indicators* (Washington, D.C., various years).

a. In case of a tie for the longest downturn during a regime, the downturn of largest magnitude is reported.
b. Economic data on North Korea are limited to the period 1990–2002.
c. Data on Cuba are limited to the period 1985–1996. Figures are reported for within this period only and are based on chained real GDP per capita (constant prices).
d. Economic data for Syria are based on the period 1970–2002.
e. Economic data for Haiti are based on the period 1960–1986.
f. Economic data for Kenya are based on the period 1960–2002.
g. Economic data for Togo are based on the period 1967–2002.

Finally, North Korea's neighbors have not provided sanctuary to anti-Kim political forces. There is little or no evidence of anti-Kim political organizing among the refugees in the Chinese border region, and there are no marauding guerilla insurgencies on North Korea's borders. In fact, North Korea's neighbors might be expected actively to cooperate with North Korean security services to crack down on such activity if it were to develop. The absence of antiregime organizing together with people voluntarily crossing back into North Korea suggests a more complicated politics of deprivation.

What emerges from this analysis is a regime that while facing profound political and economic difficulties, internally possesses a monopoly on social organization combined with an astonishing capacity for coercion. Externally, it faces an environment that, at least when it comes to the issue of regime survival, is fundamentally supportive. Despite evident political tensions, North Korea continues to receive more than $1 billion in foreign aid annually, including from the United States. Despite differences in opinion on this issue within the Bush administration, no foreign government today is committed to a policy of "regime change" in North Korea. Yet, in order to deflect popular discontent, the Kim Jong-il regime actively portrays its largely self-created difficulties as a product of foreign hostility. This strategy may be abetted by the "religious" nature of the regime, which may convey additional legitimacy beyond conventional performance criteria.

Modeling Change

Formal statistical modeling has been used to examine the likelihood of political instability or, more precisely, regime change.[35] The models are estimated from three separate cross-national data sets on political developments worldwide since 1960. Several dozen explanatory variables, generally falling into three categories, were considered. The first category consists of political, legal, and cultural variables that tend to change slowly, if at all. These variables would include such things as the origin of the country's legal system—that is, whether the system was created indigenously, adopted, or imposed by a colonial power—and proxies relating to the quality of domestic political institutions. A second group of variables involves demographic and social indicators that also tend to change slowly. These indicators include things such as the level of urbanization and the degree of ethnic or religious heterogeneity within a country. Economic policy and performance indicators make up the final category. These measures tend to exhibit the greatest temporal variability. As a consequence, the more slowly changing political and social variables

Figure 4-1. Hazard Rate of Regime Change: Baseline and under Three Scenarios, 1990–2003[a]

Percent

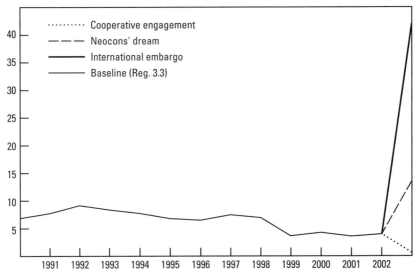

Source: Noland, *Korea after Kim Jong-il.*
a. See text for description of the three scenarios.

tend to determine whether a particular country is generally prone to instability whereas the more rapidly changing economic variables tend to determine whether the likelihood of regime change is strong or weak.

These models were estimated and then used to generate the probability of regime change in North Korea. The results from one such model are displayed in figure 4-1. In this particular model, the hazard of political regime change is a function of per capita income, per capita income growth, openness to international trade, inflation, the share of trade taxes in total tax revenue, aid receipts per capita, and whether the country has a tropical climate—an inverse indicator of institutional quality. (Stability is a positive function of income level and growth, trade openness, institutional quality, and aid, and is a negative function of inflation and trade taxes.) According to this particular model, the probability of regime change peaked at nearly 10 percent in 1992, declined, peaked again in the late 1990s, and has since declined to approximately 4 percent in 2002, the most recent year in the simulation.[36]

An implication is that economic performance critically influences regime stability and that North Korea's external relations play a crucial role in this regard. To explore this theme, the models were simulated under three alternative scenarios. Under one scenario, which might be labeled "cooperative engagement," diplomatic tensions are eased, and North Korea successfully globalizes in a diplomatically supportive environment so that it receives higher levels of aid from South Korea, China, the United States, and other countries as compared to the status quo. It normalizes diplomatic relations with Japan and begins to receive postcolonial claim settlement payments. It joins the multilateral development banks and begins receiving aid from them as well. Total aid reaches $3 billion annually. Under the less threatening environment, it liberalizes its economy, the share of trade in national income rises to what it would exhibit if it were as integrated into the world economy as a "normal" country with its characteristics, and trade taxes are cut to the South Korean level. The rate of economic growth rebounds to its 1999 peak of 6 percent. All other variables stay at their 2002 values.

After the July 2006 missile launches and the October 2006 nuclear test, the United Nations Security Council authorized limited sanctions on North Korea. This action followed on the heels of an ongoing U.S. campaign to squeeze North Korea financially in response to its counterfeiting and other illicit financial transactions. These events suggest the "neocon's dream" scenario, where the global community puts the squeeze on the Kim Jong-il regime: aid is cut off, growth falls to its previous low of –6 percent, and the inexpertly enacted July 2002 economic policy changes drive inflation up to 300 percent, reputedly its rate over the course of the year from 2002 to 2003.

In 2006 concern centered on the possibility of a North Korean nuclear test, but given attitudes in Seoul and Beijing, it is doubtful that this action would generate comprehensive sanctions. Greater provocation would be required for the international community to react in such a way.[37] In this "international embargo" scenario, North Korea's relations with the rest of the world deteriorate precipitously, perhaps under suspicion of exportation of nuclear weapons, and all international trade is cut off. Admittedly this scenario is a stretch for the underlying statistical model, which does not distinguish between food, oil, and video games in the maintenance of a society, and some might object that a total embargo is politically unrealistic as well. It may not be without some utility, however, revealing something about the nature of regime dynamics, at least in a cross-country sample.

For heuristic purposes, the predicted hazard rates associated with each of these alternatives are appended to the graph as "2003," although there is nothing unique in the scenarios to link it to that date, and indeed, some of the changes envisioned in the "cooperative engagement" scenario would probably take more than one year to realize. Nevertheless, the simulations may be revealing in terms of how outside forces might affect regime survival in North Korea.

According to these results, under the "cooperative engagement" scenario, the likelihood of regime change falls to less than 1 percent. Kim Jong-il dies in his sleep, and one of his sons dons their grandfather Kim Il-sung's mantle. In the "neocon's dream," the likelihood of regime change rises to about a one in seven probability, growing thereafter, and in all probability, Kim Jong-il is out of power within a few years. In the final scenario, "international embargo," the likelihood of regime change is over 40 percent in the first year, and the Kim Jong-il regime probably collapses within two years.

One caveat should be underlined: there may be psychopolitical phenomena that are not well captured by these models. In particular, foreign pressure may provide the regime with a rationale for poor performance, while a lack of foreign pressure (that is, an absence of enemies) may conversely deprive the regime of an excuse. The models may overstate the impact of these alternative scenarios on regime stability—the good scenario may not be quite as good and the bad scenario not quite as bad as depicted in figure 4-1, regardless of how one defines "good" and "bad" outcomes.

Character of Successor Regimes

Suppose that the current regime is unable to manage this transition. Regime change—at least the internally generated variety—would not necessarily imply the disappearance of the North Korean state, though it is surely one possibility. The key issues would be the viability and character of the successor regime. Would any regime that breaks with the Kim Il-sung model be viable? Would it be able to legitimate itself, or would this simply be a transitional state toward unification? Is a post-juche North Korean state possible?

The current military-first ideological campaign, which at first blush would appear to signal the ascendance of the most reactionary element of the polity, may actually be the mechanism through which a broad-ranging, top-down modernization of a society subject to external threat is justified.[38] By elevating the military to the vanguard, the military-first ideology justifies all manner of departures from past practice—including the jettisoning of socialism in practice if not as a teleological ideal—in pursuit of military modernization. One could imagine this militarized nationalism being used to remove the current leadership in favor of a more technically competent group of nationalist modernizers.

There is historical precedent: in the Meiji Restoration and in the founding of modern Turkey under Mustafa Kemal Ataturk, revolutionary changes were justified as responses to external threats and legitimated in terms of restoring past historical glory. (Current propaganda that emphasizes military-first politics to build a "powerful and prosperous country" out of the "barrel of a gun" oddly echoes the "wealthy nation and a strong army" slogan of Meiji-era Japan.) Yet, in this North Korean production, Kim Jong-il would be playing the roles of both the Tokugawa Shogun and the Emperor Meiji. Doing so may be consistent with the interest he expressed to former secretary of state Madeleine Albright in the "Thai model." He would reign but not rule.[39]

In a positive sense, top-down military-centered modernization may be a successful political development strategy. Of course, from a normative perspective, the results of that strategy—a nuclear-armed and possibly proliferating North Korea—may be antithetical to U.S. interests. And there is no guarantee that a military modernizer would be the Park Chung-hee or Augusto Pinochet of North Korea and not its Alexander Kerensky or Lothar de Maizière. The legitimization challenges for a post-juche North Korea could be profound, and there is no certainty of success—even if the regime were supported by a South Korea fearful of the implications of collapse and absorption.

South Korea is key, not only because of the resources that it could provide to a new North Korean regime but also because of the challenge that its very existence poses for legitimizing any successor regime in North Korea. (In theory, several of North Korea's neighbors have the economic wherewithal to support the regime materially. By Chinese standards, North Korea, with its population of 22 million, is akin to a relatively small province.) Ironically, one can imagine a situation in which the most radical forces in North Korea would be revolutionary nationalist unifiers who might well be opposed by a South Korean government that, fearing a collapse and absorption scenario, might try to prop up the North Korean state.

Indeed, there is talk in some quarters that under the proper political conditions, South Korea might make "reconciliation transfers" to North Korea of 1 percent of GDP, or about $6 billion, multiples of the estimated $2 billion a year of "survival rations."[40] Whether the existence of this South Korean 911 line would be sufficient to guarantee the political survival of the Kim Jong-il regime is an existential question, though it suggests that the reality that the country may be headed toward lies somewhere between "cooperative engagement" and the "neocon's dream."

The American dilemma in a nutshell is that its top priority is to denuclearize North Korea, but that result is unlikely to be achieved without the active cooperation of South Korea, China, and Japan. Indeed, its principal ally, South Korea, appears willing to extend virtually unconditional assistance to North Korea. Even if one is doubtful about the prospects of eliminating the North Korean nuclear program through negotiation with a Kim Jong-il regime, earnest and sincere participation in the ongoing Six Party Talks is essential to put the onus on Pyongyang for any failure to make consensual progress, and thereby to secure multilateral support for more coercive measures. To use a sports metaphor, the February 2007 joint statement amounts to a first down, not a touchdown; it represents a positive incremental step in a process that may ultimately achieve the goal of the denuclearization of the Korean peninsula, but carries no guarantees of accomplishing such an objective. Committing the parties to particular actions in a specified time frame should contribute to uncovering fairly quickly whether the participants are truly committed to a negotiated solution.

The same sort of dilemma operates in the humanitarian sphere: the North Korean regime in effect holds its populace hostage, creating an ethical quandary for the world community, torn between the impulse to ameliorate the suffering of vulnerable people and the understandable reluctance to prop up a totalitarian regime that at base is the source of the problem. As tempting as it may seem to cut off assistance with the hope that an intensification of misery could provoke collapse of the regime, in the end, it is unpersuasive to bet increased suffering now against possible gains in an uncertain future. As a consequence, the international community is forced to make incremental improvements in the status quo, for example, by increasing the transparency of humanitarian relief operations with the aim of improving their effectiveness. In this regard, the unwillingness of North Korea's two primary benefactors, China and South Korea, to direct their assistance through multilateral channels, and their acting, in effect, as lenders of last resort, undercuts, perhaps fatally, the efforts of the United States, the European Union, and others to strengthen the effectiveness of humanitarian relief efforts in the DPRK.

Notes

1. North Korean propaganda has described Kim Jong-il "as a contemporary god," "superior to Christ in love, superior to Buddha in benevolence, superior to Confucius in virtue, and superior to Mohammed in justice," and, ultimately, "the savior of mankind." Marcus Noland, *Avoiding the Apocalypse: The Future of the Two Koreas* (Wash-

ington, D.C., 2000), 62. After Kim Il-sung's death, the office of the presidency was abolished, and he was designated the "eternal president." See also David Hawk, *Thank You, Father Kim Il Sung* (Washington, D.C., 2005).

2. On North Korea's internal classification system, see Aidan Foster-Carter, "Korea: Sociopolitical Realities of Reuniting a Divided Nation," in Thomas H. Hendricksen and Kyong-soo Lho (eds.), *One Korea?* (Stanford, Calif., 1994); Helen-Louise Hunter, *Kim Il-sung's North Korea* (Westport, Conn., 1999); Charles Armstrong, *The North Korean Revolution* (Ithaca, N.Y., 2002); Korea Institute for National Unification (KINU), *White Paper on Human Rights in North Korea 2004* (Seoul, 2005).

3. For examples of this argument, see Han S. Park, "Human Needs, Human Rights, and Regime Legitimacy," in Moon Chung-in (ed.), *Understanding Regime Dynamics in North Korea* (Seoul, 1998); Bruce Cumings, *Korea's Place in the Sun* (New York, 1997); and Bruce Cumings, *North Korea: Another Country* (New York, 2003).

4. For detailed examinations of the prison camp system, see David Hawk, *The Hidden Gulag* (Washington, D.C., 2003); KINU, *White Paper*. For a memoir of one camp survivor, see Chol-hwan Kang, *The Aquariums of Pyongyang* (New York, 2002).

5. Regulations under the 2004 penal code appear to have codified the differential treatment between economic refugees and those cases deemed political. If the authorities conclude that a repatriated refugee crossed the border for economic reasons, the new code stipulates sentences of up to two years of "labor correction." The government has even signaled the promise of a pardon under the 2004 penal code, and several nongovernmental organizations operating in the region have confirmed that punishments seem to be less severe than in the past. On the other hand, if the authorities decide that a refugee crossed the border for political reasons, this individual will be charged with the crime of treason and is subject to longer-term detention. Soo-Am Kim, "The North Korean Penal Code, Criminal Procedures, and Their Actual Applications," Studies Series 06-01 (Seoul, 2006). Those assisting refugees in escaping the country have been publicly executed. Changes in the legal code specify relaxed treatment for pregnant women, though in practice these protocols are breached, and in some cases forced abortions continue to be practiced. Keumsoon Lee, "The Border-Crossing North Koreans: Current Situations and Future Prospects," Studies Series 06-05 (Seoul, 2006).

6. U.S. Department of State, "North Korea," in *2004 Country Reports on Human Rights Practices* (Washington, D.C., February 28, 2005). See Amnesty International, "Starved of Rights: Human Rights and the Food Crisis in the Democratic People's Republic of Korea (North Korea)" (London, 2004), web.amnesty.org/library/index/engasa240032004; KINU, *White Paper*.

7. A survey found that for 19 percent of 200 recent defectors, foreign radio broadcasts such as Korea Broadcasting System, Radio Liberty, Voice of America, and Radio Free Asia were their main source of news. Twenty-one percent knew someone who had modified their North Korean fixed tuner radios to listen to foreign broadcasts, and

more than half reported knowing someone who had been punished for listening to unauthorized broadcasts. None reported receiving information through foreign newspapers. There is no way of knowing how representative these defectors are of the general public.

8. Hawk, *The Hidden Gulag*; State Department, *Reports on Human Rights*; KINU, *White Paper*.

9. In addition to North Korean citizens, North Korea reportedly detains 486 South Koreans and an unknown number of non-Koreans. KINU, *White Paper*.

10. KINU, *White Paper*; Dae-Kyu Yoon, "Analysis of Changes in the DPRK Criminal Code," *CanKor*, no. 194 (Seoul, January 31, 2005), www.cankor.ca/issues/194.htm.

11. Alternative death estimates are analyzed in Marcus Noland, "North Korea: Famine and Reform," *Asian Economic Papers*, III (2004), 1–40; Stephan Haggard and Marcus Noland, *Famine in North Korea: Markets, Aid, and Reform* (New York, 2007), 73–76.

12. KINU, *White Paper*; Stephan Haggard and Marcus Noland, *The North Korean Refugee Crisis: Human Rights and the International Response* (Washington, D.C., 2006).

13. Noland, *Avoiding the Apocalypse*, 179. Table 5.2 in *Avoiding the Apocalypse* provides nine examples of "food for talks." A more recent example is the February 2003 U.S. government announcement, in the run-up to diplomatic talks over the North Korean nuclear weapons program, that it would provide 40,000 metric tons of grain to North Korea, despite the fact that the North Koreans had not fulfilled the June 2002 aid transparency and monitoring conditions, which had been reaffirmed the previous month, January 2003, by USAID administrator Andrew S. Natsios. China implicitly linked donations to political behavior in the diplomatic maneuvering around the Six Party Talks over the North Korean nuclear program in 2003 and 2004. The termination of support by Japan in 2002 and its resumption in 2004 were explicitly linked to diplomatic developments.

14. Amnesty International, "Starved of Rights"; Stephan Haggard and Marcus Noland, *Hunger and Human Rights: The Politics of Famine in North Korea* (Washington, D.C., 2005).

15. "U.S. More Dangerous than NK? Most Seem to Think So," *Chosun Ilbo* (January 12, 2004).

16. Young-shik Bong, "Anti-Americanism and the U.S.-Korea Military Alliance," in James M. Lister (ed.), *Confrontation and Innovation on the Korean Peninsula* (Washington, D.C., 2003), 18–29.

17. Noland, *Avoiding the Apocalypse*, 302–309.

18. One result of these changes has been a noticeable upsurge in small-scale retail activity. Peter Gey estimates that 6 to 8 percent of the workforce is engaged in informal trading activities. See Peter Gey, "North Korea: Soviet-Style Reform and the Erosion of the State Economy," *Internationale Politik und Geschellschaft*, I (2004), 115–133, www.fes.de/ipg/ONLINE1_2004/ARTGEY.HTM (in German). For an English version, see *Dialogue and Cooperation* (Singapore), no. 1 (2004).

Although this is usually interpreted as household-level entrepreneurial activity, Han Shik Park, a frequent visitor to North Korea, argues that most of this activity is sponsored by state-owned enterprises, which own the capital, such as carts used by peddlers. According to Park, state-owned enterprises, partly deprived of state subsidies, have entered small-scale retailing as a means of generating revenue. Han Shik Park at the "Korean Peninsula Peace and Security Forum," Washington, D.C., July 20, 2004.

19. Noland, "North Korea: Famine and Reform," table 4.

20. Marcus Noland, "Transition from the Bottom-Up: Institutional Change in North Korea," *Comparative Economic Studies*, XLVIII (2006), 195–212.

21. Noland, *Avoiding the Apocalypse*, 76, table 3.7.

22. Anders Åslund, Peter Boone, and Simon Johnson, "How to Stabilize: Lessons from Post-Communist Countries," *Brookings Papers on Economic Activity*, no. 1 (1996), 217–313.

23. Ibid.

24. The first such zone was established in the Rajin-Sonbong region in the extreme northeast of the country in 1991. It has proved to be a failure for a variety of reasons, including its geographical isolation, poor infrastructure, onerous rules, and interference in enterprise management by party officials. The one major investment has been the establishment of a combination hotel-casino-bank. Given the obvious scope for illicit activity associated with such a horizontally integrated endeavor, the result has been less Hong Kong than "Macau North."

25. North Korea's relationship with China is complicated. In January 2006, North Korean leader Kim Jong-il visited China. Notably, as in his 2004 trip, he visited not only the capital, Beijing, but also the economically dynamic cities of southern China, implying that there was more on the agenda than simply extracting aid from the Chinese government. In fact, upon his departure, Kim acknowledged the "correctness" of the Chinese model. Although there are enormous differences between North Korea and China, one can hope that this experience spurs further experimentation and reform in North Korea.

26. Marcus Noland, "How North Korea Funds Its Regime," testimony before the Subcommittee on Federal Financial Management, Government Information, and International Security, Committee on Homeland Security and Government Affairs, U.S. Senate (April 25, 2006).

27. World Food Programme, "Public Distribution System (PDS) in DPRK," DPR Korea Country Office (Pyongyang, May 21, 2003).

28. Food and Agricultural Organization (FAO), *The State of Food Insecurity in the World 2003* (Rome, 2003), table 1. See Noland, "North Korea: Famine and Reform" for an evaluation of the WFP and FAO data.

29. Haggard and Noland, *Famine in North Korea*, 196–197.

30. See Ruediger Frank, "A Socialist Market Economy in North Korea? Systemic Restrictions and a Quantitative Analysis," unpublished paper, Columbia University (New York, 2003); Noland, *Korea after Kim Jong-il*, 7–8.

31. See Bank of North Korea, www.bok.or.kr/contents_admin/info_admin/eng/home/press/pressre/info/timeseriesnk1.xls. For a discussion of the extremely poor quality of the data for North Korea, see Marcus Noland, "The Two Koreas: Prospects for Economic Cooperation and Integration," *East-West Center Special Reports*, VII (Honolulu, 2002).

32. Former U.S. vice president Walter Mondale once observed that anyone who described themselves as an expert on North Korea was a liar or a fool; my corollary would be to distrust any figure on North Korea that comes with a decimal point attached.

33. Noland, *Avoiding the Apocalypse*, 252.

34. Andrei Lankov, "Pyongyang: Rules of Engagement," *Pacific Review*, XVI (2003), 617–626.

35. Noland, *Korea after Kim Jong-il*, 21–41. The underlying sample consisted of seventy-one countries. In some applications, the sample size was reduced due to missing data on the explanatory variables. See the appendix to Noland, *Korea after Kim Jong-il*, for a more complete description of the data used in this analysis.

36. Other models generally yield higher probabilities though a similar time-series pattern. Ibid., 39.

37. Marcus Noland, "The Economic Implications of a North Korean Nuclear Test," *Asia Policy*, II (2006), 25–39.

38. It could also be the mechanism through which a skeptical military is reassured that the primacy of its status will not be challenged by the reform process.

39. Madeleine Albright, *Madame Secretary* (New York, 2002), 466.

40. Anthony Michell, "The Current North Korean Economy," in Marcus Noland (ed.), *Economic Integration on the Korean Peninsula* (Washington, D.C., 1998), 137–164.

five
Turkmenistan under Niyazov and Berdymukhammedov

Gregory Gleason

With the death in late 2006 of Saparmurad Niyazov, founding leader and despot of Turkmenistan, that natural gas–rich ex-Soviet satrapy began tentatively charting a post-Niyazov era under the unexpected leadership of Gurbanguly Berdymukhammedov. Potentially a cautious reformer, Berdymukhammedov may conceivably attempt to modernize and humanize the country's ruling regime. Or he may plunge the country into deep pools of repression. The rise of Berdymukhammedov and what that means is discussed in a postscript to this chapter.

The Niyazov Era

Citizens of Turkmenistan gathered each September 12 to celebrate Ruhnama Day in honor of the *Ruhnama*, the book of spiritual teachings written by the country's late president-for-life, Turkmenbashi, the "head of all Turkmen." Turkmenbashi was not only both head of state and government, he was also the moral leader of the country. Turkmenistan citizens were familiar with the *Ruhnama* because its passages were ubiquitous elements of everyday life in this remote, arid, southern borderland of the former Soviet Union. The words of the "Glorious Leader" were inscribed at all public places.[1] Grandiose public monuments extolled the Glorious Leader's virtues. Towns, mountains, canals, streets, libraries, and schools were named in his honor. The wisdom of the "Great Leader" offered guidance for all the Turkmen who sought the path of enlightenment. Knowledge of key passages of the *Ruhnama* was not only required for those who would become government officials, judges, or civic leaders but was also necessary for ordinary citizens attempting more mundane achievements, such as passing a driver's license test. To ensure that Turkmen citizens did not lose sight of their Glorious Leader in their everyday affairs, Turkmenbashi found ways to remind citizens regularly of his presence. He declared that the months of the calendar be renamed: January was named in his honor, and April was named in honor of Turkmenbashi's deceased mother.

State Repression in Turkmenistan

Before he chose to become known as Turkmenbashi and become the spiritual father of a country, Niyazov's political influence was based on a more profane political institution, the Communist Party of the Soviet Union. Until the collapse of the Soviet Union in 1991, Saparmurad Niyazov appeared to be an unexceptional, faceless, gray, local party bureaucrat, a staunch communist ideologue devoted to the Soviet Union and the highest Communist Party official in Turkmenistan. But as the Soviet Union began unraveling, Niyazov changed his ideological colors, quickly assuming the position of a Turkmen nationalist. He chaired the Communist Party's last formal convocation, presided over a decision to dissolve the party, adjourned the group for lunch, and then reconvened the same membership in the same hall to establish the Democratic Party of Turkmenistan. He publicly took the position of a proponent of a national renaissance oriented toward building a democratic, market-oriented state that functioned in accordance with international standards. It was as the head of the Democratic Party of Turkmenistan that Niyazov began in the early 1990s to forge one of the world's most exaggerated tyrannies.

Consolidating control over all aspects of the society, economy, and government in the early postcommunist period, Niyazov manipulated the structural remnants of the disintegrating Soviet system to create a political machine based on coercion, fear, and patronage. The key to Niyazov's grasp of political power was his monopolization of the country's ample natural gas reserves, its primary export earner. The country's natural gas industry was initially developed during the Soviet period. The Soviet command and control economic system was based on the extraction of resources for the priorities of the Soviet system. Turkmenistan's gas was shipped out through pipelines to Russia for distribution to other parts of the USSR and for sale to

European trade partners. Little of the revenue from gas sales remained in Turkmenistan during the Soviet period.

When the Soviet Union dissolved, the gas reserves and physical facilities of the Soviet gas industry fell into Niyazov's hands. Niyazov turned the industry into an engine of his own design for transforming the country. In the early days of independence, shadowy intermediary companies marketed Turkmen gas in ways that channeled revenue into Turkmenbashi's individual accounts—revenue that served as the major source of income for financing his political consolidation of power and elimination of his opponents.

As Turkmenbashi's regime consolidated, he embarked on grandiose state projects. Ostentatious government-financed public demonstration projects were designed to realize Turkmenbashi's bold pretensions of transforming Turkmenistan into a "new Kuwait." The capital city of Ashgabat was transformed from an underdeveloped village into a foreign-built showcase of majestic white marble public buildings, public parks, and architectural displays. A city where water shortages were commonplace during the Soviet period was transformed into a "city of a thousand fountains." Assuring citizens that the country's gas and oil revenues would produce such a surfeit of wealth that Turkmenistan's citizens would be guaranteed a life of leisure in a land of plenty, Turkmenbashi sought to create an image of progress toward Turkmenistan's glorious future.

The image is a mirage. Behind the facade of shimmering public buildings in the capital, Turkmenistan is a country marked by isolation, poverty, social malaise, and the systematic elimination of the capacity for governance and sustainable development beyond the existence of the leader. Turkmenistan has become one of the most repressive and bizarrely governed states in the world. Government decisionmaking is basically at the whim of the leader. All government posts are filled at the pleasure of the president. There is no independent legislative authority or judicial independence. There is no political space for civic initiative or individual autonomy. The government routinely violates civil legal protections and human rights and exclusively controls the information media. The public sector has crowded out the private sector, quashing individual initiative and making all business activity dependent upon government decisions.

The administrative institutional capacity necessary to sustain a modern system of governance has been eviscerated. The rule of law has been supplanted by the rule of caprice, and political institutions such as courts and parliamentary institutions have been transformed to carry out merely ceremonial and theatrical functions. Isolation and dependency have been encouraged through the systematic dismantling of the educational system and the mass media. The system of public health is in a shambles.[2]

Turkmenbashi combined aspects of hero worship with brutal police state tactics to eradicate not only his political opposition but anyone whom he even imagined would be capable of "failing to maintain his trust." As he eliminated political opponents and competitors one by one, Niyazov created a fiction of paternal rule for the public as a whole. In the assessment of one Turkmen journalist who succeeded in escaping to the West,

> Over the past twelve years he [Turkmenbashi] has plunged the country ever deeper into neo-Stalinist torpor. Institutions such as the courts and parliament are merely a facade for thuggish, arbitrary, one-man rule. Niyazov has cut school to nine years and college to two, the easier to hold sway over an ill-educated populace. Despite abundant natural resources, Turkmenistan's people are increasingly impoverished while a coterie of courtiers gorges itself on pilfered wealth.[3]

Turkmenistan's "neo-Stalinist torpor" has made criticism within the country dangerous. But Turkmenbashi did not succeed in perpetuating the mirage outside of his country. In the international community, there was a universal denunciation of the Turkmenistan government's policies. Governments, news and broadcasting organizations, international organizations, and nongovernmental organizations evaluated the Turkmenistan government as violating international standards.

Turkmen government policies regarding economic opportunity, media freedom, civic and human rights, education, health care, and the environment have provoked international expressions of alarm and protest. The State Department's *2005 Country Reports on Human Rights Practices* summarized that "Turkmenistan is an authoritarian state dominated by president-for-life Saparmurat Niyazov who retained his monopoly on political power." It said that "the government continued to commit serious abuses and its human rights record remained extremely poor."[4] The Organization for Security and Cooperation in Europe and the Commission on Security and Cooperation in Europe (the Helsinki Commission) criticized Turkmenistan for failing to observe fundamental standards of human rights and good governance.[5] On October 3, 2006, the European Parliament's International Trade Committee voted to suspend consideration of an interim trade agreement with Turkmenistan until the Turkmen government made an effort to improve significantly its human rights record. In 2006 Freedom House ranked Turkmenistan as one of the most repressive countries in the world.[6] Human Rights Watch considers Turkmenistan to be in flagrant violation of international standards.[7] Reporters without Borders put Turkmenbashi on the international list of thirty-five "predators of press freedom" and listed Turkmenistan 165th in its press freedom index, placing it third from the bottom just above Eritrea and North Korea.[8] The 2006 State of the World Liberty Index ranked Turkmenistan 154 out of 159 countries surveyed for individual liberties, economic freedom, and the ratio of government size to levels of taxation.[9]

Mechanisms of State Control

In the years after the USSR collapsed, Turkmenistan created a unique and bizarre psychological environment of repression. Rivaling and in some aspects surpassing the repressive extremes of Soviet totalitarianism during the late stages of Stalin's rule, the political context in Turkmenistan was characterized by sham political institutions; capricious government; a cult of personality around the supreme leader; neutralization and in some cases physical elimination of political opposition; systematic elimination of alternative views as represented in the media and competing parties; and widespread violations of civil and human rights.

Sham political institutions are the hallmark of postcommunist Turkmenistan. While the country adopted a constitution soon after independence that conformed to international standards, the constitution in fact did not establish the rule of law, create or reflect a true social compact, serve to constrain the government, or establish protections for civil liberties. Formal descriptions on paper have little or no relationship to the actual practice of government and economics. Leadership is idiosyncratic, government is capricious, and process is ad hoc. Turkmenistan has had popular elections, but they have never met international standards of being free and fair. Turkmenistan's elections on December 19, 2004, were the first parliamentary elections held in five years. The elections were dismissed by international monitoring organizations as neither free nor fair.[10] So was the 2007 presidential election.

Turkmenistan's system of public finance is concealed from the public. Information regarding government revenue and expenditures is held as a state secret.[11] No standard operating procedures are in place to ensure the equitable, nondiscriminatory, and nonpreferential interaction between the public and private sector. Government tenders are personally decided by the leader.[12] Much of the government's revenue and expenditure appears to be channeled through extrabudgetary funds and off-budget accounts.

The cult of the leader has been the most distinguishing feature of Turkmenistan's politics. Adulation of the leader was extreme and ubiquitous. Turkmenbashi practiced the "big lie," exaggerating the country's progress, insisting that Turkmen citizens lived in a country of advanced freedoms and liberties, and claiming that anyone who questioned the country's progress did so at the behest of foreign enemies. Turkmenbashi was the spiritual leader and routinely castigated foreign sources for spreading lies about the country, claiming that no one was abused or had his or her rights violated in Turkmenistan. As he announced on Turkmen television, "Not a single person's right is abused in Turkmenistan regardless of his nationality, religion, language, his place in society, and regardless of whether the person is poor or rich. All people are equal before law, and no one is being offended."[13] Hero worship even extended beyond the leader himself to his revered mother, Gurbansoltan eje.

Neutralization or physical elimination of political opponents and competitors has been the main instruments of control. Competing political parties and organizations were routed by Turkmenistan's feared Ministry of National Security. This policy of divide and conquer applied not only to opponents but also to otherwise loyal but questioning members of the political elite. Purges of the high state apparatus were so regular as to be routine. Niyazov regularly appointed unqualified individuals to high posts so that they were dependent upon his largesse. He removed them with no warning.

Eradication of competing political figures and parties was also accompanied by the elimination of sources of information that questioned the government's story that Turkmenistan was in its "golden age"—which is also the name of the Turkmen television broadcasting company. Through a process of attrition, the journalist corps was pared down, and the independence of the press was systematically undermined and replaced with a journalistic community fully subordinated to the state. The last remnant of an even partially independent view, the Russian media, was eliminated in 2004.[14]

Violations of human rights have been widespread and flagrant and even occurred in full view of the public as celebrations of the country's devotion to unity and the will of the leader. Human rights abuses have been frequent and severe. Nongovernmental civic initiative was routinely curtailed. International human rights organizations such as Freedom House and Human Rights Watch have ranked Turkmenistan as among the world's worst offenders of human rights.[15]

This list of the mechanisms of tyranny in Turkmenistan is not comprehensive. There are additional elements of political control and manipulation.

Cumulatively, these factors give the Turkmenistan state a character of poor governance based in and contributing to a systemic resistance to change. While World Bank governance indicators placed Turkmenistan in the top fiftieth percentile in 2005 in terms of "political stability," they ranked Turkmenistan in the bottom tenth percentile of countries in terms of "regulatory quality," "voice and accountability," and "government effectiveness."[16]

Turkmenistan's Isolation

Turkmenistan's political uniqueness developed in the context of its growing economic and political isolation. Turkmenistan is bordered by Iran and Afghanistan to the south, Kazakhstan to the north, Uzbekistan to the north and east, and the Caspian Sea to the west. Sandy deserts dominate the country's physical terrain. Low-lying mountain ranges in the south form the borders with Iran and Afghanistan. The northern border with Uzbekistan is in part defined by the watercourse of the Amu Darya River, one of Central Asia's most important natural resources. The oases and river valleys of Turkmenistan have supported civilization since ancient times. But although the area was controlled by Turkmen tribes for many centuries, Turkmenistan never existed as an independent state within its present borders.[17]

During the Soviet period, Turkmenistan was a largely underdeveloped socialist republic. The Soviet economy was organized on the principle of cooperative production, which meant that Turkmenistan served as a supplier of primary commodities such as raw cotton fiber, oil, and natural gas. These were transported to existing manufacturing centers, located primarily in the Russian areas of the USSR, for high-value secondary processing. Industry unrelated to the gas and oil complex was generally not commercially viable, and the minimal economic activity that existed in Turkmenistan was maintained by Soviet subsidies.

Turkmenistan's agriculture heavily emphasized cotton production. Given the country's arid environment, expansion of its cotton-based agricultural economy required development of an extensive irrigation system. The massive subsidies that supported this system promoted highly inefficient and environmentally damaging agricultural practices.

Water flow from the Amu Darya River is drawn off by Turkmenistan and transported to farms and municipal users through the Karakum Canal. However, this diversion has contributed to the desiccation of the Aral Sea and fueled disagreements among the Central Asian states regarding water use. Given its great gas reserves, Turkmenistan could exchange power for water with Tajikistan if it were not for the fact that it shares no border with Tajik-istan due to an intervening strip of Uzbekistan.

With the end of Soviet-era subsidies, most of the agriculture and non-gas-related industry immediately became insolvent. The Turkmenistan govern-ment quickly sought to liberalize prices for external trade while maintaining price supports domestically. It adopted a development strategy that stressed increasing foreign trade earnings while ensuring domestic political stability under the rubric of "positive neutrality." According to this policy, Turk-menistan sought, first, to maintain as much distance as possible from Russia without giving up access to northern and European gas markets that, for the first few years of independence at least, would continue to be controlled by Russia by virtue of geography. Second, the policy of positive neutrality im-plied expansion of trade with Turkmenistan's southern neighbors on the basis of self-interest. Third, it meant that the country would seek to attract foreign investment to the extent possible to revitalize the gas-related industry and build a Kuwait-style emirate in Turkmenistan. With an estimated 2.7 tril-lion cubic meters in natural gas reserves and additional potential reserves estimated at 14 trillion cubic meters, Turkmenistan was the second largest natural gas producer in the former Soviet Union and the tenth largest pro-ducer in the world. In more recent times, its proven gas reserves have grown significantly (see "Postscript").

However, the Turkmenistan government has been unwilling to enact seri-ous postcommunist structural reform by reducing the dominance of the gov-ernment, liberalizing the price structure, and monetarizing the economy to allow a true private sector to emerge. A weak financial and banking infra-structure continues to hobble economic growth. The government has sought to increase direct foreign investment but has pursued this goal primarily through efforts to woo strategic investors with concessions rather than by establishing a level playing field for economic activity. The government's credit policy has been expansionary, based on "directed credit programs" and sweetheart deals. These policies have led to lax budget constraints and re-sulted in a predictably high number of underperforming loans.

The transfer of the state's most valuable assets to the private sector—"pri-vatization"—started slowly and then came to a standstill. While small-scale trading and service operations have largely been privatized, the Turkmenistan government has delayed the transfer to the private sector of medium- and large-scale enterprises, preferring to hold them as state-managed trusts or parastatal enterprises. The Turkmenistan government continues to play a highly interventionist role in the economy. All decisions affecting business involve some political considerations. The fusion of political and economic decisionmaking requires that businesspeople "facilitate" necessary decisions by offering inducements, in the forms of bribes and payoffs, to avoid capricious and quixotic regulatory delays. Rather than creating greater oversight, this form of control creates opportunities for corruption.

Turkmenistan has sought to be an attractive commercial partner, particularly for foreign enterprises interested in participating in the development of Turkmenistan's gas, oil, and agricultural sectors. However, the foundation of economic partnership in a market economy is the establishment of fair conditions for trade and commerce, not a system of favors and special treatment for preferred parties.

International financial institutions such as the International Monetary Fund, the World Bank, and the European Bank for Reconstruction and Development (EBRD) have tried to help Turkmenistan to develop its economic institutions. While the International Monetary Fund has no formal lending program in Turkmenistan, it has provided technical assistance and policy advice. The World Bank initiated major institution-building investments in privatization, modernization of the financial and banking sectors, joint venture administration, training in the energy sector, and improvement in water quality and urban transportation. The EBRD made significant investments in key institutional programs.

However, all of these multilateral lending programs have come to a standstill. The international development community has not been satisfied with Turkmenistan's progress toward the adoption of international standards of policy and practice. Turkmenistan became a member of the Asian Development Bank in 2000, but the bank has not opened an office in Turkmenistan. In April 2000, the EBRD took the unprecedented step of suspending its public sector lending programs to Turkmenistan because of the government's unwillingness to implement agreed-upon structural reforms.[18] In 2004, the EBRD announced that Turkmenistan was unwilling to abide by the bank's articles of incorporation. A 2004 letter to Turkmenbashi from Jean Lemierre, president of the EBRD, noted that the bank's directors "expressed grave concerns about the continuing lack of progress with regard to democratic and economic reform" and observed that Turkmenistan "has made little progress in structural and institutional reforms." In this situation, "the Bank is unable to expand its activities and will continue to focus on promoting private sector investments . . . providing that such investments are genuinely private and not controlled directly or indirectly by the State or government officials."[19] International financial institutions have remained cautious. The

EBRD slimmed down activities to what it regarded as "baseline" level, warning that if the Turkmenistan authorities did not

> move forward with democratic and critical market reforms, the Bank [would] not be able to move beyond the Baseline scenario. In this scenario, the Bank's activities will be focused on the promotion of private sector activities, particularly in the SME [small- to medium-enterprise] and micro-finance areas, provided it can be shown that the proposed investments are not effectively controlled by the state or by state entities and Government officials will not personally benefit from such investments.[20]

Officially, the international financial institutions concentrate on preparatory work, such as policy dialogue and nonlending analytical support, rather than on technical assistance and direct project lending.

Despite some economic gains in recent years, much of Turkmenistan's population is living below the poverty level.[21] International institutions regard Turkmenistan's economic reporting to be exceptionally unreliable. Turkmenbashi regularly reported economic statistics that appeared to be delusional. For instance, in a television appearance in 2004, Turkmenbashi reported an annualized economic growth rate for the country of over 20 percent.[22] In a television appearance in August 2006, Turkmenbashi again reported an annualized growth rate of 20 percent.[23]

It is difficult to make clear assessments about poverty, in part because there are differing estimates of the size of Turkmenistan's population. Recent public figures announced by Turkmenistan put the population at just over 6.4 million.[24] Outside estimates put the population at 5.7 million.[25]

The government has adopted populist policies to support the social safety net. Since 1992 the government has subsidized housing and related utilities (electricity, water, gas, sanitation, heating, and hot water) as well as key consumer goods (for example, bread, flour, and baby food). According to social indicators, however, the safety net is far from sound. Local gas and water supplies, while without cost to the consumers, are frequently interrupted. The country's infant mortality rate (39.6 per 1,000 live births) is among the highest in the region, and life expectancy (63.9 years) is among the lowest in the former USSR.

It is difficult to assess the state of Turkmenistan's contemporary macroeconomic conditions and public finances because in 1997 the government began to treat economic statistics, including gas output figures, as state secrets. Since then the government has sought to create the impression of economic progress in order to sustain public support and possibly influence international bond market ratings. For instance, in 2000 a Turkmenistan government spokesman claimed that the country appreciated international advice but was "following its own way to solve problems related to the process of transition" and was experiencing steady economic progress, with GDP growth rising from 5 percent in 1998 to 16 percent in 1999 and 14 percent in 2000.[26] The Turkmenistan government routinely claimed 15–20 percent per year growth rates each year until 2005. International financial institutions have not been satisfied with Turkmenistan's success in economic policy or structural reform and have generally dismissed Turkmenistan's growth statistics as instrumental rather than descriptive in character.

The Politics of Tyranny

Capricious leadership was the most distinguishing characteristic of Turkmenbashi's rule. He threatened, persecuted, and eliminated opponents of the regime, and journalists and political activists were targets as well. A recent incident concerned the arrest of three journalists and pro-democracy activists. On June 16, 2006, Turkmen government authorities arrested Ogulsapar Muradova, a correspondent for Radio Free Europe–Radio Liberty, and Annakurban Amanklychev, a correspondent for Galaxie Presse. Sapardurdy Khajiev, a human rights activist, was arrested by Turkmen government authorities on June 18, 2006. A Turkmen court issued a six-year sentence to Muradova and seven-year sentences to Amanklychev and Khajiev for violations of the Turkmenistan criminal code, ostensibly for possessing ammunition. In reality, the charge was political activism. All three were associated with the Turkmen Helsinki Foundation, a nongovernmental organization based in Bulgaria that monitors human rights conditions in Turkmenistan.

While in detention, Ogulsapar Muradova died. On September 12, 2006, the Turkmen authorities revealed her death to family members, claiming that she had died from natural causes. At first her family members were not allowed to see her body, and no autopsy was permitted. Eventually her adult children were allowed to see her body before burial, and they concluded that Muradova had been tortured and killed while in detention. Her death provoked alarm and objections from major world governments, international organizations, and nongovernmental bodies.

The Muradova case is an example of an arrest, torture, and murder for political means. It is certainly an illustration of capricious rule. But the Turkmen regime goes beyond this level of brutality and travesty to the very extreme of political tyranny. Dictatorial leaders often rule by forming a type of contract with political elites that rewards loyalty with protection; such pliant and subservient supporters usually become the principal beneficiaries of the regime. Turkmenbashi indeed surrounded himself with supporters, but his policies appeared to be of unparalleled unpredictability. Members of the political elite faced even fewer prospects of protection than did people accused of opposition or even sedition. Appointments and dismissals of high government officials occurred almost continuously.

When Turkmenbashi fired Rashid Meredov as deputy prime minister on March 7, 2005, he removed one of the longest-serving high officials. The opposition website gundogar.org claimed that Turkmenbashi had fired fifty-eight deputy prime ministers in the past thirteen years, an average of over four appointments a year. Of the fifty-eight, only six former deputy prime ministers continued to work for the government. The opposition site alleged that sixteen were imprisoned, eight fled the country, and the rest were unemployed and black-listed for other work—or were under house arrest.[27]

The cavalier character of Turkmenbashi's rule dates from the earliest days of independence, but it worsened as Turkmenbashi consolidated his political control. The "power organs"—the security and internal affairs agencies— were responsible for implementing Turkmenbashi's rule, yet these organs were not exempt from his capriciousness. In early 2002, the head of the Turkmenistan Ministry of National Security was removed on charges of corruption. After investigations directed by Turkmenbashi, more than 100 senior members of the country's security agency were imprisoned. In September 2002, another wave of scandals swept through the country, as President Niyazov announced that the new security agency head would also be removed.

In November 2002, events in Turkmenistan took a truly bizarre turn. According to government reports, on November 25, 2002, Turkmenbashi survived an assassination attempt in the midst of an attempted coup d'état. The Turkmen government media soon announced that former foreign minister Boris Shikhmuradov and three other government ministers had masterminded the coup attempt. The reports claimed that a truck had blocked the president's motorcade. Gunmen opened fire on Turkmenbashi's car, but he escaped the attempt unscathed. The following day, the Turkmenistan government announced the arrest of sixteen people in connection with the assassination attempt. On December 2, 2002, General Prosecutor Gurbanbibi Atajanova announced that after investigations, twenty-three people were arrested for involvement in the coup attempt. According to Atajanova, the government discovered proof that Shikhmuradov had coordinated the assassination plot from Russia in order to take power himself.

On December 18, 2002, Atajanova provided a public report on Turkmenistan national television in which she detailed a sequence of events. She claimed that Boris Shikhmuradov directed the assassination attempt from inside Turkmenistan, claiming that he had entered the country in 2002 from Uzbekistan with the help of Abdurashid Kadyrov, the Uzbek ambassador to Turkmenistan. The report claimed that Shikhmuradov, together with other conspirators, remained in the Uzbek embassy in hiding until late 2002. On December 24, 2002, a website under the direction of Shikhmuradov issued a statement in which he claimed that he had been in Turkmenistan since September 2002. The following day, Turkmenbashi announced that Shikhmuradov had been captured. Four days later, Turkmen national television aired footage of Shikhmuradov publicly confessing to the assassination attempt.[28] In the aftermath of these events, the Turkmenistan government authorities detained hundreds of relatives of those implicated in the plot, some of whom, according to reports, were physically abused and denied access to medical treatment. Relatives of those implicated in the attack also were said to have lost jobs and were evicted from their homes without compensation. At year's end, many remained under house arrest and were not allowed to leave the country or travel internally.[29]

Atajanova became known as the "iron lady" of Turkmenistan for her grand inquisitor status. Her power serving as prosecutor general was uncontested until early 2006 when Turkmenbashi became suspicious that she was misusing the unlimited power that she exercised over imagined and real opponents of the Turkmen regime. In April 2006, Turkmenbashi personally accused Atajanova of corruption and misuse of the prosecutor's office. Faced with this criminal accusation, Atajanova publicly confessed to bribe taking and corruption on a state television broadcast.[30] She allegedly pleaded in tears to Niyazov for forgiveness and asked the Turkmen leader not to put her in prison. Eventually she was stripped of her possessions and privileges. Atajanova's case made it abundantly clear that no one in Turkmenistan was above, beyond, or out of the range of Turkmenbashi's exercise of power.

Looking Ahead: Handing over the Mantle of Repression

Turkmenistan's political evolution from a Soviet-era dependency into a rogue tyranny has been made possible by political exchange relationships financed primarily through natural gas revenues. Although the Turkmenbashi-as-great-spiritual-leader phenomenon was primarily psychological in origin, it was supported by economic compromises with the managers of key sectors, particularly energy, banking, and agriculture. The beneficiaries of this system were the primary supporters of the system; therefore threats to the system represented threats to the largesse that they enjoyed. There were only two choices for these beneficiaries—unquestioning and unconditional fealty to the Great Leader or the risk of elimination. Servile obeisance before the Great Leader was demanded; any lapse of obsequious devotion ran the risk of being identified as opposition. "There is no opposition in Turkmenistan," the Great Leader was often quoted as saying. This statement was no doubt intended to function as both a political observation and a political threat. But the experience of Turkmenbashi's servile, sycophantic entourage vividly illustrated that the country's administrative elite had no assurance that loyalty would be repaid with protection and security.

Postscript: After Turkmenbashi

Niyazov's death in Ashgabat on December 21, 2006, opened a new, potentially positive, period for Turkmenistan. If his successor continues on an early path of cautious reform, a new Turkmenistan could well emerge out of the discredited remains of one of the globe's more odious, repressive nation-states.

Turkmenistan's enormous mineral resource wealth and the country's crucial geopolitical location on the fabled Silk Road intersect with dynamic forces of change. Resource-hungry China and India, an economically resurgent Russia, an energy-dependent Europe, a recovering Afghanistan, and a politically unstable but energy-rich Middle East are factors that are creating new forces of change throughout the entire region. Turkmenistan, located at the intersection of Asia, Europe, and the Middle East, possesses the potential for playing a role in the region far out of proportion to the size of its population or its historical influence. For these reasons, foreign diplomatic and commercial interests carefully observed the initial changes introduced by the new, post-Turkmenbashi government.

Turkmenbashi's funeral ceremony took place in Ashgabat on December 24, 2006, ceremonially headed by Gurbanguly Berdymukhammedov, a member of Turkmenbashi's inner circle during his last days. The funeral gave Berdymukhammedov the opportunity to represent Turkmenistan to foreign dignitaries and suggest new directions for the country's development. Heads of state from Turkmenistan's immediate neighbors, Tajikistan and Kazakhstan, were in attendance at the funeral ceremonies. But the positions of distinction in the funeral procession went not to heads of state but heads of government. Russia's Prime Minister Mikhail Fradkov and Ukraine's Prime Minister Viktor Yanukovich, the two men who hold the key positions in Turkmenistan's foreign gas trade, were accorded positions in the funeral ceremonies that illustrated the new government's sensitivities to its primary sources of revenue.

Although Berdymukhammedov ranked among the closest supporters during Turkmenbashi's last period, he was not visibly in contention for political succession. Yet Berdymukhammedov quickly stepped into the position of "temporary acting president" as well as supreme high commander of the armed forces with the first official announcement of Turkmenbashi's death. Berdymukhammedov then expeditiously convened a special meeting of the country's parliament, the Halk Maslikhat. At this meeting, the 2,466 members listed in attendance unanimously endorsed the appointment of Berdymukhammedov to serve as "acting president" until formal presidential elections could take place on February 11, 2007. The Halk Maslikhat then proceeded to approve a list of six nominees for the election, including Berdymukhammedov. The body also approved a constitutional amendment that sanctified this unusual sequence of events. At the same time, Berdymukhammedov maneuvered the presumed constitutional successor, Ovezgeldy Atayev, the chairman of the Halk Maslikhat, out of a position of influence by announcing that Atayev had been charged with corruption.

Berdymukhammedov easily swept the presidential election on February 11 and was sworn in as president on February 14, 2007. The head of the Turkmenistan Central Election Commission announced that Berdymukhammedov had captured nearly 90 percent of the votes. The Turkmenistan political opposition living in exile joined international monitoring organizations and civil rights groups in denouncing the elections as neither free nor fair. While the elections were not monitored or witnessed by international observers, Turkmen television announced that the president's inauguration had been attended by heads of state from Kazakhstan, Tajikistan, Georgia, and Afghanistan as well as heads of government from Iran, Ukraine, Russia, and Turkey.

Even before his election, Berdymukhammedov pledged that Turkmenistan would hold firm to the policy of "neutrality," based on neighborliness, mutual respect, equal rights, and beneficial cooperation with all countries of the world, faithfully fulfilling international obligations and commitments. At his inauguration, Berdymukhammedov stressed the importance of continuity in Turkmenistan's national traditions but also suggested that he would cautiously carry out reforms to improve health care, promote private business development, and revitalize education. As this book went to press, it was too early to know whether he would in fact follow through effectively on his promises. It was also too soon to know whether he had the full support of the Turkmenbashi coterie.

It is not surprising that continuity is the favored theme of Berdymukhammedov and those who have supported him in preventing electoral competition regarding the future of post-Turkmenbashi Turkmenistan. Every one of the members of Turkmenbashi's closest circle of power was a product of the era. Every one has witnessed how those government officials who fell out of favor in Turkmenistan were rebuked, isolated, banished to obscurity, fined, punished, sent to prison, tortured, and even sent to their death. Every one of them has contributed to the country's hero worship by participating in sycophantic adulation of the "Great Leader." Yet for precisely these reasons, each one of them is also invested in the continuation of the course that Turkmenbashi laid for the country. Not one is likely to be willing to turn comfortably to the future before being sure that all the necessary steps have been taken to evade the revenge of the past.

As in the past, Turkmenistan's sizable gas reserves likely will continue to shape the country's relations with its neighbors as well as its internal politics. The country's trade and foreign relations potential has made the stakes very high and has convinced many of Turkmenistan's political elite that the cost of mistakes will be equally great. At the same time, it is not clear exactly what the stakes are. It is clear that the development of Turkmenistan's natural resources would require substantial investment in prospecting, drilling, processing, and transportation in order to produce and market the gas. Such investment implies considerable interaction with other countries, international organizations, and international commercial firms in a way that assumes a level of conformity to international standards. Turkmenbashi succeeded in postponing internationally acceptable behavior by attempting personally and cannily to manage the country's neomercantile foreign policy.

It has never been particularly clear how much gas exists for Turkmenistan to export. Assessments of the country's reserves vary widely, ranging from 3 to 6 trillion cubic meters. In 2002, the Asian Development Bank began helping Turkmenistan to arrange an independent gas assessment. It financed the American firm DeGoyler and MacNaughton in 2005 to provide an independent audit. Although the audit results have not been made public, Turkmenistan government sources have indicated that the Dovletabat gas field alone contains some 4.5 trillion cubic meters and that the country's total reserves exceed 6 trillion cubic meters. In 2006, Turkmenistan exported about 55 billion cubic meters and announced plans to increase exports in 2007 to 100 billion cubic meters.[31] Turkmenistan renegotiated gas prices from $40 per thousand cubic meters in 2005 to $100 per thousand cubic meters beginning in 2007. However, the situation changed dramatically in October 2006 when Turkmenbashi announced the discovery of new and unanticipated reserves in the Yolotan gas field, which is said to contain 7 trillion cubic meters alone. If the reserves of the Yolotan field are even close to the figure that Turkmenbashi used, it will surely signify a business opportunity that none of the countries interested in Caspian energy resources can afford to ignore.[32]

In the decade and a half since Turkmenistan's independence, Turkmenbashi managed to remain at the helm of what certainly was one of the world's most bizarre, brutal, corrupt, capriciously governed, and, if the assessments of its natural gas reserves are even roughly accurate, potentially prosperous countries. The secretive rule of Turkmenbashi undermined Turkmenistan's business environment. The unwillingness of the Turkmenistan government to adopt standard statistical reporting, generally accepted accounting practices, internationally accepted banking standards, and sound public administration greatly increased the risk entailed in operating a business in the country. But now the possibility that there is much more gas than was previously expected provides great opportunities for a government that may liberalize politically.

Turkmenistan under Berdymukhammedov finds itself in a delicate and potentially enviable situation. If Berdymukhammedov simply perpetuates Turkmenbashi's methods, however, Turkmenistan may not grow. Nor will its people advance socially.

Notes

1. The second volume of the *Ruhnama* was presented by Turkmenbashi to the Turkmen Mejlis (parliament) on September 12, 2004.

2. For instance, see the analysis of the removal of some 27,000 health workers from their positions, in Institute for War and Peace Reporting, "Turkmenbashi Wields the Axe: Third Wave of Medical Cuts Closes Hospitals Everywhere Except the Capital" (London, March 11, 2005), iwpr.net/?p=rca&s=f&o=238797&apc_state=henirca2005.

3. Saparmurad Ovezberdiyev, "In Turkmenistan, Thugs and Tyranny," *Washington Post* (August 6, 2004).

4. U.S. Department of State, "Turkmenistan," in *2005 Country Reports on Human Rights Practices* (Washington, D.C., March 8, 2006).

5. The Commission on Security and Cooperation in Europe introduced a resolution in the U.S. Congress calling on the Turkmen government to make significant improvements in human rights as well as to end "the diversion of state funds into President Niyazov's personal offshore accounts, and adopt international best practices as laid forth by the International Monetary Fund regarding the disclosure and management of oil and gas revenues." See Representative Christopher Smith, "Human Rights Abuses in Turkmenistan," *Congressional Record: Proceedings and Debates of the 109th Congress*, 2nd session, CLII (September 27, 2006), 123.

6. For Freedom House coverage of Turkmenistan, see "Worst of the Worst: The World's Most Repressive Societies 2006" (September 6, 2006), www.freedomhouse.org/template.cfm?page=138&report=40.

7. See Human Rights Watch, "Turkmenistan" (January 2007), hrw.org/doc/?t=europe&c=turkme.

8. Reporters without Borders, "Worldwide Press Freedom Index 2005" (October 2005), www.rsf.org/article.php3?id_article=15331.

9. See State of World Liberty Project, "The 2006 State of World Liberty Index: Countries Listed by Ranking/Score" (August 12, 2006), www.stateofworldliberty.org/report/rankings.html. The ranking derives from a composite of indexes: the Heritage Foundation–Wall Street Journal's "2006 Index of Economic Freedom," Frasier Institute–Cato Institute's "2005 Economic Freedom of the World," Freedom House's "2005 Freedom in the World," and Reporters without Borders's "Press Freedom Index."

10. These elections were only announced by the president in September 2004, with little preparation time for political competition. See "Turkmen Parliamentary Elections Set for 19 December 2004," BBC Mon Alert CAU 310804 ak/ov (August 30, 2004), in Russian, from www.turkmenistan.gov.tm. The Organization for Security and Cooperation was not allowed to observe the elections and thus made no comment on them. Gulnoza Saidazimova, "Turkmenistan: Election Noteworthy for Lower Official Voter Turnout," Radio Free Europe–Radio Liberty Report (December 20, 2004), www.rferl.org/featuresarticle/2004/12/fee317cc-ba38-4891-ac32-5a411bd2b9d3.html.

11. "Turkmen President Calls for 20 Per Cent GDP Growth in 2005," BBC Mon Alert CAU 260804 cb/mn/ (August 26, 2004), in Turkmen, from TV Altyn Asyr, Ashgabat.

12. "Niyazov Commissions Tenders on the Construction of Provincial Theaters," Watan TV News (August 26, 2004).

13. BBC Mon CAU 220604 ak/ov/ (June 21, 2004), in Turkmen, from TV Altyn Asyr, Ashgabat.

14. According to Russian media, Turkmenistan disconnected Russia's Mayak radio station in July 2004, explaining that equipment failure required renovation that would

take at least a year to complete. BBC Mon CAU MD1 Media 120704 ag/bs (July 12, 2004), in Russian, from ITAR-TASS News Agency, Moscow.

15. Freedom House, "Worst of the Worst"; Human Rights Watch, "Turkmenistan."

16. World Bank, *Development Indicators 2005* (Washington, D.C., 2005).

17. For a recent survey of Turkmenistan, see Rafis Abazov, *Historical Dictionary of Turkmenistan* (London, 2005).

18. "EBRD Cuts Turkmen Loans, Slams Political System," Reuters (April 18, 2000).

19. See European Bank for Reconstruction and Development, "EBRD Adopts New Turkmenistan Strategy" (July 16, 2004), www.ebrd.com/new/pressrel/2004/102 july16.htm.

20. European Bank for Reconstruction and Development, "Strategy for Turkmenistan: As Approved by the Board of Directors on 23 June 2004" (London, 2004).

21. There is considerable disagreement over the reliability of economic data gathered and distributed by the Turkmenistan government. World Bank analysts collect and analyze data but often do not report the data for public distribution. A World Bank study of poverty conducted between 1988 and 1998 "found the proportion of people living in absolute poverty to be increasing." The surveys in 1998 found that 79.4 percent lived on U.S.$4.30 per day or less and almost 44 percent on U.S.$2.15 per day or less. See World Health Organization, "Highlights on Health, Turkmenistan 2005" (2006), www.euro.who.int/eprise/main/who/progs/chhtkm/demographic/20050131_1. See also World Bank, *World Development Indicators 2005* (Washington, D.C., 2005).

22. See "Turkmen Leader Details Robust Economic Growth This Year," BBC News (May 3, 2004), in Turkmen, from TV Altyn Asyr, Ashgabat. Regarding the reliability of economic statistics for the country, see International Monetary Fund, "Turkmenistan: Recent Economic Developments," Staff Country Report 99/140 (Washington, D.C., December 10, 1999).

23. Turkmenistan Project, "Turkmenistan to Boost Fuel and Energy Sector" (August 4, 2006), www.eurasianet.org/turkmenistan.project/index.php?page=wnb/editor/wnb20060811&lang=eng#2a.

24. According to the data of National Institute of State Statistics and Information, the population of Turkmenistan reached 6,408,600 people on June 1, 2004. Watan TV News (June 23, 2004).

25. Population Reference Bureau, "2004 World Population Data Sheet" (Washington, D.C., August 2004).

26. International Monetary Fund, "Statement by the Hon. Seyitbay Kandymov, Governor of the Fund and the Bank for Turkmenistan, at the Joint Annual Discussion," Press Release 15 (September 26–28, 2000), www.imf.org/external/am/2000/speeches/pr15tme.pdf.

27. See a review in the *Turkmenistan Weekly News Brief* (March 4–10, 2005).

28. An account of these events is available in Emmanuel Decaux, "OSCE Rapporteur's Report on Turkmenistan," Office for Democratic Institutions and Human

Rights, Organization for Security and Cooperation in Europe (Vienna, March 12, 2003).

29. See U.S. Department of State, "Turkmenistan," in *2002 Country Reports on Human Rights Practices* (Washington, D.C., March 31, 2003).

30. Bruce Pannier, "Turkmenistan: Former Prosecutor 'Confesses' on State TV," Radio Free Europe–Radio Liberty (April 25, 2006), www.rferl.org/featuresarticle/2006/04/3a1ec544-e90b-4d7c-93ac-810bb1a5b84b.html.

31. In February 2006, the Turkmenistan official government website published an article that was viewed by many analysts as designed to popularize rising expectations regarding the country's export potential. See "Export Capacity of Turkmenistan Exceeds 100 Billion Cubic Meters of Natural Gas per Annum" (February 15, 2006), www.turkmenistan.ru/?page_id=3&lang_id=en&elem_id=7753&type=event&sort=date_desc.

32. On November 3, 2006, in a meeting with foreign diplomats, President Niyazov was reported to have announced the discovery of unexpectedly large gas deposits in the Yolotan field. See "Weekly News Brief on Turkmenistan" (November 3–9, 2006), www.eurasianet.org/turkmenistan.project/index.php?page=wnb/editor/wnb20061111&lang=eng.

six
Burma: Poster Child for Entrenched Repression

Priscilla A. Clapp

When Burma emerged from colonial rule in 1948, it was the wealthiest, best educated, and most progressive country in Southeast Asia. In fact, it was Asia's original democracy. Today it is one of the most economically backward, politically stagnant, and repressive countries in the region and, indeed, in the world. How did a country with such a promising start come to be identified as one of the world's leading "outposts of tyranny" fifty years later?[1] What made things go so wrong for Burma?[2]

Historical Factors

In many respects, Burma's failure to develop sustainable democracy is rooted in its colonial legacy. As part of the British Raj, it was divided into two distinct entities: lower Burma, which was dominated by ethnic Burmans, and upper Burma, which was a collection of non-Burman tribal entities. In lower Burma the British established a well-trained Burman civil service to run the government, whereas upper Burma consisted of self-governed ethnic states answering directly to the British but retaining their tribal structures, many of which were primitive.

When Burma won its independence from Britain at the close of World War II, it was faced immediately with the task of uniting these two Burmas under a single government. Recognizing this reality, General Aung San negotiated the original constitution with the major tribal groups to create a union of seven relatively autonomous ethnic states (Karen, Karenni, Shan, Chin, Kachin, Mon, and Arakan) and seven largely ethnic Burman divisions, governed by a national parliament.[3] Unfortunately, Aung San was not able to prevent some of the ethnic groups from insisting that the constitution should allow them to secede from the union after ten years if they were not satisfied with its governance.[4] He probably hoped that he would be able to deliver the necessary reassurance once the young democracy had begun to function, but that was not to be.

Tragically, Aung San was brutally killed, along with most of his convening committee, in July 1947, just months before independence. Nevertheless, one or another of the small group of nationalists that he had formed to fight for independence, known as the Thirty Comrades, continued in one form or another to govern the country for the next forty years. U Nu—one of the Thirty Comrades—inherited the mantle of leadership as prime minister of the newly elected parliament, but he was not a strong leader and did not manage over the years to develop effective institutions of central government and instill a sense of nationhood among the ethnic nationalities. The country became so wracked by insurgency that the elected parliament soon found itself controlling very little territory beyond Rangoon. In 1958, with more than one state threatening to secede from the union, the elected government invited the head of the armed forces, General Ne Win—yet another of the Thirty Comrades—to hold the country together under martial law. Ne Win did so and returned the country to parliamentary government after new elections were held in 1960, but the nation soon began to fall apart again under a bickering and ineffectual parliament. Ne Win staged a coup d'état in 1962, imprisoning the entire cabinet, including U Nu, and thus ending Burma's experiment with democracy.[5]

Ne Win launched the "Burmese Way to Socialism" and nationalized the country's economy in 1964, instituting a new constitution in 1974 to establish perpetual single-party government under the Burma Socialist Programme Party (BSPP). The BSPP parliament and the occasional parliamentary elections were at best only a flimsy disguise for Ne Win's military dictatorship. Developing his own "cult of personality," he was an absurdly whimsical ruler who treated the country as his private domain. Apparently resenting colonial and other external influence on Burma's earlier educational and economic achievements, he proceeded to dismantle many of the country's economic and social structures and plunged it willy-nilly into serious political and economic decline. Anyone who appeared to challenge his authority was dismissed from government and usually imprisoned. Only sycophants remained unscathed.

The cumulative impact of Ne Win's incompetent governance, particularly with regard to economic mismanagement, began to take its toll in the late 1980s. A series of ill-considered economic measures to shore up the declining currency in 1987 generated a public protest that grew eventually into a wide-scale rebellion against the government in 1988. At about this time, Aung San's daughter Aung San Suu Kyi, who had been living abroad for decades, returned to Burma to nurse her ailing mother.[6] As the antigovernment demonstrations grew in intensity, she was drawn into politics and, with her charismatic public presence and unflinching bravery in the face of military intimidation, soon became an emblem of a nascent democracy movement. In the midst of the turmoil, Ne Win abruptly resigned, ordering his cabinet to return the country to multiparty democracy. Instead, the military attacked hundreds of street protesters in August 1988. In September what remained of Ne Win's government was ousted in a military coup by the State Law and Order Restoration Council (SLORC), which promptly announced that elections would be held soon for a multiparty parliament. Although the SLORC vowed to turn authority over to a new civilian government after the elections, it is clear in hindsight that they had every intention of using the elections to create a civilian shell for continued military rule.

By the time that the elections were held in 1990, the world was in the midst of a dramatic political evolution. In Europe the Berlin Wall had come down and Germany was heading for reunification, the Soviet Union was falling apart, and China's communist regime had suffered a major political challenge in Tiananmen Square. The SLORC felt obligated to carry out Ne Win's order to return to multiparty parliamentary government, but it was determined to avoid the political liberalization that seemed to be overtaking its neighbors. Thus the generals attempted to engineer the elections to produce a majority for the government party and were deeply dismayed when the opposition National League for Democracy (NLD) won more than 80 percent of the vote.

The SLORC quickly backtracked on its earlier plan, announcing instead that a National Convention would first have to decide on a new constitution before the elected parliament could be seated. They insisted that military and government delegations would dominate the convention rather than the newly elected members of parliament. Thus originated the political stalemate that has persisted in Burma ever since. After a hiatus of nearly ten years, in

2004 the National Convention began to sit once again, without the participation of the political party that had won the elections and with its agenda dictated by the generals and the prospect of a new constitution no more apparent than it had been a decade ago.

Burma's political history is critical to understanding the reasons behind the country's seemingly unending cycle of military rule and economic decline, even as its neighbors have been achieving dramatic political and economic advances. First and foremost among these reasons has been the lingering perception that Burma's union of various ethnic groups was fragile and could disintegrate at any moment. This fear kept the young Burmese democracy from delivering peace and prosperity to its people. It provided a justification for Ne Win to impose martial law and govern the country with an iron hand for decades, and it has remained alive in the minds of the current military regime, despite its success in bringing the major insurgencies to an end. Sadly, this fear—whether real or imagined—has excused decades of institutionalized repression against Burmese of all ethnic backgrounds.

A second and related factor is the historical division between lower and upper Burma. Over the years, the military regime has thoroughly penetrated all aspects of economic and political life in lower Burma, systematically squeezing civilians out of positions of significant responsibility and subverting the country's institutions to military goals and objectives. Upper Burma, on the other hand, has been allowed a certain degree of local autonomy, with former insurgents and their militias controlling the structures of local government in many areas. The "cease-fire" agreements negotiated by the government with different insurgent groups have tended to ratify varying degrees of local autonomy. There is also a significant economic gap between these two Burmas. Not surprisingly, some of the most remote areas of the country along the Indian and Chinese borders are not connected to the rest of the country by roads and railroads and remain woefully underdeveloped.

A third important historical factor has been Burma's seeming inability to develop new political leadership outside the legacy of its original liberation movement. The generals in charge today are derivatives of Ne Win. The leadership of the democratic opposition traces its origins to Aung San and Ne Win. While Aung San Suu Kyi is, by any standards, one of the world's most talented and inspirational political figures, her rise to prominence in Burma began because she was Aung San's daughter, seeking to complete his unfulfilled mission. Other senior members of her NLD party first rose to prominence with Ne Win. The long history of these personal relationships and interconnections permeates Rangoon's political milieu, as if it has been frozen in time.

Finally, it is clear that Ne Win's autocratic rule abruptly arrested the development of democratic institutions in Burma. Subsequently, the leadership of the SLORC and its successor, the State Peace and Development Council (SPDC), has systematically dismantled, outlawed, or militarized the remaining institutions of government and civil society that survived the Ne Win years. They have forced talented civilians to resign from government ministries and replaced them with retired military officials. Nearly all cabinet ministers are now retired or active-duty military officers.

Successive military leadership has further compounded Burma's poverty of talent in governance by continuing Ne Win's practice of excluding the best and brightest from government for fear of being challenged. The minicoup within the upper ranks of the SPDC in October 2004 has effectively accelerated the process of political impoverishment by eliminating the sector of the leadership that managed both the country's external relations as well as SPDC relations with the ethnic cease-fire groups. Any promise of productive dialogue between the government and its opponents—both internal and external—that appeared in the 2001–2002 period was extinguished by 2006.

Characteristics of the Military Government

Although they pretend to rule by committee rather than by force of personality, the generals who control Burma today have retained many of the strange practices, prejudices, fears, and personal idiosyncrasies that characterized Ne Win's rule. While less overtly xenophobic than Ne Win, they are still paranoid about external influence and the perceived external manipulation of Burma's internal affairs. Although they crave recognition by the international community, they believe that foreign influence diminishes Burma's sovereignty; they will even engage in self-destructive behavior to avoid foreign influence. For example, the SPDC has failed to carry through on its promise to move to a free-market economy, at least in part because it and its business cronies resent it if foreign companies make any profit in Burma or succeed in any particular sector of the economy. Burma's leaders have harmed their own export potential in order to deny profits to foreign trade companies. Most important, they believe that "democracy" is a foreign device to gain political influence in Burma and that the political opposition acts at the behest of foreign powers.

Burma's generals are, by and large, politically unschooled and fear free speech, open debate, and political complexity because they associate openness with the period of weak democratic government during which ethnic insurgencies spread and the army had to restore order. Most of the senior military leadership served on the front lines of battle against communist-inspired insurgencies along the Chinese border and home-grown insurgencies elsewhere in the country. Even today the military remains heavily armed and guarded. The more senior generals are highly risk averse and most comfortable sticking closely to accepted dogma. They will play only by their own rules of government, which are published daily in the government-controlled press, although they readily change those rules to fit their own purposes. Not surprisingly, their political jargon is salted with the words *order*, *discipline*, *duty*, and *obedience*. The utter refusal of Burma's military leadership to tolerate any degree of debate has time and again stifled even the most gradual moves toward transition away from total military dictatorship.

Finally, it is clear that the top general, Than Shwe, like Ne Win before him, has become highly adept at suppressing any form of dissent or disobedience within the military ranks, ensuring that the small group of generals at the top remains highly unified in its determination to retain an iron grip on political power. For more than fifteen years after 1988, the top leadership group was required to spend every night at military headquarters, supposedly to be close by should there be an emergency. They met with each other the first thing in the morning and the last thing at night. Than Shwe appears to control the essential levers of power within the military. He determines who gets promoted and does not hesitate to purge senior military ranks regularly, as he has demonstrated dramatically several times in recent years. In October 2004, he arrested General Khin Nyunt, his prime minister, head of military intelligence, and third in power; fired or arrested all the people answering to Khin Nyunt; and demolished the military intelligence structures under Khin Nyunt's control, some 30,000 uniformed military in all.[7] With the removal of Khin Nyunt, several key ambassadors who reported to him, and the foreign, home, and labor ministers, Than Shwe appears to have deliberately purged the SPDC of anyone who might wish to see Burma gradually return one day to pluralistic civilian government.[8]

The Nature of Repression in Burma

There is no question that repression in Burma is widespread and pervasive.[9] Through its control over all major organs of political and economic power in the country, the military regime brooks no challenge to its authority whatsoever. While it has not repeated the wide-scale slaughter, imprisonment, and exile of its opponents that occurred in 1988–1990, it has continued to employ a variety of judicial and extrajudicial punishments to prevent any form of political opposition or challenge to military rule from gaining strength. The chief among these are discussed below.

Use of Military Force against Domestic Opposition

In the postcolonial period, Burma's armed forces have been organized and employed almost exclusively to establish and maintain security at home and not against a foreign enemy, although in recent years they have, from time to time, engaged in sporadic border skirmishes with Thailand, India, and Bangladesh in the course of pursuing insurgent militia. Ne Win expanded and substantially strengthened Burma's army to fight the extensive insurgencies being supported by Communist China along the eastern borders during the 1970s and 1980s. The SPDC continues to strengthen the armed forces, which have expanded from 200,000 to 450,000 since 1988, even though the insurgencies have largely been quelled.[10]

Unfortunately, the tactics developed to fight insurgencies included extremely harsh measures against civilians seen to be supporting insurgent militias, including rape, pillage, forced relocation, "scorched earth" destruction of villages and farmland, and the slaughter of women and children. The SLORC and SPDC have used these tactics liberally throughout Burma, and they are still common today in the areas where small insurgencies remain on the Thai border, laying large areas to waste and leaving tens of thousands homeless. The army has also been known to turn its counterinsurgency tactics on other ethnic civilian populations (including Burmans) when it has perceived a political threat to the regime or when it simply wants to seize land for its own use.

The liberal use of forced labor has been a corollary form of military repression, growing out of the need to support an army extended into remote areas of the country. The army is known to round up young men and boys on the streets of population centers and dragoon them into army service, either as forced labor or as recruits. Forced labor is used to portage army supplies through dangerous areas, build roads into remote areas, and perform other support services for the army. The military government has also tolerated, perhaps sometimes encouraged, the use of forced labor by local municipalities for public works projects.[11]

Use of Military Intelligence to Spy On and Intimidate Civilians

Government surveillance of the civilian population is pervasive in Burma. Until 2005 this surveillance was centered in a well-resourced and relatively sophisticated military intelligence corps (commonly referred to as MI) bearing a strong resemblance to the former Soviet Union's KGB. The activities of MI included regular tapping of telephones, e-mail, and other forms of electronic and written communication. MI kept close tabs on all persons, including military, who were suspected of disagreeing with the government in any form. It employed many civilian organs of government, such as the Ministry of Posts and Telecommunications, as well as business enterprises, particularly those engaged in communications and tourism, to extend its surveillance capabilities. In fact, elements within MI even owned companies providing e-mail service, high-tech communications, and news and tourism services. Local government organizations, such as the police and the neighborhood warden system (which patrols urban and rural neighborhoods to ensure that people are not away from home without official notification), also reported to MI. The organs of MI were particularly interested in the activities of foreigners and any unauthorized contacts they might have with Burmese nationals.[12]

In a surprising move at the end of 2004, Than Shwe abolished the entire military intelligence structure, including MI, the Directorate of Defense Services Intelligence, and the National Intelligence Bureau, as part of his effort to destroy the power base of Khin Nyunt. Because the National Intelligence Bureau and the directorate coordinated intelligence functions government-wide, it is likely that some separate intelligence services still continue to function, but without strong central coordination within the military. It is clear that responsibility for surveillance of political dissidents and their possible connections with foreigners now rests primarily with the Police Special Branch under the authority of the home minister. For example, police authorities have taken the place of MI in watching over Aung San Suu Kyi's compound, where in 2006 she remained under formal house arrest. Similarly, political arrests and threats to opposition politicians in 2006 were carried out by police instead of military intelligence. After MI was disbanded, a new military intelligence unit was formed, headed by a relatively senior general, but it has neither the resources nor the power of its predecessor. It would be a surprising aberration in the long history of military rule in Burma, however, if the leadership did not eventually recreate a means of ensuring strong military control over an intelligence function that is so critical to its political power.

Subversion of the Legal System

Based on British common law, Burma's legal system was one of its proud legacies. Although the shell of the common law system remains today, decades of military rule have turned it into a vehicle for punishing enemies. Courts continue to operate, but the judges are not independent of the military leadership. Criminal and civil cases initiated by the SPDC are kept on a separate set of records, and their outcomes are dictated by the military leadership. Judges must regularly reach absurd interpretations of law to justify the judicial results required by the military. People brought to court for political reasons are generally not allowed to have legal representation in court. Many of those convicted of political crimes are also deemed a security threat, which can leave them languishing in prison for a lifetime because there is no set time limit on their sentences. Most of the well-known political prisoners from 1988 and the decade of the 1990s, estimated to number more than 1,000, remain in this predicament.[13] The military regime also punishes people quite arbitrarily for economic crimes, the basis for which is unpredictable because the generals change the rules governing the economy almost whimsically from day to day.

Ironically, Ne Win and subsequent military regimes have not hesitated to turn the perverse legal system against their own kind. Ne Win jailed many colleagues, friends, and family during his leadership. The SPDC has repeatedly ostracized and jailed its own cohorts on trumped-up charges. In 2002 Ne Win's son-in-law and grandsons, who had lived their lives ostentatiously confident that they were above the law, were sentenced to life in prison on a long list of both political and economic charges. Ne Win himself and his favorite daughter were placed under house arrest. Ne Win died several months later, still under house arrest. In 2005 hundreds of military officers were charged with a variety of trumped-up legal infractions, ranging from corruption to subversion, in the ongoing effort to purge Khin Nyunt and his associates.

Outlawing Civil Society and Political Activity

According to the rules of the military regime, it is illegal for more than five people to gather in public without official permission. Police and intelligence services keep all potential political activity under close surveillance and do not hesitate to bring it to a halt. Since the 1990 elections, the National League for Democracy and other political parties have been under close scrutiny with severe restrictions on their activities. All telephones, computers, and other electronic equipment must be authorized by the government. Gatherings at NLD party offices have been restricted or halted many times. In the late 1990s, the government closed down most of the local NLD party offices and forced party members to resign, apparently so that the regime could claim that the NLD no longer had a large enough base to warrant official status as a political party. This process was suspended, however, during 2000–2002 when the military leadership engaged in "confidence-building" discussions with the NLD leadership. Many of the restrictions on the NLD were then reinstated in mid-2003, when Aung San Suu Kyi and other party members were attacked at Depayin by government stooges and then taken into custody. Since then the SPDC's civilian arm, the Union Solidarity Development Association (USDA), has been harassing and forcing NLD members to resign and close offices. Only the headquarters in Rangoon still operated in 2006. The types of constraints and punishments placed on the NLD are also visited on other political parties and independent civil society organizations.

As part of its strategy to control and contain the rise of civil society institutions, the SPDC has in recent years created a number of "government organized" nongovernmental organizations (GONGOs) to support and supplement government programs and to participate in the expanding international nongovernmental organization arena. Prominent among these are women's groups, led by the top generals' wives, engaging in business promotion or humanitarian activity. Burmese and foreign donors have been encouraged, perhaps even forced, by the military leadership to channel contributions to humanitarian causes through these GONGOs, often in return for special business considerations.

The most egregious and blatantly coercive GONGO, however, is the USDA, whose patron is the top general. All government, military, and paramilitary officials, the national Red Cross, the fire brigades, and all officially sanctioned civic organizations are required to be members of the USDA. Most observers expect that the military regime will eventually register the USDA as a political party. With its vast membership beholden to the government, it would be expected to dominate any future parliamentary elections. In fact, the majority of delegates to the reconvened National Convention are undoubtedly members of the USDA. It has also been used by the military to organize attacks, both physical and verbal, on the NLD.

Economic Repression

When Ne Win nationalized the economy in the name of socialism, he institutionalized military control of the economy. It was only natural for the army to keep a firm grip on the levers of centralized economic control once the generals had replaced Ne Win's BSPP with their own regime. Thus Burma's economy today remains a military economy in which the needs and objectives of the armed forces take precedence. The SPDC and the army control the vast majority of land and have confiscated additional land when they felt the need for it. They operate agricultural and manufacturing enterprises, and they own logging and mining concessions. Most of Burma's population subsists on farming, fishing, and small-scale entrepreneurship around cities and population centers. Larger-scale private enterprise, however, operates at the pleasure of the military and must accommodate the generals, commonly by paying bribes and catering to the needs of the army and its businesses. Military families tend to be highly placed in both business and government. People who fall out of favor with the military leadership are likely to lose their economic livelihoods and have their families banished from educational and employment opportunities. In the move against Khin Nyunt, Than Shwe also arrested his family and colleagues for a variety of economic crimes, ostensibly because of corruption but in reality to disenfranchise Khin Nyunt's "empire" and to gain control over its economic assets.

Population groups have been moved arbitrarily around the country for economic reasons. For example, when the regime wanted to clean up the slums of Rangoon in anticipation of a tourist boom in the early 1990s, the army moved whole sections of the city to rural suburbs, dumping people in the middle of rain-filled rice paddies to fend for themselves. Burmans have been moved from the impoverished dry zone to "model villages" in northern Rakhine State, ostensibly for their own economic benefit, but in reality to counterbalance the large Muslim population in that area. Moreover, the movement of Muslims in the northern Rakhine area is severely restricted, making it very difficult for them to engage in commerce. The SPDC has recently assisted the Wa tribal leadership to relocate some 60,000–80,000 poor hill tribes from the northern areas of the Wa State along the China border, where they subsisted on opium production, to the lowlands of the Shan State along the Thai border, where they have taken over the rich farmland of the local Shan, in turn displacing them into Thailand.

Religious Discrimination and Intolerance

The generals give pride of place to Buddhism in Burma, parading themselves prominently in Buddhist temples around the country. As might be expected, they maintain firm control over the Buddhist clergy and strongly discourage any political activity by monks, placing government informants among them and readily jailing monks who step over the line. Christianity is fairly widespread in Burma, thanks to extensive missionary activity during the colonial period. The generals tolerate Christianity but do not trust Christians, who thus rarely rise to prominence in the government or military. In some areas of the country, such as the Karen, Chin, and Kachin states, the military regime perceives Christianity to be related to antigovernment political or insurgent activity and often persecutes activist church figures for this reason. Burma's Muslim population is large and growing, despite the regime's efforts to keep it under control. Outbreaks of violence between Buddhist and Muslim groups in cities are fairly common and appear to be largely spontaneous, that is, not necessarily inspired by the regime. Animosity between Buddhist and Islamic clergy appears to be deep seated. If the authoritarian hand were to be lifted from Burma, religious violence could become a more serious problem in urban areas, where the expanding Muslim population is especially apparent.

Censorship

The SPDC strictly controls all forms of media in Burma. Daily newspapers are produced by the government; television and radio stations are government owned and controlled. The Internet and e-mail can only be accessed through government servers, and only government-approved Internet sites are available to the public. The government allows publication of popular journals provided they are totally devoid of political content; journalists are often jailed for stepping over the line. The political content in newspapers is strictly propagandistic, designed to promote the image of the military. (In fact, it has just the opposite effect with most of the population.) Some foreign publications are available in tourist hotels, at times in censored form. In recent years, however, access to foreign news via satellite TV has become widespread in areas of the country that have electricity and satellite coverage. The government appears to have been unsuccessful in controlling satellite dishes by requiring licenses.

Measuring Repression in Burma

It would take a writer like Lewis Carroll to capture the full absurdity of military governance in Burma. Indeed, it is precisely this "Alice in Wonderland" quality, with all its whimsy, illogic, and internal contradiction, that makes it very difficult to measure repression in Burma by any set of standards. Furthermore, it is virtually impossible to collect reliable statistics. The SPDC, for example, does not even know the size of Burma's population—the most basic of national statistics—because there has been no census for nearly twenty-five years. (The 52 million figure used today is an estimate, derived more or less unscientifically from the last official count.)

Although it can be confidently stated that for decades political prisoners in Burma have numbered in the hundreds, it is not possible to arrive at an exact count by matching it with individual souls. The numbers used by foreign governments and humanitarian organizations—currently ranging from 1,000 to 1,500—are compiled from a variety of largely anecdotal sources, including families of political prisoners, opposition political parties, and insurgent groups. When the International Red Cross began to interview the prison population in Burma in 1999, it soon became apparent that neither the government nor the NLD and other opposition political organizations had a reliable record of political prisoners.[14] In January 2005, the NLD estimated that there were 400 political prisoners, of whom 135 were NLD members, saying that this number was the most that they could account for directly. In any case, whether there are about 500, 1,000, or 1,500 political prisoners, they represent a minuscule portion of the Burmese population in sheer numbers and only 1 to 2 percent of the total population in Burmese prisons and labor camps.

Yet it is precisely the existence of political prisoners—and not the number—that is generally used to illustrate the egregious nature of political repression in Burma because these people have been imprisoned solely for trying to promote democracy and political pluralism in the face of decades of obstinate, autocratic, military rule. The military regime uses imprisonment to decapitate opposition political movements and send a harsh message to others who might emerge. Thus, once the number of political prisoners can be counted in the hundreds, it represents a significant loss to political movements. Arriving at the exact number brings little additional value as a measurement of repression.

Economic repression is similarly impossible to catalogue statistically in Burma, not least because the government either classifies as secret or does not collect statistics on the economy, since the numbers would reflect badly on military management. In the aggregate, it is clear that Burma is one of the poorest nations in the world, certainly in Asia. According to the Australian Department of Foreign Affairs, the International Monetary Fund (IMF) projected Burma's GDP at U.S.$4.7 billion in 2006 (with a negative growth rate) and per capita GDP at U.S.$83 for the same year (with U.S.$1,751 purchasing power parity)—among the world's lowest.[15] An inordinate proportion of the country's resources are diverted to support a bloated military force at the expense of the social services and the civilian economy.[16] Health services and education have been degraded by extreme neglect. Agricultural land, on which the bulk of the population ekes out a subsistence living, is losing its productivity for lack of fertilizer and proper use. Water is in scarce supply in many parts of the country. Investment in public works is determined almost solely by military requirements.

Scarce resources are deployed by the regime to buy military equipment, maintain one of the largest armed forces in Southeast Asia, and ensure that the military itself enjoys a higher quality of life than the general population. Military schools and universities are well equipped, and the military has its own health and hospital system and access to food supplies. The officer corps is allowed to profit liberally from extralegal activities.[17]

The more salient reality, however, is that the SPDC controls the country's economy precisely to ensure that no power centers can develop outside the purview of military structures. It purposely denies economic development to its civilian population to guarantee continued military predominance. The unchecked ability of the military leadership to manipulate the economy to its own purposes leaves the vast majority of the country with little or no economic access, stifling economic growth and preventing the development of a business class of any significance outside that strictly controlled by the government. Those individuals or groups who appear to be developing a separate economic strength are purposely cut down. There is no question that, in the hands of the generals, the economy is an instrument to reinforce political repression.

Finally, it is important to note that repression in Burma is more intense in some parts of the country than in others. Not surprisingly, the military government concentrates its venality on those areas of the country where it has the most control and on the remaining pockets of insurgency. In general, areas of the country controlled by ethnic leaders who have concluded ceasefire agreements with the military government have a considerable degree of economic and even political autonomy. Northeastern Burma, for example, where there are large numbers of ethnic Chinese, receives Chinese satellite television and uses Chinese cell phone services and Internet access. In the Wa, Kokang, Pa'o, and several other autonomous areas, local ethnic militia are in charge, and their populations are largely insulated from the SPDC, although it is likely that the rule of local militias is far from enlightened.

On an international scale, Burma probably ranks in the ninetieth percentile for repression. The World Bank's statistics on governance and anticorruption from 1996 to 2002 rank Burma in the lowest tenth percentile worldwide in five of its six categories: voice and accountability, government effectiveness, rule of law, regulatory quality, and control of corruption.[18] Only in the sixth category, political stability, does Burma rise slightly above 10 percent. The SPDC's score for the voice and accountability category is the lowest of all, descending from 1.6 percent in 1996 to 0 in 2002. (Transparency International's "Corruption Perceptions Index" ranks Burma 160th—tied with Guinea and Iraq—of the 163 countries rated in 2005.)[19] Because the systematic institutionalization of repression in Burma through decades of military rule has deliberately incorporated all of these categories of governance, the SPDC voice and accountability ranking is perhaps the most comprehensive and illustrative statistical measure of repression in Burma on a comparative basis.

Is Burma Also Aggressive?

Despite its severely repressive history, Burma's military government has not had aggressive intentions toward its neighbors in modern times. On the contrary, the military leadership has consistently maintained a policy of strict neutrality and justified the strength of its military forces, as well as its iron grasp on political power, on the basis of internal security and preserving the union. It has taken pains to prevent "external forces" of all kinds from influencing the internal affairs of the country, and it has promoted neighborly relations with the five countries sharing its borders.

This is not to say that Burma's insurgencies have not from time to time complicated its relations with neighbors. During the Ne Win years, when Mao's China was actively supporting the Communist Party of Burma's campaign against the government and infiltrating communist leadership into the insurgencies on the China-Burma border, Burma's relations with China were very frosty, and Ne Win refused to visit China. When Deng Xiaoping withdrew China's support from the insurgencies, creating the conditions for cease-fire agreements between the insurgent militias and the Burmese government, Rangoon's relations with Beijing improved rapidly. Today, China is Burma's largest financial supporter and source of military equipment.

There have been similar strains in Burma's relations with Thailand from time to time as a result of active insurgencies on the Thai-Burma border. Burma's military leadership has been dismayed by what it sees as Thai support and encouragement for the insurgents by allowing them refuge in Thai territory and providing them with material support, as well as Thailand's tolerance of international support for large, long-term refugee settlements on the Thai side of the border. During 2001, as the Thaksin government was coming into office in Bangkok, Thai and Burmese military forces actually came into direct conflict briefly in an area of the border where there is a substantial territorial dispute. Prime Minister Thaksin Shinawatra moved quickly, however, to defuse the tension with a series of diplomatic overtures to Rangoon and some senior reassignments in the Royal Thai Army. There have also been brief, small-scale skirmishes between Burmese and Bangladeshi forces and Burmese and Indian forces on Burma's western borders, but these tensions have been quickly defused diplomatically.

India and China now compete for the attention of Rangoon's military leadership, and the senior generals bask in their popularity with these two elephantine neighbors, trying to reap maximum benefits from the two relationships while simultaneously keeping their influence on Burma to a minimum. Burma's military leaders have long appreciated the danger of becoming a battleground in Sino-Indian competition and undoubtedly see membership in the Association of Southeast Asian Nations (ASEAN) as a valuable counterbalance.

Some observers argue that Burma's neighbors should consider the intractable military leadership in Rangoon as a serious threat to the neighborhood because the country's creeping social, economic, and political deterioration is spilling across borders in the form of refugees, narcotics, disease—particularly HIV/AIDS—and black marketeering. While it may be true that retrograde governance in Burma is a potentially destabilizing factor in the region, it does not actually constitute aggression. Nor is Burma a source of or refuge for terrorist activity aimed at the outside world. On the whole, therefore, Burma cannot be considered to rank high on any aggressive scale.

Conditions and Prospects for Change

As with most countries that have endured decades of heavy-handed dictatorship, Burma's socioeconomic and political structures are at present extremely underdeveloped and potentially unstable. Ultimately, the creation of a stable democracy in Burma will require a total overhaul of government and the development of civil society and the institutions of pluralistic democracy. Abrupt or violent transition would most likely leave the country in turmoil for years to come. It would also lead to the return and continuation of authoritative, inevitably military rule. On the positive side, however, unlike most other repressive rogue states, Burma did at one point enjoy a nascent and growing civic, economic, and political base that could still provide the impetus for building democratic institutions if military rule were to recede in a paced manner. Two areas of development in particular would be required to create fertile ground for democratic institutions to grow and take root in Burma: the first is political; the second, economic.

Political Development

Above all, there must be real political dialogue to frame a new constitution that ensures non-Burman ethnic nationalities enough local autonomy to retain their identities and exercise some control over local political, economic, law enforcement, and educational structures. In reality, none of these groups still aspires to independence or the secession option stipulated in the 1947 constitution. Serious, productive dialogue on constitutional issues can only be achieved if all three parties are present: the major ethnic leaders, the democracy movement leaders, and the SPDC. Major ethnic leaders and the democratic forces within Burma already appear to support a general framework for a reasonable solution because there has been underground dialogue among them for years. The major obstacle is the SPDC's reluctance to engage seriously with the other two parties. Beyond their own inability to cope with political give-and-take, the generals also tend to view cooperation and agreement among ethnic and democracy parties as de facto collusion against the regime. They see in it a potential for instability and disorder, harking back to the experience of earlier decades.

This dilemma is apparent in the way the regime has structured and conducted the reconvened National Convention when it met in 2004 and then resumed in 2005. The regime has invited only chosen ethnic leaders, hoping to dictate terms to them, and has engineered the exclusion of the NLD by stubbornly refusing to release Aung San Suu Kyi from detention or allowing her to participate in the convention. Without her and the NLD in the process, the convention can have no international legitimacy. To make matters worse, in the run-up to the February 18, 2005, resumption of the National Convention, after the purge of Khin Nyunt, the SPDC arrested prominent Shan leaders, including the senior leadership of the Shan NLD. They also extended by one year the house arrest of NLD General Secretary Aung San Suu Kyi and Vice Chairman U Tin Oo. The international community interpreted these moves as SPDC's deliberate defiance of international calls for inclusion of democratically elected groups in the constitutional process.[20]

Indeed, without Aung San Suu Kyi and the NLD, there is probably no hope for a democratic solution in Burma in the foreseeable future. Decades of severe repression, unenlightened military rule, and isolation have kept serious political talent from emerging.[21] While there is an aspiration for freedom and democracy in principle among the people, the great majority of Burmese have no clear understanding of the responsibilities, flexibility, and patience that stable democracy entails. They have received no political education, it being forbidden in Burmese schools and universities. Aung San Suu Kyi, on the other hand, was raised and educated largely outside Burma and has a profound grasp of the challenges of democracy. She has spent her years and decades of internal exile and repression imparting this ethos to her followers in the NLD. With party activity on the streets largely prohibited, activity inside NLD party headquarters has been lively in recent years, incorporating a substantial educational program, with seminars, classes, guest speakers, and political debate. This situation diminished dramatically in 2004–2005, when Aung San Suu Kyi was put under official house arrest, Khin Nyunt was purged, and communication between the NLD and SPDC ended. Nonetheless, despite the regime's deliberate impoverishment of the NLD, Aung San Suu Kyi and NLD officials are still capable of forming the essential nucleus for the regeneration of democratic principles and institutions in the course of a real political transition. Furthermore, only with the participation of the NLD would a process of political transition in Burma have sufficient credibility internationally to muster strong economic and political support.

Economic Development

The second critical area for development is economic. To lay the basis for stable democracy in Burma, serious economic reform must be undertaken with strong assistance and firm guidance from international financial institutions. The World Bank, International Monetary Fund, and Asian Development Bank have compiled extensive studies over the years, with recommendations on how to approach essential reforms. The Japanese government worked with the Burmese government for several years, exploring how to institute some of the restructuring recommended by the World Bank, but the SPDC refused to accept its conclusions. The regime undoubtedly fears the potential destabilization that can come from structural and monetary reform and recognizes that once it embarks on reform, it will begin to lose control of the economy and, consequently, the ability to finance its vast military structures.

Related to economic reform is the problem of weeding out corruption. It is no surprise that Burma under military rule is one of the most corrupt countries in Asia. Although many less autocratic Asian governments also suffer from debilitating corruption, the SPDC in many respects promotes corrupt practices as a norm for economic activity. Senior military officers are allowed to use their official positions to personal economic advantage, and the regime's business cronies are given wide license to profit personally from the exploitation of public properties and resources. Foreign investors are usually required to partner with a military enterprise and employ family members of their military partners; when their joint ventures begin turning a profit, military partners often expropriate the business by fiat, leaving foreign investors high and dry. The military will be loath to relinquish this perquisite. Thus it will take decades of strong pressure from both inside and outside the country to eliminate the most damaging corrupt practices.

As mentioned earlier, the military regime, particularly in recent years, has substituted military officers for civilians in many government positions to ensure that the civilian ministries are responsive to military objectives and that the armed forces can maintain strong control over government structures in the future. It is widely believed among Burma's military leaders that civilians are undisciplined and inadequately alert to the country's security needs. In their minds only people with a proper military background, who adhere to the regime's doctrines on political and security matters, can be trusted in positions of government responsibility. Therefore, as long as the military plays a deciding role in political governance, it will be difficult to improve governance in civilian ministries.

Furthermore, the permeation of civilian ministries with military and ex-military leadership at top and middle levels greatly exacerbates the degree of corruption throughout the civilian ministries. Until serious economic reform manages to release the military's stranglehold on the economy at both the macro- and micro-levels, the culture of corruption promoted by the military leadership will continue to affect the civilian ministries. While this problem is not unique to Burma in the developing world, it greatly complicates the question of how to structure international development assistance to strengthen and empower the institutions of central government essential to sustain development at both national and local levels.

Current Prospects

If the aforementioned elements are key to stable transition in Burma, addressing them is, unfortunately, anathema to the current military regime. There seems to be very little hope of achieving a breakthrough as long as the current leadership, particularly the top general, remains solidly locked in place. The scene is even bleaker with the purge of Khin Nyunt and the ascendancy of an apparently hard-line group as potential heirs to the throne.[22] The hard-liners, led by Senior General Than Shwe, have consistently resisted efforts by the international community to encourage political reconciliation and transition. They refuse to ease internal restrictions and repressive measures and, even more important, to engage with the democracy forces. And they have been unresponsive to recommendations for economic reform, demanding instead that the international financial institutions should give them money and resources to spend as they see fit.

U.S. and International Policy Considerations

Burma resides, for better or worse, in the backwaters of U.S. foreign policy priorities. It is not of strategic security concern, only coming into play on the margins of conflict in the area since World War II, for example, with the Kuomintang in China and the communists in Indochina. In the post-September 11 age of terrorism, the SPDC has kept itself on the right side of U.S. counterterrorist policy, responding positively to Washington's concerns about dealing with militant Islamic groups, despite a general deterioration in overall U.S.-Burmese relations.

Burma has few, if any, resources of strategic interest to the United States. The United States has no commercial interest in Burma. It has been cost free, therefore, for the United States to use economic sanctions as a political tool against the military regime—first in 1997 by outlawing any new U.S. economic investment, and later in 2003 by prohibiting Burmese exports to the United States and the use of U.S. financial services, including the dollar, in Burma.[23] The sanctions have also served to ensure that the United States will have little economic interest in Burma for the duration of military rule.

The United States is concerned about narcotrafficking from Burma, which is the second largest producer of heroin in the world and a major source of amphetamine-type stimulants (for example, methamphetamine) in Southeast Asia. The SPDC has responded to this concern, achieving impressive annual decreases in opium production for the past five or six years, especially in 2003, but failing to stem the growing production of amphetamine-type stimulants, which are flooding into Thailand and China. Political concern about continued military rule in Burma has prevented the United States from substantially assisting the SPDC in its counternarcotics effort.[24] In January 2005, the U.S. Drug Enforcement Agency indicted eight high-ranking leaders of the United Wa State Army (a major cease-fire group) for drug trafficking, presenting the SPDC with a dilemma since at least one of these people was a delegate to the National Convention.

Support for the democratic forces in Burma, exemplified by Aung San Suu Kyi, has been the main thrust of U.S. policy toward Burma since 1988, drawing bipartisan endorsement in Congress and solid agreement between the legislative and executive branches. Congress annually earmarks more than $7 million of U.S. foreign assistance to support Burmese exile groups and other activities aimed at restoring democracy in Burma. In recent years, Congress has also supported $1 million in assistance annually for HIV/AIDS programs in Burma, conducted by international nongovernmental organizations (NGOs).[25]

The United States has played a central role in promoting and supporting international efforts, led by the United Nations, to encourage democracy and human rights improvements in Burma. For more than a decade, the UN secretary general has maintained a special envoy for Burma, most recently retired Malaysian diplomat Tan Sri Razali Ismail, who resigned this position in 2005 out of frustration and has not been replaced. The UN Human Rights Commission has a special rapporteur for Burma, currently Brazilian academic Paulo Sergio Pinhiero, who has not been allowed to visit the country since 2004. Both managed to visit Burma on a regular basis until 2004, submitting reports to the secretary general and the Human Rights Commission, respectively. These reports provided substantial grist for the annual UN General Assembly resolutions on Burma. Although the United States managed to bring the situation in Burma to debate in the Security Council in 2006, the proposed resolution was vetoed by China and Russia in early 2007. The UN has also provided the venue for an informal consultative group on Burma, consisting of representatives from a number of interested governments, which backstops the UN special envoy and attempts to coordinate broad policy issues.[26]

The UN's International Labour Organization (ILO) has taken a very active interest in curbing the widespread use of forced labor in Burma. Working through labor unions internationally, the ILO raised a serious enough threat to Burma's trade relations several years ago to elicit a response from the SPDC. Through a number of special missions to Burma and the presence of a representative in Rangoon, the ILO has succeeded in surveying the country's labor practices rather extensively and, at least before Khin Nyunt's purge, seemed to convince the SPDC to reduce the most blatant forms of forced labor that had been common around population centers. During 2005, after the purge of Khin Nyunt, the SPDC diminished even its limited cooperation with the ILO. Similarly, the International Committee for the Red Cross (ICRC), after a ten-year effort, finally managed to gain access to Burma's prisons in 1999 and, at least for a while, achieved marginal improvements in prison conditions, particularly for political prisoners or so-called security detainees. Although its program operates on strict confidentiality, it is probably fair to say that ICRC's effort contributed to the release of many of the political prisoners who emerged during 2001–2002 and again after the attack on the NLD in May 2003.[27] In early 2006, the SPDC levied new restrictions on international NGOs, including the ICRC, requiring that they be accompanied in their activities by representatives from the Union Solidarity Development Association, and the ICRC decided that it could no longer visit prisons without jeopardizing the prisoners they were interviewing.

UN assistance agencies and a small number of international NGOs conduct modest assistance programs focused largely on humanitarian needs. The SPDC places both constraints and demands on these programs that greatly complicate the ability of the international agencies to deliver effective assistance and achieve sustainability. The most extreme example is the UN High Commissioner for Refugees (UNHCR) resettlement program in northern Rakhine State, where UNHCR has spent more than fifteen years repatriating and stabilizing communities of Rohingya returnees who fled to Bangladesh in 1991. Despite this long investment, however, it is clear that the Rohingya population in this area would come under threat from the army if the UNHCR were to depart. Even without government interference, conditions in Burma—particularly the remote areas controlled by ethnic groups—make assistance programs challenging and costly.

The major international financial institutions are not present in Burma and are prohibited by their largest donors, chiefly the United States, from providing any assistance beyond minor technical support. Burma does benefit from some ASEAN programs funded by the Asian Development Bank. The World Bank and IMF regularly conduct surveys of economic conditions in Burma and recommend structural and monetary reforms, which in turn are rejected by the SPDC so as not to risk the destabilizing effects of reform without substantial financial assistance from the international community. In 2000, probably in response to the embarrassing economic conclusions reached by the World Bank and IMF, the SPDC ceased publishing most essential economic statistics, making it more difficult since then to obtain a full picture of the country's economic performance.

Because the post–cold war environment, unconstrained by superpower competition, places a greater premium on human rights and governance, international scrutiny of the situation in Burma has been much more intense than previously. The international response to the military's harsh attack on public protesters in 1988 undoubtedly took Burma's military leaders by surprise and contributed to decisions taken at the time to return to parliamentary government. However, as the generals struggled with the dilemma of how to do so without relinquishing their own ability to exercise control and maintain stability and security, they came to resent deeply the intrusion of the international community into Burma's internal affairs and developed elaborate evasion tactics to keep their critics at bay. The first of these was the elections of 1990, in which they badly miscalculated and subsequently had to regroup. The second was the National Convention of 1992–1996, in which they believed they could achieve roughly the Golkar arrangement that appeared to have been acceptable in Indonesia. At about this time, they managed to join ASEAN to acquire a regional buffer against pressure from the UN, United States, EU, Japan, and others. With ASEAN's support during this period, the SPDC refused to allow the rapporteur from the UN Human Rights Commission to visit the country and largely succeeded in foiling Alvaro De Soto, the UN secretary general's special envoy.

The post–cold war world, however, also brought political evolution within ASEAN, notably the rise of civilian democracy in Thailand and Indonesia, making Burma's ASEAN security blanket much less comfortable. New governments in several ASEAN countries became frustrated with the recalcitrant, hermetic generals in Rangoon and began more actively to support UN efforts to encourage transition, particularly with the appointment of Razali as special envoy. As the twentieth century was drawing to an end, the generals began to engage with UN bodies on questions of human rights and forced labor, appearing to soften some of the rough edges on their unrelenting scorn for international standards of domestic behavior. This softening, combined with their willingness in 2000 to talk directly with Aung San Suu Kyi as part of the "confidence-building" process, brought a period of relative relaxation in external pressure.

When the SPDC finally gave Aung San Suu Kyi freedom to travel around the country in 2002 and then failed to honor its stated intention to enter into serious dialogue with the NLD on transition, both internal and external pressure began to build again. In the eyes of the generals, Aung San Suu Kyi was risking internal instability because of the size of the crowds that she was drawing during her travels. It was time to bring things back under control, regardless of the international repercussions. When they jailed her in May 2003, they appeared once again to have been somewhat taken aback by the strength of the international reaction, particularly from ASEAN and China. To mollify their neighbors, they returned to their original plan to engineer a new constitution in preparation for a managed transition. Khin Nyunt was promoted to prime minister and put in charge of the so-called seven-step process. His new status also put him in a better position to deal directly with

ASEAN prime ministers in attempting to obtain their backing for the junta's plan. On the surface at least, this ploy appeared to achieve its objective of keeping the ASEAN buffer intact.

The purge of Khin Nyunt in late 2004, however, presented a serious setback to the promised seven-step program when the remaining leadership made it clear that they had no intention of including democratic forces in the constitutional process, significantly tightening the terms of Aung San Suu Kyi's house arrest and rounding up new crops of political detainees.[28] The loss of Khin Nyunt also had broader repercussions for Burma's diplomatic relations in the Asian region and beyond because he and his faction had been the architects of the country's foreign policy after 1990 and carried the burden of responsibility for managing the country's relations with the outside world. The loss of the ministers, ambassadors, and senior government and military officials, who were imprisoned or forced to resign with Khin Nyunt, left the international community with no effective means of engaging the SPDC. It also left the SPDC woefully unprepared to deal with the opprobrium of ASEAN and the UN in response to the backtracking on political reform. Popular pressure on ASEAN governments brought pressure, in turn, on Rangoon to step back from assuming the ASEAN presidency in 2006. In July 2005, the SPDC agreed to this request, motivated undoubtedly by a combination of diplomatic weakness, uncertainty about its ability to host and ensure security for an ASEAN summit, and increasingly undisguised insouciance about the concerns of the outside world.

The SPDC's resurgent xenophobia also brought increasing restrictions on the activity of UN agencies and international NGOs in Burma, which reached a breaking point in August 2005 when the Global Fund to Fight HIV/AIDS, Tuberculosis and Malaria decided to withdraw from Burma and renounce its five-year, $100 million assistance commitment. Those seeking dialogue with the SPDC leadership found little opening left. At the July 2005 ASEAN foreign ministers meeting in Laos, Foreign Minister Nyan Win even refused to meet with UN Special Envoy Razali. During 2006, prodded by ASEAN parliamentarians, several ASEAN governments, especially Malaysia, Philippines, Indonesia, and Singapore, began openly to voice frustration with the SPDC's refusal to honor its commitment to the seven-step plan, reaching a crescendo at the Asian Regional Forum in Kuala Lumpur in July 2006.

At the same time, the SPDC's relations with China, India, and Russia gathered new momentum as China and India vied for rights to develop promising natural gas reserves off the coast of Burma's Arakan State and Russia sought further commercial military deals, probably in anticipation of the large profits the SPDC would reap from its energy sales. The SPDC's reenergized diplomacy with China, India, and Russia was undoubtedly designed also to offset the loss of its ASEAN buffer with the international community and to ensure protection against negative repercussions in the UN Security Council.

Conclusion

As recent political regression in Rangoon amply demonstrates, many years of international efforts at persuasion via both engagement and disengagement have had precious little impact on Burma's stubborn military leadership. If anything, in 2006 the generals seemed to be more determinedly dug in than they were before. Although it is difficult to predict *when*, it is nonetheless certain that change *will* come to Burma one day, probably not so much as a result of international pressure but because of internal tensions, particularly within the military. The massive purge of 2004 opened a serious breach in the solidarity of the top military leadership, which had been so carefully guarded during the post–Ne Win years, and may mark the beginning of the end for the SPDC.

The consequences of the ill-considered purge began to rock the regime in 2005. In mid-May three unusually sophisticated bombs wracked several civilian population centers in downtown Rangoon, sending the military leadership into a frenzied attack on all its perceived enemies—except perhaps those responsible for the bombs. Although several alleged Karen National Union activists were arrested in July and charged with responsibility for the bombings, they were soon released for lack of evidence. Many Burmese observers suspect that the real culprits may be inside the military itself. In any case, the bombs were seen as proof of the regime's new vulnerability in the absence of an effective military intelligence force and indisputable evidence of strife in the upper reaches of the SPDC. Than Shwe's decision to force large sectors of the military and key ministries to move in toto to a new town halfway between Rangoon and Mandalay by the end of 2005 only fed popular perceptions of the regime's paranoia and potential instability.

Indeed, an internal purge of this depth and breadth inevitably sparks unintended and unpredictable consequences for those who engineer the housecleaning. A body of over 30,000 dishonorably discharged or demoted military forces represents a powerful source of grievance against the SPDC, adding new fuel to the widespread despair and disdain for the generals among the population as a whole. While doubtless bringing a certain amount of satisfaction to the long-suffering Burmese people, the spectacle of hundreds of military officers being jailed, subjected to secret trials, and summarily sentenced does not reflect well on the integrity of the military leadership as a whole. (If there are so many rotten apples in the basket, are not the rest of the apples also infected by the same rot?) Furthermore, it suggests serious strife and instability inside the opaque cocoon in which the generals have enveloped themselves for so long. In light of these growing signs of insecurity within both the regime and the Rangoon environment, it is not hard to imagine that the precipitous decision to move the capital to a location near Pyinmana in late 2005 was driven as much by security concerns as by anything else. This theory is strongly reinforced by the bunker-like appearance of the new city, called Naypyitaw, that had emerged there by 2007.

Despite the past failure of international engagement or pressure to set Burma's military regime on a course toward political transition, with the SPDC leadership appearing increasingly fragile and the likelihood of a change in leadership in the relatively near future, it is especially important for the international community to remain actively engaged in promoting change. This should be a deliberate collective effort in which different governments play different roles. The general strategy should be two-pronged: to maximize pressure on the SPDC to fulfill its promise of political transition, and to seek opportunities to build and strengthen institutions and groups outside the military to meet the task of civilian governance one day.

Having made political transition the sine qua non for Burma's assuming the presidency in the future, ASEAN must maintain strong pressure on the SPDC to meet its commitments. Other Asian powers and the EU, United States, and UN must support and encourage ASEAN's efforts and remain consistent on the issue of transition. The UN, for example, will be a critical arbiter of the eventual results of the National Convention, particularly as they may affect ASEAN's judgment of when Burma should be allowed to assume the group's presidency. There can be no question among the major international players that the current situation in Burma is unacceptable. At a minimum, the country's deterioration under military rule has reached a dangerous level and will be increasingly problematic for the region if it is not reversed as soon as possible.

Despite growing SPDC efforts to restrict the work of UN and other international agencies in Burma, the international community should continue efforts on all fronts to build and develop the country's civilian institutions, whether by promoting observance of human rights, working to eliminate the practice of forced labor, improving the health and education systems, addressing basic human needs, educating competent civilian cadres who can eventually be placed in government, building modern communications, or encouraging private sector economic development. Many of these activities have been under way for years on a limited scale without, in effect, improving the efficacy of military government. At the same time, it should be made clear that donors who engage in large-scale enterprises with the government's military business structures are knowingly contributing to the corruption and enrichment of the generals themselves. Chinese and Russian arms sales and infrastructure projects fit into this category. The proposed Chinese and Indian gas deals run the same risk unless properly structured.

The United Nations must play an even more active role in organizing and orchestrating pressure on the SPDC to observe international norms of governance and to bring popularly elected political elements into the constitutional process. The UN secretary general must continue to set benchmarks for performance, as he has in recent statements, and to insist strongly that his representatives and UN agencies should have adequate access to the country to meet their responsibilities.

At this juncture, however, the most critical roles are those of Burma's Asian neighbors, specifically India, China, Japan, Malaysia, Thailand, and other key ASEAN members. Their past strategies of engagement have proved just as fruitless with the SPDC as U.S. and EU pressure and sanctions. They have all been fooled by the generals in one way or another. It is high time for them to begin setting some minimum performance standards for Burma. China, India, and Japan, for example, as major Asian economic powers, should make their economic dealings with the SPDC contingent on basic economic reforms. They should use the access that they claim to have achieved through "engagement" policies to press the SPDC for both political and economic reforms. In addition to pressuring the SPDC to release Aung San Suu Kyi and other NLD prisoners and to follow through with the promised political transition, ASEAN should use its programs and structures to help build nonmilitary economic, political, and nongovernmental capacity in Burma.

The international community should recognize that Burma has the best chance of making a stable political transition from military rule if it can be achieved while Aung San Suu Kyi and the elderly NLD leadership are still in place. Not only do they have the best grounding in democratic tradition of any other group in the country, but they provide the leadership and sense of continuity that will be necessary to bring along the ethnic groups and the wider population. This reality was amply demonstrated during the year 2002–2003, when Aung San Suu Kyi was free to travel around the country.

She gained the respect of ethnic leaders and drew huge crowds of common people everywhere she went—people who were not so much concerned with the politics of the NLD as they were with finding a charismatic leader who could begin to turn the country around. Burma has no other political leader with wide appeal and is not likely to have one in the foreseeable future. As Nelson Mandela demonstrated in South Africa, a charismatic, intelligent personality can be a priceless beacon during periods of difficult change.

At the same time, the international community should also be prepared to accept a solution in Burma that includes an active, perhaps even temporarily dominant role for the military. While the current leadership's concerns about internal stability are overdrawn, they are not totally misplaced. Political transition will have to be managed with a firm hand if Burma is not to slide into another form of misrule or perhaps the anarchy of corruption. With more enlightened military leadership (that is, not the current leaders but those who will eventually replace them), it would be entirely possible for fundamental agreement to be reached between the SPDC, Aung San Suu Kyi's NLD, and both elected and self-appointed ethnic leaders on how to proceed with transition. Having led the international community in applying pressure on the SPDC, the United States, in particular, must be prepared to accept a Burmese solution that is less than a return to 1990 and to relax its restrictions on economic assistance as soon as such a process is under way.

Finally, the World Bank and IMF should continue to press the SPDC on fundamental economic reforms, perhaps in tandem with Burma's large Asian neighbors. (At the appropriate time, the United States should relax its restrictions on the activities of the World Bank and IMF in Burma and allow some critical support for economic reform.) Even in the most optimistic scenario, it will take years to sort out the structural problems caused by decades of misguided socialism and centralized economic control in the hands of the military. The sooner this process begins, the more it will encourage and support political transition.[29]

Notes

1. Quote from Secretary of State Condoleezza Rice in her confirmation hearings before the Senate Foreign Relations Committee (January 18, 2005), www.senate.gov/~foreign/testimony/2005/RiceTestimony050118.pdf.

2. David Steinberg makes a salient comparison between the nature of military rule in Thailand and South Korea, on the one hand, and that in Burma, on the other, which allowed these two countries to make the transition to pluralistic, civilian gov-

ernment while Burma went in the other direction. See David Steinberg, *Burma: The State of Myanmar* (Washington, D.C., 2001), 32–37.

3. Aung San was the freedom fighter who gained Burma's independence from Britain after World War II.

4. The Shan and Karenni states were granted the right of secession after ten years, and the question was left open for the Mon, Karen, and Arakan states.

5. By 1962 Ne Win had succeeded in building the army into the most effective branch of government. See, for example, Mary Callahan, "On Time Warps and Warped Time," in Robert Rotberg (ed.), *Burma: Prospects for a Democratic Future* (Washington, D.C., 1998), 57.

6. Burmese do not have a first and last name, but rather a single compound name. Perhaps as a sign that he expected his children to continue his mission, Aung San—contrary to Burmese practice—gave all his offspring his name in addition to their own name. This chapter will use Aung San Suu Kyi's full Burmese name throughout.

7. Larry Jagan, "Deposed PM's Allies Face Sentencing," *South China Morning Post* (February 21, 2005).

8. Andrew Selth provides convincing evidence that internal divisions have preoccupied Burma's military leaders for decades, resulting in frequent purges and command shifts, with the most contentious issues being the distribution of wealth within the military, the question of whether the army should remain in political power, and the degree of dependence on China. Andrew Selth, "The Armed Forces and Military Rule in Burma," in Rotberg (ed.), *Burma,* 87–103.

9. The State Department produces annual reports detailing repression in Burma. See U.S. Department of State, "U.S. Support for Democracy in Burma Reports" (December 2006), usinfo.state.gov/eap/east_asia_pacific/burma/burma_reports.html.

10. International Institute for Strategic Studies, *The Military Balance* (London), for the years 1988–2004. These figures include both regular military and paramilitary forces.

11. In February 2005, several local officials were sentenced to sixteen months in jail for using forced labor on road and public works projects, but this is as yet the only such example. Officials are usually pardoned or not formally charged with using forced labor.

12. See Emma Larkin, *Secret Histories: Finding George Orwell in a Burmese Teashop* (London, 2004), 56–58. This book contains excellent firsthand observations of various forms of military repression in Burma and provides the historical context for these practices.

13. See U.S. Department of State, "Conditions in Burma and U.S. Policy toward Burma for the Period September 28, 2003–March 27, 2004" (April 13, 2004), www.state.gov/p/eap/rls/rpt/31335.htm. In his August 2005 report to the UN General Assembly, UN Special Rapporteur for Human Rights Paulo Pinheiro claimed there were some 1,100 political prisoners. United Nations General Assembly, "Situation of Human Rights in Myanmar," A/60/221 (August 12, 2005), 3.

14. During their 2001 confidence-building period, the NLD and Home Ministry tried to arrive at a common notion of how many NLD members were in prison, but they discovered that many names had been incorrectly recorded and that there had been considerable double counting.

15. Government of Australia, Department of Foreign Affairs and Trade, "Burma Country Fact Sheet" (Canberra, 2005).

16. Although reliable figures are not available, Selth estimates that the SPDC devotes 35–40 percent of the government budget to defense. In addition, the military finances most of its support costs from its own business and farming enterprises. See Selth, "Armed Forces and Military Rule in Burma," 89. Steinberg estimates that military spending accounts for 50 percent of the national budget, in addition to its extensive business enterprises, returns on joint ventures, and the like. Steinberg, *Burma: The State of Myanmar*, 78.

17. For a full description of the extensive privileges the military reserves for itself, see Steinberg, *Burma: The State of Myanmar*, 73–77.

18. Daniel Kaufmann, Aart Kraay, and Massimo Mastruzzi, "Governance Matters III: Governance Indicators for 1996–2002," World Bank (Washington, D.C., May 2003).

19. Transparency International, "Corruption Perceptions Index 2006" (Berlin, October 2006), www.transparency.org/policy_research/surveys_indices/cpi/2006.

20. On February 15 and 17, 2005, the United States, European Union, and United Nations issued statements of concern that the NLD had been excluded from the National Convention and that Shan leaders had been arrested just before the convention resumed. They questioned the legitimacy of the constitutional process without the participation of elected officials from the opposition.

21. Some Burmese argue that the SPDC has allowed a vestigial NLD to survive to promote the impression that it is the only opposition and thus keep diverse centers of opposition from emerging.

22. Prime Minister General Khin Nyunt and his faction presented a more amenable face to the international community, agreeing to engage in discussion of economic and political change and pursue dialogue internally with the NLD.

23. See U.S. Department of State, "Report on U.S. Trade Sanctions against Burma" (April 28, 2004), www.state.gov/p/eap/rls/rpt/32106.htm.

24. See U.S. Department of State, "2003 International Narcotics Control Strategy Report" (March 1, 2004), www.state.gov/p/inl/rls/nrcrpt/2003.

25. U.S. Department of State, "Conditions in Burma."

26. Included among members of the group are the United States, EU governments, Japan, Korea, Australia, Canada, Thailand, Malaysia, India, and, from time to time, other ASEAN governments.

27. Furthermore, the former head of the ICRC delegation in Rangoon, who negotiated the 1999 agreement with the SPDC, served as an adviser to UN Special Envoy Razali, as well as to the ILO and other international organizations.

28. The amnesty for thousands of prisoners in late 2004 and early 2005 included only a small number of political prisoners. Observers in Rangoon believe there were roughly 10,000 prisoners released, with fewer than 100 being political prisoners.

29. For a representative checklist of measures that all parties, including the international community, can take to support stable transition in Burma once it is under way, see International Crisis Group, "Myanmar: Sanctions, Engagement or Another Way Forward?" (April 26, 2004).

seven

Winning the African Prize for Repression: Zimbabwe

Robert I. Rotberg

Zimbabwe, Togo, and Equatorial Guinea are the leading repressive states in sub-Saharan Africa. Some of their neighbors may be poorly managed, corrupt, and barely democratic, but only those three bear comparison with the extreme kinds of nation-states that are the subjects of this book. None in sub-Saharan Africa is so odious. None treats its citizens and taxpayers so harshly. None governs with such massive deficiencies. In recent times, Zaire and Kenya might have qualified, or Malawi, the Central African Empire, and Uganda under an earlier set of potentates. Togo recently starred as Africa's longest autocracy; Equatorial Guinea represents a classic case of family despotism. Except for Equatorial Guinea's petroleum deposits, both of the last countries are small, poor, strategically irrelevant nation-states. Zimbabwe, on the other hand, is large. It is a key African state, traditionally prosperous and, until 1998, reasonably well run.

Repression Defined

A repressive state preys on its own citizens. It denies human rights and civil liberties, eschews or makes mockery of democracy, is fundamentally patrimonial, uses the mailed fist to compel obedience and achieve compliance with the demands of its ruler or ruling junta, follows the laws of the jungle, assassinates opponents and takes political prisoners, often is capricious and unpredictable in its policies and actions, totally commands the state's economy, almost always is seriously corrupt, inhibits individual prosperity, need not be more than superficially ideological, and operates outside the norms of world order.

At the center of a repressive state is its architect, the man (in all cases) around which the functions and purposes of the state revolve. (The Burmese junta was, until recently, an example of carefully calibrated power balancing, mostly between its two dominant personalities.) Each of the African cases discussed in this book features a would-be monarch or a real monarch—a supreme ruler who has forcefully gathered more and more power into his own hands, terrified or eliminated potential rivals, brooks no dissent, employs a secret police of enforcers (the Central Intelligence Organization [CIO] in Zimbabwe), sequesters state resources and funds, and controls every level of decisionmaking.

Some of the repressive states discussed in this volume are, like Zimbabwe, nominal democracies, that is, they abide by the forms of democracy. They hold elections and pass or rubber-stamp legislation in parliaments. Opposition parties can voice their opinions in parliament, albeit with difficulty. There are courts and judges. The president can claim to have been chosen by the people at the ballot box, even at repeated intervals. If these kinds of authoritarian nation-states thus mimic the norms and employ the nomenclature of democracy, should they be rated less repressive than the states that dispense with such façades? Clearly it is hard to function as a thoroughly totalitarian entity if a regime claims all the while to follow democratic practices. Does the democratic pretension make a difference, and does it separate the truly irredeemable repressors from the redeemable ones?

Zimbabwe's Meltdown

Zimbabwe and its president, Robert Gabriel Mugabe (in power since 1980), raise these and other taxonomic questions.[1] As examples of repression, they satisfy all of the criteria set out above, as do most of the nation-states featured in this book and nearly all of the principal rulers discussed. Zimbabwe indeed is Africa's Burma—a once proud and successful nation brought to its knees by the actions of a venal leader and his leadership cadre. Before 1998, Zimbabwe boasted the best balanced economy in all of Africa; the best educated population per capita; decent relations between 4,000 white settler farmers and the emerging indigenous middle class, their rulers, and even legions of underpaid farm workers; and an independent judiciary. Although the governmental system was fundamentally hostile to participation, transparency, and accountability, it observed democratic prerogatives and was not notably repressive.

In 1998, Zimbabwe counted more university-trained Africans per capita than any other country on the African continent. With commercial crops of tobacco, sugar, and maize, its agricultural sector contributed substantially to the prosperity of the nation. Gold, ferrochrome, nickel, iron, and coal also boosted Zimbabwe's wealth. Tourism produced significant sums, based on visits to the magnificent Victoria Falls, the ruins of Great Zimbabwe, and several outstanding national parks filled with the fauna and avifauna of Africa. Mugabe was an acknowledged authoritarian ruler, but the courts remained independent, and their judgments were respected. Television and radio were state controlled, but there were a number of freethinking weeklies, and dissent was more ignored than stifled. Opponents, either within or outside the ruling Zimbabwe African National Union–Patriotic Front (ZANU-PF), were harassed and intimidated, often physically. But voices of criticism were heard within the national parliament, and such repressive tendencies as doubtless existed were muted.

Unexpectedly, after fifteen to eighteen years of reasonably effective governance, Zimbabwe from the late 1990s descended headlong into tyranny. Every vital sign turned downward. Mugabe, threatened by growing opposition and increasingly contemptuous of differing viewpoints, became ever more imperious and despotic. He and his state started systematically preying on his and its subjects. The result, as the following analysis indicates, was the transformation of Zimbabwe over a remarkably few years into Africa's most malevolent state. The state and the ruler's instruments of repression became finely honed. By 2007, the nation's once high levels of good governance had fallen to the floor. Educational and health services were in shambles, rule of law had largely vanished, crime rates had escalated, corruption was rife, economic growth was strikingly negative, inflation was at Weimar levels, unemployment rates were among the very highest in the world, food shortages and hunger were constant, infant and maternal mortality rates were extraordinarily high and life expectancy correspondingly low, political freedoms were universally denied, and even the ruling political party had come to chafe under the exactions and Duvalier-like capriciousness of the nation's Pol Pot–like ruler.

Worst of all, as this chapter went to press in April 2007, no uprising of the downtrodden masses, no purple or rose revolutions, and no alliances between opposition politicians and soldiers and police appeared likely. Powerful neighbors were not going to intervene, as Tanzania had done so successfully in Idi Amin's Uganda and as Rwanda and others had done with equal force in Mobutu Sese Seko's Zaire. External sanctions seemed ineffective, as they had been against white Rhodesia in the 1960s and 1970s, and Mugabe, aged eighty-three, appeared as strong and alert as ever. Since the state was in shambles, even Mugabe's natural death would not (as in post-Niyazov Turkmenistan) necessarily result in more than cosmetic improvements. In 2007, the forces of repression and despotism ran roughshod over civility, tolerance, and human rights. The regime attacked opponents ferociously throughout March and April, killing a dozen or so and maiming more than 500. For the first time, however, such brutal assaults drew condemnation from African leaders as well as from heads of state and government outside of Africa. How the tragedy developed, and how it was created, were easier questions to answer than predicting how and when Mugabe's reign would end and Zimbabwe would recover.

Corruption and the Invasion of the Congo

Mugabe and the associates who helped him to pillage the state became noticeably more high-handed, arrogant, and corrupt in the mid-1990s. Contracts for major new construction projects were routinely awarded to unqualified bidders, most of whom were part of or connected to Mugabe's family. Mugabe was aging, of course, and had a new second family.[2] Both considerations, or simply the natural progression from authoritarian to all-powerful and not-to-be challenged ruler, encouraged escalating levels of corruption. Then Laurent Kabila's Congo imploded when Rwandan troops invaded. Mugabe, without parliamentary, cabinet, or central committee approval and with no fiscal authority (the minister of finance was informed after the event), gleefully dispatched 11,000 Zimbabwean soldiers to defend Kabila or, more accurately, to pretend to defend Kabila while appropriating for Mugabe and his cooperating generals wealth from diamond mines, cobalt and cadmium tailings, and almost any portable mineral resources in and around the Mbuyi-Maji area of southern Congo.

Although Mugabe and his associates enriched themselves from the resulting loot, the hapless Zimbabwean taxpayer paid the costs—roughly $5 million a week—of sending soldiers to the Congo and fueling their equipment. At the same time, at home, Mugabe had been compelled by a series of strategic demonstrations to promise expensive pensions to 39,000 supposed veterans of the 1971–1979 guerrilla war against Rhodesia. Those two extravagances, plus Mugabe's outright attack on his country's most productive export sectors, effectively bankrupted Zimbabwe. By mid-1999, Zimbabwe had consumed its foreign exchange reserves and was living month to month and petroleum shipment to petroleum shipment. Urban consumers began to notice shortages first of gasoline and diesel, and then of basic staples—even bread. To keep his national economy at home marginally operative, Mugabe and his associates had to cut special deals for petroleum with shady patrons. The government also changed domestic banking rules, forced insurance companies to purchase bonds paying negative interest, maintained a fixed exchange rate that favored officials and Mugabe's cronies (they gained preferential access), manipulated the proceeds of tobacco auctions and mineral sales, and stashed their own cash skimmings in the British Virgin Islands and the Isle of Man. But the downward economic spiral continued, affecting the poorest of the poor most of all.

Corruption is fundamental to the transformation of Zimbabwe (and other such repressive states) from a weak democracy into a flamboyant tyranny. Whether naked greed moved Mugabe to become unalterably repressive is debatable. Nevertheless, patrimonial states are impossible to sustain without impressive flows of cash into ruling pockets. Mugabe's bankrupting of Zimbabwe in the late 1990s and his assault on the Democratic Republic of Congo in 1998–2002 were motivated in large part by the drive to self-aggrandize and keep apparatchiks loyal. No edifice of power can easily be sustained without regularly renewed coffers of enrichment. Transparency International's 2006 Corruption Perceptions Index rated Zimbabwe 130 of 163 countries (tied at 130 with Azerbaijan, Burundi, Central African Republic, Ethiopia, Indonesia, Papua New Guinea, and Togo).[3]

Discontent and Protest

By 1998, urban Zimbabweans were demonstrably discontented. Whereas they and their rural compatriots (Sindebele speakers excepted) had always supported and believed in Mugabe as "the father of the nation," and with a friendly smile tolerated his anachronistic retro-Marxism and constant use of "comrade," that complaisance ended sometime early in that year. Their economic pain, their awareness of new heights of corruption, and the arrogance of the Congo caprice caused disaffection, even the rise of an aroused opposition. It emerged out of the strong and well-disciplined trade union movement.

Army helicopters sprayed tear gas on rioting trade unionists several times in 1998 and 1999 after they had taken to the streets of Harare and Bulawayo, protesting against the collapse of the Zimbabwean dollar, wildly escalating food prices, and Mugabe's newly lavish lifestyle. He and his second wife had constructed a number of mansions locally, and the ZANU-PF mayor of Harare had outraged workers by building a great $1.5 million mansion for himself during a period when luxury houses cost $130,000 and the municipality of Harare could not find $685,000 to pay for a water pump; consequently, the people of the country's capital went without water in their homes.

Given growing national concern regarding Mugabe's methods of governance—even among the upper ranks of the ZANU-PF—a national constitutional conference convened in 1999. Stage-managed mostly by Mugabe and his henchmen, it gave him the power to take white-owned farms without compensation, thus overruling legal restrictions. It also recommended a few other alterations to the existing constitutional provisions and extended his ability to continue to contest the presidency without limits of term or time.

The proposed new constitution had to be put to a national referendum. Mugabe's mistake was to demand approval of the new amendments—thus giving the electorate a real choice for the first time. The embryonic opposition, led by Morgan Tsvangirai of the trade union movement and what had now become the Movement for Democratic Change (MDC), coalesced around a national "no" vote in the referendum of February 2000. Fifty-five percent of those who cast ballots voted "no." Mugabe had never before lost an electoral contest, which infuriated him and emboldened the MDC and its adherents.

The MDC was a truly multiracial, multiethnic party, drawing support from urban Shona and Ndebele speakers, professionals and workers, the Ndebele and eastern Shona rural areas (but not from Mugabe's central Zimbabwe Shona-speaking heartland), and from whites of all backgrounds, especially farmers. The MDC channeled and encouraged a sense of outrage and a national search for change.

Racism and the Land Issue

In the past, Mugabe had always played the racial card when challenged. Doing so was easy, for Rhodesia had been uncompromisingly racist; whites had always exploited blacks. Beginning in the 1890s, powerful whites had heartlessly pushed Africans off the nascent nation's best lands. This process of expropriation continued through the 1920s and was confirmed, even sanctified, by a 1930 commission chaired by Sir Morris Carter. It relegated Africans to the less well watered, stonier, and less loamy soils of the colony. After independence in 1980, that gross disparity was meant to be rectified by official purchases of white-owned farms and the resettlement of truly landless African peasants. Some of that shift in ownership occurred gradually, but much of the transferred farmland—especially the choicest segments—somehow found its way into the arms of Mugabe's close associates. The recovered estates were used as patronage spoils—and still are. Moreover, in those few cases of genuine distribution to the land-poor, no state resources were provided to maintain irrigation facilities and other equipment. Compounding the problem, the government's agricultural extension services collapsed for want of funding, and the few new farmers had nowhere to turn for help. The 8.3 million acres that had been purchased during the 1980s were "grossly underutilized," declared the government's own auditor general in 1997.[4]

Mugabe failed to resettle the landless in the 1980s when he had access to British funds. Moreover, to boost Zimbabwe's prosperity during his first decade in office, Mugabe's regime approved the sale of several thousand farms from one white farmer to another. New buyers received specific approval for their purchases from the government. Very few of the farms subsequently confiscated in 2000–2004 had themselves been taken from Africans by original families or, indeed, by families that had entered the country before the 1950s.

Mugabe believed in 1998, 1999, and 2000 that he could undercut the MDC and its white supporters by declaring a pogrom on whites and white-owned farms. At the beginning of 1998, he began confiscating 12 million acres from 1,500 white farmers, and the country's currency promptly plummeted. Mugabe sent "war veterans" onto the targeted farms to take them back, theoretically in order to transfer the white-owned lands to landless peasants. Ninety-nine percent of the land, however, was given to cabinet ministers, wives, political cronies, relatives, and girlfriends of the Mugabe machine.[5] Even when the nation's courts ruled that such actions were illegal, the attacks on white-owned farms continued. Mugabe unleashed a crusade designed to buttress his own control and maintain ZANU-PF hegemony but instead destroyed what was left of his country's once prosperous economy—one of the best breadbaskets of Africa.

Stolen Elections

A parliamentary election had been scheduled for June 2000. None had ever been seriously contested since 1980 and certainly not since ZANU had forcibly merged with the Zimbabwe African People's Union in 1988 to form the Patriotic Front. The campaign between Mugabe's ZANU-PF and the

MDC was vicious, with the police and ZANU-PF thugs breaking up MDC meetings, invading its offices, and especially intimidating rural chiefs and rural voters. Ultimately, by rigging the returns in several key constituencies, the ZANU-PF won 62 of the contested seats; the MDC, 57; and the Zimbabwe African National Union, 1 (out of 120 elected seats; another 30 were appointed by Mugabe). The MDC won all of the country's urban seats and a majority of all votes cast.

The election itself was a shambles, with doctored voter rolls and Mugabe-designed constituency boundaries finalized a mere three weeks before the election and released to the opposition only by court order. The UN, which led an election-monitoring effort, learned that 10–25 percent of registered voters were in fact deceased (also true for the 2005 election); its monitors threw up their hands in despair two weeks before the polling date. Other outside monitors were similarly discomfited, leaving Mugabe's party hacks to oversee a campaign in which MDC candidates were beaten up and had their houses firebombed. A week before the election, the head of the Zimbabwe Human Rights Forum reported "a complete subversion of the democratic electoral process."[6] European and other foreign observer teams, and even one group representing Africa, denounced the election as not free and not fair. Later the MDC took the ZANU-PF and electoral officials to court in thirty-eight of the sixty-two constituencies won by the ZANU-PF, alleging fraud; of the twelve cases adjudicated in the high court before 2005, the MDC won seven and lost five. The latter were appealed, but only two were heard. Both were won by the MDC. Allegations regarding the other twenty-six constituencies were not heard by the court system before the 2005 election, when the parliament was dissolved and all of the cases stemming from 2000 became moot.[7]

In 2002, after a stepped-up campaign to oust white farmers—during a period when Zimbabwe experienced great shortages and the economy worsened—the country again went to the polls. This time there was a straight contest for president between Mugabe and Tsvangirai. Official intimidation was rife. Hoodlums regularly attacked MDC campaigners; in some areas, MDC campaigners had to go underground for fear of being killed. Tsvangirai himself was often ambushed on rural roads. The official result showed a Mugabe victory by 56 percent of the 3 million votes cast, but few independent local or foreign observers credited the results. The United States refused to recognize the outcome, terming it "flawed." Secretary of State Colin L. Powell said at the time that "Mr. Mugabe can claim victory, but not democratic legitimacy."[8] Even a mission from the Organization of African Unity, now the

African Union, deprecated the results.[9] The count had been falsified, especially in a number of constituencies that had cast many fewer ballots in 2000. One estimate suggested that purposeful congestion at urban polling stations (where Tsvangirai and the MDC were strong), and the reduction of the number of stations days before the poll, denied about 400,000 people the right to participate. It is also estimated that 800,000 extra shadow ballots were counted.[10] Tsvangirai and his supporters cried foul, but the electoral commission and virtually all of the media were controlled by Mugabe.

The 2005 parliamentary election was less violent but still characterized by the usual tactics to ensure a ZANU-PF victory: Mugabe's regime limited public gatherings through a policy of prior permission, allowed the police to detain suspects for weeks without bringing charges, put the already partial electoral commission under tighter state control, and continued to prohibit public scrutiny of voter registration lists. The voters' rolls for 2005 were replete with false names and listings of the dead; an independent audit calculated that 2 million of the 5.6 million names on the list were suspect. Of the 2 million, an estimated 800,000 were names of dead persons; another 900,000 were names of persons no longer residing at the addresses where they originally had registered.[11] Traditional constituency boundaries were manipulated to reduce the number of seats in urban areas and increase those in rural constituencies. Zimbabweans outside the country were prohibited from voting for fear that they would favor the MDC. Soldiers in uniform were permitted to vote in any constituency. Few objective external and internal observers were permitted to monitor the election; even teams from the South African-based Electoral Institute of Southern Africa and a Southern African Development Community (SADC) parliamentary forum were barred. Polling stations were more numerous and more effectively situated in areas favorable to the ZANU-PF. Government-run radio and television permitted MDC candidates derisory amounts of time to campaign while Mugabe and ZANU-PF candidates talked for hours. Independent radio broadcasts were jammed, the two independent weekly newspapers were harassed, and commercial printing establishments preparing MDC fliers were firebombed. Food, especially maize, was used to reward support for ZANU-PF candidates and was available to party members in ZANU-PF areas only. ZANU-PF candidates received official funding while the MDC was not allowed to accept overseas contributions and received no monies from the state. Registration fees for candidates rose 2,000 percent to discourage the MDC and independent candidates. Until a few days before the election, police patrolled MDC rallies, intimidating potential voters. On the eve of the election, Mugabe declared that anyone who voted for the MDC was a traitor. He declared that his party would win two-thirds of the total seats (120 contested and 30 appointed).[12]

After a lower than usual voter turnout (under 50 percent), Mugabe's assertion proved correct. The polls were organized and manned by ZANU-PF supporters and loyal security forces; MDC observers were often locked out. Ballot boxes were stuffed. One MDC analyst suggested that there had been 500,000 false ballots, down from 800,000 in 2002.[13] Counting was manipulated; in many constituencies, ZANU-PF officials walked off with ballot boxes and later announced counts that were inflated by more than the number of persons who had registered their votes—according to observers. The MDC claimed its bedrock urban seats in Harare and Bulawayo and defeated Emmerson Mnangagwa (Mugabe's speaker of parliament and long-time henchman) in Kwekwe, but it lost key periurban and a number of supposedly secure rural constituencies. Mugabe's men and women racked up surprisingly one-sided victories in virtually all of the rural areas, even in MDC-dominated Chimanimani, and emerged with 78 seats out of 120. One independent was victorious, leaving the MDC with 41. Washington, London, and Brussels all condemned the result, declaring it false. Only governmental delegations from South Africa, Malawi, Mozambique, the SADC, and the African Union reported that the election was fully free and fair.

In 2007, Mugabe still ruled. Presidential elections are supposed to be held again in 2008, but Mugabe wants to stay on, postponing the scheduled poll until 2010. Meanwhile, he continues to prey on a despondent, largely lifeless land. Despite elections, it is a country repressed and terrorized by the state.

Slaying the Fatted Calf

Commercial farming, which once supplied 18 percent of the nation's total GDP and 30 percent of its export earnings, is essentially defunct. Mugabe has chased nearly 4,000 white and black families off their farms. Their land and equipment has not been given to landless peasants but rather to Mugabe's political cronies and other politically connected black entrepreneurs. Nearly all of the land remains untilled, too, and precious irrigation systems have been wrecked and expensive equipment scrapped and sold. Some 400,000 African farm workers have lost their livelihoods and are destitute. Without the people who know how to work them, the farms grow nothing and contribute to national starvation. Finally, by late 2005, Mugabe's own governor of the Central Bank of Zimbabwe began criticizing the wanton destruction of the country's farming capacity. He, but not Mugabe, admitted that the wholesale land grab had been a mistake. Likewise, in late 2005, Zimbabwe's deputy minister of agriculture acknowledged that Mugabe had given "land to people lacking the passion for farming, and this is why every year production has been declining."[14]

The tragedy of Zimbabwe is that one man's overweening ambitions, avarice, and lust for power destroyed everything positive that a free Zimbabwe had come to embody. From 1998 to 2006, Zimbabwe's GDP per capita dropped from about $700 to $350.[15] According to one study, the purchasing power of the average Zimbabwean had fallen in 2005 back to 1953 levels.[16] By 2005 and well into 2007, Zimbabwe's foreign exchange reserves had vanished into personal pockets, and there were constant consumer shortages of soap, salt, sugar, cooking oil, and other basics, and of gasoline and diesel fuel. Inflation soared from a mere 30 percent per year in 1998 to 1,200 percent per year in 2006 and 3,700 percent in 2007; Zimbabwe's currency exchange rate against the U.S. dollar plummeted from 38:1 to 12,000:1 and beyond. In early 2007, the exchange rate was over 5,000:1, but because of the changes in Zimbabwe's currency, that was the equivalent of a massive 5,000,000:1. Unemployment increased to 80 percent, and economic growth turned negative, losing 10–20 percent each year since 2000.[17] The government's official fiscal deficit rose alarmingly from 8 percent of GDP in 1998 to 20 percent in 2000 and close to 60 percent in 2005. In 2005, Zimbabwe dollar notes had stopped circulating, replaced by easily counterfeited locally printed bearer bonds in Z$10,000, Z$20,000, and Z$50,000 denominations; the state could not afford to pay for the printing overseas of proper bills. Allegedly, Zimbabwe was able to continue to function in 2005 only because major foreign-owned banks were allowing the regime to write large overdrafts, month to month.

Other 2005 statistics contributed ongoing alarm: local manufacturing had shrunk by 51 percent since 1997 and exports had halved; foreign direct investment had fallen from U.S. $444 million to U.S. $9 million between 1998 and 2004. Consequently, 80 percent of the country's population was living below the official poverty line.[18]

In mid-2006, the consequences of Zimbabwe's economic collapse became even more obvious. Without warning, the governor of the Central Bank revalued the national currency, lopping three zeros off the existing currency denominations (sacks of local dollars had been needed even to buy bread) and permitting the exchange of only limited quantities of old dollars for new dollars.[19] Businesses struggled to re-create their account books, holders of ill-obtained old currency hoards spent wildly on luxury goods (for later resale), and even more chaos than usual was injected into the country's deranged economy.

Schools have stopped teaching for want of textbooks or wages. Hospitals have run out of basic medicines and staff although the wards are still full. Fewer than 900 physicians remained in Zimbabwe in 2004, a ratio of one doctor for every 13,500 Zimbabweans.[20] (Malawi has a more deplorable ratio; Zambia, Botswana, and South Africa have much better numbers.) The HIV-AIDS pandemic rolls on relentlessly, with no provision of retroviral drugs and almost no government attention. Most of all, thanks to governmental errors of commission (not natural causes), Zimbabweans have begun to starve: in mid-2004, the city of Bulawayo reported 152 deaths from hunger since January, 29 in July alone. The UN World Food Programme meanwhile reported that 4.6 million Zimbabweans were officially at risk of dying from hunger.[21] In 2005, the Zimbabwe Vulnerability Assessment Committee (comprising the SADC, UN, nongovernmental organizations [NGOs], and government officials) reported that under the most optimistic scenario, 2.9 million Zimbabweans would require substantial food aid. More would be at risk, it said, if the government's Grain Marketing Board were not able to procure and provide adequate supplies of maize at reasonable prices.[22] That was a proper caution since the board failed to obtain such amounts, and the 2006 harvest was puny. In August 2006, the World Food Programme was feeding 1 million Zimbabweans.[23]

Millions of ordinary Zimbabweans fled and continue to flee to Botswana, Mozambique, and South Africa. This outpouring of refugees also includes journalists, physicians, lawyers, and several thousand tried and true farmers, the backbone of Zimbabwe's once powerful economy.

The people of Zimbabwe are at least 50 percent poorer than they were at independence in 1980. The modern look of Zimbabwe's cities belies their new poverty and the depths to which the living standards of most Zimbabweans have tumbled. Health outcomes are a result of this new impoverishment under Mugabe. With the onset of AIDS, Zimbabwean infant mortality rates have risen alarmingly to almost 10 percent of every 1,000 live births. The mortality rate of children under five years of age has risen from 80 deaths for every 1,000 live births in 1990 to 132 in 2005. Meanwhile, life expectancy has plummeted. In 1990, the average Zimbabwean could expect to live to sixty. In 2006, Zimbabwean women had a reduced average life expectancy of thirty-four years; men, thirty-seven.[24] An estimated 40,000 Zimbabwean women died in childbirth in 2006. The local press reports incidents of infanticide on a large scale, as women without hope kill their newborns and discard corpses into Harare's sewers.

Countries cannot easily be bankrupted, but, since 1999, Zimbabwe has been unable to pay its petroleum or energy bills. It has only with difficulty covered the running costs and salaries of its overseas diplomatic missions. Kuwait, Libya, and Malaysia have all provided petroleum in exchange for land or other kinds of payback. In 2006, China agreed with Mugabe to build barracks for the Zimbabwean army and construct several coal-fired thermal electric power generating plants. In exchange, Mugabe gave the Chinese favored access to Zimbabwe's mineral riches, especially ferrochrome, platinum, copper, zinc, nickel, and gold. He mandated the teaching of Chinese, by Chinese, at the University of Zimbabwe. Mugabe also "purchased" three new Chinese fighter aircraft, having obtained three others in 2005, along with three passenger aircraft (two of which had serious technical flaws) for Air Zimbabwe. But it is primarily due to the misguided benevolence of South Africa that Zimbabwe has survived. A total collapse of the Zimbabwean economy, which most independent observers believe has already occurred, would devastate South Africa.

For Zimbabwean consumers, life since 1999 has been a succession of interminable lines for gasoline for their cars, diesel fuel for their tractors, kerosene for heating, cooking oil, and bread. In an agricultural land where national self-sufficiency has been assumed except in years of dramatic drought, wheat and other staples (including the white maize that most Africans eat) have mostly been unavailable—except to the politically favored few. Even local vegetables have been scarce and expensive. (In 2004, Mugabe's thugs attacked the country's largest grower of vegetables, trashing the vast farm, dispersing the farm workers, and taking over one of the last large agricultural spreads that was still in non-ZANU-PF hands.)

An observer commented:

This week we watched helplessly as the Zimbabwe government continued with its systematic destruction of security of tenure. Eric Harrison is losing his small farm—he bought it thirty years ago, and only last year was he finally free of debt. He is sixty-five and is now being dispossessed by political thugs financed and sent by senior figures in ZANU-PF who are stealing a Z$3 billion dollar orange crop while the police watch. We are witnessing a hotel resort owner with a ninety-nine-year lease on his site, on which he and his wife have built up a complete infrastructure for tourist visitors and whose table is well known, being dispossessed by ZANU thugs. They are also in their sixties and will walk away with nothing. Kondozi farm—3,000 workers,

5,000 outgrowers, the largest single exporter of fresh vegetables to Europe. The work of two men—one black, the other white, both Zimbabweans—now taken over illegally by force. All exports halted and the equipment being stolen. Billions of dollars of investment have gone down the drain. The banks [are] left holding billions of dollars of useless debt.[25]

In late 2005, Christopher Dell, the American ambassador to Zimbabwe, integrated most of these issues and concerns in an outspoken speech in Mutare, eastern Zimbabwe. "Neither drought not sanctions are at the root of Zimbabwe's decline. The Zimbabwe government's own gross mismanagement of the economy and its corrupt rule has brought on the crisis." Zimbabwe had been fiscally reckless. "Chaotic disruptions on commercial farms" had led to the collapse in food production. "The land grab" had intensified the suffering of the nation's "most vulnerable segments of society—the rural and urban poor." Dell reminded Zimbabweans that American humanitarian assistance would continue to be generous but that it would support the regime financially only when it restored the rule of law, conducted free and fair elections, put security forces under effective civilian control, repealed repressive legislation, and developed a legal and transparent land reform program.[26]

Tyranny and Brutality

Mugabe's regime routinely brutalizes both its opponents and persons or groups critical of or suspected of being critical of the policies and procedures of the government. There is no forced labor, on the Burmese model, and there were no compulsory removals of populations until 2005, when 700,000 to 1.2 million urban dwellers were forcibly evicted from Harare and Bulawayo. They were dispatched in midwinter to rural areas, their houses and shops destroyed. Nearly all were suspected of supporting the MDC. But Mugabe may additionally have been flexing his muscles—showing who was boss. Arbitrary arrests, detentions without trial, sexual assaults, torture, political assassinations, and the spread of generalized mayhem are all tools used by the Mugabe machine to repress and terrorize Zimbabweans.[27]

When the presses of the country's only independent daily newspaper are bombed, and when it and several independent weekly newspapers fall afoul of hastily introduced legislation and are shut down, and only official media outlets—television, radio, and the press—remain, freedom of expression obviously is severely challenged. Similarly, when the government effectively bans all foreign correspondents and deports media representatives who happen to hold local residency permits, it is easier for a nondemocratic regime to recede into the global background. The key to this kind of control is a scheme of special permits: journalists have to be registered and so do newspapers and other outlets of expression. An additional announced step is to censor e-mails and the Internet, as Burma and China do, but possibly with less effect.

On the eve of the 2005 elections, the government employed Iranian-supplied jamming transmitters to drown out independent radio voices beamed into the country from medium-wave transmitters in neighboring Botswana. One respondent tried to find SW Radio Africa's evening newscast on a March evening: "At first I thought there was no signal, but then I was able to pick . . . up a faint signal right next to . . . a muffled roar." Soon it became impossible to discern anything over the continuous stream of noise. The professional jamming was conducted from studios of the Zimbabwe Broadcasting Corporation in Gweru.[28]

In 2006, the government tightly controlled seven daily newspapers, four radio stations, and the only television channel. The weekly *Financial Gazette*, long critical of the government, was purchased by financiers closely allied to Mugabe. Only the *Standard on Sunday* and the *Independent*, both private weeklies, continued to publish, albeit always with an eye on official restrictions and by virtue of a modicum of self-censorship. The country's commercial printing establishment has also been attacked. A Bulawayo firm that was printing fliers for the MDC was firebombed. The CIO regularly visits commercial printing concerns, uttering dark warnings.

In 2004, the government of Zimbabwe moved menacingly against civil society—private charities, religious groups, aid organizations, and all manner of NGOs. At the state opening of parliament in Harare in July 2004, Mugabe accused Western-funded church and human rights groups of siding unconscionably with his opponents and with Britain, the former colonial power. He threatened to close the most offensive NGOs and arrest their officials because they had long been "interfering" in politics. He objected particularly to their criticisms of him and his government for violating human and democratic rights. NGOs must work for the betterment of the nation, said Mugabe. Zimbabwe could not allow NGOs to be used as conduits and instruments of foreign interference in national affairs.[29]

Mugabe's Orwellian Non-Governmental Organisations and Churches Act imposes strict registration requirements on civil society. All groups engaged in charity and educational works are required to seek an official license, disclose sources of funding, and identify foreign donors. Even if they do fulfill those requirements, the government can still deny registration to any group, no matter how large or well connected, just as it refused to license the *Daily News* despite high court orders to the contrary.[30] This civil society legislation enables Mugabe's government to weed out foreign-financed groups that support human rights or participatory democracy, thus effectively chilling contributions from abroad and emasculating all NGOs.

Mugabe's object was to eradicate civil society, just as the free press has been destroyed, the independent judiciary neutered, foreign criticism muted, the opposition emasculated, local protest curtailed by the meting out of exemplary punishments, and African criticism deflected by a vigorous nationalistic propaganda campaign. Equally, the Mugabe regime has denied the existence of widespread hunger and starvation. It has effectively channeled internationally supplied food assistance to cities and rural areas dominated by the ZANU-PF, hoarding available rations for his own favorites in order to influence political results in 2005 and in subsequent years. As Roman Catholic Archbishop Pius Ncube has oft complained, Mugabe uses maize rations to "reward supporters and punish dissidents."[31]

In 2004, Zimbabwe, again Orwellian like so many Potemkin-style democracies, signed a South African Development Community protocol that prescribes procedures for transparent elections and mandates a free press, freedom of assembly, and outside electoral monitors. Zimbabwe pledged to abide by these provisions of the new SADC charter and to provide for full participation of all citizens, establish an independent voting authority, not interfere with the competitive process, give opposition parties every advantage available to the ruling party, and so on.

Yet, at the same time, Mugabe's parliament passed the aforementioned new restrictions on civil liberties and renewed strictures on the press. Mugabe also appointed a new electoral supervisory body of toadies. A spokesman for the MDC said that the government had "put into place a whole array of laws that make[s] it impossible to compete. We have to go to ZANU-PF for permission even to hold a meeting."[32] In addition, according to the Public Order and Safety Act of 2004, it is illegal to put up posters in public places. Painting graffiti on a wall became a serious offense.

There is no question that Zimbabwe under Mugabe has breached democratic norms and is a repressive state. Archbishop Ncube says that "they burn homes. They kill people. They torture people with electricity. They intimidate people to make them feel afraid."[33]

Criticism from Africa and the West

President Bush, then-secretary of state Powell, then-British foreign minister Jack Straw, and a host of international missions and other delegations agreed with Ncube's criticisms. Powell, in his 2001 visit to Johannesburg, urged Mugabe to "submit to the law and the will of the people."[34] In 2003, President Bush stated that since 2000 "the government of Zimbabwe has systematically undermined that nation's democratic institutions, employing violence, intimidation and repressive means . . . to stifle opposition to its rule." In announcing an executive order barring Mugabe and seventy-six of his cronies from entering the United States, President Bush also said that the Mugabe government had not only harmed Zimbabwe's people but had also posed an "unusual and extraordinary threat to the foreign policy interests of the United States."[35] President Bush announced a freeze on the U.S. assets of Mugabe and the others.

Even a committee of the African Union (AU) declared Zimbabwe in breach of fundamental African values. Africans never criticize each other, and the new African Union has been careful about interfering in the sovereign powers of its members. Nevertheless, in early July 2004, a report adopted by the AU executive council slammed Zimbabwe for arresting and torturing opponents and human rights lawyers, arresting journalists, stifling freedom of expression, and denying civil liberties to its citizens.[36] Mugabe had never before heard such comments from his peers.

The report emanated from the AU's own African Commission on Human and People's Rights, but it reflected an investigation in 2002, following the flawed presidential elections.[37] After speaking to victims of political violence and torture in Zimbabwe, the investigators said that "at the very least" human rights violations and arbitrary arrests had occurred during and after the 2002 elections. The AU mission had been particularly alarmed by the arrest in 2002 of the president of the Law Society of Zimbabwe. "The mission is prepared and able to rule that the government cannot wash its hands from responsibility for all these happenings," read the report.

"It is evident that a highly charged atmosphere has been prevailing," said the AU investigators, "and activists undertook their illegal actions in the expectation that the police would not act against them." Moreover, "government did not act soon enough and firmly enough against those guilty of gross criminal acts."

"By its statements and political rhetoric, and by its failure at critical moments to uphold the rule of law," the investigators continued, "the government failed to chart a path that signaled a commitment to the rule of law."

The mission was not able to find definitively that the human rights violations were part of an orchestrated plan by the ZANU-PF government. But the report said that the Zimbabwean state did acknowledge to the observers that "excesses did occur."

The AU commission concluded that the media in Zimbabwe should "be free from the shackles of control" so that they may "voice opinions and reflect societal beliefs freely." The report also called for a repeal of draconian laws and asked the government to abide by the judgments of its supreme court, which should, it pleaded, be free of political pressure.

The report also said that on the whole, the mission found Zimbabwean society to be highly polarized— presumably in 2002, but its conclusions are apposite for 2004 to 2007 as well. Nevertheless, it argued, "The land question is not in itself the cause of division. It appears that at the heart [of the problem] is a society in search of the means for change and divided about how best to achieve change after two decades of dominance by a political party that carried the hopes and aspirations of the people of Zimbabwe through the liberation struggle into independence."[38] That last sentence well captures the fundamental political issue in Zimbabwe today, as well as in 2002.

In the *2003 Country Reports on Human Rights Practices*, the State Department's Bureau of Democracy, Human Rights, and Labor quietly understated its conclusions: Zimbabwe continued during 2003 to commit numerous, serious human rights abuses. Mugabe and the ZANU-PF were accused of fostering a "systematic government-sanctioned, campaign of violence targeting supporters and potential supporters of the opposition." Moreover, "security forces committed extrajudicial killings." In some cases, with explicit government support, extralegal militias "killed, abducted, tortured, beat, abused, raped, and threatened farm owners, their workers, opposition party members," and sympathizers. Security forces and government youth militias "tortured, beat, and otherwise abused persons." There were politically motivated disappearances, arbitrary arrests and detentions, and lengthy pretrial detentions. Prison conditions remained harsh.[39]

Additionally, the report stated that the government restricted freedom of speech and the press; beat, arrested, and prosecuted journalists; denied academic freedom; and curtailed freedom of assembly and forcibly dispersed nonviolent public meetings. It eliminated freedom of association for political organizations, restricted freedom of movement, and attacked and arrested members of human rights nongovernmental organizations. At a time of severe hunger, the official Grain Marketing Board "routinely and publicly denied handouts of maize meal to suspected MDC supporters."[40]

The 2004 report by the same State Department bureau noted little improvement. Three MDC supporters had been killed: one was beaten to death by thirty ZANU-PF youths, another was shot by "war veterans" and soldiers, and the third was shot by a ZANU-PF cabinet minister.[41] According to the Zimbabwe Human Rights Forum, there were also 8 politically motivated attempted murders, 33 death threats, 399 assaults, and 189 cases of enforced internal displacement. There were sixty-two reports of similarly motivated kidnapping of MDC supporters and candidates by ZANU-PF cadres. Other "disappearances" may have gone unreported due to intimidation. Seven MDC members of parliament were arrested, one of whom was imprisoned for fifteen months.

In January 2004, two editors and a reporter for the weekly *Independent* were charged with criminal defamation and released on bail. In May, an editor and a reporter from the weekly *Standard* were charged with publishing false statements prejudicial to the state, arrested, and released on bail. An American reporter with Zimbabwean permanent resident status was deported despite a high court ruling in his favor. He had lived in and reported from Zimbabwe for twenty-four years.[42]

During the first eleven months of 2004, according to the Zimbabwe Human Rights Forum, there were 170 cases of torture of MDC personnel and supporters (versus 391 cases in twelve months in 2003). The Forum also noted two politically motivated rapes, a number that seems low and explicable only because of cultural taboos against the admission of rape. A total of 389 MDC followers were arrested and detained unlawfully. The Human Rights Forum further indicated that ZANU-PF thugs or soldiers participated in 145 instances of theft or property damage. In May, for example, a mob of ZANU-PF activists armed with machetes attacked the MDC during a memorial service, and CIO agents kidnapped and brutalized the president of the Zimbabwe National Students Union.[43]

In 2005, torture numbers were slightly reduced to 136 incidents for the year, and only 4 rapes were reported. However, unlawful arrests and detentions soared to 658 and 628, respectively, almost triple the number for 2004. In 2006, through November, 368 persons were tortured, there were 2 attempted murders and 6 death threats, 11 kidnappings, 1 rape, and 1,468 persons had been unlawfully arrested and detained.[44]

"I'm No Idi Amin"—The Causes of Mugabe's Mayhem

Zimbabwe became a repressive state gradually, inexorably, and as much because of the natural progression of tyranny as because of any grand design.

But it grew repressive specifically because of its ruler's lust for power and unquestioned dominance. No structural factors contributed. There were no national emergencies, no unusually poisonous opponents, no threats of terror, and no challenges by neighboring countries.

Repressiveness in Zimbabwe may reflect ninety years of colonial rule and the discriminatory policies that were inherent in settler domination. It may similarly stem somehow from decades of oppression of Africans by whites: broad denials of opportunity and advancement, limited access to good land and water, and a fundamental lack of decency. It also may have origins in the frustrated pangs of indigenous nationalism in the late 1950s and early 1960s, the harsh crackdown on African political aspirations from the mid-1960s, and the traumatic war of independence from 1971 to 1979. Mugabe and many other African politicians were imprisoned from 1964 to 1974. For the next five years, Mugabe had to claw his way to the top of the nationalist ladder by outmaneuvering, ousting, and overcoming the appeals of several key Shona-speaking military men and their political allies. This was no gentle contest, but Mugabe was always the most focused, ascetic, and ruthless of contenders for primacy within the upper levels of the ZANU hierarchy.

Mugabe consolidated his victory after 1980 by allying with whites, especially white farmers, and by suppressing and massacring his Sindebele-speaking opponents (about 30,000 were slaughtered in southwestern Zimbabwe on Mugabe's orders in 1982–1984). Shackled, however, by the provisions of the British-imposed independence constitution, Mugabe governed relatively tolerantly (except for the unfortunate massacres) through 1987, when he was able to become executive president after seven years as prime minister. Then the shift to a more repressive style of leadership occurred, becoming more pronounced after 1990.

Repression reflects the visible hand of individual or collective rulers. In Africa, despite the dismal records of Togo and Equatorial Guinea, no single exemplar of repressive, failed, leadership surpasses Mugabe. In the annals of human-made disasters in Africa, he even approaches the inspired debacles of Mobutu in Zaire (Congo), Amin in Uganda, and Jean-Bedel Bokassa in the Central African Empire.

"I'm no Idi Amin," Mugabe resentfully told the London *Sunday Times*.[45] Indeed, because he is educated and sophisticated and Amin, Bokassa, and Mobutu were anything but—being poorly educated tyrants pursuing peculiar personal visions and vendettas in countries less robust than Zimbabwe—Mugabe is doubtless correct. Yet he may be considered worse for his own people than an Amin because the gifted Mugabe had inherited a well-run, well-off country. He proceeded to rob Zimbabwe of its potential, repressing a population that knew less suffering under settler rule.

Mugabe is no mere thug. He is well educated and capable of matching wits with the world's best and brightest of leaders—as is true of so many of the rulers discussed in this book. Mugabe was taught by Jesuit missionaries in rural Zimbabwe, became a teacher, and studied for a B.A. in English and history at the University College of Fort Hare (in South Africa), then one of the five best institutions of higher learning in Africa. After graduating from Fort Hare in 1951, Mugabe taught school first in Zimbabwe and then in Zambia at a teacher-training institution. Along the way, he obtained a diploma and a bachelor's degree in education from the University of South Africa and another bachelor's degree in economics from the University of London, all by correspondence. Subsequently, Mugabe taught in a teacher-training school in Ghana, from 1956 to 1960, where he met Sally Heyfron, his first wife.

Because Mugabe is genuinely talented and because Zimbabwe is a modern state that was once one of Africa's best, his reckless abuse and headlong flight into repression has been that much more tragic. There is no doubt that he alone is the architect of Zimbabwe's collapse into ignominy and pauperism. He has had a raft of helpers, many of whom have profited thereby, and the loyal acquiescence for two decades of the aging revolutionaries of ZANU-PF's controlling politburo, central committee, and ministerial cabinet, and most of the members of parliament. But Mugabe always gave the orders, denounced or demoted those who had second thoughts, kept dossiers on his henchmen, and acted resolutely and relentlessly as a much more polished version of Haiti's François (Papa Doc) Duvalier. After 1990, Mugabe sought no consent or consensus, contemptuously ignored his own cabinet ministers, and gave peremptory orders even to the members of his hand-picked central committee.

Mugabe consolidated his grip on power in the early 1990s, becoming simultaneously more autocratic and more avaricious. Those close to Mugabe then and since have attributed his increasing arrogance and vanity to age (he was born in 1924), a noticeable anger at being eclipsed as a key leader of southern Africa by Nelson Mandela after South Africa held its first democratic elections in 1994, and the waning influence of Sally Heyfron. About 1990, the president and Grace Marufu, a young secretary, became increasingly intimate. She subsequently gave birth to Mugabe's three children, his only child with Sally having died very young. After Sally herself died in 1992, Mugabe married Marufu, initially in a nonpublic, indigenous ceremony. The upsurge in Mugabe's repressive tendencies and greed has closely tracked her rise to prominence and power. Senior ZANU-PF central committee members call her "grasping Grace" behind her back.[46]

Lord Acton's dictum that "absolute power corrupts absolutely" is suggestive in Mugabe's case and perhaps in the case of many of the other repressive examples in this volume, but it is hardly conclusive. In Zimbabwe, as in so many other nations in Africa since 1960, a weak civil society provided openings for autocracy; the cold war, with its tolerance for strongmen, offered others. Zimbabwe, again like so much of the developing world, lacked an independent media to hold politicians accountable. Mugabe also cleverly created a party-dominated socialist state. Given the comparative prosperity of the 1980s, the growth in schooling and medical care for Africans, the absence of any serious victimization of whites, and the co-optation of the then-main opposition party, anti-Mugabe voices were largely stilled. Moreover, the ZANU-PF was ethnically and politically formidable. The few politicians who opposed Mugabe and the ZANU-PF lacked national legitimacy or could easily be intimidated. The CIO kept internal dissidents in line, and Mugabe's patronage machine was lavish. By the early 1990s, Mugabe was unassailable within the party and outside, and the resultant sense of entitlement engendered excesses.

Even after the end of the cold war era and its tolerance for developing-world dictators, no one in Africa publicly called Mugabe to account. President Julius Nyerere of Tanzania was greatly displeased when Mugabe rebuffed his plea not to send troops into the Congo. Mandela regarded Mugabe as an insufferable autocrat. But neither of them nor any of their peers expressed criticism publicly. Only much later, when repression was wholesale and elections had been stolen, did a few courageous African leaders, led by neighboring Botswana's President Festus Mogae, demand better from Africa and Mugabe. However, throughout Mugabe's rule, neither South Africa nor SADC has publicly expressed its horror at the cataclysm that Zimbabwe has become.

Likewise, the international lending institutions always thought it wiser to woo Mugabe than to criticize him. Although Mugabe and his finance ministers repeatedly refused to obey conditions imposed by the World Bank and the International Monetary Fund or to fulfill promises that they had made, both lending institutions continued to back Mugabe. Even after he sent troops into the Congo, the IMF rewarded Zimbabwe with tranche after tranche of support. The World Bank and other donors never flagged in their backing, even as Mugabe grew increasingly repressive.

In early 2007, Mugabe's apparatus of control was not total. As intensive and thoroughgoing as is his own cult of personality, and as repressive as the state definitely is, nonpolitical, urban, middle-class, non-property-owning individuals go to work and enjoy their weekends without much fear of informers or direct intimidation. They may have difficulty finding bread or cooking oil, of course, and certainly gasoline. The police cannot be trusted, having become thoroughly politicized. Crime rates have escalated, too. Furthermore, savings are not secure, and the banking system provides no comfort. Nevertheless, the façade of pre-1998 existence can persist, with only occasional glances over one's shoulder.

What does it mean that ordinary life somehow continues, if with heavy shadows? Is Zimbabwe thus somewhat less repressive than the other cases covered in this volume? Or should repression not be calibrated on an absolute scale but rather be considered relative according to where and how a state began? Zimbabwe represents no rapid shift from a Soviet communist, overweening, hegemonic enterprise to a post-Soviet regime that appears and behaves much the same. Nor has Mugabe's Zimbabwe always existed as a tight-fisted autocracy in the manner of Syria. Zimbabwe had a political culture, much honored in the breach, of democratic decisionmaking. Independent Zimbabwe and its predecessor polities prided themselves on efficient governance. Mugabe still pays lip service to those old shibboleths. Is Zimbabwe therefore a less repressive rather than more repressive state? Or should that judgment relate primarily to how well advanced a state it was and thus how far it has fallen—how far it has deviated from its political traditions? In our sample of countries, Zimbabwe may have slipped the most because of its harsh new levels of repression.

How Repressive, How Aggressive?

There can be no substantial doubt that Zimbabwe is a repressive state that employs the usual physical means—the excesses of paramilitary militias and selected assassinations, torture, and kidnappings—to create a pervasive atmosphere of fear and destruction. Furthermore, the state's total control of the available media (including the jamming of opposition broadcasts beamed from outside the nation's borders) allows Mugabe's henchmen to intimidate and oppress opponents and keep citizens on edge. More pernicious in 2004–2007 has been the regime's use of food aid to reward its followers or supposed followers, and to punish those suspected of adhering to the MDC or at least showing inadequate support of the ZANU-PF. In this manner, millions of Zimbabweans have been at risk of starvation, and some hundreds, at least, have starved.

Zimbabwe is as regimented as Niyazov's Turkmenistan, and some of its policies of repression are as bizarre as those foisted on Turkmen by Turkmenbashi. There may be as many political killings and disappearances as in Equatorial Guinea or Uzbekistan. Yet Zimbabwe is less a police state in appearance than almost any of the Central Asian satrapies, Burma, and North Korea. In many respects its atmosphere is reminiscent of Belarus and Tunisia.

Highly repressive as it is, Zimbabwe is not particularly aggressive. It has withdrawn its troops from the Democratic Republic of Congo. It engages in doubtful dealings with China, Libya, and Malaysia but has not been accused of drug trafficking, gun smuggling, or money laundering. It does not attack its neighbors, except by forcing the flight of millions of emigrants. For our purposes, Zimbabwe is a corrupt nation-state that preys on its citizens, immiserates them, but does not project its in-state power beyond its borders.

Policy Implications

In this case, the policy implications are limited. Washington has already imposed travel and financial sanctions on members of the upper echelon of the ZANU-PF, as has the European Union. A Zimbabwean minister of sport was prevented from attending the Olympic Games in Athens. The British Treasury has sequestered substantial funds belonging to Mugabe's coterie. But the West is preoccupied with Iraq, Afghanistan, and the Sudan, while Zimbabwe poses a minimal strategic threat. Given the absence of obvious overt genocide, the reluctance of the rest of Africa to criticize Zimbabwe publicly, and South Africa's refusal to oust Mugabe or even to curtail his and other leading Zimbabweans' travel abilities, the United States, Britain, the European Union, and other world players feel powerless to act, however hungry Zimbabweans become, however more despotic Mugabe grows, and however much he defies the forces of world order, South Africa, and SADC.

It would not take too many South African or Western troops to oust Mugabe. The Zimbabwean defense forces are ready for political change. Nor would it be hard politically for South Africa to send Mugabe into exile. What is lacking is a casus belli—a misstep regionally or internally that threatens neighbors or produces a bloodbath within the country. Then regional and outside intervention would have more immediacy and legitimacy. Meanwhile, despite the intense suffering of millions of Zimbabweans and the denial of their human rights and civil liberties, and despite world order's acceptance of the "responsibility to protect" norm, no one acts, and Mugabe's mayhem continues unchecked.

Notes

1. Much of the analysis in the early part of this chapter is drawn from Robert I. Rotberg, "Africa's Mess, Mugabe's Mayhem," *Foreign Affairs*, LXXIX (September–October 2000), 47–61.

2. A senior cabinet member reported to me that Mugabe entered a grandly acquisitive phase in the middle 1990s and beyond. See Robert I. Rotberg, "Mugabe Seen as Bar to Zimbabwe's Progress," *Southern Africa Report* (February 21, 1997).

3. Transparency International, "Corruption Perceptions Index 2006" (November 5, 2006), www.transparency.org/policy_research/surveys_indices/cpi/2006.

4. *Christian Science Monitor* (January 21, 1998).

5. Michael Wines, "Corruption and Despair Are Choking Zimbabwe," *New York Times* (October 19, 2003).

6. Rotberg, "Africa's Mess," 48.

7. No ZANU-PF member of parliament, even the two whose seats were forfeited to the MDC, was forced to leave his or her seat. Such is the rule of law in contemporary Zimbabwe.

8. Quoted in Rachel Swarns, "Mugabe's Aides Declare Him Winner of Zimbabwe Vote," *New York Times* (March 13, 2002).

9. See section in this chapter on "Criticism from Africa and the West."

10. "Solidarity Peace Trust," BBC News (July 21, 2004).

11. See *Southern Africa Report* (March 18, 2005).

12. *Boston Globe* (March 30, 2005); *Economist* (March 26, 2005).

13. Eddie Cross, "Sitrep 4" (April 5, 2005), www.eddiecross.africanherd.com.

14. See *Southern Africa Report*, XXIII (November 4, 2005).

15. Economic statistics were collected from domestic press and personal sources, as international databases were only current up to 2002.

16. Todd Moss and Stewart Patrick, "After Mugabe, Zimbabwe Will Need Post-Conflict Response," *CGD Notes* (December 2005); Michael Clemens and Todd Moss, "Costs and Causes of Zimbabwe's Crisis," *CGD Notes* (July 2005), 2.

17. "Not Quite a Row of Sixes," *Economist* (June 17, 2006); "Can It Get Worse?" *Economist* (May 27, 2006); "U.S. Diplomat Rips Mugabe's Government," CNN.com (May 3, 2006). For inflation in 2002–2004, see Andrew Meldrum, *Where We Have Hope: A Memoir of Zimbabwe* (London, 2004), 5

18. Christopher Dell, "Plain Talk about the Zimbabwean Economy," speech delivered at Africa University (Mutare, Zimbabwe, November 2, 2005), 3.

19. *Economist* (August 26, 2006); Center for Security Studies, "Zimbabwe Reins in Runaway Currency," *ISN Security Watch* (August 22, 2006), www.isn.ethz.ch/news/sw/details.cfm?ID=16561.

20. Compare this number with about 1,800 physicians and a ratio of 7,194 Zimbabweans per physician in 1995. (Calculations based on World Bank, *World Develop-*

ment Indicators [Washington, D.C.]). See Michael Wines, "With Health Systems in Tatters, Zimbabwe Stands Defenseless," *New York Times* (February 5, 2004).

21. *Southern Africa Report* (August 13, 2004), 4–5.

22. See "Zimbabwe: Rural Food Security and Vulnerability Assessments," Report 5 (Harare, June 2005), www.zimrelief.info/files/attachments/doclib/0003.pdf.

23. UN World Food Programme, "World Hunger—Zimbabwe" (January 2007), www.wfp.org/country_brief/indexcountry.asp?country=716.

24. In 1992, life expectancy was fifty-six years. By 2002, it had fallen to thirty-nine years of age. Also, in 2002, the infant mortality rate was 79 per 1,000 life births. See World Bank, *World Development Indicators*; "Zimbabweans Have Shortest Lives," BBC News (April 8, 2006).

25. Eddie Cross, personal communication, August 7, 2004.

26. Dell, "Plain Talk," 7, 13–14.

27. The excessive use of force is documented in Human Rights Watch, "'You Will Be Thoroughly Beaten.' The Brutal Suppression of Dissent in Zimbabwe" (November 1, 2006), 7–22.

28. Eddie Cross, personal communication, March 16, 2005.

29. *Southern Africa Report* (July 23, 2004).

30. A few weeks before the 2005 elections, the country's supreme court decided that the *Daily News* should in fact have been licensed under the pernicious Access to Information and Protection of Privacy Act and that the Media and Information Commission, having barred the *Daily News* in 2003, should take another look at its original decision. But the government blocked further action favorable to the *Daily News*.

31. *New York Times* (August 28, 2004).

32. Welshman Ncube, quoted in Sharon Lafraniere, "Opposition Plans Boycott of Elections in Zimbabwe," *New York Times* (August 26, 2004).

33. Ibid.

34. See Colin L. Powell, "Remarks at the University of Witwatersrand" (Johannesburg, South Africa, May 25, 2001), www.state.gov/secretary/former/powell/remarks/2001/3090.htm.

35. Quoted in David Stout, "Bush Orders Sanctions Imposed against Leaders of Zimbabwe," *New York Times* (March 8, 2003).

36. Beauregard Tromp, "AU Slams Abuses in Zimbabwe," *Sunday Independent* (Johannesburg) (July 4, 2004).

37. It was not submitted to the AU's 2003 summit of heads of state because the document had not then been translated into French. It was also voted down by the 2004 summit after strenuous objections by Mugabe and was ignored at the 2006 summit.

38. Christopher Munnion, "United Africa Condemns Mugabe Regime," *Daily Telegraph* (July 5, 2004).

39. U.S. Department of State, "Zimbabwe," in *2003 Country Reports on Human Rights Practices* (Washington, D.C., February 25, 2004).

40. Ibid., 1–2.

41. U.S. Department of State, "Zimbabwe," in *2004 Country Reports on Human Rights Practices* (Washington, D.C., February 28, 2005).

42. See Meldrum, *Where We Have Hope.*

43. See Zimbabwe Human Rights NGO Forum, "Monthly Political Violence Reports—2004," and "Monthly Political Violence Reports—2005," www. hrforum zim.com/frames/inside_frame_monthly.htm.

44. See the Zimbabwe Human Rights NGO Forum, "Monthly Political Violence Report" (December 2005, June 2006, and November 2006), www.hrforumzim.com/ frames/inside_frame_monthly.htm. See also Zimbabwe Human Rights NGO Forum, "An Analysis of the Zimbabwe Human Rights NGO Forum Legal Cases, 1998–2006" (June 2006), www.hrforumzim.com/special_hrru/analysis_1998_2006.pdf; U.S. Department of State, "Zimbabwe," in *2005 Country Reports on Human Rights Practices* (Washington, D.C., March 8, 2006).

45. David Dimbleby, "Mugabe No Idi Amin," *Sunday Times* (London) (June 25, 2000).

46. Rotberg, "Africa's Mess," 58.

eight
Understanding Repression
in Belarus

Margarita M. Balmaceda

The fall of the Berlin Wall in 1989 ushered in a period of democratization and market reform that has extended across Central and Eastern Europe, with one important exception: Belarus. The Belarusian experience as an exception to the broader regional trend toward reform offers a valuable opportunity to analyze how democratization can fail in a post-Soviet context. The case of Belarus also presents important and interesting issues in the study of repressive regimes, in particular concerning the sources of repressiveness and international rogue behavior, and the interrelationship between structural and personal factors in the maintenance of such regimes. Last but not least, the case of Belarus presents complex policy choices for the United States and the international community.

Many of the political systems that have developed in the former Soviet Union have (rightly) been characterized as "semiauthoritarian."[1] At first glance, it would seem that the case of Belarus represents just another variation in this universe of post-Soviet semiauthoritarian regimes. A closer examination of Belarus, however, reveals a very different kind of phenomenon than that observable in Russia or pre–Orange Revolution Ukraine, countries also frequently labeled as semiauthoritarian. A variety of relatively subtle and less subtle repressive measures combine to create a regime that is not only totally out of step with political developments in the region but that poses a clear threat to its own citizens and to the still-fragile European security system. Thus my hypothesis is that despite levels of physical repression that may seem "moderate" by international comparison, the way that these elements of repression synergize with each other and have been institutionalized by the regime creates a repressive situation no less problematic than that of several severe Asian and African cases.

This chapter presents a brief historical background to the Belarusian case, followed by a discussion of the interrelationship between "hard" and "soft" repression under the current Lukashenko regime and an evaluation of the regime's aggressiveness in terms of its international behavior. The main engines of governance of the current Belarusian regime are analyzed, as well as its sources of stability and instability and the possibilities for change. The chapter concludes by asking what the level of repression of the regime means in this particular case, and what should be the appropriate response from the international community.

Belarus in a Post-Soviet Context

How is the Belarus case different from that of other post-Soviet states? In comparison with Ukraine, where significant human rights abuses were common during the regime of Leonid Kuchma (1994–2004), Belarusian repression has been more systematic—well institutionalized and internalized both in the workings of the regime and the psychology of its population. In comparison to the Central Asian states of Turkmenistan and Uzbekistan, the level of repression and cult of personality of the ruler remains relatively low. One way to explain these differences may relate to the high levels of education and relative welfare that characterize the Belarusian population. It may also imply a higher degree of separation between ruler and ruled and a greater resiliency in civil society in comparison to these other states. The 2006 United Nations Development Programme's Human Development Report gives Belarus relatively high grades in terms of human development indicators, ranking it 67th worldwide, at approximately the same level as the Russian Federation (65th) and ahead of Ukraine (77th), Turkmenistan (105th), and Uzbekistan (113th).[2] In terms of newspapers printed daily, Belarus, with 151.36 per 1,000 population, was well ahead of both the Russian Federation and Turkmenistan, with 105 and 6.37 per 1,000 population, respectively.[3]

Background

One of the main sources of stability for the Lukashenko regime is his ability to tap deep into the sources of conservatism in Belarusian society with his own brand of demagogic rhetoric. When one compares the values and beliefs of a regime with those of its community, the question of *which* political communities are chosen for comparison is crucial. Evaluating the Lukashenko regime in the context of Soviet (and post-Soviet) values and understandings of human rights versus Central European ones will make a significant difference in whether or not this regime is viewed as "deviating" from the values of its community. In many ways, this same question—whether to see their own country in a pro-Western, Central European context or in a post-Soviet, Eurasian one—is the central issue dividing the national consciousness of Belarusians today.

Belarus was an exception to broader trends in the region's democratic development even before Lukashenko came to power in 1994. During the Soviet period, Belarus was considered exceptional, if only in the sense of how well the Soviet system seemed to work there and how little underground opposition to the regime existed. With a highly Russified population, towns rebuilt from scratch "by the whole Soviet Union" after World War II, a high level of industrialization, and a highly educated population that saw its living standards rise steadily after 1945, Belarus was referred to by many as "the most perfectly Soviet" republic of the USSR. During the period of perestroika, its difference from other neighboring Soviet republics, such as Ukraine and Lithuania, became increasingly clear. The relative weakness of Belarusian national identity, together with the determination of its entrenched communist elite, prevented the growth of a broad-based nationalist independence movement. Instead, the opposition Belarusian Popular Front remained limited to a small group of intellectuals, and the new Belarusian state was established by those same communist leaders who had opposed independence only a year earlier.

During the first years after independence, it was not obvious in what direction Belarus would go, with the government and the political elites split between those who wanted neutrality for the country and those favoring a close relationship with Russia. Stanislau Shushkevich, Belarus's first head of state, placed a high priority on establishing Belarusian sovereignty, especially vis-à-vis Russia, and on developing constructive relationships with international institutions such as the European Bank for Reconstruction and Development, the International Monetary Fund, the World Bank, and the Conference on Security and Cooperation in Europe (now the Organization for Security and Cooperation in Europe [OSCE]). Yet infighting over relations with Russia, uneasiness over what many saw as the forced introduction of Belarusian as the official language, and popular frustration over failed economic reforms and corruption led to the election as president of Aleksandr Lukashenko, who ran on an anticorruption platform in July 1994.[4]

Lukashenko's authoritarian tendencies emerged soon afterwards. In 1995, riot police acting on Lukashenko's orders beat up Belarusian Popular Front deputies on the steps of the parliament building; shortly thereafter, the number of internal security forces rose to double that of the armed forces.[5] In late 1996, Lukashenko moved closer to consolidating absolute power by carrying out a referendum (widely seen as manipulated) dissolving the country's last democratically elected parliament and allowing extended presidential powers.[6] This critical hurdle passed, Lukashenko was left "unopposed in his drive to create a personal dictatorship, based on a classic combination of force and a cult of personality."[7]

In 2007, Aleksandr Lukashenko celebrated thirteen years in power. In the course of these years, Lukashenko was able to institutionalize his regime significantly while avoiding needed reforms in the Belarusian economy and failing to find a clear role for Belarus in the international system.

The domestic record sheet is mixed. Lukashenko has been able to maintain social and economic stability in the country but at the expense of not engaging in any significant reforms. The long wage arrears workers often experienced in mid-1990s Ukraine and Russia seldom occurred in Lukashenko's Belarus, and monthly salaries have continually increased since the mid-1990s.[8] Large state-owned companies have remained basically intact. Of all the Eastern and Central European countries, Belarus is the only one where the economic system has not fundamentally changed since the demise of the Soviet Union. There is no doubt that reforms—possibly very painful in social terms—must come to Belarus one day; they have simply been postponed.

How Repressive Is the Lukashenko Regime?

The repressiveness of the Lukashenko regime can be categorized as moderately high. This repression is not limited to or even principally characterized by the imprisonment and killing of political opponents but rather operates through lower-key and less spectacular activities such as restricting freedom of the press and administrative harassment of those with opposing views. It would be incorrect to state that Lukashenko rules by sheer force against a population that actively opposes him. Rather, his power is based on a combination of appeal to tradition, demagoguery, harassment, intimidation, and control of the media.

"Hard" Political Repression

Lukashenko's regime has employed overt political repression. Between 1999 and 2000, four prominent opposition figures (TV cameraman Dimitry Zavadsky, former minister of internal affairs Yury Zakharenko, Thirteen Supreme Soviet speaker Viktor Honchar, and businessman and opposition sympathizer Anatoly Krasovski) disappeared under unclear circumstances. It is assumed they were killed at the order of internal security forces.[9] A full investigation of these disappearances has been hindered by Lukashenko, and some investigations of individual cases were ended altogether. In early 2004 alone, both the United Nations Human Rights Commission and the Parliamentary Assembly of the Council of Europe (PACE) censored Belarus over these disappearances; PACE recommended the cessation of all contacts with Belarus until the situation was clarified.

Long-Term Political Prisoners. It is difficult to gather accurate data on the number of political prisoners in Belarus. Amnesty International's reports mention "at least two long term prisoners of conscience."[10] In 2004, two opposition politicians received two-year sentences for defaming the president in a poem, and one of them was also given a thirty-month sentence for handing out leaflets accusing the president of the 1999–2000 disappearances.[11] A third prominent opposition figure, former presidential candidate Mikhail Marynich, was accused of stealing computers (which he had been given as part of a grant) from the U.S. embassy in 2004 and sentenced to five years in prison in what was widely seen as a show trial intended to intimidate the opposition.[12] In early summer 2005, three new sentences for political activists announced the beginning of a new wave of repression. Mikola Statkevich, head of the Belarusian Social Democratic Party (Narodnaya Hramada) and Pavel Sevyarynets, head of the Young Popular Front Organization (Malady Front) were sentenced to three years in a labor camp (under article 342, outlawing the organization of protests that "disrupt public order") for fomenting protests in Minsk after the October 2004 referendum.[13] Andrei Klimov, a former member of the outlawed Belarusian parliament, was sentenced to eighteen months in detention under the same article. In July 2006, Aleksandr Kazulin, former rector of the Belarusian State University and opposition candidate in the March 2006 elections, was condemned to five and a half years for alleged hooliganism and disorderly conduct related to protest demonstrations held after the March 17, 2006, elections, widely considered as rigged. He gained international attention through his hunger strike in the fall of 2006; even after the end of the fifty-three-day hunger strike, his health remained precarious.

The longest-serving political prisoner of recent times is Professor Yuri Bandazhevsky, sentenced to eight years in a labor camp in 2001 on bribe-taking charges but widely believed to have been punished because of his criticism of official responses to the 1986 Chernobyl catastrophe.[14] In 2004, his health failing, he was transferred to a lower-security, "conditional freedom" labor camp but was denied early release until August 2005, when he was unexpectedly freed.

Despite the relatively small number of long-term political prisoners, much larger numbers (possibly several hundred) are subject to short-term imprisonment yearly. The hallmark of the Belarusian situation, however, is not the number of political prisoners per capita but the way in which medium-level repression is able to permeate all aspects of life through self-censorship, fear, and intimidation. Among the most common types of repression observable in Belarus is the beating of opposition politicians and sympathizers by plainclothes thugs at the service of the state, as a way of sowing fear among the opposition. The severe beatings of opposition leaders Valery Frolov and Anatoly Lebedko in 2004 are examples.[15]

"Soft" Political Repression

The hallmark of the Lukashenko regime, however, has not been "hard," open repression but rather more indirect forms of control and intimidation. These methods range from short-term detention and economic harassment of opposition sympathizers to control of the media and educational and political institutions.

Detentions and Arrests. The short-term arrest and subsequent release of opposition protesters (several hundred a year) is also a common intimidation tactic used by the regime.[16] Although the terms of detention may be relatively short (hours or days), political detainees are purposely subjected to especially harsh treatment in a prison system already condemned internationally for its poor conditions and treatment of the prisoner population at large.[17] The judicial system, largely a part of Lukashenko's "presidential vertical" system of power, has little independence from his political dictates.[18] More generally, the presumption of innocence, although enshrined in the Belarus constitution, means little since an overwhelming number of individuals facing criminal charges are found guilty.[19]

Control of the Media. Despite Belarus's high levels of newspaper circulation per capita, access to independent newspapers and media, especially outside the capital, is greatly restricted. The nationwide TV and radio stations are owned by the state and present an exclusively pro-presidential perspective, vilifying the opposition when giving it coverage at all. Although some independent TV and radio stations exist, their coverage is limited to local areas, and to steer clear of conflict with the regime, they focus on entertainment, not information. The foreign radio and TV stations that are accessible— including Radio Liberty–Radio Free Europe, Radio Racija, Deutsche Welle, and Russia's Channel One—broadcast uncensored information, including criticism of the Belarusian regime, but Lukashenko has been known to jam their signals when particularly affronted by the content or when coverage of Belarus is expected. On other occasions, rebroadcasted Russian Channel One programs have been manipulated, with Belarusian footage inserted but presented as part of the Russian program.[20]

Several independent newspapers exist, but they are in a precarious economic condition as they receive no advertising revenue from the state, are regularly subjected to short-term closings, and are seldom available outside Minsk.[21] In late 2005, the state tightened its grip on independent newspapers by denying them access to printing presses, removing them from the centralized subscription list, and denying them distribution rights through the state-owned postal service and the state newspaper kiosk network. Given the lack of alternative mail and retail systems, these measures de facto made it impossible for most readers to access such newspapers.[22]

An existing law punishing insults or libel of the president with up to four years of imprisonment has also been used to intimidate the opposition press. In 2003, the Committee to Protect Journalists ranked Belarus as one of the ten "worst places to be a journalist."[23] The situation of journalists worsened in 2004, as exemplified by the beating of Russian TV journalist Pavel Sheremet and the murder of independent journalist Veronika Cherkasova, the investigation of which was promptly dropped by the police. As a result of these factors, most of the widely available newspapers are either unabashedly pro-Lukashenko or focus on lifestyle features with little political information. Thus the average media consumer—Internet access is limited in Belarus—has practically no access to alternative information sources.

In 2006, restrictions on the distribution of independent newspapers tightened further. The additional limitations placed on the print edition of the daily newspaper *Narodnaya volia* further hampered its ability to reach subscribers. Thus the voice of Belarus's largest remaining nationwide-circulation newspaper—and its only independent daily—has been largely silenced.

Manipulation of Political Institutions. Lukashenko manipulates political institutions for the purpose of remaining in power. Through a 1996 referendum, Lukashenko was able to extend his presidential term, originally scheduled to end in 1999, for two additional years, disband the democratically elected parliament, and gain approval for the establishment of an undisclosed presidential administration budget.[24] Although barred by the constitution from being reelected to a third term, Lukashenko pushed for a referendum in 2004 that approved a constitutional amendment removing presidential term limits.

Economic Harassment of Opponents. Another important form of soft repression has been the harassment of opponents through economic means. A 1999 ban on registering associations at residential addresses created significant problems for nongovernmental organizations. Many local authorities, who continue to control most real estate (and even private landlords fearing government reprisals), refuse to rent to organizations not enjoying the blessing of the regime. For example, most of the real estate in downtown Minsk is controlled by the Presidential Administration. Thus anybody wanting to open a business, register an association, or even hold a meeting has to have the approval of the Presidential Administration. With few other places to choose from, those out of favor with the president are often left with literally no place to go. The European Humanities University, one of the country's few non-state-controlled universities and one actively engaged in academic exchanges with the West, was forced to close down in 2004 when the Presidential Administration refused to renew its rental contract and the Ministry of Education subsequently cancelled the university's license, saying that it lacked adequate physical premises.[25] Similarly, businesses suspected of having connections to the opposition are subjected to extra taxes and other inspection, or are forced to undergo cumbersome registration procedures.[26] Similarly, independent research institutes have been forced to close.[27] Critical newspapers have not received government advertisements—a major potential source of revenue in an economy still largely controlled by the state—for many years.

Some examples of soft repression exercised by the Belarusian regime include a historian's dismissal from her position at the Academy of Sciences ("because positions were being cut") after she ran for parliament in the September 2004 elections as an independent candidate, and pressuring a political scientist to resign from his faculty position at the Belarusian Agrarian Technical University after he published an article in a Moscow academic journal calling the Belarusian regime a dictatorship. Another faculty member who participated in the elections as an opposition candidate was dismissed from his position at the Brest Pedagogical University for "professional unsuitability" on the basis of his "poor record of ideological work" and "lack of sports achievements."[28]

International Behavior

How aggressive is the Lukashenko regime internationally? Is it a threat to its neighbors? Together with Russia, Ukraine, and Kazakhstan, Belarus was one of the four Soviet republics possessing nuclear weapons on its territory at the time of the dissolution of the Soviet Union in 1991. In 1992, the Belarusian government gave up its inherited nuclear weapons and acceded to the Nuclear Non-Proliferation Treaty. The renunciation of nuclear weapons means that the country now has fewer military resources that can be used for playing a dangerously aggressive role in international terms. Nevertheless, Belarus has been able to act as an international outlier in several other areas.[29] Belarus has been suspected of providing weapons to other rogue regimes; Lukashenko has frequently visited Libya and other Middle Eastern states, and supported Slobodan Milosevic's regime in Serbia and Saddam Hussein's in Iraq. In 2003, it became clear that Belarusian passports had been issued to several high-ranking Iraqi officials under Saddam Hussein.[30] As of 2004, Belarus was one of the top twenty weapons exporters in the world, with most weapons going to unstable areas such as the Sudan and Iran.[31] There have been reports that Belarus derived yearly more than $2 billion in weapons sales, "much of which goes into a secret fund controlled directly by the president."[32]

Another security concern centers on Belarus's role as a surrogate for some of the less attractive sides of Russian foreign policy. Russia uses Belarus as a clandestine—or at least little publicized—route for the profitable export of Russian weapons to unstable areas such as Yemen, Algeria, and Syria.[33] In the mid-1990s, Belarus gained increased prominence as a purveyor of unregulated weapons to warring sides in hot conflicts as well as to "rogue states" around the world.

Belarus has also pursued weapons re-sale opportunities without Russia's knowledge.[34] For example, during the 1999 NATO campaign against Serbia, Yugoslav foreign minister Zivadin Jovanovic visited Minsk. Discussions were held on "possible weapons supplies concerning air-defense systems."[35] (Much of Belarusian military-technical cooperation with Russian factories is in the area of air defense systems, so Belarus has much to offer.) Indeed, the real danger seemed to be that by supplying Belgrade with Russian weapons, Minsk enmeshed Moscow even deeper in conflicts where the latter would rather remain on the sidelines. The title of a 1999 *Izvestia* front-page article on this topic was telling: "Minsk Invites Moscow to the Balkans."[36]

Relations with Western institutions such as the European Union, the Council of Europe, and the Organization for Security and Cooperation in Europe remain tense due to their criticism of Lukashenko's repressive policies and the Belarusian regime's unwillingness to engage in real dialogue. Indeed, of all the Central and Eastern European states, Belarus is the only one that has not sought good relations with these institutions. At the same time, it would be simplistic to characterize Belarus policies as pro-Russian.[37]

Lukashenko's voluntaristic and authoritarian means of policymaking may also create tensions with his neighbors and the international community at large. His policymaking style has been characterized by a disregard of formal institutions, including hardly democratic ones such as the government-controlled National Assembly and the various ministries. Instead, Lukashenko has used direct appeals to the masses as well as his own system of keeping high state functionaries in fear. While formal institutions remain in place, the president's practice of issuing direct commands to his ministers limits their role in making important policy decisions. Examples of this leadership style were seen during energy negotiations with Russia, where Lukashenko greatly restricted the negotiating power of relevant actors and their experts, and sought to deal with the issues at a purely political level.[38] One example of this approach was his 2005 call for the building of a new nuclear reactor as a way to break the country's energy dependence on Russia. With 20 percent of its territory still contaminated by the 1986 Chernobyl nuclear accident and as the country that suffered most from it, it is unlikely that the Belarusian population would agree to such a step. Moreover, the prospect of an internationally isolated Belarus building a nuclear reactor when it cannot finance the purchase of advanced technology with adequate safety safeguards worries most of its neighbors.

Whereas Belarus's brand of open repression may be relatively moderate compared to that of other cases analyzed in this book, it is exactly the country's geographical location that makes it such a threat to the regional security system. First, by maintaining a certain degree of social stability "financed" by a close relationship with Russia while simultaneously ignoring both economic reform and real democracy, the Belarusian regime constitutes a dangerous model that politicians in other parts of the former Soviet Union may be tempted to emulate. Second, the Belarusian exception to larger democratization trends in the region is a hole in the web of regional security, diminishing the effectiveness of the pan-European security and political structures built in Europe since 1991.

This consideration became painfully clear in 2005, when Lukashenko, unhappy with the election results in the Union of Poles of Belarus (where an antigovernment leadership was elected), engaged in a systematic harassment of the 20,000-member organization, including the arrest of its leaders. The issue had worrisome international effects, as the preexisting "cold war" between Belarus and Poland escalated rapidly. The Belarusian government expelled several Polish diplomats in mid-2005 and publicly accused the Polish government of intervening in Belarus's internal affairs and masterminding the change of leadership in the Union of Poles. Nearly 500,000 ethnic Poles live in Belarus—equivalent to 5 percent of the population—and such anti-Polish vilification, once consumed by simple people in the countryside with little access to alternative information, can have a very negative impact on interethnic relations in Belarus.[39] The Polish government responded by calling for some kind of intervention by the EU, which in turn reinforced the biggest fears of the Lukashenko regime but also provided it with an excuse for remaining domestically repressive and internationally isolated.

Belarus and Russia

The Belarusian-Russian relationship is complex. On the one hand, Belarus has acted as spokesman for some views and attitudes from which Russia would officially like to distance itself to avoid attracting the wrath of the West. On the other hand, on some occasions, Lukashenko has gone above and beyond Moscow's "expectations," at times embarrassing Russia with extreme declarations, especially concerning attitudes toward the West and NATO expansion. One of Lukashenko's favorite roles has been to show himself as Russia's defender in the face an "aggressive and encroaching" Western alliance. In the words of a prominent member of the outlawed Belarusian parliament, "The 'demand' for Lukashenkism can only exist in the context of a divided Europe, in the context of an atmosphere of enmity and suspicion—and that is why it is to Lukashenko's advantage that that atmosphere is maintained."[40] In other words, Lukashenko can only maintain his position as Russia's steadfast ally by actually undermining Russia's relationships with other partners, especially the West. Doing so might not be difficult, as Lukashenko has become a "public relations disaster" for Moscow.[41] Based on size, population, and economic and military power, it makes sense to regard Belarus as the junior partner in the relationship with Russia; yet for political reasons,

Lukashenko has been in a position to "blackmail" the Russian leadership into accepting his proposals.

Lukashenko's self-appointed role as Russia's spokesman and defender vis-à-vis NATO has also been convenient for Russia. It is only through Lukashenko's lips that Russia could afford to make some of its most aggressive comments about the North Atlantic Treaty Alliance, positions that the Russian leadership could not afford to voice openly until 2007 without endangering its often tense but polite relationship with the West.[42] However, such a role for Belarus has been complicated by the challenges of the post–September 11 world, as Russia's participation in the antiterrorist alliance left little space for Lukashenko's anti-NATO rhetoric. At the same time, Belarus's growing isolation in the wake of EU expansion has put the country more on the spot than before: now surrounded on all but two of its borders by EU members (Poland, Latvia, and Lithuania), Belarus's abnormality becomes even more obvious and problematic.

Isolation and Self-Isolation

These modest manifestations of active aggression in international affairs have been compounded by isolationism. Some aspects of this isolation are the result of concrete policies by the Lukashenko regime to keep Belarusians from enjoying Central and Western European standards of political and economic freedom. What the Belarusian regime has denounced as Western isolationist attitudes toward Belarus (referring to resolutions and sanctions by PACE, the EU, OSCE, and the UN) are, first and foremost, responses to Lukashenko's repressive policies. Belarus's answer to UN and OSCE resolutions calling for attention to human rights issues has been to call for the reform of those organizations, questioning both their interest in Belarus and the basic values expressed in their resolutions.[43]

The story of Belarus's response to a 2002 World Bank program to fight AIDS, malaria, and tuberculosis is a telling example of the way in which the country has dealt with Western interests: the $28.8 million aid project was rejected because Belarus could cope on its own with "decreasing" levels of AIDS, malaria, and tuberculosis.[44] Given the high growth rates of both HIV/AIDS and tuberculosis in the former Soviet Union (with Russia, Ukraine, and Belarus having one of the fastest-growing rates of HIV/AIDS infection in the world) and Belarus's role as part of the Eurasian transit route for illegal immigrants from Africa and Asia to Western Europe, the country's refusal to participate in such projects has implications that go well beyond its borders.

As a result of these and similar experiences, the World Bank, International Monetary Fund, the United Nations, and the European Union have significantly downgraded or eliminated their offices in Belarus. The Organization for Security and Cooperation in Europe, one international organization that sought to maintain a high profile and a real presence in Belarus, has been subject to constant pressure and harassment by the Belarusian government since the mid-1990s.

One important source of stability for Belarus is the country's relative isolation from foreign influences. It allows the regime to keep part of its population (especially the population outside Minsk) in the dark about both what is really happening in Belarus and about the results of a decade and a half of reform in the neighboring states of Lithuania and Poland. In the official Belarusian version, economic reform in these states, as a result of Western-inspired shock therapies, has led to mass unemployment and pauperization, in contrast to the largely "stable" economic situation in Belarus. The Belarusian regime has been able to maintain this largely inaccurate picture through control of print and electronic media and through its policies concerning nongovernmental organizations (NGOs).

NGOs in Belarus not only defend human rights but also disseminate accurate information regarding internationally accepted Western human rights standards. Through a variety of measures, the Belarusian regime has sought to undermine both aspects of their work. The regime has engaged in veiled and outright repression of Western-related NGOs through taxation of humanitarian aid, constant calls for reregistration, and closure. By 2004, human rights-related NGOs were "effectively prohibited" from receiving support from foreign sources.[45] Registration rules were tightened in 2004, with only NGOs involved in "social work," "social-ecological work," and "Chernobyl work" (as defined by the state) allowed to register; as a result, most human rights NGOs were denied official registration. These and other unregistered NGOs are condemned to invisibility (the law prohibits the media from disseminating information on behalf of unregistered NGOs) and to work outside the law, thus making them a constant target.[46]

Other policies have attempted to counteract the effects of globalization and of growing international interest in NGOs in Belarus by creating filters between these organizations and their foreign sponsors. An example of this policy was an announcement that the Belarusian government would require organizations to be prequalified by a state agency before being allowed to apply for EU-funded programs such as Technical Assistance to the Commonwealth of Independent States. Such policy was also related to the government's effort to create regime-sponsored pseudo-NGOs (akin to what Priscilla Clapp refers to as "sham civic organizations" in Burma), giving them preference in the EU grant-seeking process by excluding other, legitimate organizations from the competition.[47]

How the Regime Retains Power

Lukashenko has been able to remain in power by relying on sources of stability, using hard and soft repression, limiting the development of private economic activities, and increasing the regime's use of ideology.

While subjecting the opposition to hard and soft repression, the Lukashenko regime also blackmails and even terrorizes its own parliamentary deputies.[48] Although "government by blackmail" is not unique to Lukashenko's regime, he has taken this tactic to new heights, having one of his own ministers arrested during a cabinet meeting, in front of the TV cameras.[49] Accumulating incriminating evidence on his closest associates is not hard for Lukashenko, given that most possibilities for lucrative economic activities are concentrated in the powerful Presidential Administration. While it may be hard to refuse an invitation to serve on Lukashenko's staff, accepting a post often entails the risk of landing in jail.[50] After the 2004 referendum, legislation was passed subjecting business leaders to dismissal, fines, or criminal prosecution and jail should they fail to comply with expected production targets, be found responsible for worsening the economic situation, or for "seriously endangering the state of societal interests"—thus providing Lukashenko with additional means to keep the highest members of the *nomenklatura* under control.[51]

This system of making officials dependent on the approval of the regime was widened to reach lower-level state employees in 2004, when all state employees (and employees of state-owned businesses) were moved to short-term contracts (usually six months or a year). This new contract system helped the regime solidify its control by giving the state an easy means of dismissing independent union members and opposition activists and, more generally, causing employees to fear loss of employment if they oppose Lukashenko. More concretely, the timing of the measure—just before the referendum—was seen as exerting pressure on state employees working in election commissions to acquiesce in the manipulation of the voting process.[52]

Lukashenko's frequent rough handling of his own staff not only reflects his own personal fancy but is also part of a political strategy. Keeping middle- and high-level officials in fear of the president gives them less opportunity to organize as a possible "nomenklatura opposition." At the same time, periodically "cleaning up" corruption in the upper ranks of government strengthens Lukashenko's image as a "benevolent czar," prevented from carrying out policies for the masses only by the interference of self-interested officials. Lukashenko thus creates the perception of a direct, unmediated link between himself and the population—which explains why he has not created his own political party.

While securing some form of stability in the short term, the widespread use of blackmail actually reflects the weaknesses and lack of real institutionalization of the Lukashenko regime. Indeed, the Lukashenko regime remains fundamentally noninstitutionalized in the sense that it is fully dependent on the dictator's own charismatic appeal to the population and his system of control over subordinates at all levels (the so-called presidential vertical). These dynamics reveal the personalistic nature of the regime and may also help in understanding the resistance to the Lukashenko regime that could potentially come from within the ranks of his own administration.

The Lukashenko regime has also sought to hinder the development of private enterprise, which fits well with a state-controlled economic model.[53] According to the Index of Economic Freedom, Belarus ranks near the bottom worldwide in terms of economic freedom, listed 145th among 157 countries.[54] Moreover, Lukashenko's antientrepreneurial rhetoric resonates easily with a population in need of scapegoats to blame for a decline in living standards since the dissolution of the Soviet Union. Lukashenko also fears the political competition that could arise from strong economic actors independent of the state.

Lukashenko fears the emergence of other domestic or foreign centers of economic power (besides the Presidential Administration, which de facto controls much of Belarus's business). His techniques for exerting almost total political power include preventing the emergence of autonomous sources of economic power, "privatizing" the shadow economy to use it for his own purposes and to augment the shadow budget available to the Presidential Administration, and ensuring that all major political and economic players in the country—from entrepreneurs to cabinet-level ministers—remain dependent on his personal favor.[55] Such strategies can only work where no strong interest groups exist and where the impact of any interest group is severely limited by a centralized system of national interest articulation and policymaking.

Most important, the relative lack of alternatives to state employment—an estimated 80 percent of the population depends on government salaries, stipends, or pensions—gives economic intimidation much more impact than it would have in a situation in which individuals were more economically independent of the state. The fact that state institutions continue to have a near-monopoly on individual advancement opportunities also means more opportunities for the Lukashenko regime's brand of low- to medium-level coercion and control.

The Lukashenko regime has also used as a central mechanism "Belarusian ideology," which stresses the importance of sovereignty in the face of outside interference but lacks much concrete content.[56] Starting in 2002, Lukashenko began to emphasize the need to develop such a national ideology and to establish the institutional vehicles to promote it.[57]

Some of these vehicles have been the establishment of pro-Lukashenko youth organizations and "ideological education" at educational institutions and in the workplace. Membership in the government-controlled Belarusian Republican Youth Movement, modeled on the Soviet Komsomol, is a prerequisite for students hoping to maintain good academic standing and housing.[58] Since 2004, students at Belarusian universities must pass a course on "Foundations of the Ideology of the Belarusian State," based on instructions in a 700-page textbook.[59] In the workplace, ideological control has been furthered by the appointment of a person in charge of "ideological work" at each institution—even in private companies—and the establishment of mandatory monthly workplace meetings to discuss ideology.[60] Although not necessarily related to the promotion of a pro-regime ideology, a 2004 law allowing military units to adopt orphans between the ages of fourteen and sixteen (under the condition that they join the unit when they reach eighteen) is another worrisome indication of the growing role of the state in citizens' lives.

The centerpiece of Belarusian ideology is the elevation of Belarusian sovereignty. The importance of sovereignty is used to justify ignoring calls for change in the regime's domestic policies. With a periodic deterioration of Lukashenko's relations with Russia, this anti-Western rhetoric sometimes turns into something resembling North Korea's *juche* (self-reliance), but in a mild and rather pathetic form since Belarus cannot in practice isolate itself from the rest of the world. It is located in the very heart of Europe, and its very livelihood depends on its role as an important transit route from Western Europe to Russia and vice versa. In fact, one of the main sources of the regime's stability from 1994 to 2006 was Russia's heavy subsidization of Belarus's economy. This support was related to Belarus's role in gas and oil transit, and in oil refining and the subsequent export of high-priced petroleum products.[61]

Changes after the October 2004 Referendum and March 2006 Presidential Elections

On October 17, 2004, a referendum occurred in Belarus regarding whether presidential term limits should be removed. In fact, preparation for the referendum highlighted the various forms of repression used by the regime: intimidation, control of state media, and economic pressure. The poll followed pro-Lukashenko propaganda on state-controlled radio and TV and was widely characterized as undemocratic. Lukashenko won what he called an "elegant victory" of 77 percent in favor of removing term limits, opening the way for him to run again for president in 2006. In the parliamentary elections that took place on the same day, not a single opposition candidate managed to be elected to the National Assembly. This result was not surprising, as many opposition candidates were not allowed to register, and many of those who managed to register were often intimidated, subject to dismissal from their workplaces, and not allowed to advertise in the national media.

Lukashenko's "victory" in the 2004 referendum gave the Belarusian regime a new burst of self-confidence. Thus, after 2004, Lukashenko's regime entered a new stage of development toward a greater institutionalization of its authoritarian and isolationist features. Pressure on the opposition intensified, as demonstrated by the show trial of opposition leader Mikhail Marynich. The Law on Organs of State Security was modified to allow the State Security Committee (*Komitet gosudarstvennoi bezopasnosti* [KGB]) officers to enter any home—by force if necessary—without previous permission by a judge, with the provision that they inform a prosecutor within twenty-four hours.[62] Another law, passed in late 2005, made "defaming" the country's government abroad a criminal act.

This trend toward increased self-confidence further strengthened after the presidential elections of March 2006, in which Lukashenko won 82.6 percent of the votes. Although there is little doubt that Lukashenko had a plurality of voters' support, the official results were hard to take seriously. Leaving aside the fact that the opposition had little access to the media, the elections themselves were plagued with irregularities (for example, high levels of officially sponsored early voting, which made the process much more difficult to monitor by international observers), and the entire process was characterized by a lack of transparency.

The United States and the European Union declared the 2006 election invalid, illegitimate, and rigged. They said that the election had been conducted in an atmosphere of intimidation and called for a new race. Answering such criticism, Lukashenko defiantly said that the outcome had "convincingly demonstrated who the Belarusians are and who is the master of the house."[63]

Alexandr Milinkevich, the chief opposition candidate and former physics professor with broad international experience (he was a visiting fellow at the University of California in the late 1990s), received 6 percent of the vote. However, he refused to recognize the results, calling for a revote free of arrests or harassment. Before the poll, Lukashenko had promised to "wring the necks" of protesters. His police had arrested hundreds of opposition activists and beaten Aleksandr Kazulin, a key presidential candidate, during a rally. The police had also expelled students and dismissed state workers suspected of opposition sympathies.[64]

The opposition responded to the manipulation of the elections with a peaceful and rather small tent city in central Minsk, which was allowed to stand for about five days, so long as the international press remained. But this façade of tolerance did not last. Further emboldened by the results of the election, the president felt even less constrained in his power. Repression increased—he declared in March 2006 that "the opposition will be dismantled in a tough way after the elections."[65] These trends were confirmed with the arrest, trial, and sentencing to five-and-a-half years in jail of Kazulin in mid-2006 on charges of organizing antigovernment demonstrations after the election.

Shortly thereafter, four local election observers were sentenced to jail terms for up to two years under a 2005 law restricting public protests. After arresting them in February, before the presidential poll, the chief of the KGB publicly accused the four of plotting a violent coup. (The observers had received some of their support from Washington's National Democratic Institute.)

Stability and Instability

To understand the Lukashenko regime's sources of stability and instability, one must also understand the roots of its power. Examining long-term (history, culture, identity), medium-term (demographic changes, Soviet legacies), and short-term factors (Lukashenko's own charismatic role, Russian economic support) can help explain why, of all the Central and Eastern European countries, Belarus is the only one where a demagogical, repressive regime emerged, and also why this regime has been able to remain in power despite significant domestic problems and changes in its immediate international environment.[66]

Sources of Stability

Some of the most important sources of the Lukashenko regime's stability lie in Belarus's history and culture. (However, a historically or culturally deterministic view cannot fully explain the situation in Belarus.) During World War II Belarus was devastated, its capital was largely destroyed, and its previously richly multiethnic population was decimated. This legacy has led a significant part of the population to adopt a resigned and even passive attitude, best reflected by the Russian-language phrase *"lish by ne bylo voiny,"* loosely translated as "we can bear anything—just spare us war."[67]

Other sources of stability for the Lukashenko regime rest in the demographic, urbanization, and industrialization processes occurring in Belarus since the end of World War II. As a result, Belarus became "the most perfectly Soviet of the Soviet republics." These legacies and memories of the Soviet period largely explain Lukashenko's appeal to the Belarusian population. In addition, despite high levels of urbanization, most city dwellers come from the countryside and are not highly politicized.

Factors based in Lukashenko's personality are also at work, in particular his charisma and his ability to connect with the "common people" and provide easy answers to some difficult questions concerning the effects of the dissolution of the Soviet Union on Belarus.[68] Lukashenko's personal appeal to the less-educated and rural population stands in clear contrast to the opposition, which has the image of being dominated by intellectuals from Minsk and has been unable to establish a direct connection to the population.(Furthermore, it has been weakened by infighting.) The 75, 77, and 92 percent figures showing support for Lukashenko in the 2001 presidential elections, the 2004 referendum, and the 2006 referendum, respectively, are clearly overstated; a variety of polls place real popular support for Lukashenko at around 30–40 percent, with an additional 30 percent disliking him strongly and 30 percent being unsure.[69] However, it should not be assumed that the 30 percent of the population strongly disliking Lukashenko supports the opposition or is politically active.

Despite the ups and downs of Belarusian-Russian relations in recent years and the stalling of the much-heralded Russian-Belarusian unification process, Russian support remains essential for the survival of the Lukashenko regime.[70] Belarus has received significant direct subsidies in the form of currency stabilization programs related to the integration process with Russia, as well as subsidized oil and gas supplies. More indirectly, the Lukashenko regime, riding on Russia's oil boom, derives substantial income from its own oil refining industry. Revenues from legal and illegal transit services (taking advantage of the open border with Russia) also provide substantial income to Lukashenko's Presidential Administration and to a large group of small-scale "shuttle traders" who sell imports from Russia and other countries at open-air markets.[71]

To understand Belarus's importance for Russia, it is important to keep in mind the country's important geographical position as the former Soviet Union's westernmost state. From a Russian perspective, this has become even more important since the dissolution of the USSR and the expansion of NATO. Given its complicated relationships with Lithuania and Ukraine, Russia's "most convenient and direct access to the West is through Belarus."[72] Since the fall of the Soviet Union and the exodus of the Baltic states, Belarus—together with Kaliningrad Oblast—remains the only zone of Russian influence on the borders with NATO. As part of its military agreements with Russia, Belarus maintains an air defense system in the western area of the Commonwealth of Independent States, acting as Russia's air safety "shield." These arrangements help explain why Russia has continued to support the Lukashenko regime despite its often less than friendly tirades against Russia.[73]

Sources of Instability

Despite Lukashenko's tight control over Belarusian society and the non-Minsk population's general distrust of the opposition and aversion to change, the Lukashenko regime is potentially weak. Belarus has boasted a degree of economic and wage stability in comparison with neighboring Russia and Ukraine, but this comparative advantage is diminishing as incomes averaging $218 a month are eaten away by inflation.[74] In addition, Belarus's isolation from the EU is becoming increasingly difficult to maintain, particularly as post–Orange Revolution Ukraine moves closer to the West.

Changes in Russia's value-added tax structure in 2005 created a wave of small-entrepreneur mass mobilization. The application of value-added tax on an importing-country basis means a 10 to 18 percent increase on final prices, which represents a double threat to the regime as it reduces the availability of low-cost products on which the population can rely to maintain a minimally acceptable standard of living.[75] Shuttle traders have emerged among the lower middle class, and the trade has become an important source of additional income for underemployed citizens who might otherwise turn their frustration into political activism.[76]

Russian support, essential for maintaining the regime in power, may come to an end as the contradictions in the Russian-Belarusian relationship become increasingly clear. Domestically, the most important factor, however, is the mounting frustration of middle- and high-level officials, who find themselves powerless in the face of Lukashenko's whims. Should Russia eventually decide not to support Lukashenko and instead put its weight behind a nomenklatura candidate, dissatisfied high-level officials may become important as agents of change.[77]

Since late 2006, the Belarusian-Russian relationship has deteriorated sharply because of Russia's imposition of steep increases in the price of natural gas sold to Belarus, the reduction of oil trade arrangements bringing Belarus several billion U.S. dollars annually, and the near-cessation of refined beet sugar imports from Belarus. The reduction of these important sources of income may have significant implications for Lukashenko's ability to remain in power, as well as for the regime's international "rogueness." In the medium term, a reduction of Russian support may lead to deteriorating living standards and a loss of economic legitimacy for the regime. However, in the short term, Lukashenko has been able to use the conflict with Russia to emphasize his own nationalist credentials. In international terms, the results of the growing conflict with Russia are twofold. The European Union has seized this window of opportunity to make special efforts to engage Belarus in a political dialogue. However, the partial loss of Russian subsidies may prompt the regime to expand weapons export operations.

U.S. Policies toward Belarus

For many years, one main challenge to U.S. and Western policy in Belarus was the West's limited opportunities to exert influence.[78] Many of these limitations remain, reinforced by Lukashenko's policy of isolation. Yet two trends may open the door to new means of constructive influence in the Belarusian human rights situation: the enlargement of the European Union to Belarus's borders and Russia's own uneasiness about the relationship. The United States is already well respected among the Belarusian opposition for remaining firm in its positions concerning human rights violations in Belarus. It should continue to support local NGOs with an eye toward gradual, long-term results. Lukashenko's personal role is undoubtedly the driving force behind his repressive regime, but large structural factors, such as the weakness of NGOs, have facilitated the regime's emergence and consolidation. These longer-term factors are likely to remain as obstacles to democracy even when Lukashenko eventually leaves the political scene. Thus, the United States should adopt a two-pronged policy, pressing the Belarusian government to live up to its official human rights commitments in the short term and promoting the development of a truly democratic society in the medium and long term. In doing so, it should not be afraid to push Belarus into an "even closer embrace with Russia." Rather, the United States should use the contradictions and tensions existing in the Belarusian-Russian relationship to support greater respect for human rights.

Conclusion: Measuring and Understanding Repression in Belarus

There are several problems involved in seeking to measure repression in Belarus using conventional measures, such as the number of long-term political prisoners and the number of people executed for political reasons. First, Belarus has not attracted enough interest from the international community to have very detailed human rights reports devoted to it. Although the U.S. State Department's *2006 Country Report on Human Rights Practices* devotes a full thirty-five pages to Belarus (many of them analyzing current legislation), other annual reports, such as those of Human Rights Watch and Amnesty International, usually devote only three or four pages to Belarus.[79] Most of the materials available, especially those collected firsthand by Belarusian organizations, are devoted to documenting specific cases of human rights violations rather than to creating a quantitative database. Second, human rights organizations working in Belarus are themselves subject to significant repression and thus are not in the best position to monitor the situation.

The most serious challenge to measuring the level of repression in Belarus has to do with the type of repression. While serious physical violence against the opposition exists, the kind of repression most often seen in Belarus is not blatant or violent but indirect. It ranges from widespread "mild" physical violence to short-term arrests on administrative grounds to the threat of economic reprisals. Many of these subtler forms of repression work on the subconscious level, meaning that the regime need only hint at them, not always apply them, in order to be effective. This combination of a multitude of small and medium-level repressive and intimidating measures makes the Belarusian system under Lukashenko a qualitatively very different regime compared to the semiauthoritarianism observable in places like Russia, Azerbaijan, or (until recently) Ukraine. The institutional changes that Lukashenko has introduced since 1994 make it increasingly impossible for common citizens and high functionaries to escape the web of his control.

According to most standard understandings of repression, Belarus is simply not a highly "repressive" state. That is, if one defines repression as the use of open violence against opponents of a regime, then Belarus would not be considered a state actively fighting against a population that is decidedly set against the regime. Instead, the Belarusian government uses a variety of means to prevent its population from being informed and becoming politically engaged in the first place. So, subjectively, the population may not feel as if it is being heavily repressed.

In Belarus, repression is a way of life and something that many people largely take for granted. That it can operate largely at a subconscious level is a result of the fact that it builds upon the pre-Soviet and Soviet Belarusian experience, especially the valuation of personal safety above all else, a hard-learned lesson of a war that decimated the Belarusian population. Many Belarusians do not feel unqualifiedly free, but many of them—especially in the countryside—see this as natural in the context of a direct, almost father-child relationship between them and the leader, and not necessarily as active repression.

Urban dwellers and those with a larger degree of exposure to the foreign world, however, feel more subjectively repressed. But even in these cases, people's concepts of repression, self-repression, and the available alternatives are often colored by their view of the opposition. Indeed, in the case of Belarus, there is a connection between the subjective feeling of repression and the perception of available alternatives. The opposition's lack of popularity means that confronted with the choice between making themselves vulnerable to repression by supporting an opposition that they see as ineffective anyway, or falling back upon the well-learned traditions of self-repression and political passivity, many Belarusians will naturally choose the latter. The point is not that the regime would be unwilling to use even more brute force to suppress opposition if it saw fit but that the effectiveness of isolation, preemptive censorship, and intimidation, which build upon Belarus's history and experience, makes even higher levels of open repression unnecessary.

Notes

1. A scholarly literature has started to develop around this issue. See, for example, Marina Ottaway, *Democracy Challenged: The Rise of Semi-Authoritarianism* (Washington,

D.C., 2003); Steven Levitsky and Lucan Way, "The Rise of Competitive Authoritarianism," *Journal of Democracy*, XIII (2002), 51–65.

2. United Nations Development Programme, *Human Development Report 2006: Beyond Scarcity: Poverty, Power, and the Global Water Crisis* (New York, November 2006), hdr.undp.org/hdr2006/statistics/. Belarus's HDR rankings have been declining recently, however.

3. The figures for Belarus and Turkmenistan are from "Newspaper Circulation (per Capita) by Country" (2007), www.nationmaster.com/graph/med_new_cir_ percap-media-newspaper-circulation-per-capita, citing UNESCO Institute for Statistics, March 11, 2003. The latest available data for Russia are from 1996; see "Russia Facts and Figures" (2007), encarta.msn.com/fact_631504846/Russia_Facts_and_ Figures.html, citing the UNESCO database.

4. For a discussion of the situation leading to Lukashenko's election in 1994, see Rainer Lindner, "The Lukashenko Phenomenon," in Margarita Balmaceda, James Clem, and Lisbeth Tarlow (eds.), *Independent Belarus: Domestic Determinants, Regional Dynamics and Implications for the West* (Cambridge, Mass., 2002), 77–108.

5. John C. Reppert, "Belarus and European Security," in Balmaceda, Clem, and Tarlow, *Independent Belarus*, 256–269.

6. The so-called Parliament of the Thirteenth Convocation was disbanded by Lukashenko in 1996 and replaced by the pro-Lukashenko National Assembly. The "old" parliament continued to function underground for some time and distinguished itself from the new, Lukashenko-controlled parliament by using the name "Thirteenth Supreme Soviet" or "Supreme Soviet of the Thirteenth Convocation."

7. Margarita Balmaceda, James Clem, and Lisbeth Tarlow, "Introduction," in Balmaceda, Clem, and Tarlow, *Independent Belarus*, 3–20.

8. If in 1997 average monthly salaries amounted to $100, by early 2007 they had increased to nearly $300. For 1997 data, see Human Rights Watch, "Human Rights Watch World Report 1998: Republic of Belarus" (1998), www.hrw.org/worldreport/ Helsinki-04.htm. For 2007 data, see "Average Inflation-Adjusted Monthly Pay Reported Down 9.5 Percent in January," *Belaruskie novosti* (February 28, 2007), naviny. by/rubrics/inter/2007/02/28/ic_news_259_267457/.

9. In early 2004, the Parliamentary Assembly of the Council of Europe published a report accusing high-ranking officials of involvement in the disappearances. See Human Rights Watch, "Human Rights Overview: Belarus" (January, 2005), hrw.org/ english/docs/2005/01/13/belaru9878.htm.

10. Amnesty International, "Amnesty International Report 2002: Belarus" (2002), web.amnesty.org/web/ar2002.nsf/eur/belarus!Open.

11. Current law provides for up to four years of imprisonment or two years of detention in internal exile for those found guilty of public insults or libel against the president.

12. The equipment had been given free of charge by the U.S. embassy to the Business Initiative organization for temporary use. See Charter 97, "Belarus News Update" (February 14, 2005), www.charter97.org. Marynich was freed in April 2006.

13. The sentence was automatically reduced to two years under the terms of a general amnesty announced to commemorate the sixtieth anniversary of Soviet victory against fascist Germany in World War II.

14. Amnesty International, "Belarus 2003" (January 2007), www.web.amnesty.org/web/web.nsf/print/7D1E4C692F67CE3780256E860041C911. See also David Marples, "Bandazhevsky Case Highlights Chernobyl Controversies," *Eurasia Daily Monitor*, II (March 7, 2005), www.jamestown.org/publications_details.php?volume_id=407&issue_id=3253&article_id=2369374.

15. Frolov was beaten up by "thugs" at the entrance of his apartment building, while Lebedko was beaten during a political demonstration.

16. See Amnesty International, "Belarus 2003." During March 2000 Freedom Day protests, for example, around 500 demonstrators were arrested for several hours.

17. As of 2006, the total number of prisoners was officially reported to be 35,000. See U.S. State Department, "Belarus," in *2006 Country Reports on Human Rights Practices* (Washington, D.C., March 6, 2007), www.state.gov/g/drl/rls/hrrpt/2006/78802.htm. The 2001 Belarus Helsinki Committee's report described overall jail conditions as "not only unsanitary but also life-threatening." For an English summary, see International Helsinki Federation for Human Rights, "Belarus" (January 2007), www.ihf-hr.org/viewbinary/viewdocument.php?doc_id=2691.

18. In addition, all lawyers are subordinated to the Ministry of Justice, and some of those defending nongovernmental organizations or opposition figures have been denied official registration.

19. In 1998—the last year that the Belarusian Helsinki Committee made statistics available—more than 99.5 percent of those accused were found guilty. Cited in U.S. State Department, "Belarus," in *2003 Country Reports on Human Rights Practices* (February 25, 2004), www.state.gov/g/drl/rls/hrrpt/2003/27827.htm.

20. Human Rights Watch, "Belarus."

21. The government reserves the right to close a newspaper after two warnings. In mid-2003, for example, the highly regarded independent newspaper *Belaruskaya delovakia gazeta* (*Belarusian Business Newspaper*) was closed down for three months after government warnings concerning its publication of news about the trial of Mikhail Leonov, a former Lukashenko associate, and about Lukashenko's use of the presidential airplane to fly a Russian model visiting him. In 2004, twenty-five independent newspapers were temporarily suspended. See U.S. State Department, "Belarus," in *2004 Country Reports on Human Rights Practices* (Washington, D.C., February 28, 2005), www.state.gov/g/drl/rls/hrrpt/2004/41671.htm.

22. U.S. State Department, "Belarus," in *2005 Country Reports on Human Rights Practices* (Washington, D.C., March 8, 2006), www.state.gov/g/drl/rls/hrrpt/2005/ 61638.htm.

23. See Human Rights Watch, "Belarus."

24. The size of this secret budget has been estimated at between $3 and $10 billion, compared to the country's official budget of $12 billion. This money is directly available to the president, with no oversight attached.

25. Before it closed, the European Humanities University had joint programs in place with French (political science), German (European studies), and U.S. (American studies) universities and was a frequent host to Fulbright visiting lecturers. In 2005, with support from the European Union, international foundations, and the Lithuanian government, some degree programs were reestablished in Vilnius.

26. Most businesses not controlled by the Presidential Administration fall into this category.

27. On March 15, 2005, the supreme court of Belarus ordered the closing of the Independent Institute of Socio-Economic and Political Studies (NISEPI) on the basis of formal violations of registration rules, such as not lodging its main office at the registered address and repeated use of the abbreviated name of the organization. The government's wrath fell on NISEPI after it conducted Gallup-supported exit polls at the October 2004 referendum that showed the real level of support for the president to be much lower than that officially announced.

28. Other university administrators have lost their jobs due to smaller offenses. For example, in 2005, two officials of Baranovichi State University lost their positions after a group of students from the university performed a sketch critical of President Lukashenko on a national TV student show. See Charter 97, "Belarus News Update" (January 21, 2005), www.charter97.org.

29. See Gary K. Bertsch and William C. Potter, *Dangerous Weapons, Desperate States: Russia, Belarus, Ukraine and Kazakhstan* (New York, 1999).

30. Human Rights Watch, "Belarus."

31. From 1997 to 2004, Belarus ranked tenth in weapons deliveries to developing countries, with a total of $1.6 billion in sales. Congressional Research Service, "Conventional Arms Transfers to Developing Nations, 1997–2004" (Washington, D.C., August 29, 2005), 65. See also Stockholm International Peace Research Institute, "SIPRI Arms Transfers Database" (January 2007), www.sipri.org/contents/armstrad/access. html#twenty. For a detailed discussion of alleged sales of Russian weapons to Yemen, Syria, the Sudan, and Algeria between 1995 and 2005, see Simon Araloff, "Clandestine Routes of the Russian Weapons" (July 27, 2005), www.axisglobe.com/article.asp?article=280. However, the information he provides should be taken with a grain of salt, as few sources are provided.

32. Adrian Bloomfeld, "White House Report Alleges Belarus Has Sold Arms to Iran," *Telegraph* (March 19, 2006), www.telegraph.co.uk/news/main.jhtml?xml=/news/2006/03/19/wbelarus19.xml.

33. Araloff, "Clandestine Routes for Russian Weapons."

34. Belarus and Russia have not reached agreement on the issue of prohibiting the reexport of Russian weapons. See Yuri Golotiuk, "Minsk priglashaet Moskvy na Balkany," *Izvestia* (March 4, 1999).

35. Aleksandr Kozyr, president of the Foreign Affairs Commission of the (official) parliament. Ibid.

36. Golotiuk, "Minsk."

37. Belarusian policy can be characterized as clearly pro-Russian only during the mid-1990s. For most of the period after 1997, however, these relations can be characterized as highly ambiguous. See Yuri Drakokhrust and Dmitri Furman, "Perepety integratsii," in Dmitri E. Furman (ed.), *Belorusia i Rossia: Obshestva i gosudarstva* (Moscow, 1998); Yuri Drakokhrust and Dmitri Furman, "Belarus and Russia: The Game of 'Virtual Integration,'" in Balmaceda, Clem, and Tarlow, *Independent Belarus*, 232–255; Margarita Balmaceda, "Myth and Reality in the Belarusian-Russian Relationship," *Problems of Post-Communism*, XLVI (1999), 3–14.

38. For example, during negotiations about gas supplies from Russia in 2004, even though the country was nearly cut off, Lukashenko delayed resolution by not giving the high-level negotiators sent to Moscow any real power to sign agreements. See Alexander Blokhin (Belarus's ambassador to Russia), in Tatiana Manenok, "Premeri ne dogovorilis," *Belorusski rynok*, XVI (April 28, 2004). Similarly, negotiations over possible Russian investments in the gas transit company Beltransgas have been significantly slowed due to Lukashenko's desire personally to control each step of the process.

39. See Marek Ziolkowski, "Relations with Belarus," *Yearbook of Polish Foreign Policy* (Warsaw, 1997), cited in Agnieszka Magdziak-Miszewska, "Belarus: Poland's Strange Neighbor," in Balmaceda, Clem, and Tarlow, *Independent Belarus*, 344–365.

40. Anatoly Lebedko, interview with author, December 22, 1997.

41. See Kathleen J. Mihalisko, "Belarus: Retreat to Authoritarianism," in Karen Dawisha and Bruce Parrot (eds.), *Democratic Changes and Authoritarian Reactions in Russia, Ukraine, Belarus, and Moldova* (Cambridge, 1997), 275.

42. Lebedko, interview.

43. See Aleksander Feduta and others, *Belarusskii ezhegodnik 2003* (Vilnius, 2004), 106.

44. See Olga Birikova, "Na konu budusche sotrudnichestvo," *Belorusski rynok*, XX (2004), B13. On the World Bank proposal, see also *Belorusski rynok*, XV, XXI, XXXI (2002) and XIII, XXI, and XXXVII (2003).

45. State Department, "Belarus," *2004 Country Reports*. Presidential Edict 24 of November 28, 2003, prohibits foreign funding to educational and political activities. Human Rights Watch, "Belarus."

46. State Department, "Belarus," *2004 Country Reports*.

47. Priscilla Clapp, "Burma," paper prepared for Rogue States II Conference, John F. Kennedy School of Government (Cambridge, Mass., April 28–30, 2005), 6. See also Priscilla Clapp, chapter 6 in this volume.

48. For an excellent discussion of how these mechanisms work in practice and how the use of fear affects officials at all levels, see Viktor Dashuk, "Bal satani," *Narodnaya volia* (Minsk) (May 17, 2005), 3–6. Dashuk is a well-known Belarusian film director who was deprived of work after falling out with the regime.

49. See Keith A. Darden, "Blackmail as a Tool of State Domination: Ukraine under Kuchma," *Eastern European Constitutional Review*, X (2001), www.law.nyu.edu/eecr/vol10num2_3/focus/darden.html.

50. Such was the case for Tamara Vinnikova, former head of the National Bank of Belarus, arrested in the mid-1990s (and later allowed to leave the country secretly) and for Galina Zhuravleva, one of the heads of the Presidential Administration, who was arrested in 2003 on accusations of large-scale corruption. The harshest sentence imposed on a former Lukashenko ally was an eleven-year prison term for corruption against Yegor Rybakov, former head of the government-controlled Belarusian State Television and Radio Company.

51. See Andrei Podvitskii, "Nari dlia nomenklatury," *Belarusskaya gazeta*, LI (December 27, 2004).

52. See State Department, "Belarus," *2004 Country Reports.*

53. As of 2004, the private sector produced only 20 percent of Belarus's GDP, while in neighboring countries it was responsible for 60–80 percent of GDP. Leonid Zlotnikov, "Faktor nomer 1—Rossia," *Belorusski rynok*, XVI (April 28, 2004).

54. Heritage Foundation and Wall Street Journal, "2006 Index of Economic Freedom" (January 2007), www.heritage.org/research/features/index/countries.cfm.

55. Lukashenko has not only annihilated any possible sources of independent economic power but is believed by many to have largely privatized Belarusian mafia activities for himself or for the Presidential Administration. Lukashenko's personal presidential machinery is estimated to employ up to 5,000 people and have a very substantial budget; it seems to have become a shadow government itself. The Belarusian opposition asserts that the size of the Presidential Administration's budget is commensurate with the country's yearly budget. Author's interviews, Minsk, November–December 1997, November 2001, and March 2004.

56. One might consider the question of why Lukashenko decided to develop a "national ideology" after 2003. At a certain level, it could be argued that this was a logical response to the failure of the integration process with Russia, as the development of such a "national ideology" would be a natural way to justify the now undeniable reality of a more distant relationship with Russia. At the same time, it is clear that for Lukashenko the main purpose in establishing a national ideology was further to strengthen his personal control over the country. Soon after coming to power in 1994, Lukashenko sought to create a national ideology to accompany his regime but did not succeed then because the institutional mechanisms for exerting his personal power had not yet been established. See Georgii Antoniuk, "Bolshaya stirka mozgov mozhet ne poluchitsia," *Belorusski rynok*, VIII (March 1, 2004).

57. The requirement, in effect since 2005, that 75 percent of the music broadcast by radio stations be composed by Belarusians, must also be seen in the context of these larger trends.

58. In at least one instance, administrators at state universities warned students that "they would be deprived of their benefits and stipends if they did not join the BRYM." State Department, "Belarus," *2003 Country Reports*; "Belarus," *2005 Country Reports.*

59. See Alexandra Goujon, "Nationalisme et identité en Biélorussie," paper presented at the International Conference on Belarus at the Crossroads of Postcommunism, Center for Advanced Studies in Education (Vilnius, Lithuania, May 24–26, 2005).

60. According to Presidential Decree 111 of February 2004, the heads of both state and nonstate organizations are personally responsible for the quality of ideological work in their organizations. In the case of private higher educational institutions, the person responsible for ideological work (vice-chairman for ideology) can be named or dismissed only with the approval of the Presidential Administration. See Sergey Valikin, "Vozbrashchenie 'komissarov,'" *Belorusski rynok*, VIII (March 1, 2004).

61. For more information, see Margarita M. Balmaceda, *Belarus: Oil, Gas, Transit Pipelines and Russian Foreign Energy Policy* (London, 2006).

62. The law on "*O vnesenie izmenienie i dopolnenie v zakon ob organakh gosudarstvennoi bezapasnosti Resopubliki Belarus,*" passed on April 18, 2005. See Marina Koktysh, "KGB prikhodit bez zvonka i stuka," *Narodnaya volia* (Minsk) (May 21, 2005), 1.

63. "Lukashenko Says Revolution 'Failed,'" *Radio Free Europe–Radio Liberty* (March 20, 2006), www.rferl.org/featuresarticle/2006/03/854f7645-a015-4317-8386-d89f2ba5e90f.html.

64. See Alex Rodriguez, "Thousands Protest Belarus Election," *Boston Globe* (March 20, 2006).

65. Lukashenko, as cited in "Opposition Candidate Arrested in Belarus," *Boston Globe* (March 3, 2006).

66. For an analysis of Belarus as a demagogical state, see Elena A. Korosteleva, "Is Belarus a Demagogical Democracy?" *Cambridge Review of International Affairs*, XVI (2003), 527–535.

67. Twenty-five percent of Belarus's overall population, including almost the entire Jewish population, was killed during World War II.

68. Survey and focus group research conducted in Belarus supports this view. One important source is the European Union INTAS project "Charismatic Political Leadership in Russia, Belarus and Ukraine" (99-00245). For preliminary results based on these data, see Korosteleva, "Demagogical Democracy"; and Olga Gille-Belova, "The Nature of Relations between Political Leaders and Their Supporters: The Case of Russia, Belarus and Ukraine," unpublished manuscript for the conference "Russia, Ukraine, and Belarus: Political Leadership, International Security and Public Opinion," Centre d'Études et de Recherches Internationales (Paris, July 1, 2002), www.bath.ac.uk/eri/pdf/intas-belova.pdf. See also European Commission, "Central and Eastern Eurobarometer," nos. 4 (1994), 5 (1995), and 6 (1996), www.europa.eu.int/comm/public_opinion/archives/ceeb_en.htm, for surveys done in 1993, 1994, and 1995, respectively. For a sample of results based on these data, see Richard Rose and William Mishler, "Political Patience in Regime Transformation: A Comparative Analysis of Post-Communist Citizens," Studies in Public Policy 274 (Aberdeen, 1996).

69. Most independent prereferendum polls pointed to 40 percent support for lifting presidential term limits; in Gallup–Baltic Survey exit polls, 53 percent of those voting (equivalent to 48.37 percent of all registered voters) reported voting to lift presidential term limits.

70. This relationship is perhaps best exemplified by Russia's brief but total suspension of gas supplies to Belarus in February 2004 and Lukashenko's assertion that this action amounted to "war" on Belarus. See also Balmaceda, "Myth and Reality."

71. On legal and illegal transit revenue, see Margarita Balmaceda, "Belarus as a Transit Route: Domestic and Foreign Policy Implications," in Balmaceda, Clem, and Tarlow, *Independent Belarus*, 162–196.

72. Vasily Sholodonov, Belarusian deputy minister for Commonwealth of Independent States affairs, as quoted in *Zvyazda* (Minsk) (September 25, 1997), 2.

73. In a certain sense, one could find a parallel with North Korea, where, as Marcus Noland notes, despite widespread criticism of its human rights record and "facing profound political and economic difficulties . . . externally it faces an environment that, at least when it comes to the issue of regime survival, is fundamentally supportive." See Marcus Noland, chapter 4 in this volume.

74. One indicator of Belarus's declining economic well-being is the fact that since Lukashenko's ascent to power in 1994, the country's population has dropped by over 6 percent, and the economically active population has decreased even more. For data on monthly income, see "Special Report: Waving the Denim—Belarus," *Economist* (March 18, 2006), 23.

75. For January 2007 data, see "Average Inflation-Adjusted Monthly Pay."

76. See Kirill Spotykovich, "Ne do smekha: Komu zabostovka, komu—basta," *Belarusskaya gazeta*, IX (March 7, 2005).

77. On the possibilities and limits that the mid- and high-level nomenklatura will eventually challenge Lukashenko, see Leonid Zlotnikov, "Possibilities for the Development of a Private Economic Sector and a Middle Class as a Source of Political Change in Belarus," in Balmaceda, Clem, and Tarlow, *Independent Belarus*, 122–161.

78. See Balmaceda, "Myth and Reality."

79. See State Department, "Belarus," *2006 Country Reports*; Human Rights Watch, "Belarus"; Amnesty International, "Belarus 2003."

nine

Equatorial Guinea and Togo: What Price Repression?

John R. Heilbrunn

Although a heart attack ended the life of Togolese dictator Etienne Gnass-ingbé Eyadéma on February 5, 2005, it left intact the clan-based autocracy that he had established after a bloody coup thirty-eight years earlier. Initially, his death opened questions about succession and whether Togo would resume a democratic transition that had collapsed thirteen years before.[1] However, the Gnassingbé clan could hardly allow their father's death to leave it vulnerable to retribution from vengeful compatriots. A brutal campaign of killings and beatings of opponents in southern Togo accordingly preceded the elections.[2] Although the exact number of deaths may never be known, the U.S. State Department's *2005 Country Reports on Human Rights Practices* details multiple cases of brutality and many deaths.[3] On April 24, 2005, thirty-nine-year-old Faure Gnassingbé won highly flawed elections, corrected any mishaps that had followed Eyadéma's unexpected infarction, and consolidated the ruling clan's grip on Togo.

The Dilemma of Entrenched Autocracy

The Togolese experience highlights the dilemma of removing an entrenched autocracy from power. A critical question confronting reformers in Togo during 2006 is how might they remove from office a clan that has showed little compunction in its use of ruthless brutality to capture and hold power? Widespread violence accompanied preparations for the April elections. As the clan closed ranks around Faure Gnassingbé, his opponents decried the rapid scheduling of the vote and launched demonstrations to protest a campaign of violent intimidation.[4] The Gnassingbé clan opposed free and transparent elections since a loss of power carried potential and real risks for the family and its corrupt associates. These fears are no less the case for dictators of other African predatory autocracies, notably Equatorial Guinea and Zimbabwe. Risks of prosecution and retribution are constant fears for African autocrats who use common strategies to hold power and enrich their extended families and associates.[5]

Extremely authoritarian states typically undergo periodic popular protests followed by breathtakingly brutal human rights abuses. To counter domestic threats and vengeance, despots use routine violence, collusion with selected economic actors, corruption, and most important, clan politics as primary strategies to hold on to power. Indeed, a willingness to employ the most extreme forms of repression characterizes the strategies of these regimes and deepens the tragedy of numbing levels of poverty and political isolation. Removing the tyrant's clan from office and moving the country toward the crucial processes of reconciliation pose serious challenges to citizens of these states. Indeed, a dismal equilibrium enables extreme autocrats to protect their regimes and as a consequence, their clans and venal associates.

This chapter compares the closed systems of rule imposed by the Gnassingbé clan of Togo and Nguema clan of Equatorial Guinea. It argues that their political systems are trapped in a dilemma that perpetuates dysfunctional and extremely repressive rule. Entrenched practices of violence, nepotism, collusion, and corruption deny the ruling clan an option of liberalization and reform. On the one hand, Equatorial Guinea and Togo operate through the informal relations characteristic of clan politics.[6] On the other, Togo and Equatorial Guinea exemplify the dilemma of extreme authoritarianism: the clans that surround their leaders cannot permit meaningful reforms since decades of human rights abuses and corrupt administration have intensified demands for revenge and retribution. Indeed, the longer a clan retains power, the harder it is to resolve the crisis, which contributes to inequitable economic opportunities and stunted political development.

Equatorial Guinea and Togo are repressive states; their people are dominated by clans that have perpetrated a litany of human rights abuses. As a consequence, their opponents' demands for revenge have discouraged the clan from stepping down or enacting any substantive relaxation of authoritarian rule. Indeed, an extreme dictator undoubtedly recognizes that he is playing a high-stakes game; the sole means to remove him from power is through violent overthrow.[7] Both Teodoro Obiang Nguema and Gnassingbé Eyadéma came to power through violence and killed their predecessors, and their families and cronies may expect little more than the same treatment. Each regime is institutionally paralyzed; the dictator, his clan, and cronies have incentives to block reform for fear of prosecution, imprisonment, or fatal retribution.

Such autocrats are willing to incur the isolation and censure that is a cost of being identified as a repressive state. International criticism from potential partners may be the cost of holding onto power. The most extreme despots acknowledge by their actions that they will accept restricted donor assistance, limited access to credit, and international isolation even within their immediate community of states. When the calls for reform become too strong to ignore (as occurred with Faure Gnassingbé in 2005), the clan's principals regroup, adopt a more conciliatory stance, and undertake a campaign of domestic terror to prevent opportunistic behavior by their opponents in temporarily weak times.

Superficially, these two countries appear to be very different cases. In the 1980s, oil companies discovered substantial petroleum reserves in Equatorial Guinea's territorial waters. Togo exports phosphate rock, cocoa, and limited quantities of cotton. However, similarities abound in the practices of their repressive, clan-based regimes. Legacies of policy decisions made at critical junctures have directly influenced the paths that each state has taken in its development.[8] These legacies are present in the regimes' seeming resistance to reform and their leaders' rejection of calls for liberalization that have come from domestic and international actors. This chapter examines why the Togolese and Equatorial Guinean regimes are so resistant to change and proposes an explanation of the causes of these regimes' dilemma. First, the regimes' strategies are introduced, followed by comparisons of four dysfunctional practices in Equatorial Guinea and Togo: routine violence, nepotism and clientelism, collusion with foreign and domestic economic actors, and systemic corruption. These practices are embedded in both states and account for persistent repression. Since reports of widespread human rights abuses have marred the reputations of both Equatorial Guinea and Togo, I assess throughout how the perpetrators of these abuses have impeded reforms of the authoritarian state. The chapter concludes with a consideration of how Equatorial Guinea and Togo might emerge from their dismal yet seemingly stable equilibriums.

Strategies

These two dictatorships routinely use nepotism, collusion, corruption, and terror to ensure regime longevity. Terror here refers to a political leadership's routine use of violence to quiet opposition. In her brilliant study of totalitarianism, Hannah Arendt trenchantly noted that terror is a mechanism of control by which the most extreme authoritarian leaders ensure obedience.[9] One can assume that a tyrant is a purposive actor, enforcing policies with the principal goal of self-preservation and enrichment. The most common strategy is violence that quiets potential opponents by forcing populations to live in fear. Routine intimidation prevents competitors from coalescing into an effective, unified opposition movement. Despite incentives to avoid an overuse of terror, violence is a common practice in extreme authoritarian states.

Routine violence contributes to a dependence on the army, secret police, and informal agents of repression. Dependence on the state's coercive apparatus is a critical weakness since military leaders present formidable challenges to a ruling clan's hegemony. Powers granted to leaders of security agencies enable them to pose credible threats to an autocrat and his clan. The problem is how to control the exercise of force by the military and police detachments to which responsibility has been delegated. An oft-used strategy to minimize risks in this high-stakes game is nepotism. Since the most trustworthy collaborators are immediate kin, an autocrat has an incentive to appoint clan members to important positions in the army, police, and administration.

In both Togo and Equatorial Guinea, members of the ruling families occupy key positions in government, and, as a consequence, may have been implicated in serious crimes. In Togo, for example, Eyadéma appointed his children as ministers and commanders of major army camps, where they have remained. The appearance that the Togolese coup had been transformed into an electoral mandate failed to resolve many important issues. First, Gnassingbé was a member of a clan that operated much like the mafia: it dominated business in Togo.[10] Second, calls for prosecution of selected members of the Gnassingbé family were never rescinded. Although members of the clan had committed diverse crimes for which they should answer, demands for retribution remained obstacles to a resolution of the crisis. Third, the Forces Armées Togolaise (FAT) needed to be reformed for the sustainable reconstruction of the Togolese state.

Equatorial Guinea's Obiang has been all too aware of the dangers of using even family members to staff the security apparatus; he came to power after leading a bloody coup that toppled and executed Macías Nguema, his uncle.

To offset these dangers, the Equatorial Guinean president's family, known as the Mongomo or Nguema clan, has been given a joint stake in the petro-economy.[11] Before Mobil opened the Zafiro field in 1995, Equatorial Guinea was among the world's poorest countries. Since the discovery of significant oil reserves in offshore waters, the Mongomo clan has captured the state and distributes oil revenues for its personal enrichment with the assistance of international oil firms and European and American banks, including the now defunct Riggs Bank of Virginia.[12] These discretionary seizures provided access to wealth and reinforced the neopatrimonial bonds that sustained the Nguemist regime and ensured the loyalty of its officials.

Authority in clan-based African autocracies recalls the Weberian concept of "sultanism," an extreme form of patrimonialism that "operates primarily on the basis of discretion."[13] In sultanistic regimes, "the ruler exercises his power without restraint, at his discretion and above all unencumbered by rules or any commitment to an ideology or value system."[14] Such a despot employs various strategies to repress opposition and create allegiances among diverse groups in society. A dictator may use populist political rhetoric or personality cults to justify the regime's occasional excesses. What makes Togo and Equatorial Guinea distinctive is that Eyadéma and Obiang used constitutionalism and populist rule to provide their regimes with a veneer of legitimacy.

Asymmetrical access to political liberties and economic opportunities are indicative characteristics of predatory autocracies. Both Obiang and Eyadéma enjoyed considerable latitude in deciding electoral rules. They manipulated their constitutions to prevent opponents from winning parliamentary seats or gaining an external audience while maintaining the international legitimacy necessary to retain development assistance and economic relations. Economic institutions were similarly manipulated to protect property rights in lucrative sectors. In less profitable activities, the clan has an incentive to seize assets of domestic business actors, as occurred in Equatorial Guinea's forestry sector. Any potentially successful venture faces a risk of expropriation by clan members. This threat of predatory seizure has a chilling effect on entrepreneurial activity. For example, when Eyadéma was faced with a potential inability to pay his armed forces in 1992, he simply seized a local bank and distributed its cash to the army. A similarly instructive example is the Mongomo clan's claim to the lucrative property on Bioko Island, where Western oil firms have located their corporate offices and housed their expatriate staff. This capture of desirable real estate has provided extraordinary benefits for the Nguema family. It expropriated properties from their Bubi owners and rented them out to international oil companies for huge gains.

The despots who control extremely repressive authoritarian regimes have incentives to collude with private international capital as a strategy to hinder any nonclan business coalitions that might challenge the status quo. In some sectors, the despot might encourage domestic producers to create supportive business coalitions. In Togo, for example, Eyadéma established a partnership with retailers in the commercial sector to bring import duties and prestige to his authoritarian regime. Combined with his efforts to create an image of Togo as the "Switzerland of Africa," the effect was to secure the country's reputation as a pro-Western liberal economy and increase state revenues from import duties.

In less profitable economic sectors, a tyrant might choose to allow some production as long as such factions never threatened the regime. If a business coalition exists that tries to compete with the regime, the response is brutal. Such was the fate of Bubi traders who thrived for a short time until the Nguema family seized their assets and real estate. The Bubi traders were thereafter arrested and harassed. Many of those who were unable to escape from Equatorial Guinea were left destitute.

In other productive sectors, clan members control potential rents and allocate contracts, often to highest bidders of bribes. When confronted by a decline in export revenues or a suspension of international donor assistance, dictators have incentives to enter profitable relationships with criminal actors and organizations for their mutual benefit. These relationships might be damaging for the country but still enable the regime to continue to pay its army and secret police. For example, Eyadéma became increasingly isolated from the international community after members of his family and regime were implicated in serious human rights abuses. Through his collusion with criminal actors, he succeeded in gathering needed revenues. For instance, as is discussed below, Eyadéma hosted Angolan rebel leader Jonas Savimbi's family for a period while Lomé served as a transit point for export of conflict diamonds and for illicit arms going to Angola.

In Equatorial Guinea, the Nguemist regime completely disregarded the needs of its people. Numerous contracts awarded to foreign timber firms without any provision for domestic producers reflected the regime's utter disconnection from its society.[15] The contracts were an organized effort to strip domestic owners of forestry stocks of their wealth. In other activities, the list of criminal practices that implicates Obiang Nguema includes arms trafficking, illegal toxic waste dumps, drug smuggling, and money laundering.[16] These activities lend credence to Bayart and coworkers' depiction of certain African regimes as criminal states, where the leaders have a disregard for accepted international norms of behavior even if it should result in censure and isolation.[17] Indeed, the profits are evidently high enough to make isolation and censure preferable to losing control.

African despots have multiple reasons to encourage systemic corruption in the public sector. The World Bank has defined corruption as the abuse of public office for private gain. Daniel Kaufmann has provided a useful distinction when he writes that corruption is "'the privatization of public policy,' in which public policy is seen as including access to public services."[18] In a tyranny, bureaucrats limit all access to public services and consume available rents. Corruption becomes a means to reward supporting coalitions and family members. In addition, corrupt relationships bind clients to the state and, in that sense, provide the glue for the regime to coalesce and survive. Members of the inner circles are able to extract revenues from the state and distribute a portion to the select few who support the regime. Systemic corruption is manifest in patron-client networks headed by members of the autocrats' immediate families, who engage in vulgar malfeasance and criminal activity.[19] Patrons of clientelist networks receive benefits that they distribute to their younger or more distant clansmen, which is a characteristic of many dictatorships. However, when coupled with routine violence and collusion, it is intrinsic to the survival of an extremely repressive state.

Dysfunctional Politicoeconomic Institutions

Political institutions include the constitutional provisions that define the powers accorded to the branches of government and methods for electing representatives. Electoral rules and norms established by constitutions affect the idiosyncratic manner in which autocrats in rogue states exercise power. The constitutions of Equatorial Guinea and Togo, for example, grant the executive preponderant influence over the other branches of government, whose mandates are ambiguous and subject to presidential whims. Constitutional ambiguity contributes to remarkable latitude given to executive decisionmaking since the rules are vague and subject to redefinition according to circumstances. This latitude poses a quandary for the putatively democratic opposition parties since they must operate within the rules established by constitutions even when dictators routinely ignore or redefine key provisions at their convenience. Hence, the democratic opposition parties in Equatorial Guinea and Togo are at the mercy of autocratic machinations. Brutality is routinely visited on the populace, which deepens uncertainty since interactions with the state result in unpredictable outcomes.

Routine Violence: The Despot's Game

Routine violence is a common practice in an autocracy. What makes these despots distinctive is the dictator's willingness to use lethal force against real, potential, and imagined opponents. The unrestrained use of violence, however, has a negative impact on investments and economic predictability. Despite the costs inherent in violent outbreaks, autocrats are likely to violate basic human rights and use terror to hold onto power. In the worst cases, human rights violations attain genocidal dimensions, such as the mass killings perpetrated by the Janjaweed in the Darfur region of the Sudan or the genocidal campaign unleashed by Radovan Karadzic in Bosnia-Herzegovina in 1992.[20] Genocidal practices are unsustainable; the nightmare that Cambodians suffered under Pol Pot shows that a genocidal regime lacks the rules and norms that prevent elite politicians from consuming their own.[21] Most despots therefore avoid a threshold of violence that destabilizes their regime or provokes international intervention. Therefore controlled violence and an underlying threat of potential brutality constitute one of the political system's defining characteristics.

Poverty is related to violence in that both poverty and violence debilitate a population; an impoverished people is less likely to rebel against an entrenched autocracy even when faced with profound inequities. Income distribution in Equatorial Guinea and Togo is highly unequal and favors presidential clans and their cronies. Presidents of both countries enact policies that enrich their families while contributing to a deepening of the already numbing level of poverty among the Togolese and Equatorial Guinean people. Poverty is often a by-product of predatory rule, a lack of information, uncertainty, and high transaction costs. Worse, poverty contributes to poor health and low levels of human capital. Such conditions are useful for political rogues since they impede an organized opposition from emerging, and exiled groups are unable to communicate effectively with sympathizers in-country. The autocrat deliberately limits economic opportunities to strengthen his control over the economy's few productive sectors and guarantees the subservience of potential entrepreneurs. Competition for resources is therefore restricted to a select number of clan members, retainers, and elite politicians. As a consequence, a substantial portion of the population is denied the benefits of education and employment. These allocation decisions are evident in the statistics presented in Table 9-1.

In Equatorial Guinea and Togo, violence has affected development in different ways. Extreme violence in Togo during the late 1990s had the impact of

Table 9-1. National Statistics, Togo and Equatorial Guinea
Units as indicated

Statistic	Year	Togo	Equatorial Guinea
Surface area (sq. km.)	...	56,800	28,100
Population (millions)	2003	5	0.494
Per capita income (U.S. dollars)	2003	310	700
Life expectancy (years)	2003	49	44
GDP change (percent)	2003	2.7	14.7
Literacy rate (percent)	2002	74 (male) 45 (female)	n.a.
Percent below poverty line	1987–1989	32.3	n.a.

Source: World Bank, *World Development Indicators 2005* (Washington, D.C., 2005).

alienating the international community. After Eyadéma's death in 2005, the Gnassingbé clan followed his wishes, and rule was passed to one of its most internationally presentable members, Faure Gnassingbé. Charles Debbasch, former president of Aix-Marseille III University and counselor to both former French president Valéry Giscard d'Estaing and Eyadéma, helped engineer a veneer of constitutional succession via the parliament.[22] It appeared as if Eyadéma's cronies and children could cry, "The king is dead! Long live the king!" Yet before and after the April 2005 presidential elections, the Gnassingbé clan's desperation was evident in the excessive violence that it perpetrated on Togo's people. As a consequence, international development assistance and investment have been minimal in Togo since the election. Even attempts to reach an accord among different parties failed, and the European Union remained at odds with Togo's dynastic state throughout 2006.[23] By contrast, a constant level of intimidation and risk of violence has only marginally deterred oil companies from investing in Equatorial Guinea.

Both Equatorial Guinea and Togo control rigorously any information about human rights abuses in their prisons or during periods of electoral "competition." While celebrity cases receive the attention of international human rights organizations like Amnesty International (Amnesty), the exercise of violence against common citizens has been reported anecdotally, with little hard evidence to substantiate allegations. In Equatorial Guinea, the 2002 arrest and incarceration of Felipe Ondó Obiang prompted a letter of protest from Amnesty. Similarly, Amnesty reported the incarceration in October 2003 of Pastor Bienvenido Samba Momesori, who had been imprisoned and sentenced to death along with 110 others in 1998.[24] Shortly afterward, an Amnesty press release reported that Momesori was being held with thirty other "prisoners of conscience."[25] And in April 2005, Amnesty revealed the horrific conditions at Equatorial Guinea's Black Beach prison, where at least seventy prisoners were at risk of starvation.[26]

Even the paltry reporting in Equatorial Guinea is more open than in Togo, with its 2000 Press and Communications Law that is among the most restrictive in Africa and imposes serious penalties on the press for a range of infractions.[27] These policies were consistent when Eyadéma was alive and have continued under the regime of his son, Faure Gnassingbé. After the elections, reports on the actual numbers of dead and wounded at hospitals and morgues were banned, and Suzanne Aho Assouma, the minister of health, instructed that any requests from journalists were to be forwarded to ministry staff.[28] Agence France-Presse reported in early 2005 that eleven people died and ninety-five were wounded in riots in the capital city of Lomé.[29] These figures are in stark contrast to the list of at least 150 victims that Amnesty compiled in a process it describes as "very difficult to establish and is a controversial matter."[30] Indeed, since the 1999 Amnesty report detailing multiple political murders, the Gnassingbé clan has strictly controlled the release of figures on the number of detainees and deaths.

Routine Violence in Equatorial Guinea

Violence in Equatorial Guinea has been at proportions that few states have ever experienced. According to one journalist, Macías Nguema had on occasion crucified prisoners along the road to the airport to show his resolve to visiting dignitaries.[31] From this vantage point, the use of force in Obiang's Equatorial Guinea is relatively less oppressive than his predecessor. Yet violence is a distinct characteristic of the Equatorial Guinean regime and shapes everyday life in the country. As one visitor to the capital, Malabo, remarked, "You have to go there. It's ever so pretty. Other than the fact that they beat people up rather a lot, it's really nice."[32] Despite the peculiar naïveté of this observation, violence in Equatorial Guinea attains surreal levels of banality; Amnesty reports that beatings, disappearances, and arbitrary incarcerations in the notorious Black Beach prison occur with disturbing regularity.[33] "From the family inner circle to the poor, Equatorial Guineans live in fear of arbitrary detention, harassment, beatings, and the seizure of personal property."[34]

Obiang has used repression along with the more passive violence of an extraordinary poverty. Statistics for social sector spending, including health and education, are dismal. "In 1997–2002, the country spent a mere 1.23 percent of its government expenditure on health [and] . . . 1.67 percent on education."[35] These statistics are telling considering the incredible economic growth rate (15 percent) since the advent of oil production. It is evident that little of the revenues are earmarked for social sector spending, which accounts for the International Monetary Fund's cautions that the Equatorial Guinean government needs to build capacity and make more non–oil sector investments.[36]

Equatorial Guinea has chilling statistics for poverty in a country experiencing an oil boom. In 2003, its 494,000 inhabitants had an average annual income of $700. Yet, Equatorial Guinea is a middle-income country: its figures for GDP growth are 41.6 percent between 1997 and 2001, and the economy grew by 14.7 percent in 2002–2003, making it among the world's fastest growing.[37] Although literacy rates are unavailable, the nature of rule in Equatorial Guinea makes it reasonable to suggest that extreme poverty is common among less favored groups (for example, the Bubi). Indeed, repressive policies have pushed some regions of Equatorial Guinea into poverty and, in some areas, economic collapse. All the while, Obiang and his family have been amassing fortunes from offshore oil fields.

The persistence of violence and its relationship to corruption in Equatorial Guinea leaves the Mongomo clan vulnerable to retribution should they ever leave power. In addition, it is questionable that these people have any incentive to open the regime to wider participation or to reduce the levels of violence. The effect is that the regime is caught in a dilemma: liberalization might create the conditions that could lead to retribution for decades of crimes. Hence the governing clan has every incentive to resist inclusive politics and to protect the exclusive political regime.

Routine Violence in Togo

Violence in Togo has been a political strategy to intimidate opponents, prevent them from organizing, and entrench the dictatorship. When Eyadéma was alive, his use of violence was an implicit admission that his family was in physical danger should he be removed from power. As a consequence, elections and periods of political activity were extremely dangerous for members of the opposition. This use of violence has been no less a strategy of the Gnassingbé clan since the 2005 elections. Although concrete numbers are unavailable, estimates count hundreds of alleged victims during the campaign period.[38] Diplomatic costs have been extremely high as critical sentiments against the Gnassingbé clan have gelled internationally. As a result, Togo is paralyzed; its leadership is incapable of reform. The effect of such violence has been that the Gnassingbé clan can neither liberalize its economy for fear of enriching potential opponents nor relax its grip on political processes.

Togo's 1998 elections were extraordinary for the brutality and arbitrary violence that the regime perpetrated on its population. An insecure Eyadéma unleashed the army and militia in the months before the elections; hundreds of people were killed and thousands fled into exile. In that environment, a national electoral committee was to supervise polls, place international observers, and count the votes. However, when it appeared that Gilchrist Olympio, son of Togo's first president, might win, the FAT seized ballot boxes, disbanded the electoral commission, expelled international observers, and declared Eyadéma the winner. International observers condemned the elections as neither free nor fair and left the country. Togo descended into a period of strikes, protests, and economic stagnation. Opposition parties boycotted the 1999 legislative elections; the Togolese People's Rally "won" an overwhelming majority.

After the 1998 elections, Amnesty released a series of scathing reports on Togo. The first, entitled "Togo: Rule of Terror," alleged that during the 1998 presidential campaign period, hundreds of bodies had been found on the beaches of Ghana, Benin, and Togo; soldiers had reportedly bound their hands and feet and thrown them from military aircraft into the Atlantic Ocean.[39] Reports in the international press depicted Eyadéma as a pariah and included him among the world's most repressive dictators. At first, the government reacted angrily and accused Amnesty of releasing untrue and unverified information.[40] In July 2005, a new report entitled, "Togo: Will History Repeat Itself?" documented the cruelty and ferociousness of the Forces Armées Togolaises and pro-Gnassingbé militia in their repression of opponents. Amnesty depicted a renewal of arbitrary shootings and terror after the allegedly fraudulent election of Faure Gnassingbé.[41]

Such allegations create an impression of a clan that is out of control and preys upon the citizens of southern Togo. Since the FAT is 75 percent composed of people from northern ethnic groups and overwhelmingly Kabyé, it has formed what Amnesty called an "army of cousins."[42] Togo's ethnic army indicates the low levels of development in the far-flung northern regions; few young men presently in the FAT or militia have alternative employment opportunities. During the turbulent 1990s, it was common to read in the opposition press that any new "democratic" government would send these Kabyé men "back to their rocks." Such fears were undoubtedly among the reasons in 1963 that a small group of recently decommissioned Kabyé soldiers assassinated President Sylvanus Olympio and seized power when they were denied employment. Poverty in Togo makes the stakes of seizing power strikingly high. Ethnic violence remains among the emotional undercurrents in Togolese politics.

The Gnassingbé regime governs a society of people who live in conditions of abject poverty. In 2003, Togo's 5 million people lived on an average per capita income of $310 a year. Statistics suggest that in 1989, almost a third of the population lived below the poverty line; however, conditions were exacerbated by the extreme economic decline that followed the stillborn 1991 national conference. Togo's poverty may be even worse since the aggregate figures fail to capture the wide gap between people in urban centers, notably Lomé, and those in the far-flung regions. Social indicators are even more telling: in 2002, the illiteracy rate was 26 percent for adult men and 55 percent for women. This relatively high illiteracy rate persists in a country that at independence had one of the highest school attendance rates in Africa. For example, in 1957, Togo had a 42 percent school attendance rate that surpassed most of Francophone Africa; only Cameroon had a higher rate at 59 percent.[43] These statistics show that the progress that Togo enjoyed while a darling of the World Bank and Western donors has been reversed by the Gnassingbé clan's brutal rule. Poverty is a passive form of repression that has enabled the regime to prevent the populace from rebelling effectively.

Nepotism: The Despot's Insurance

Extremely authoritarian regimes, such as the autocracies in Togo and Equatorial Guinea, are characterized by high levels of insecurity and uncertainty regarding their longevity. Opponents contest the dictator's legitimacy of rule from exile or through small groups scattered throughout society. In turn, the dictator overcomes the shortened time horizon created by an active opposition through a strategy of brutal violence and the appointment of clan members to key positions of state. It is thereby possible for the autocrat to ensure as much as possible the long-term security of his family and cronies by establishing dynastic rule. However, excesses of family members and close associates may counter such goals by fueling movements directed against both the autocrat and his family. In Equatorial Guinea and Togo, nepotism has been among the primary strategies both dictators used to ensure their tenure in office. However, nepotism is a high-risk strategy that requires distribution of diverse resources as inducements for loyalty. The method by which Obiang

Nguema and Eyadéma imposed their clans on political processes in Equatorial Guinea and Togo is instructive for an appreciation of the role of nepotism in an extreme authoritarian state.

Nepotism in Equatorial Guinea

The institutional arrangements inherent in nepotism are consistent with the oligarchic misrule that characterized the preceding Spanish colonial administration. For the last three decades, Equatorial Guinea has been dominated by tyrants who have employed the most intense forms of repression to ensure compliance with their rule. Macías Nguema allegedly killed around 50,000 people—one-tenth of the total population—between 1969 and 1979.[44] Those who remained behind were either part of the regime or stayed at great risk to their physical security. Obiang replicated many of the elements of his predecessor's rule, in particular a reliance on family members to administer the state. However, a crucial difference between Macías and Obiang is the abundant oil resources that have transformed Equatorial Guinea into a petroeconomy. This transformation increased incentives for the clan to reinforce its grip on political power.

Nepotism in Equatorial Guinea is enabled by the small size of the country. Obiang is able to exert greater control over his administrators by appointing his children, nephews, and nieces to positions of great influence (see table 9-2). These appointments have resulted in the capture of Equatorial Guinea's oil rents by members of a clan-based autocracy. However, as indicated by the attempted coup in 2003 that was led by his half-brother Agustín Ndong Ona, and then by the 2004 mercenary plot, even clansmen may aspire to seize power.[45] To address such threats, Obiang has used destitution and brutality as his primary methods for discouraging clansmen from fomenting coups.

Nepotism in Togo

Nepotism has been a critical strategy in Togo's rogue state to ensure continued dominance of the public sector and minimize unpleasant surprises. Members of the Gnassingbé clan had been placed in their positions by the patriarch, Eyadéma. Two sons had served as commanders of the most important military garrisons in Togo. Until he became ill, Ernest Gnassingbé commanded the Landja-Kara garrison in northern Togo. Another son, Rock Gnassingbé, has commanded the Tokoin garrison in southern Togo. Both Ernest and Rock Gnassingbé have been implicated in specific assassinations and violent crimes perpetrated against opponents of their father's regime. Since seizing power in the clan's name, Faure Gnassingbé has continued his

Table 9-2. Pattern of Nepotism in Equatorial Guinea

Government office	Individual	Family relation	Village–Mongomo	Ethnicity–Fang Esangui
President	Teodoro Obiang Nguema Mbasongo	. . .	Yes	Yes
Cooperation with Missions	Alejandro Evuna Owono Asangano	None	Yes	Yes
Labor and Social Security	Ricardo Mangue Obama Nfube	Brother-in-law	No	No
Forestry, Fisheries, and the Environment	Teodorín Nguema Obiang Mangue	First son, first wife	Yes	Yes
Mines and Energy	Gabriel Mbega Obiang Lima	First son, second wife	Yes	Yes
National Security	Manuel Nguema Mba	Uncle	Yes	Yes
Economy and Finance	Rosendo Otogo Meneng	Uncle	Yes	No

Source: Max Liniger-Goumaz, "Equatorial Guinea: 'We Saw Hell in Malabo': A Country Dominated by Foreign Companies, Human Rights Violations, and Political Authoritarianism," *Africa Contemporary Record: Annual Surveys and Documents*, CCVII (New York, 2004), B326–B328.

father's practice by naming his brother Kpatcha Gnassingbé as minister of defense, delegated to the presidency. Faure's choice of appointments indicates the centrality of the clan and the military to the regime's survival.

Faure Gnassingbé began his political career as minister of mines under his father, who appeared to be grooming him as his successor. Other sons occupied high-profile positions as well. One was director of the free trade zone at the Lomé port and another headed international cooperation relations. Indeed, the clan had evolved to dominate key positions throughout the political economy. However, since Togo is a country of approximately 5 million inhabitants, ten times the size of Equatorial Guinea, nepotism has its limitations in effective domination of the state. Consequently, the Gnassingbé clan has depended on coalitions of individuals who either come from the north, preferably their natal village of Pya, or are members of coalitions dependent on the autocracy for their economic and physical well-being.

Collusion: The Despot's Income

If a government requires taxes for its operating revenues, taxpayers demand a minimal democratic rule that brings a degree of accountability, or they will exercise mobility and transfer their capital out of the economy.[46] However, a rogue state cannot anticipate a steady revenue flow from taxes since most of its citizens are impoverished. Dictators of rogue states must at a minimum pay their security forces and therefore seek funds from off-budget sources. The search for off-budget sources of revenues leads to collusion between the dictator and selected private sector actors or, in the extreme, criminal elements.

The need for off-budget revenues indicates an exigency to prevent independent nodes of social and economic power from emerging that might challenge the regime. In the Togolese case, funds had initially come from international donors, who rewarded Eyadéma's pronounced commitment to free markets and property rights. He developed close relations with the World Bank and the U.S. Agency for International Development from which his regime received substantial support that was indispensable to its survival. When that source of revenues ended, Eyadéma turned to other strategies, including the illegal sale of end-user certificates for conflict diamonds. In the case of Equatorial Guinea, Obiang has enjoyed the benefit of oil windfalls that have enabled the clan to establish close relations with international oil firms and one U.S. bank. These collusive relations helped members of the Equatorial Guinean "aristocracy" amass huge fortunes that they have expatriated to a number of international accounts.

Collusion in Equatorial Guinea

Whereas the Spanish colonial state actively repressed most political movements in Equatorial Guinea, an exception was an administrator named García Trevijano, who mentored a Fang civil servant named Macías Nguema. His interest in Nguema was "because of his limited intellect and poor education, he was the ideal tool for the Franco dictatorship."[47] When Spain acceded to pressure from the United Nations to grant Equatorial Guinea independence, Nguema was seen as the optimal candidate to protect Spanish interests.

Independence came in 1967 after the people of Equatorial Guinea approved a constitutional referendum. On October 12, 1968, Macías Nguema won the presidential elections, and Equatorial Guinea became an independent state. The reality of life under Macías Nguema was unpredictable and extremely violent. Within three years, he had allocated important government posts to close family members and people from Mongomo, his natal village on the mainland. Equatorial Guinea quickly acquired a reputation as one of the most horrific dictatorships in the world. Indeed, by 1975, the economy had collapsed, members of Nguema's Esangui Fang family occupied all the key posts, and per capita GNP had fallen to $70.00 a year.[48] Macías Nguema became increasingly irrational and started killing imagined rivals, including his nephew, the brother of Colonel Obiang Nguema, then his army chief of staff.[49] This killing proved too much for the clan; in August 1979, Obiang

Nguema led a military coup that ended his uncle's career and life.[50] Immediately upon taking power, Obiang replicated many of Nguema's practices, allocating posts to relatives and close accomplices, mostly from Mongomo. As a result, Equatorial Guinea experienced considerable continuity in its political system.

President Obiang Nguema governs through personal discretion and the selective rewarding of privilege and wealth. Although this pattern of rule reflects continuities from Spanish colonialism, Obiang has the added benefit of oil windfalls that he allocates to ensure regime stability. By 2001, total proven reserves were estimated at over 1.1 billion barrels, and oil constituted almost 90 percent of exports.[51] Indeed, the U.S. Geological Survey has suggested that unproven reserves might be as high as 13.5 billion barrels.[52] Oil production has accordingly jumped from 60,000 barrels a day in 1997 to over 300,000 in 2005.[53] Equatorial Guinea's economic performance has been marked by growth that averaged 37 percent a year between 1996 and 2006.[54] With such increases of wealth, it is likely that Equatorial Guinea might emerge as an equal among oil-exporting countries, in spite of its leadership.

Considerable evidence suggests that Obiang's clan has siphoned off oil revenues paid to the state for its personal use. Reports of accounts opened and closed for family members in the Virginia-based Riggs Bank show that a collusive relationship had developed between the regime and selected banks in the United States and Europe. It is hardly surprising that when asked about the transfers of funds into accounts held by a shell company called Kalunga, for example, Obiang refused to divulge any information about those holdings, thereby forcing Riggs to close all the Equatorial Guinean accounts.[55] His refusal to discuss oil revenues points to the influence of long-serving Gabonese President Omar Bongo Ondimba, who has treated Gabon's oil income as a personal account. When asked about Equatorial Guinea's petroleum windfalls, Obiang has asserted that how government uses its oil revenues is a matter of national security.[56]

An unwillingness to reveal amounts received from oil exports is troublesome and indicates a lack of transparency in revenue management in Equatorial Guinea. Since oil fields in Equatorial Guinean territorial waters were first discovered in the early 1990s and came into production in 1996, substantial payments have been deposited in government accounts as signature bonuses and other fees and licenses. From the limited available evidence, it is clear that these revenues have largely gone to the Nguema clan. Steady enrichment of the president's clan has contributed to its members' sense of impunity and a decline in non–oil sector production.

Before discovery of the offshore reserves, Equatorial Guinea was extremely poor; the country exported timber and cocoa. Although cocoa had been primarily an activity of the Bubi people who inhabit Bioko (formerly Fernando Po), the earlier nationalization of cocoa plantations by Macías Nguema reduced cocoa production to negligible levels. One impact of the systematic violence visited on the Bubi people was a decline in agricultural production. For example, in 1995, agriculture accounted for 51.6 percent of GDP; in 2002, it constituted 10.5 percent. This decline of cocoa's importance reflects both the disproportionate economic power of oil and, consistent with theories of the "Dutch disease," an overall decline of other nonpetroleum tradable sectors.

Timber was the traditional export from the mainland province of Rio Muni, and it represented 12.4 percent of exports for 1996–1997. After the collapse of cocoa production, forestry products gained importance. Licenses were granted by Obiang's son, who became popularly known as "the minister for chopping trees."[57] The younger Obiang Nguema developed a close relationship with the Malaysian timber company Schimmer. He granted Schimmer a concession totaling 200,000 hectares, and within a short period, the Malaysian company dominated 42 percent of the entire lumber sector.[58] The extent to which this sector enriched the president's son to the detriment of indigenous producers demonstrated how Equatorial Guinea had evolved into a private domain of the Nguema family. In many respects, both the Nguema regimes have adopted the politically and economically repressive policies of Spanish colonialism.[59]

The presence of a constitution is paradoxical in these extreme dictatorships. An appearance of democracy resonates with the international community even if the dictators ignore other norms consistent with republican government. The experiences of Equatorial Guinea imply that perhaps Obiang accepted a constitution to enable international oil companies operating there to protect their reputations. In 1982, Obiang proposed a constitutional referendum that created a parliament and established a seven-year term for the executive. However, the electoral law limited parliamentary candidacy only to members of the Democratic Party of Equatorial Guinea (*Partido Democrático de Guinea Ecuatorial* [PDGE]), thus establishing a single-party state.[60] In 2002, several rival political parties emerged to challenge Obiang's PDGE. Although the constitution provides for both presidential and parliamentary elections, reports are that elections are far from free and that opposition candidates are in mortal danger if they remain in the country.[61] For example, in the 2002 presidential elections, Celestino Bacale, the main opposition leader, withdrew from the contest due to his fear that he and his family might be vulnerable to incarceration, torture, and even death.[62]

Collusion in Togo

Cold war politics and a radicalization of West African regimes allowed Togo to pose as a bastion of capitalism surrounded by three radical regimes: the People's Republic of Benin, Ghana, and Upper Volta. Throughout the 1980s, Eyadéma successfully established alliances with donors, Western diplomatic missions, and domestic and international entrepreneurs in commerce, manufacturing, and banking. It is ironic that the first collusive relationship that the Eyadéma regime enjoyed was with the World Bank and Western donors. The government was an early recipient of financing from the International Monetary Fund's Structural Adjustment Facility and was held out as a model of economic probity. Infusions of development assistance transformed Lomé into an international center for conferences, meetings, and an entrepôt for goods transiting to Niger, Upper Volta, and Mali. The infusions of international assistance enabled Eyadéma to consolidate his single-party regime and accumulate a sizable personal fortune, as demonstrated by the construction of palatial homes in Lomé and his natal village of Pya.

With the expansion of Lomé into an entrepôt, Togo's economy boomed. Eyadéma seized a number of international investments to create a state-owned enterprise sector. Foremost among these nationalizations were the phosphate rock mines at Kpémé on the coast near Lomé. During the 1970s, the phosphate mines were consolidated under the Office Togolais de Phosphate. Eyadéma was careful to reimburse international investors rapidly.[63] Selected banks were then nationalized to receive party dues paid to the single party, the Togolese People's Rally. During the 1970s, Togo's cloth retailers collaborated with the regime to monopolize the regional distribution of printed cloth.[64] Eyadéma favored this sector by lowering import duties on cloth and benignly ignoring the extraordinary accumulation of capital that was occurring among Lomé's successful cloth retailers, known as the "Nana Benz" for the cars they drove to the markets. Eyadéma colluded with the cloth retailers to promote his image as a proponent of free trade and capitalist property rights. However, that relationship was unsustainable. The cloth retailers had replicated the exclusive, indeed oligarchic traditions of Togolese development, and when political events caused an unraveling of the bonds with Eyadéma, they fled Lomé and established new warehouses in Accra, Cotonou, and Lagos.[65]

The democracy movement and systematic repression by the Eyadéma government caused Togo's economy to slow. Reports of hundreds of people being summarily executed during the 1998 presidential campaign horrified and embarrassed Eyadéma's allies. His regime was obviously acting far outside accepted norms, and international developmental assistance was suspended. In 2000, the "Fowler Report" to the UN Security Council showed that Eyadéma had provided Savimbi with end-user certificates to purchase arms in Bulgaria in exchange for "conflict diamonds."[66] This evidence was corroborated by reports that a former Soviet KGB officer named Victor Bout had transported at least nineteen arms shipments through Togo to Angola.[67] Possibly Eyadéma was acting on his personal friendship with Savimbi; members of Angolan rebels' immediate family resided in an opulent hotel in Lomé.[68] However, the Fowler Report provided evidence that Eyadéma had taken payment in diamonds, enabling him to pay his army and protect his family. The disclosures of involvement in the illicit diamond trade suggest that Eyadéma had abandoned his persona as a progressive, pro-Western leader in order to enrich himself and consolidate control over Togo's unruly southern population.

Corruption: The Despot's Glue

Corruption enables a dictator to pay people and effectively to bind them to the regime. It is difficult to measure corruption since predatory autocrats enjoy absolute rule to an extent unsurpassed by less authoritarian regimes. Hence, as in the absolutist regimes of seventeenth-century Europe, the president is the state and all revenues are in his domain. This identification of the dictator with the state complicates a contemporary definition of corruption as the abuse of public office for personal gain since practically all aspects of the autocracy are abusive. For example, the separation of powers that limits most rulers, even in authoritarian regimes, fails to constrain the despot. Such an absence of accountability mechanisms is particularly salient in both Equatorial Guinea and Togo, where the autocrat dominates all governmental operations.

Despite the problem of defining corruption, wholesale looting of state revenues constitutes an abuse of a most basic contract between a ruler and his subjects. Indeed, looting exceeds the "stationary bandit" concept, wherein the bandit steals but not so much as to impoverish his victim.[69] The relevant question about corrupt practices is to understand what shifts are possible and whether the dictator has any incentives to accept limits on his prerogative to consume state revenues.

Corruption in Equatorial Guinea

Macías Nguema established a brutal police state that perpetuated legacies of colonial corruption. By 1979, the country was destitute, largely due to corruption. Corruption has been a common practice under Obiang, and it favors overwhelmingly the Nguema family. Shortly after coming to power, Obiang annulled the 1973 constitution, transferred discretionary powers to the executive, and eliminated any separation of powers. An utter lack of accountability characterizes the actions of the government in Equatorial Guinea. In addition, officials have no fear that they may be held accountable for any malfeasance unless their actions offend Obiang. Hence the clan is free from the rules that constrain officials in most states.

Most pertinent, Obiang granted his clansmen immunity from crimes that include the theft of state revenues. Evidence of the regime's rapacity has been reported in newspaper accounts of the enrichment of Obiang's family.[70] Other accounts are recorded in an astounding U.S. Senate Subcommittee on Investigations report released in July 2004. Hundreds of millions of dollars were deposited into over sixty accounts held by Obiang, his family, and associates at the Riggs Bank. For example, inquiries were made in vain about Kalunga, a shell company that received wire transfers totaling $26,483,982 from Equatorial Guinean government accounts at Riggs. Letters sent about Kalunga's accounts at Banco Santander in Madrid received no response about authorized signatures or ownership of the shell company. Banco Santander responded that Spanish statutes prohibited disclosure of bank information even in the event of suspected money laundering.[71] Since July 2004, all the accounts at Riggs Bank have been closed, and funds have undoubtedly been transferred to more receptive banking environments. From evidence presented in the Senate subcommittee report, it is clear that the Mongomo clan diverted to its accounts substantial sums from the signature bonuses and tax payments made by a consortium of oil companies.

In other sectors, the Mongomo clan has dominated all economic activities and serves as a gatekeeper for any transactions.[72] For example, Obiang's second son, Gabriel Mbega Obiang Lima, is head of the ministry of mines and hydrocarbons. He held numerous accounts at Riggs Bank that regularly received transfers and even cash deposits.[73] Another son, Teodorín Obiang Nguema, the minister of fishing, forests, and water, controls access to forestry resources and is reputed to demand heavy commissions from firms seeking to enter that sector.[74] Teodorín Obiang Nguema has made huge investments in the Hollywood music industry as well as real estate in Southern California.[75] In Malabo, the capital of Equatorial Guinea, the elder Obiang and his wife own a real estate company that leases properties to oil companies for large sums of money.[76] What has evolved is a system that denies other groups access to rents while a small clique controls all lucrative sectors.

Corruption in Togo

The extent of corruption in Togo must be measured by proxy and inference. Some reports that may be attributed to members of one or another opposition party have accused Ernest Gnassingbé of embezzlement.[77] However, hard evidence for these actions is absent. Strict controls over information restrict exposures of official corruption. In the last years of Eyadéma's life, the government established a National Anti-Corruption Commission to investigate allegations of malfeasance. It quickly became a political tool. For example, Minister of Justice General Seyni Mémène criticized Mayor of Lomé Amouzouvi Akakpo for providing lackluster support for Eyadéma during the 1998 presidential campaign; shortly thereafter an investigation was launched into graft in the Lomé municipality.[78] Similarly, when Claude Améganvi reported that Eyadéma had amassed a personal fortune of $4.5 billion, he was arrested, and the newspaper that had published his allegations was closed for defaming the president.[79] Under Faure Gnassingbé, control over information criticizing the regime has tightened.

The analytic problem in Togo is similar to that in Equatorial Guinea: the state is dominated by a dictator who enjoys absolute power; hence transparency in official exchanges is absent. Accountability that might be provided by the other branches of government is similarly nonexistent. The lack of judicial and legislative independence inhibits any investigation into executive malfeasance. Hence it is reasonable to conclude that the president enjoys access to the country's (scarce) wealth and that he will make use of it when he so desires.

Conclusion

African predatory regimes are often dominated by clans that can neither loosen the restrictive bonds on society nor relinquish power. Rule is dependent on the use of nepotism, collusion, corruption, and violence. These strategies are the means by which the despots control their populations. In Equatorial Guinea and Togo, the impact of international norms is less than in states with abundant natural resources. The Gnassingbé clan has been able to protect the autocracy, commit flagrant human rights abuses, and ignore international calls for censure through an iron grip on the territory and those few resources that it possesses. Equatorial Guinea is a contrast since its resource base requires the dictatorship to establish and maintain relations with international oil firms. Although these relations may overwhelmingly favor the Nguemist regime, some concessions to international norms are necessary. These concessions leave open the possibility of change toward a more equitable regime.

The policy implications of this comparison suggest that emerging from the dismal equilibrium of despotic rule requires shifting the clan's incentives toward a relaxation of autocratic rule to escape the rogue's dilemma. This relaxation of authoritarianism must occur through internal policies that respond to international and domestic pressures. First, the regime must incrementally open the political process to relax the more onerous restrictions on basic liberties. What is critical is to phase in the liberalization to avoid a bloodbath perpetrated by the oppressed populations. Second, the clan might retire older members of the regime in order to replace them with younger citizens who entertain moderate solutions. Third, in both Equatorial Guinea and Togo, the armed forces need to be representative of the country. Staffing changes require an effort to avoid confrontation and civil war. Finally, domestic policies should distribute appropriations more equitably to offset the legacies of asymmetrical development.

International pressures are ultimately limited by the willingness of clan members to accept conditions. First, it is necessary to employ governance conditions to ensure due diligence in the use of development funds. These rules already exist in donor organizations. However, it is possible to condition aid eligibility on specific political developments. Second, the national governments of firms that engage in business with these states should enforce rigorously any violations of antibribery laws that are modeled on the U.S. Foreign Corrupt Practices Act. The effect would be to impose the rules and norms defined in those laws on the state. Third, international organizations are effective forums in which to condemn despotic regimes. Silence is in many respects acquiescence to the most egregious actions. The use of isolation by international organizations is a final strategy that may restrict or eliminate the links that autocrats enjoy with international firms and agencies.

These strategies or some combination thereof might be effective in promoting the positive reform of despotic regimes.

Notes

1. John R. Heilbrunn, "Togo: The National Conference and Stalled Reform," in John Clark and David Gardinier (eds.), *Political Reform in Francophone Africa* (Boulder, Colo., 1997), 225–245.

2. Amnesty International, "Togo: Will History Repeat Itself?" (London, July 2005), web.amnesty.org/library/index/engafr570122005.

3. U.S. State Department, "Togo," in *2005 Country Reports on Human Rights Practices* (Washington, D.C., March 8, 2006), www.state.gov/g/drl/rls/hrrpt/2005/ 61597.htm.

4. Agence France-Presse, "Manifestations à Lomé: Heurts entre forces de sécurité et manifestants," *Le Monde* (April 6, 2005).

5. The terms *dictator* and *autocrat* are used interchangeably in this chapter.

6. Kathleen Collins, "The Logic of Clan Politics: Evidence from the Central Asian Trajectories," *World Politics*, LVI (2004), 224.

7. Ronald Wintrobe, *The Political Economy of Dictatorship* (New York, 1998), 26, 39.

8. This point agrees with Engerman and Sokoloff's critique of the overdeterminism in arguments of "path dependency" in favor of path influence. See Stanley L. Engerman and Kenneth L. Sokoloff, "Factor Endowments, Institutions, and Differential Paths of Growth among New World Economies: A View from Economic Historians of the United States," in Stephen Haber (ed.), *How Latin America Fell Behind: Essays on the Economic Histories of Brazil and Mexico, 1800–1914* (Stanford, 1997), 262.

9. Hannah Arendt, *The Origins of Totalitarianism* (1948; reprint, New York, 1976).

10. Diego Gambetta, *The Sicilian Mafia* (New York, 1993).

11. Mongomo is the natal village of the Nguema clan. This clan is a member of the Esangui subgroup of the larger Fang ethnic group that lives on the mainland portion of Equatorial Guinea. Mongomo is located in the far east of the country, and its people have historic ties with Fang peoples of Congo-Brazzaville and Gabon.

12. U.S. Senate, Permanent Subcommittee on Investigations, "Money Laundering and Foreign Corruption: Enforcement and Effectiveness of the Patriot Act. Case Study Involving Riggs Bank," report prepared by the Minority Staff of the Permanent Subcommittee on Investigations (Washington, D.C., July 15, 2004).

13. Max Weber, *Economy and Society: An Outline of Interpretive Sociology* (Guenther Roth and Claus Wittich, trans. and eds.; Berkeley, 1978), 232.

14. Houchang E. Chehabi and Juan J. Linz, "A Theory of Sultanism: A Type of Nondemocratic Rule," in Houchang E. Chehabi and Juan J. Linz (eds.), *Sultanistic Regimes* (Baltimore, 1998), 7.

15. Janet Roitman and Gérard Roso, "Guinée-Équatoriale: Être 'off-shore' pour rester 'national,'" *Politique Africaine*, LXXXI (2001), 126.

16. Geoffrey Wood, "Business and Politics in a Criminal State: The Case of Equatorial Guinea," *African Affairs*, CIII (2004), 547–567.

17. Jean-François Bayart, Stephen Ellis, and Béatrice Hibou (eds.), *La criminalisation de l'état en Afrique* (Paris, 1997).

18. Daniel Kaufmann, "Myths and Realities of Governance and Corruption," in *The Global Competitiveness Report 2005–2006* (Davos, 2006), 82.

19. See the list of Nguema family members engaged in smuggling exposed by Santos Pascual Bikomo, "Guinea Conexión," *La Diáspora* (July 24, 1997), www.afrol.com/es/Paises/Guinea_Ecuatorial/documentos/guinea_conexion_97.htm.

20. Samantha Power, "Dying in Darfur: Can Ethnic Cleansing in Sudan Be Stopped?" *New Yorker* (August 30, 2004); Norman Cigar, *Genocide in Bosnia: The Policy of Ethnic Cleansing* (College Station, Tex., 1995).

21. Ben Kiernan, *The Pol Pot Regime: Race, Power, and Genocide in Cambodia under the Khmer Rouge, 1975–79* (New Haven, 1996).

22. Debbasch currently lives in Togo under the regime's protection. See Philippe Bernard, "Malgré un mandate d'arrêt, Charles Debbasch a séjourné en France," *Le Monde* (July 6, 2006).

23. "Togo—Conclusion d'un accord politique partiel," *Le Monde* (July 7, 2006).

24. Amnesty International, "Equatorial Guinea: Possible 'Disappearance'/Fear for Safety" (October 30, 2003), web.amnesty.org/library/Index/ENGAFR240122003?open&of=ENG-GNQ.

25. Amnesty International, "Prison Conditions/Detention without Charge/Possible Prisoner of Conscience/Fear of Torture or Ill-Treatment" (November 13, 2003).

26. Amnesty International, "Equatorial Guinea: Prisoners Starving to Death" (April 14, 2005), web.amnesty.org/library/Index/ENGAFR240062005?open&of=ENG-360.

27. Freedom House, "Freedom of the Press—Togo (2005)" (Washington, D.C., 2005), www.freedomhouse.org/inc/content/pubs/pfs/inc_country_detail.cfm?country=6847.

28. Amnesty International, "Will History Repeat Itself," 10.

29. Agence France-Presse, "Togo: Au moins once morts et 95 blessés dans les émeutes de Lomé," *Le Monde* (April 27, 2005).

30. Amnesty International, "Will History Repeat Itself," 9.

31. Ken Silverstein, "U.S. Oil Politics in the 'Kuwait of Africa': An Investigative Report," *Nation* (April 22, 2002), 13.

32. Mathew Engel, "Happy Days for the Great Dictators," *Guardian* (December 21, 1999); also cited in Wood, "Business and Politics in a Criminal State," 563.

33. For example, see Amnesty International, "Equatorial Guinea: Former Exile Held in Isolation without Charge" (August 2004), web.amnesty.org/appeals/index/gnq-010804-wwa-eng.

34. Wood, "Business and Politics in a Criminal State," 561.

35. Jedrzej George Frynas, "The Oil Boom in Equatorial Guinea," *African Affairs*, CIII (2004), 527–546.

36. International Monetary Fund, "Republic of Equatorial Guinea: 2005 Article IV Consultation—Staff Report" (Washington, D.C., 2005), 20.

37. Frynas, "The Oil Boom in Equatorial Guinea," 527.

38. Amnesty International, "Togo: A High Risk Transition" (March 18, 2005), web. amnesty.org/library/index/engafr570082005.

39. Amnesty International, "Togo: Rule of Terror" (May 5, 1999), web.amnesty. org/library/Index/engAFR570011999.

40. Stephen Smith, "Amnesty dénonce des exécutions au Togo en 1998," *Libération* (May 5, 1999).

41. Amnesty International, "Will History Repeat Itself."

42. Amnesty International, "Togo: Rule of Terror," 24, emphasis in original.

43. République Française, *Annuaire statistique de l'union française outre-mer, 1939–1959* (Paris, 1960), D226.

44. Silverstein, "U.S. Oil Politics in the 'Kuwait of Africa,'" 13.

45. Wood, "Business and Politics in a Criminal State," 551–552.

46. Although this idea is not particularly new, see the excellent reformulation by Carles Boix, *Democracy and Redistribution* (New York, 2003), 25.

47. Max Liniger-Goumaz, *Small Is Not Always Beautiful* (Lanham, Md., 1988), 48.

48. Ibid., 60.

49. Wood, "Business and Politics in a Criminal State," 549.

50. Liniger-Goumaz, *Small Is Not Always Beautiful*, 61.

51. Energy Information Administration, "Equatorial Guinea: Background" (2004), www.eia.doe.gov/emeu/cabs/eqguinea.html.

52. Wood, "Business and Politics in a Criminal State," 549.

53. Arnim Schwidrowski and others, *Equatorial Guinea: Selected Issues and Statistical Appendix* (Washington, D.C., October 29, 2003), 3; Esther Pan, "China, Africa, and Oil" (January 12, 2006), www.cfr.org/publication/9557.

54. International Monetary Fund, "Public Information Notice (PIN) No. 06/66" (June 14, 2006).

55. U.S. Senate, "Money Laundering and Foreign Corruption," 107.

56. Jean-Dominique Geslin, "Pétrodiplomatie," *Jeune Afrique l'Intelligent*, MMCLXXV (September 16–22, 2002), 33.

57. Engel, "Happy Days for the Great Dictators."

58. Wood, "Business and Politics in a Criminal State," 554; Roitman and Roso, "Guinée-Équatoriale," 127.

59. Liniger-Goumaz, *Small Is Not Always Beautiful*, 49.

60. Max Liniger-Goumaz, *A l'aune de la Guinée Équatoriale* (Sierre, Switzerland, 2003), 164.

61. Max Liniger-Goumaz, "Equatorial Guinea: 'We Saw Hell in Malabo': A Country Dominated by Foreign Companies, Human Rights Violations, and Political Authoritarianism," *Africa Contemporary Record: Annual Surveys and Documents*, CCVII (New York, 2004), B323.

62. See Amnesty International, "Equatorial Guinea" (2003), web.amnesty.org/report2003/gnq-summary-eng.

63. In January 1974, Togo took control of 51 percent of the mines; on February 2, Eyadéma announced seizure of the remaining 49 percent. "Le Togo prend contrôle total de la Compagnie togolaise des mines du Bénin," *Marchés Tropicaux et Méditerranéens, M* (February 8, 1974), 329.

64. Rita Cordonnier, *Femmes africaines et commerce: Les revendeuses de tissu de la ville de Lomé (Togo)* (Paris, 1987).

65. John R. Heilbrunn, "Commerce, Politics, and Business Associations in Benin and Togo," *Comparative Politics*, XXXVII (2005), 473–492.

66. Tony Hodges, *Angola from Afro-Stalinism to Petro-Diamond Capitalism* (Bloomington, Ind., 2001), 155. See also Ewen MacAskill and David Pallister, "Rich Pickings That Fuel African Wars," *Guardian* (London) (June 7, 2000).

67. Ibid.

68. See the UN Forum, "Diamonds for Blood" (June 17, 2000), www.unforum.com/UNaheadlines0.htm.

69. The term "stationary bandit" is from Mancur Olson Jr., "Dictatorship, Democracy, and Development," *American Political Science Review,* LXXXVII (1993), 567–576.

70. John Vidal, "Oil Rich, Dirt Poor," *Guardian* (August 26, 2004).

71. U.S. Senate, "Money Laundering and Foreign Corruption," 56–57.

72. The depiction of the Mongomo clan as gatekeepers is from the Senate report. Ibid., 98.

73. The Senate report notes that on six occasions, Riggs accepted cash deposits of $1,000,000 or more. Representatives of the Equatorial Guinean government would arrive with suitcases filled with cash. Ibid., 51.

74. Roitman and Roso, "Guinée-Équatoriale," 128.

75. Wood, "Business and Politics in a Criminal State," 551.

76. U.S. Senate, "Money Laundering and Foreign Corruption," 99.

77. Togo-Confidentiel, "Le Lt.-Col. Ernest Gnassingbé sur les 'détournement au Togo' et les accusations de menace de mort contre l'ancien PM—démenti et contradiction" (July 31, 2002), www.togo-confidentiel.com/texte/Politique/Ernest_Gnassingbe.htm.

78. Economist Intelligence Unit, "Togo, 1st Quarter" (London, 2002), 16.

79. Economist Intelligence Unit, "Togo, 4th Quarter" (London, 2002), 15.

ten

Uzbekistan: A Decaying Dictatorship Withdrawn from the West

Martha Brill Olcott

Uzbekistan is a decaying dictatorship with a seriously flawed human rights record. The country is dominated by Islam Karimov, the country's sole president, who has physically and mentally weakened in recent years but has delegated almost no power to his cabinet, his parliament, or his judicial system. The only source of authority that has accumulated more power in recent years is the country's national security service, which oversees Uzbekistan's elaborate security system. It both guarantees the power of the president and insulates him from society and even from much of the ruling elite.

The security services permeate much of society, helping to identify "politically unreliable" persons, many of whom are charged with membership in "extremist" religious organizations said to threaten the existence of the secular Uzbek state. As a result, Uzbekistan holds thousands of political prisoners. The security network is probably not as extensive as the population fears but is large enough to create an atmosphere of self-censorship in the media and in people's private lives, making official forms of control even more effective.

The unreformed nature of the country's political system has undoubtedly increased the security risks that the Uzbek government faces, transforming initially exaggerated threats into increasingly real ones. At the same time, though, the policies of the regime have also sharply limited the population's political experiences, making the prospect of developing a Western-style political system in the immediate future highly unlikely. (See the appendix table.)

The nature of the regime and the personality of the president have left the United States and the European Union with virtually no prospect of influencing political developments in Uzbekistan. But they also reflect the conflicting messages sent to Uzbekistan since independence, by the West in general and by the United States in particular. From the Uzbek point of view, these messages became even harder to decipher after September 11, 2001.

Since then, Uzbekistan has gone from being a staunch ally of the United States to a state that is setting itself up to be a real spoiler in the region, forcing the United States to leave its Uzbek base near the Afghan border and working with Russia and China to try to restrict the U.S. presence in the region and in neighboring Kyrgyzstan. Although Karimov's domestic and foreign policies are likely to harm the Uzbek people in the long run, in the short and medium term, they thwart U.S. goals in Afghanistan and South Asia.

This lamentable situation was in no way preordained. Relatively quickly after independence, in December 1991, Uzbekistan's leader sought to carve out an independent foreign policy for his nation based on Tashkent's preferences rather than those of Moscow. The strong-willed Karimov was determined to create uniquely "Uzbek" economic and political systems, which brought him into conflict with World Bank and International Monetary Fund advisers and with virtually anyone concerned with the country's performance in the area of human rights.

In the months after September 11, 2001, Karimov seemed on the verge of achieving his dream of a strategic partnership with the United States The latter received basing rights at Karshi-Khanabad, a Soviet-era airfield that afforded good access to northern Afghanistan, and, in early 2002, the United States and Uzbekistan signed several memorandums of agreement. Tashkent pledged itself to achieve steady progress in political as well as economic reform.

The Uzbeks quickly demonstrated themselves to be reliable strategic partners, believing that they shared with the United States similar goals regarding ridding the Central and South Asian region of "international terrorism" and being willing to take this fight to Iraq as well. But with U.S. policymakers confident that the situation in Afghanistan was under control, and with Uzbekistan offering little strategic support of any value in the Iraqi battle, the United States offered far less security assistance for Tashkent than the Uzbeks expected.

At the same time, promises of free and fair parliamentary elections in 2004 clearly proved hollow, and the prospects of political reform more generally seemed dim, making it harder and harder for Uzbekistan's defenders to muster any arguments against human rights critics in both the United States and many EU capitals. These critics pressured their respective governments to hold Tashkent to its international human rights obligations. By mid-2005, both the United States and the EU had sharply limited the kinds of direct foreign assistance that could be offered to the Uzbek government; in the European case, this meant restricting foreign aid almost exclusively to nongovernmental actors.

The breaking point was reached in May 2005, when Uzbek forces fired on a crowd in Andijan, leaving hundreds dead.[1] The crowd, which included armed demonstrators, had gathered in the aftermath of a prison break, whose purpose, in part, was to liberate popular local businessmen who were part of an unsanctioned religious group and were charged with being Islamic extremists.[2] The Western press picked up this story very quickly, even though access to Andijan was denied to foreign reporters, and almost immediately labeled it a massacre of unarmed Uzbek civilians. This "massacre" in turn led to swift pressure from European capitals for an international inquiry. There was also substantial pressure from Washington, where the Bush administration was looking for ways to balance its growing interest in spreading democracy globally.

Tashkent reacted quickly and decisively, giving U.S. and European leaders little opportunity for constructive engagement. Moscow and Beijing, Uzbekistan's partners in the Shanghai Cooperation Organization (SCO), were quick to accept Tashkent's version that "terrorists" were responsible for the Andijan massacre, a conclusion that was borne out by an "international investigation" carried out by SCO member states. Although shunned by the West, Karimov was embraced in Beijing and then in Moscow. At the SCO summer summit in 2005, the member nations called upon the U.S. military to withdraw from Central Asia; shortly thereafter, the United States was given six months to vacate the base that it had been using in Uzbekistan. As the last U.S. planes were preparing to fly out, the Uzbeks and Russians signed a comprehensive military alliance. The government in Tashkent had made a clear choice to lock out the West.

A Bad Partner Left Washington with Bad Choices

Uzbekistan had posed a growing policy dilemma for the United States well before the disturbances in Andijan. Since the "Georgian Revolution" of 2003, pro-democracy nongovernmental groups (especially those with U.S. government or Open Society Institute funding) had been under considerable pressure in Uzbekistan. Their position further worsened after the Ukrainian revolution of 2004 and the ouster of Askar Akayev, president of neighboring Kyrgyzstan, in March 2005. Many in the U.S. democracy-building community also began pressing hard for the United States to end all funding to the Uzbek government in the hope that doing so might lead to a "color revolution"—as the postcommunist ousters were termed—in Uzbekistan as well.

But Washington was given some difficult choices in the first half of 2005 when the Uzbek government sought U.S. support for "democracy building" projects of its own, including prison and judicial reform, help with the procurators' offices, and work with parliamentarians and members of new political parties and groups whose formation was organized by the Uzbek government. Absent U.S. or other foreign government support, these groups are unlikely to develop any civic competence. The same is also true of the relatively small number of individuals active in independent (essentially opposition) secular groups.

As most U.S. policymakers charged with responsibility for Uzbekistan seemed to recognize, the secular opposition in Uzbekistan is not a substantial force, lacking the strength of opposition groups in Kazakhstan, Tajikistan, or Kyrgyzstan. Therefore, even before Andijan, Uzbekistan was seen as an unlikely candidate for a color revolution. The prospects for a secularly inspired and popularly supported revolution against Karimov and his entourage have grown even more remote over time.

In contrast, religious opposition groups (both those willing to cooperate with the regime and those that refuse) are increasing in numbers and will be a critical force in political coalition building in the future.

The nature of the political system that has evolved in Uzbekistan strongly reflects Karimov's personal preferences for the institutional relationships that govern how political power is exercised, but unlike the regime in Turkmenistan, which has been centered on a single person and has many aberrant qualities, the Uzbek regime is not defined around the person of the president. Instead, power is concentrated in the institution of the presidency.

It is a decaying dictatorship, defined by a very strong, but not omnipotent, president who is beginning to lose his grip on political events as he weakens physically and mentally. The regime's power is based on the threat or the use of force, and, in this regard, it builds quite heavily on the Soviet system in place at the time of independence.

Although the Tashkent government is more repressive than that of most neighboring countries, the political system that has evolved in Uzbekistan is similar to that of several other post-Soviet states. It is also similar to regimes found in parts of Africa in the first decades after independence. It is a hypercentralized presidential system, with regional governors appointed by and subordinated to the center, but at the local level, some autonomy remains through the exercise of traditional (rather than democratic) authority.

The prime minister and cabinet members serve at the president's will and are reluctant to cross him. The country's legislature has been a virtual rubber stamp, although a new professional legislature, elected in December 2004, does have limited power, albeit rarely exercised. Although formal censorship has been eliminated, de facto government control remains. Corruption is a serious problem at the national, regional, and local levels, and undermines the economic policy of the government and perverts the functioning of the legal system. Leaders of independent political forces are subject to harassment, imprisonment, or exile.

But it is hard to say just how much worse the situation in Uzbekistan is than in several other post-Soviet states. Measuring repression is very difficult and subjective. The civilian deaths in Andijan were on a scale rarely seen save in civil war conditions.

Uzbekistan certainly has more political prisoners (both in relative and absolute numbers) than Kazakhstan, Kyrgyzstan, Azerbaijan, or Belarus. As of 2006, there were several thousand political prisoners in the country, and a large proportion of them were members of Hizb ut-Tahrir, the Islamic Movement of Uzbekistan (IMU), or Jama'at, an IMU offspring.

But the challenge that the secular regime faces in Uzbekistan is also more acute than in neighboring states. There are many more devout Muslims, as well as adherents of radical or fundamentalist Islam, in Uzbekistan than elsewhere in the region. Only neighboring Tajikistan has experienced a religious revival on a scale similar to Uzbekistan; and it is precisely because of the politicization of Islam in Tajikistan and that country's civil war a decade ago that Uzbek authorities target religious believers. At the same time, the government does make regular offers of amnesty to prisoners who renounce the illegal organizations to which they belong. The number of political prisoners is a tiny fraction of the total number of religious activists (those without formal ties to state-sanctioned Islamic groups). Before the events in Andijan, the Uzbek government had grown more tolerant of unsanctioned religious activity as a means of controlling the spread of the Hizb ut-Tahrir movement, which, they argue, is an international terrorist group. But the regime did draw the line against groups that authorities in Tashkent saw as having explicit political agendas. The businessmen being tried for religious extremism in

Andijan in 2005 were accused of being members of Akramia, a group that had split from Hizb ut-Tahrir in the mid-1990s.

Explaining the Uzbek government's behavior does not excuse it, but it does underscore the difficulty of making effective comparisons. It would be hard to predict Kyrgyz or Kazakh elite behavior were the ethnoreligious cleavages in these countries similar to those of Uzbekistan. Secular opposition figures in all these countries have fared very poorly. Muggings and mysterious deaths have occurred throughout the former Soviet Union, as well as prison beatings and even suicides by those accused of crimes. But without question, Uzbekistan has a more forceful security establishment than Kyrgyzstan, in particular, where security forces stood by and watched demonstrators bring down the presidency of Askar Akayev.

Uzbekistan's security forces have grown stronger since the May 2005 events in Andijan, and, as of 2006, were firmly under the control of the chairman of the State Committee on Security. Previously there was a rivalry between this branch of security forces and the Ministries of Internal Affairs and of Defense. Even if Karimov were to disappear tomorrow, it would lead only to incremental changes in the country's political system. Uzbekistan's increasingly more important foreign partners—Russia and China—would likely throw their support behind any succession orchestrated by the security service.

Alternate Outcomes?

Uzbekistan might have developed into a more democratic system—become more like Kazakhstan and Kyrgyzstan. In fact, it would have resembled those two states had Karimov come to power with a firmer political power base in 1989, had the political system in Tajikistan not imploded in 1992, or had the West found more effective ways of engaging with Uzbekistan at key junctures in the years since independence.

Karimov probably thought that he could outmaneuver his political rivals in normal circumstances but not in extraordinary ones. These extraordinary circumstances served to legitimate Karimov's political choices for a large part of the population. Support in 2006 for the Uzbek president was obviously fading and seemed to have been severely damaged by what occurred in Andijan. But the reasons for this slide seem—and there is no reliable body of public opinion that one can look to— largely economic rather than political.

Reforming the Uzbek political and economic system has always been difficult. But if economic and political reform had been conducted in tandem, Uzbekistan would have developed differently.

For its part, the United States could have done more to influence developments in Uzbekistan, particularly in the aftermath of September 11, 2001. The United States or U.S. surrogates such as the International Monetary Fund and World Bank might have achieved quite different outcomes had they used the carrot of vastly increased economic assistance along with the stick of U.S. military withdrawal from the region.

In 2001, the Karimov government desperately wanted to increase engagement with the United States. Karimov saw the opening of the base at Karshi-Khanabad as the start of a close strategic partnership between the United States and Uzbekistan—a validation of a foreign policy strategy designed to distance the Uzbeks from Russia.

By 2004, the prospects for shaping the Uzbek political system began to diminish sharply. Washington's priorities changed after the beginning of the Iraq war, and, as they did, Russia and China showed themselves more than willing to court Uzbekistan without pressure for domestic political or economic reform.

Presidential Politics and Economic Policy in Uzbekistan

The priorities and values of the Uzbek regime mirror those of Russia and China much more closely than they do those of the United States or its European partners. As is true elsewhere in Central Asia, Uzbekistan's government reflects the personal stamp of its first and current president. Hailing from Samarkand (Tamerlane's capital) and rumored to be of both Tajik and Uzbek ethnic stock, Karimov believes that Uzbekistan has a historic mission to lead Central Asia.

This sense of mission has shaped much of his presidency. Although Karimov is often compared to the late Saparmurad Niyazov of Turkmenistan, this comparison does not do justice to the complexity of the Uzbek political system, which is fundamentally different from that of either Kazakhstan or Kyrgyzstan—less participatory, but as complex. It is more reminiscent of a country like Tunisia, where the president is the dominant power in the political system but where dispersed power is only partly delegated by presidential discretion.

Uzbekistan qualifies as a modern-day authoritarian political system. Although the power of the president and the security organs reaches down into even remote localities, their success requires the cooperation of members of the ruling elite and some degree of public cooperation. The latter has become increasingly more difficult to attain. Uzbekistan also has not been immune to the forces of globalization, and the impact of technology means that this country is unlike the totalitarian states of the 1930s. Independent sources of information do penetrate into the Uzbek population.

While news broadcasts on the state channels are closely monitored for content, it is estimated that almost half of the households in Tashkent have access to satellite programming, which includes Russian, English, and Turkish language news. Similarly, although user privacy is not as well protected in Uzbekistan as in either Kyrgyzstan or Kazakhstan, and the blocking of sites is more common, Internet cafés are found in almost every part of the country. In the end, economics more than politics defines how much access a person has to unfettered sources of information.

Karimov does not pretend to be anything other than a strong and autocratic figure, modeling himself after Timur (Tamerlane, 1336–1405), who is commemorated in downtown Tashkent with a statue and a large museum. While Uzbek diplomats try to explain the cult of Timur as a measure designed to wean the Uzbeks from the Russian-dominated Soviet-era versions of their history, Uzbekistan's neighbors understand it differently, taking it as an implicit threat. This threat is especially real to Kyrgyzstan and Tajikistan, both relatively weak states.

While doing little to directly undermine the Soviet Union in its final years, many in the Uzbek elite saw the period of Russian domination as a historic interlude that was bound to end eventually, and viewed the collapse of the USSR as allowing them to fulfill their historic destiny.

Karimov saw independence as an opportunity to depart from the constraints of Soviet-era plans for the republic. Independence made him feel empowered to carve out a model of political and economic development that he believed was attuned to Uzbekistan's specific needs. Despite the fact that he lacked the legitimacy of having participated in a struggle for national liberation, Karimov cast himself as a nationalist figure much like leaders of newly independent states in the 1960s. But for all of his claim to foster "new" Uzbek-centered thinking, Karimov has been unable to go beyond his Soviet-era training and experience.

He has been a strong supporter of a "command and control" based economy and was attracted to Chinese-style models of economic reform, where part of the economy was liberalized while most of it remained under strong state control. In particular, Karimov believed that the Soviet-era system of price supports and subsidies could be preserved through continued state control of Uzbekistan's two primary export-earning commodities—cotton and gold. Karimov believed that this formula would preserve social and political stability, especially if new responsibility were devolved to traditional local institutions, such as the *mahalla*, the neighborhood or local community. His political vision was also tailor-made to spread corruption throughout the economy.

Karimov's economic strategy was a logical complement to his political program, in which he also sought to assert a strong state presence and to counter the "uncontrolled" forces that had been spawned by Moscow's liberalizing policies of the late 1980s (Gorbachev's policies of *glasnost* and *perestroika*). In the last years of Soviet rule, Uzbekistan began to develop a culture of political participation with two pro-democracy political parties, Erk (Liberty) and Birlik (Unity), and a growing Islamic revival.

Intellectuals and writers, led by Abdurakhim Pulatov, founded Birlik in 1989 to pursue a scope of concerns from environmental to social and economic policy. Birlik was officially registered as a movement in 1991, but it was denied registration as a political party, banned in Uzbekistan, and its leaders forced into exile.[3]

Erk, which grew out of the Birlik Popular Front of Uzbekistan, was officially founded on April 11, 1990, by Muhammad Salikh and two of his friends. It was sparked in part by the appointment of Muhammad Sadiq Muhammad Yusuf, a dynamic young mufti, to head the country's religious establishment. The Erk Party distinguished itself from the rest of the Birlik movement by stressing the principle of "independence first" rather than the notion of "first democracy, then independence," which had become the slogan of pro-Moscow factions of the movement. The widespread public support for the new party caused the government to take severe repressive measures. Erk is now effectively banned in Uzbekistan.[4]

In the early 1990s, the Communist Party elite was also becoming less monolithic in its worldview than previously, and many of the country's reformist figures were more comfortable with Vice President Shukhrullo Mirsaidov than with Karimov, the more rigid and seemingly authoritarian president.[5]

Fearing his lack of popularity, Karimov began moving against his rivals. Mirsaidov was dismissed in early 1992, and the leaders of Birlik and Erk were soon forced into exile or subjected to officially sponsored harassment.[6] Since 1992, the only legal political parties have been those created by the government. These parties include Milliy Tiklanish (National Revival Democratic Party of Uzbekistan), Fidokorlar (Self-Sacrificers), Adolat (Justice), and the People's Democratic Party (former Communist Party).

The civil war in Tajikistan in the 1990s also fueled the Uzbek government's fear of violence and the seeming uncontrollability of the masses, which the fighting in Tajikistan was said to demonstrate. That war was often used as an explanation as to why Central Asian countries should proceed slowly to open up the political process. Many Uzbeks accepted the government rationale as correct, especially given lingering political instability in Afghanistan.

The country's Islamic revival proved more difficult to contain than its secular opposition. Yusuf was removed in late 1992, but radical Islamic groups centered in Andijan and Namangan continued to gain support from the thousands of young, underemployed men who lived in the densely populated Ferghana Valley. Several charismatic Islamic figures were preaching in those years (men who had received their first training in underground schools in the 1970s), and some of whom had even been able to study in other Muslim countries.[7] While the most prominent Islamists were arrested or driven into exile by the mid-1990s, radical Islamic ideas continued to be propagated in the absence of clear leaders.

Although the Uzbek government had been targeting leaders of radical Islamic groups since the mid-1990s, they did so even more ruthlessly after a series of explosions rocked Tashkent in 1999. Not content merely to target members of the IMU, the Karimov regime set out to eliminate potential as well as actual religious extremists. One particular target was the membership (or the purported membership) of Hizb ut-Tahrir, which had experienced a dramatic increase in its membership in the mid- and late-1990s.[8] Outlawed everywhere in Central Asia except in Kazakhstan, where Hizb ut-Tahrir has not been permitted to register legally, the movement's goal is the creation of a new caliphate. Its leadership claims that it is focused on using peaceful means to return Muslims to the true faith.

But the Uzbek leadership understood it and any of its offshoots or splinter groups to be treasonous, and by late 2001, over 7,000 "religious extremists" had been arrested. Those rounded up included people with known associations to seditious groups, those reputed to be devout, and those who were seemingly devout, such as bearded men or women wearing extremely chaste dress.[9] Periodic waves of arrests against religious extremists followed on a fairly regular basis, with the charges varying, based on which groups were most active at the time.

The Tashkent bombings further hardened the Uzbek government's determination to both delineate and defend its national boundaries (which the government then began mining, especially those shared with Tajikistan and Kyrgyzstan) to prevent IMU insurgents from crossing.[10] These efforts did not stop the IMU, but ordinary people paid a high price as farmers and their animals were blown up and trade was seriously disrupted.[11]

In general, the international environment in which the Uzbeks found themselves served to reinforce the ruling elite's economic conservatism, as the government was frightened of what would happen if human security were somehow compromised and social welfare commitments were not maintained. Uzbekistan stuck to price supports long after Kazakhstan and Kyrgyzstan had abandoned them, but the trade restrictions introduced to sustain this policy stifled Uzbekistan's own entrepreneurs, who were made all but extinct after Uzbekistan closed its borders in early 1999.

What price Uzbekistan paid as a result of Karimov's economic choices is hard to measure. While Uzbek statistics show a growth in GDP from 1992 to 2001, years in which other post-Soviet states experienced sharp economic declines, official statistics are subject to criticism because of the economic assumptions upon which they are based.[12] Much of this growth is a reflection of the profitability of state-owned and state-exported commodities such as gold and cotton, and does not reflect growth in any new sectors of Uzbekistan's domestic economy. Moreover, the Uzbek economy in 2006 remained highly dependent on exports of cotton.[13]

The "Threat" of Islamic Radicalism

One of the most complicated issues for political reform in Uzbekistan is the question of the relationship between religion and the state, as well as a related question of what legal protections should be afforded to Islamic fundamentalists. In the Uzbek case, as elsewhere throughout the region, the supervision of religious life is in the hands of secular authorities, and in most of Central Asia, many of these authorities were previously tied to the atheistic Soviet regime. As already noted, the country's senior cleric, the mufti, is nominally chosen by a gathering of religious elders, but in reality he serves at the explicit behest of the State Committee for Religious Affairs. While individual mosques have more discretionary authority to regulate their own affairs than was true in Soviet times, the opening of religious schools is still strictly regulated by the state, and it is very hard to secure permission. That represents a real shift from the policies of the early years after independence. The State Committee includes some believers among its membership to try to balance the influence (and bad press) from the continued presence of individuals who are tied to the Soviet era's atheistic policies. There are also occasional rumors that some of these believers are in fact members of radical Islamic groups who are interested in sabotaging the state's policy toward religion from within by pressing the state to support policies that go against the values of the Uzbek community.

In fact, much of the political activity that is in opposition to the state comes from the various and often competitive Islamic communities in the country. Restrictions on adopting religious dress in schools and public places, initially introduced in the late 1990s, remain in effect, although they appear to be less rigorously enforced, having already had the desired effect of forcing women wearing the *hijab* to withdraw from public life and getting bearded men to either shave or to go underground. The restrictions enjoyed some public support, which highlights the complexity of religious life in Uzbekistan, where secular, traditional, and radical Islamic forces have long vied for influence within the community.

Nonetheless, there seems to be strong support within the country for religious life to be regulated by the community of believers within a legal framework provided by the state. A lot of the political energy visible in 2006 in Uzbekistan was centered precisely on these questions and not on the stand of the government toward secular civil liberties.

On most other questions there seems to be very little consensus, including what should be the state's attitude toward extreme Islamic groups—those who reject the dominant Hanafi legal tradition. Hizb ut-Tahrir is one such group, and its growth in popularity speaks in part to the absence of secular and religious options.

Uzbekistan's political elite is not formally against Islam but is very wary of revivalist or fundamentalist Islam—of people who are eager to live by "the exact teachings of the book." They want to keep their republic secular and prevent devout Muslims from forcing all of their coreligionists into the public observance of the faith. Such pressure already exists even in a place as secular as Kyrgyzstan. But today, even within Uzbekistan's ruling elite, there are many who are content to see secular values overshadowed by religious ones.

While the heavy hand applied by the Karimov regime against "extreme" Islamic groups created genuine discomfort in Washington, the official Uzbek attitudes about encouraging "good" or tolerant Islam while attacking "bad" or "extremist" Islam were very much in keeping with the official U.S. thinking on such questions. If Uzbekistan's human rights record were better, it would have fitted well into the Bush administration's global strategy of encouraging the spread of "moderate" Islamic ideas while working to defeat the spread of radical ideological trends.

Before the events in Andijan and the worsening of U.S.-Uzbek relations, the U.S. embassy in Tashkent worked actively to identify moderate clerics and had invited many of them, as well as members of the state council on religion, to the United States as part of the international visitors program. The U.S. government also made fellowship money available to Uzbek scholars of Islam to come to the United States and pursue research projects on comparative Islam that were designed to encourage greater religious toleration. Virtually all of these programs were effectively frozen by the government in Tashkent in late 2005 and early 2006.

Before the events in Andijan, the Uzbek government had been willing to engage in discussions with Western officials over the treatment of political prisoners, including jailed members of the Hizb-ut Tahrir, and had introduced some limited measures to improve the conditions of at least some of those who would term themselves "prisoners of conscience," including granting them increased opportunities for prayer and some amelioration of what in many cases were dire conditions.[14]

The Uzbek government remained adamant in 2006 that Hizb ut-Tahrir was a threat to the state and, if anything, stepped up its propaganda against the group, insisting that its aim was the forcible overthrow of the state. Official representations have been made to visiting diplomats, journalists, and scholars that some members of the group were already training and taking up arms.

The Risk of Ethnic and Regional Cleavages

Much less discussed, but certainly of continued concern, is the question of interethnic relations. Ethnicity has proved more fluid in Uzbekistan than in any other place in Central Asia. Those who choose to identify themselves as Uzbeks and who learn the language are viewed as Uzbeks, even if they come from ethnically mixed families or from families who in earlier times may have identified themselves as Kazakh, Kyrgyz, or Tajik.[15] Ethnic Tajiks are the country's largest minority, and Uzbek-Tajik relations remain the most politically sensitive of all minority issues.[16]

Over the past eighty years, many among the Tajik-speaking population in Uzbekistan have gradually reidentified themselves and their families as Uzbeks on passports and official documents. Some of this reidentification has simply been a question of political urgency. An untold number of Tajiks with Uzbek indicated as their nationality still identify themselves as Tajiks and would prefer to be living in a Tajik-dominated state. The Uzbek-Tajik split continues to have a real impact on Uzbek political life. Tajiks, especially those living in the border regions, are seen as potentially disloyal, and there has even been forced resettlement of residents of some Tajik villages along the mountainous spine that Uzbekistan shares with Tajikistan (in Uzbekistan's provinces of Kashkadarya and Surkhandarya), the site of the mid-2000 IMU incursion.[17]

Similarly, any time a Tajik is the beneficiary of political favor, rumors begin to spread that he will use his new position to advance Tajik interests. When Shavkat Mirziyayev, a Tajik from Samarkand, was appointed prime minister in 2003, many Uzbeks began to complain that it was just the first step in the Tajiks' "stealing away" the cities of Samarkand and Bukhara, both of which Tajikistan believes rightfully belong in its republic.

Regionalism is also a very important political factor in Uzbekistan, and the lingering power of regional elites is another reason why Tashkent has been reluctant to engage in widespread political or economic reform. As elsewhere in the region, the president appoints provincial leaders, and Karimov has made steady use of this power, replacing officials whose loyalty is in doubt. But there has been a great deal more stability at the middle and lower levels of the provincial government, and regional elites use their political and economic levers to extract "rents" from the local population in return for delivering rents to the ruling elite in the capital.

As political conditions normalized during the first decade of independence, these subnational identities, which were stimulated in the tumultuous conditions of the final years of Soviet rule, have receded to some degree. But in a time of political transition, the country's social and political cleavages will inevitably become more important. The signals of impending transition are becoming increasingly apparent in Uzbekistan; in 2006 and 2007, even the "man on the street" has begun talking about how the president is ill and that it is time for him to leave. While it is unclear whether this transition will come in a few months or a few years, until it is completed, the political system will be difficult to transform.

Unlike in some of the other countries of Central Asia, the competing political forces in Uzbekistan are unlikely to want to use parliamentary or other Western-style participatory forms of government to mobilize political support. None of these groups feel that they have mastered such styles of political infighting. This makes replication of the political scenarios seen in Georgia, Ukraine, and Kyrgyzstan very unlikely in Uzbekistan.

Moreover, the absence of participatory institutions is likely to make the period of transition a time of potential instability, as excluded political groups seek to expand their potential power bases and influence by appealing to regional and subnational groups. For much the same reason, the role of religious opposition groups may increase as well.

There is some reason for optimism that the transfer of power will be accomplished peacefully, albeit not democratically. While the political system of Uzbekistan may appear simple to the casual outside observer, with a powerful president and a strong security system able to dictate the terms of political and economic engagement to a country of over 25 million people, in reality the political system is complex. It is also governed by an internal logic and rules of engagement that are opaque to ordinary citizens but transparent to those who need to know them.

Such a complex system transforms slowly, especially if the change comes at the hands of outside actors who do not fully understand where the levers of power lie, let alone how or by whom they are exercised. The Soviet rulers of Uzbekistan were slow to learn this lesson, and they, like the United States and Western democracy builders, argued that they were pressing for change in order to introduce a more just and equitable political system—one that would benefit the people and not the rulers.

Conclusion

Months before the deaths in Andijan, it was clear that the Uzbek leadership had not succeeded in creating a new strategic partnership with the United States and that both sides were growing more frustrated with the relationship that had evolved. The bitterness with which it ended was occasioned by Uzbekistan's refusal to allow the Organization for Security and Cooperation in Europe, the UN, or other Western-style entity to investigate what it believed was solely a domestic event.

The breach with the United States and Europe was already there and growing wider, making an eventual rupture likely, even had the prison break, demonstrations, and shootings of civilians by Uzbek security services never happened. Once the post–September 11 U.S. policy agenda began shifting from the war on terror to a fight to free the world's peoples from tyrannical rulers, it became less tenable to Karimov and the leaders of other potential "rogue" states.

Policymakers in Washington hoped that the events of November 2003 in Tbilisi, December 2004 in Kiev, and March 2005 in Osh and Bishkek served as a warning to the Uzbek authorities that they needed to engage in a fundamental reexamination of the relationship between the governors and the governed. But the message heard by those in Tashkent was different. They believed that the United States was stirring up populations that, save for self-interested foreign or domestic rabble-rousers, would otherwise remain quiescent.

Given that others, like the leaders in Russia and China, shared these views, neither Karimov nor his advisers believe that Uzbekistan is a rogue state. They believe that they are deviating from Western norms, but they see these norms as both artificial and forcibly imposed.

The government in Tashkent has been willing to accept the punishment meted out for its obstinacy. European sanctions barred key Uzbek leaders from traveling to EU countries and eliminated direct foreign assistance to the Uzbek government from member states. Uzbekistan would probably even accept full trade sanctions—simply increasing cotton, gold, and gas sales to Russian, Chinese, and Iranian partners—before choosing to change the regime's autocratic policies. In part for this reason, bilateral relations between Uzbekistan and a number of key EU states, most particularly Britain, Germany, and France, began improving in the second half of 2006, as did relations between Tashkent and Washington. The latter relationship is still hampered by Uzbekistan's poor human rights performance, and EU sanctions against Uzbekistan have yet to be removed.[18] These relationships remain problematic, but an increasing dialogue between the Europeans and Americans and the Uzbeks testifies to the West's strong concern over the indefinite isolation of Tashkent.

Karimov's behavior makes Uzbekistan's regime similar to some of the other cases considered in this volume. When under attack, it isolates the country and its citizens more completely, making the task of rebuilding a civic order after the death of the ruler even more difficult and in some cases impossible. But behavior of states like Uzbekistan is in part fueled by the lack of universally accepted international standards. As long as Tashkent can count on strong support from Moscow and Beijing, then Uzbekistan's rulers will have considerable leeway to ignore the preferences of Europe and the United States.

Notes

1. For some independent analyses of what occurred, see Shirin Akiner, "Violence in Andijan, 13 May 2005: An Independent Assessment" (July 2005), www.silkroad studies.org/new/inside/publications/0507Akiner.pdf; International Crisis Group, "Uzbekistan: The Andijon Uprising," *Asia Briefing*, XXXVIII (May 25, 2005); Radio

Free Europe–Radio Liberty, "Uzbekistan: Andijon Cover-Up Provokes EU Sanctions" (September 30, 2005), www.rferl.org/featuresarticle/2005/09/56ae1a1c-486d-4b53-9f66-bc46b6123db2.html.

2. For an account, see Martha Brill Olcott and Marina Barnett, "The Andijan Uprising, Akramiya and Akram Yuldashev" (June 22, 2006), www.carnegieendowment.org/publications/index.cfm?fa=view&id=18453. The businessmen were members of Akramia, an offshoot of the better-known Hizb ut-Tahrir religious party.

Between 1990 and 1992, Akram Yuldashev, a mathematics teacher from Andijan, wrote a theological pamphlet in Uzbek, *Yimonga Yul* (Path to Faith), which set forth his philosophy. Despite being self-taught on religious issues, Yuldashev nevertheless became a spiritual authority and was seen as a charismatic leader. He was popular across the whole Ferghana Valley, especially in Andijan. The decisive moment in the establishment of the community of his followers was his acquaintance with local Andijan businessmen

It is evident that the Andijan uprising revolved around the controversial case of Akramia. There were two opposing sets of opinion toward this group. According to one view, which was mostly presented by the Uzbek government and some local experts, Akramia was an extremist Islamic organization that harbored an intention to overthrow the secular constitutional order of Uzbekistan. The other side denied that such an organization even existed. See Alisher Ilkhamov, "The Phenomenology of 'Akramia': Separating Facts from Fiction," *China and Eurasia Forum Quarterly*, IV (2006), 39–48.

3. See "Popular Movement 'Birlik' Party" (January 2007), www.birlik.net/index.php?l=uk.

4. "The Erk Democratic Party" (January 2007), www.euronet.nl/users/turkfed/erkparty.htm.

5. Shukhrullo Mirsaidov, a former prime minister, chairman of the Council of Ministers, and vice president of Uzbekistan, left the government in 1992 after a battle with the Uzbek leadership. He formed the Forum for Democratic Forces in late 1993 to unite opposition groups, but without much success. Earlier in 1993, he faced criminal charges, such as abuse of power, and was required to pay a hefty fine. Although he was later cleared by an international tribunal, the government reportedly continued to pressure him and his relatives to pay. Mirsaidov and his family also faced physical harassment. He reported that he was subjected to five physical attacks after leaving government. See Human Rights Watch, "Uzbekistan: Persistent Human Rights Violations and Prospects for Improvement" (May 1996), www.hrw.org/reports/1996/UZBEK.htm.

6. Muhammad Salih, who had run against Karimov in the 1991 presidential elections and became leader of the Erk Party, took refuge in Turkey in late 1993. Abdurahim Polat, from Birlik, left for the United States in late 1994 after suffering a near-fatal beating in Tashkent.

7. Abdujabar Abduvakhitov, "Islamic Revivalism in Uzbekistan," in Dale F. Eickelman, *Muslim Politics* (Bloomington, 1993), 81.

8. See International Crisis Group, "The IMU and the Hizb ut-Tahrir: Implications of the Afghanistan Campaign," *Asia Briefing,* XI (Brussels, January 30, 2002).

9. U.S. Department of State, "Uzbekistan," in *2001 Country Report on Human Rights Practices* (Washington, D.C., March 4, 2002), www.state.gov/g/drl/rls/hrrpt/2001/eur/8366.htm. See also Human Rights Watch, "World Report 2001: Uzbekistan" (New York, 2001), www.hrw.org/wr2k1/europe/uzbekistan.html.

10. "Transcaucasia and Central Asia," Radio Free Europe–Radio Liberty Newsline (October 5, 2000).

11. For instance, Uzbek exports to the Kyrgyz Republic dropped from U.S.$102 million in 1994 to $51.2 million in 1998, while imports decreased from $68 million in 1994 to $19.2 million in 1997. Exports to Turkmenistan declined from $174 million in 1994 to $41 million in 1998, and imports fell from $144 million in 1994 to $10 million in 1998.

12. The Organization for Economic Cooperation and Development (OECD) reported that even with possible statistical artifacts contributing to the relatively good GDP performance since 1991, Uzbekistan indeed experienced positive economic growth since the mid-1990s. Richard Pomfret, "Central Asia since 1991: The Experience of the New Independent States," *OECD Development Centre Technical Papers,* CCXII (2003), 15 and 44.

13. In the early 1990s, agriculture accounted for 30 percent of Uzbekistan's GDP. Uzbekistan has been one of the world's five largest producers and exporters of cotton. For instance, in 1993, cotton exports constituted 41 percent of total exports and 23 percent of total GDP; in 1994, these figures were 51 percent and 26.5 percent, respectively.

14. The state-sponsored National Human Rights Center of Uzbekistan, headed by Akmal Saidov, has been instrumental in buying televisions, bedding, and even new underwear to supply some of the facilities in which political and religious prisoners are incarcerated.

15. This was not an abstract consideration, as Soviet internal passports included an obligatory line on nationality.

16. The country had a large Russian population at the time of independence, but in 2006 it is estimated that only 5.5 percent of the country's population was Russian, compared to 8.3 percent in 1989. Most of this remaining population, which is disproportionately elderly, seems grudgingly accepting of its second-class status. The Kazakh population has also diminished, as most Kazakhs who could relocated to Kazakhstan, where economic opportunities are much greater (the Kazakhs constitute 3 percent of the total population). Tajiks constitute 5 percent of the total population; Tatars, 1.5 percent; and Karakalpak, 2.5 percent. *The World Factbook: Uzbekistan,* Central Intelligence Agency (March 8, 2007), www.cia.gov/cia/publications/factbook/geos/uz.html.

17. After Uzbek security forces reportedly drove IMU militants out of the region, local officials established minefields along the border. Tajik experts also say that Uzbek security forces forcibly removed about 5,000 residents from border villages. Most of those removed were Tajiks, who were resettled about 100 miles away in Sherabad. "Inter-Ethnic Tension Threatens Fragile Tajik-Uzbek Relations" (June 28, 2004), www.eurasianet.org/departments/insight/articles/eav021403.shtml.

18. U.S. Department of State, "Uzbekistan," in *2006 Country Reports on Human Rights Practices* (March 6, 2007), www.state.gov/g/drl/rls/hrrpt/2006/78848.htm.

Appendix 10A. Nations in Transit Ratings and Averaged Scores, Uzbekistan, 1997–2006[a]

Item	1997	1998	1999	2001	2002	2003	2004	2005	2006
Electoral process	6.25	6.50	6.50	6.75	6.75	6.75	6.75	6.75	6.75
Civil society	6.50	6.50	6.50	6.50	6.75	6.50	6.50	6.50	7.00
Independent media	6.50	6.50	6.50	6.75	6.75	6.75	6.75	6.75	7.00
Governance[b]	6.00	6.25	6.25	6.00	6.00	6.25	6.25	...	...
National democratic governance	...	...	...	...	...	...	...	6.50	7.00
Local democratic governance	...	...	...	...	...	...	...	6.25	6.75
Judicial framework and independence	6.50	6.50	6.50	6.50	6.50	6.50	6.50	6.25	6.75
Corruption	...	...	6.00	6.00	6.00	6.00	6.00	6.00	6.50
Democracy score	6.35	6.45	6.38	6.42	6.46	6.46	6.46	6.43	6.82

Source: Freedom House, "Nations in Transit. Country Report: Uzbekistan (2006)" (Budapest, 2006), www.freedomhouse.org/template.cfm?page=47&nit=410&year=2006.

a. The ratings reflect the consensus of Freedom House, its academic advisers, and the author. The ratings are based on a scale of 1 to 7, with 1 representing the highest level of democratic progress and 7 the lowest. The democracy score is an average of ratings for the categories tracked in a given year.

b. Starting with the 2005 edition, Freedom House introduced separate analysis and ratings for national democratic governance and local democratic governance to provide readers with more detailed and nuanced analysis of these two important subjects.

eleven
Assessing Repression in Syria
David W. Lesch

During the last decade, scores of congresspersons, think tank and non-governmental organization representatives, and Middle East experts who have testified and commented before congressional committees assessing the regimes of Hafiz al-Asad and his son, Bashar, have, for the most part, concluded that Syria is a rogue state, terrorist state, repressive state, or any one of a number of other less-than-positive descriptions. It is argued that Syria supports terrorism, possesses weapons of mass destruction (WMD), and generally deviates from the accepted norms of the international community. In the 1980s and 1990s, terminology such as "rogue states," "backlash states," or "states of concern" became fashionable in U.S. foreign policy discourse to describe countries that went beyond internationally sanctioned behavioral patterns. In the post–September 11 environment, with the United States taking upon itself the task of evaluating countries as being for or against the terrorists, the term *rogue state* again found a receptive audience. In 2003, then White House spokesman Ari Fleischer bluntly stated that "Syria is indeed a rogue nation."[1] The appellation "repressive states" was employed by George W. Bush in his State of the Union speech in February 2005, in which he specifically mentioned Syria as a country that "still allows its territory, and parts of Lebanon, to be used by terrorists," and he called on Syria to "end all support for terror and open the door to freedom."[2] Ever since the beginning of such foreign policy categorizations, Syria has been at the forefront but also on the outside looking in.

Syrian President Bashar al-Asad, responding to a question about the use of such a negative label for his country, said, "Some see me as bad, some see me as good—we don't actually care what terms they use. It is not right to apply this term to Syria—I mean, look at the relationship that Syria has with the rest of the world; if you have good relations with the rest of the world, you are not a rogue state just because the United States says you are."[3] Imad Moustapha, Syria's ambassador to the United States, said:

> I do not immediately get offended because I understand how misinformed Americans are about the issue. I will tell you this: we are not in breach of any UN resolutions, whereas Israel is in breach of something like seventy-two UN resolutions. We do not occupy parts of Israel, Israel is occupying part of Syria. We have a small country, Israel is very powerful. [*Note:* The ambassador apparently used the word "small" to indicate Syria's relative military weakness, not its literal size.] Rather than deny the negative, I stress the positive; this so-called rogue state [Syria] has been calling for the resumption of negotiations—we have declared many times that we want a peaceful resolution of the Middle East conflict. It was us who went to the Security Council last year and submitted a draft resolution asking to declare the whole Middle East free from weapons of mass destruction and to allow the Security Council to impose modalities and mechanisms that will ensure that this will be. It was the United States that blocked this resolution, it was not Syria. So at least understand these realities, and if Americans insist on calling us a rogue state, then so be it.[4]

Then foreign minister of Syria Farouk al-Sharaa had a more biting response to the same question:

> You happened to have different teachers in school. One you respect and one you do not respect just because the style or conduct of that person is not attractive to you. But the one that you respect, if he just winks at you angrily, you spend the whole day upset because you respect him; but if you do not respect him, even if he says "go to hell," you do not accept it. You say to a friend that this man I do not respect, so whatever he says to me I am not going to respect. It would have been very harsh if it [calling Syria a rogue state] was directed at us by a respectable nation. How dare they put us in accountability, especially now with what is going on in Iraq.[5]

The actions of Hafiz al-Asad's regime in the 1970s and 1980s, especially since it was on the opposite side of the cold war as well as at the forefront of anti-Israeli hostility, established a paradigm for assessing Syria: it fit a rogue state pattern, as determined, delineated, and defined by the United States. Because of the asymmetry of power between Syria and Israel (and certainly between Syria and the United States), Damascus felt compelled, from its perspective, to adopt asymmetric means in order to survive. Adoption of such a strategy made it easier to refer to Syria as a rogue because asymmetric warfare by its very nature falls within the definition of rogueness or deviant behavior, that is, a state that is involved in terrorism and has (or is seeking to obtain or proliferate) weapons of mass destruction.

Syria, the Repressive State

Syria is a neopatrimonial authoritarian regime with only some of the trappings of democracy. Article 2 of the 1973 constitution states that Syria's "system of government is republican and sovereignty is exercised by the people," but in practice its people have no avenue or recourse to change the government, and candidates for election are vetted by the party and the government. While the constitution technically allows for a multiparty pluralist system, Syria is in reality a one-party state.

Syria is the only Arab country other than Lebanon whose constitution does not establish Islam as the state religion, although it does require the president to be a Muslim. The secular philosophy of the ruling Baath Party as well as the fact that the government is controlled by a minority Islamic sect, the Alawis (Alawites), ensures better protection of religious freedom, as well as women's rights, than in most Arab countries. Generally speaking, the country's Christian minority groups (about 10 percent of the population) and small Jewish population have been free to practice their religion without government restrictions and interference.

Governmental Structure

The constitution establishes the executive, legislative, and judicial branches of government. The unicameral parliament consists of 250 representatives elected by popular vote every four years. The parliament proposes the candidacy of the president, proposes and votes on laws (which are generated by the executive branch and the Baath Party), discusses cabinet policy, and approves the budget. The constitution guarantees that the Baath Party receives at least half of the parliamentary seats. Currently the ruling coalition, the National Progressive Front (NPF)—which is dominated by the Baath Party and includes six other leftist and communist parties—holds 172 seats while non-NPF independents, all of whom are vetted by the government, hold 78 seats.

The last parliamentary elections were in 2007. The president is elected to a seven-year renewable term after nomination by the Regional Command of the Baath Party and the parliament. The president, the party, and the cabinet can issue legislation whether or not the parliament is in session. The late president Hafiz al-Asad was confirmed by unopposed referendums five times, usually garnering 99 percent approval. Bashar ran unopposed after his father's death and received 97.29 percent of the vote in a national referendum. Political opposition to the president is not tolerated except for that of the so-called loyal opposition within the parliament. The parliament provides no check on the president.

Under Hafiz al-Asad, the regime in Damascus engineered a largely successful Faustian bargain with the Syrian people: in return for stability and security, certain freedoms are sacrificed. This bargain was welcome to a population that lived in a threatening regional environment and experienced successive coups d'état and political intrigue in the 1950s and 1960s. The regime obliged by providing security and relative stability, with a dose of economic progress from time to time when conditions were favorable. Now this Faustian bargain is being questioned. Syria has been under tremendous regional and international pressure; its economy has continued to deteriorate, it was compelled to withdraw from Lebanon in 2005, and groups in and outside of Syria are more openly agitating for political freedom.

The Baath Party is a shadow government, and the fifteen-member Regional Command of the party retains decisionmaking authority over the cabinet and the ministries. Several members of the cabinet are also in the Regional Command. This includes President Bashar, who is the head of the party as secretary general. Bashar is trying to transform the party into a more advisory body within the government rather than an entity that interferes with and dictates government policy, as has often been the case in the past. In late 2000, Bashar decided that the twenty-one members of the Regional Command should be elected by Baath Party membership rather than appointed, although all candidates first needed approval of the secretary general of the party (that is, Bashar). In July 2000, in addition to Bashar, eleven new members were elected to the Regional Command, most of whom were considered technocrats and supporters of change. However, all had been longtime party cadres, and the prime stalwarts of Hafiz al-Asad's regime—the so-called old guard—retained their positions, so it appeared that the body was not as reformist as many had hoped.

At the June 2005 Baath Party congress meeting, the first to be held since 2000, the party membership was again changed to reflect more of Bashar's vision of modernization and economic progress, if not political reform. Sixteen of the twenty-one members of the Regional Command were sacked. The command itself was also reduced from twenty-one members to fifteen, which possibly reflects Bashar's stated willingness to limit the role of the party in government affairs. Bashar is also consolidating his power base amid the rancor of the withdrawal from Lebanon and continuing international pressure, particularly from the United States.

Civil Society and the Press

Decree 39 of 1958, Syria's Law of Association, requires every civil organization to register and obtain a license from the Ministry of Social Affairs. In the months after Bashar's assumption of the presidency, during the so-called Damascus Spring, hundreds of civil society organizations, most operating from within the homes of the organizers, received licenses. Today, registration is politically motivated. Asma al-Asad, the president's wife, is very active in advocating the growth of nongovernmental organizations in Syria. In particular, she has taken a leading role in the Fund for the Integrated Rural Development of Syria.[6] Nevertheless, civil society has no opportunity to influence policy, and many of the organizations, such as the aforementioned fund, are linked to the government, calling into question the extent of their independence. In February 2001, the Ministry of Social Affairs announced that political forums (discussion groups, often with guest speakers) could not meet without its permission (as opposed to receiving licenses), which would only be granted if specific information were provided as to the location of a meeting and who was attending. Demonstrations are permitted only with the permission of the government, and often they are arranged for public show. There are no independent trade unions, but there is a government-controlled labor union.

During the 2000 Damascus Spring, Bashar al-Asad promoted freer and more pluralistic media in Syria. For the first time in forty years, private newspapers were licensed, and public criticism of the regime was permitted, even from state-controlled entities. Although publications that criticized the government—including the hugely popular satirical weekly *al-Dumari* (The Lamplighter), which ceased publication in 2003 due to government pressure—

struggled against the restrictions of the regime, the fact that such criticism was permitted indicates that there may be some cracks in the armor of political repression. Strictures on journalism became evident with Decree 50 of 2001, marking heightened levels of domestic repression and the crackdown on civil society activists that became known as the Damascus Winter. This law enabled privately owned newspapers, magazines, and other periodicals to seek licenses to publish, but they essentially did so at the discretion of the government. The prime minister's office was empowered to deny licenses for reasons "related to the public interest." In addition, the decree prohibited articles and reports about "national security, national unity, and details of secret trials." It also established harsh criminal penalties for publishing "falsehoods and fabricated reports."[7] In effect, editors could only oppose regime policies when they had official instructions to do so.

Although the state runs the Syrian media, Lebanese newspapers and pan-Arab satellite news channels such as al-Jazeera, widely available in Syria, allow open political discussion and criticism of the government to continue. In addition, the Syrian government permitted more criticism of the Baath Party in 2003–2004; in fact, the editor of the party newspaper wrote a series of articles severely criticizing the party. In late 2004, this editor became the new minister of information, a sign that Bashar may have wanted to revamp the party and its role. Public criticisms revolving around anticorruption, administrative reform, and economic performance are generally permitted, since these critiques are also emphasized by the regime. However, criticism of leading officials, as well as more specific calls for democratization or reform that are seen to undermine the legitimacy of the regime, are not tolerated—particularly when the regime is experiencing international isolation, which has been the case since the assassination of former Lebanese prime minister Rafiq Hariri and the accompanying pressure from the United States and United Nations in 2005.

Human Rights and the Judicial System

Amnesty International reports that there were fewer instances of torture in 2005–2006, although the system allowing for its application remains intact.[8] When compared to other Middle East states, including some that have close relations with the United States, Syria fares quite well in absolute numbers as well as per capita totals of political prisoners; indeed, Syria in 2005 probably had considerably fewer than 1,000 political prisoners, putting it on a par with Tunisia and well below Egypt (18,000), Algeria (4,000–7,000), and Turkey (10,000–20,000).[9] However, after accusations of Syrian complicity in the assassination of Hariri, international pressure intensified, and opposition organizations composed of Syrian exiles proliferated, so that well into 2006, the regime circled the wagons domestically and cracked down on democracy and human rights activism, arresting (or rearresting in many cases) and harassing a number of prominent individuals.

Article 25 of the constitution stipulates that citizens are equal before the law, and various articles of the penal code prescribe penalties for discrimination.[10] However, civil society organizations regularly demand equal treatment for women in their statements and manifestos, suggesting that the protection of women's rights and minority groups lags behind constitutionally mandated prescriptions. Syria supports women's rights to a degree greater than most Middle East states. Labor Act 91 of 1959 enshrines gender equality in the workplace, and Legislative Decree 4 of 1972 confirms equal remuneration between men and women. The Electoral Law promulgated in Decree 26 of 1973 grants women the right to vote in public elections and to stand as candidates in elections to the parliament, where they currently constitute over 10 percent of the total membership. Women also hold ministerial positions and are represented in the cabinet. Nevertheless, a number of discriminatory laws and practices remain in place, especially in personal status issues that fall under the *sharia* courts. For example, women are discriminated against in initiation of divorce proceedings and child custody rights.

One of the regime's prime weapons against internal dissent has been the State of Emergency Act (Decree 51), as amended and promulgated on March 9, 1963, one day after the Baath Party came to power in Syria. It declared a state of emergency that was ostensibly designed to thwart the military threat emanating from Israel but instead has been used to stifle and eliminate internal challenges to the regime. The government considers the decree a fundamental right as recognized in the International Covenant on Civil and Political Rights, which allows states to violate its provisions "in time of public emergency which threatens the life of the nation and the existence of which is officially proclaimed."[11] Under this provision, the martial law administrator (the prime minister) and his deputy (the minister of interior) are empowered to issue wide-ranging written orders restricting freedom in all areas of life. President Bashar has admitted that mistakes have been made using Decree 51 and that government officials have abused the law for their own purposes. While not committing himself to lifting the law once and for all, he has told journalists and others that it should be used genuinely to protect the people and not to abuse them.[12] However, given the international environment and the uncertainty regarding the stability and strength of the regime,

Decree 51 is likely to remain in place for the foreseeable future. Arbitrary arrests, detention, imprisonment, and lack of due process occur, although not as often as under Hafiz al-Asad.

The State of Emergency Act is extraconstitutional. Under the act, supreme state security courts (SSCs) were instituted by decree in 1968 and in principle follow the procedures of the ordinary courts. SSCs consist of two divisions, each with three presiding judges, one of whom is a military judge. Their judgments are considered final but are not enforceable until they have been ratified by the president, who has the right to annul the ruling, order a retrial, or reduce or commute the sentence. Defendants—who are almost exclusively political prisoners—appearing before the SSCs are guaranteed the same right to defense that they would enjoy before ordinary courts, but rarely have defendants actually been accorded these rights, especially as the trials have been off-limits to public scrutiny. However, between 2001 and 2004, a number of trials of activists in SSCs were opened to journalists and representatives of foreign embassies.

A number of Kurds arrested in the 2004 disturbances were tried in SSCs under cloak of secrecy and reportedly were not allowed to see their families; visits from lawyers were carefully monitored.[13] Syria's 1.5–2 million Kurds do not necessarily seek an independent state, but they do demand the right to teach their language, which is denied them by law, as well as full citizenship, which is required for state education and employment. About 200,000 Kurds were classified as stateless based on a 1962 survey.[14] Tensions between Arabs and Syrian Kurds have been ongoing. In March 2004, Kurdish riots and demonstrations occurred, apparently sparked by events in Kurdish areas of neighboring Iraq. The mid-2004 government-granted amnesty included about 100 Kurds who had been arrested after clashes with security forces in which forty people were killed after a soccer match in Qamishli. In mid-2005, a reported 50,000 Kurds protested in Qamishli over the mysterious death of a popular Kurdish preacher as well as the deaths of five other Kurds from ill treatment by police in the preceding year. Despite this unrest, there was serious discussion at the Baath Party congress in June 2005 about eliminating the state security courts, suggesting recognition of the fact that this extralegal juridical process requires significant modifications.

In general, the judicial system is corrupt and inefficient. Guilt must be proven in the normal legal process, but this provision does not hold in the SSCs. Citizens have the right to counsel in all courts but often do not have access to one in the SSCs. In the normal judicial process, they often have incompetent or corrupt counsel because of the nature of the system. In most cases independent counsel is appointed except, again, in the SSCs, where someone may be appointed only to provide the appearance of meeting the citizen's supposed right to counsel.

Article 131 of the constitution stipulates that "the judiciary shall be independent, its independence being guaranteed by the President of the Republic with the assistance of the Higher Council of the Judiciary." The latter has administrative authority over the judiciary, with the power to appoint, promote, and transfer judges. The council is presided over by the minister of justice and includes the president.

The highest constitutionally ordained judicial body in the country is the supreme constitutional court, to which five justices are appointed by the president for four-year terms. This court rules on the constitutionality of laws and election disputes and can try officials of the state, including the president, for criminal offenses.[15] In practice, there is very little judicial independence, especially above the lower-court level. Particularly with Decree 51 in place, the executive branch wields far too much power over the judiciary, and judges' appointments and decisions at all levels are ultimately subject to the approval of the executive branch or martial law representatives. In the lower-level courts, the size of payments (that is, bribes) made to intermediaries representing judges depends on the offense. Business and government connections play a major role in determining guilt or innocence, or even whether charges should be filed. At lower levels, prosecutors have some independence depending upon the case; in the higher courts and more high-profile cases, prosecutors can come under considerable government pressure or even pressure from powerful families. Capital crimes, especially murder, are less susceptible to corruption except in cases that involve a powerful figure or family. Public officials and ruling party actors are prosecuted for abuse of power and corruption but almost always at the behest of the executive, as a result of political motives rather than legal reasons. The legal educational system is extremely weak and lawyers and judges are for the most part ill prepared. Judges are often chosen based on their loyalty to the regime or the Baath Party. Thus the system generates a vicious cycle of judicial incompetence and lethargy.

Governmental authorities generally comply with judicial decisions unless they conflict with prevailing government policy; however, verdicts in cases of note are usually determined a priori, precluding the need for the executive to waive or reverse a decision. Overall, the system is weak, corrupt, and inefficient, by default leaving real judicial powers to the executive branch of government.

Corruption

The military-security apparatus has tremendous influence over the judicial and legislative branches and even at times over the executive branch, which it essentially serves. It has a symbiotic relationship with private business interests in Syria, creating avenues of influence and enrichment extending in all directions. The military is intimately involved in the political process, often vetting candidates in and outside the Baath Party for elected and appointed positions.

Syria is well known for its corrupt business environment. The Transparency International Corruption Perceptions Index of 2006 gave Syria a 2.9 score on a ten-point scale, thus ranking it 93 out of 163 countries.[16] As in most countries where the public sector plays a dominant role in the economy, the opportunities for corruption are numerous. The most common form of corruption is through what is called *wasta*, or the use of influence or connections to consummate business deals and other types of favors. It is almost an accepted form of doing business in Syria, but it establishes prescribed entrances into the Syrian economy that dampen any free market tendencies. One cannot enter into a private or public sector business situation of any significance without local mediators to provide access to decisionmakers. These "five-percenters" often multiply as the business relationship deepens. In reality, wasta is an additional form of control by the state, fragmenting bourgeois and upper bourgeois classes who might in its absence coalesce into a recognizable pressure group. In addition, it spreads the wealth to certain classes, supplements the income of government officials tied into the "five-percent" organizations, and gives more people a vested interest in maintaining the current regime.

The public sector in Syria, as a creation of the Baathist socialist doctrine of the 1960s, is dominant in the country in most industries and creates consistent opportunities for corruption. Licensing, bureaucratic regulations, and the like are oppressive, inefficiently applied, and subject to bribes. The black market economy, especially the portions intertwined with Lebanese business transactions, competes with the legal economy in terms of overall domestic product.

Although the state has launched a program to promote integrity and honesty in Syrian society in an attempt to weed out corruption as a socially accepted practice, so far legislative progress has been limited. In 2006, a number of ministries were supposedly hiring based on merit rather than connections. There are anticorruption laws on the books, but they are applied selectively by the regime only when cronies behave in an irresponsible, abusive fashion or in order to destroy someone politically through often-fabricated charges. The arbitrary and selective application of anticorruption initiatives tends to keep regime elements within accepted bounds. Individuals involved in high-profile corruption cases cannot feel secure because their fate—good or bad—is ultimately left to the discretion of the regime, the military-security apparatus, or the predetermined judicial or martial law system. Human Rights Watch reported in 2002 that people who protested against nepotism and corruption in Syria faced unfair trials on charges that included "endangering state unity" and "trying to change the constitution by illegal means."[17] Corruption allegations are often accompanied by media coverage, although the latter, being state controlled, is usually orchestrated by the government to legitimate its charges and reinforce its anticorruption campaign.

Allegations of widespread cronyism and nepotism abound in Syria. Under the regime of Hafiz al-Asad, the unswerving loyalty of his inner circle of subordinates was rewarded with a virtually free hand to enrich themselves through mostly corrupt methods of controlling business opportunities in Syria. Wealth was funneled into the hands of very powerful families who were either in or well-connected to the government. Baath Party members and sons or daughters of high-level officials and rich families have received preferential treatment in higher education, although the current regime is trying to raise the standards for Baath Party cadres incrementally before they are automatically accepted into the university.

Bashar al-Asad came into office known as someone who was decidedly against corruption, having headed a well-publicized anticorruption campaign in the year or so before ascending to the presidency.[18] Most reports suggest that overt corruption has receded in Syria since Bashar came to power, but corruption via cronyism still exists at the highest levels. This centers primarily around the powerful Makhluf family (Bashar's mother is from the Makhluf family), in particular Rami Makhluf, who runs Syriatel.

Syrians have generally embraced anticorruption campaigns by the government, but Bashar's progress in this area has experienced more success since mid-2005. Earlier lack of progress was partly because Bashar did not secure the unquestioned legitimacy and support base that would allow him to adopt tough measures. From all indications, he is incrementally attempting to create a critical mass of support in the government and the party that will allow him to implement judicial and economic reform and anticorruption policies. If the February 2006 cabinet reshuffling is any indication, Bashar may finally have that critical mass of support in the government. Even so, transparency in the Syrian judicial and business environments is minimal. The Syrian regime, with French and British assistance, has attempted to establish some mechanisms in the judicial and financial sectors (with the establishment of private banks) to create more transparency in order to build a more business-friendly environment for foreign investment and return of expatriate capital.

Cooperation and Confrontation

Syria joined the U.S.-led UN coalition that evicted Iraq from Kuwait in 1991—although most Syrians will say they joined the coalition to stand by the Kuwaitis, not the Americans. Syria was key to the convening of the Madrid Middle East peace conference in October 1991. It also negotiated *seriously* with Israel throughout much of the decade, although Damascus did not engage in the multilateral talks held in tandem with the Madrid process in which a number of countries in and outside of the region, including Israel, discussed a host of issues such as water sharing, arms control, and economic cooperation. In 2001, the United Nations General Assembly elected Syria to a nonpermanent seat on the UN Security Council. In this capacity and despite severe reservations, Syria voted for UN Security Council Resolution 1441 in 2002, which cited Iraq as remaining in "material breach" of its obligations and authorized the return of UN inspections to Iraq. The Security Council vote was unanimous.

Although not terribly enthusiastic about it, at an Arab League summit meeting in March 2002, Syria joined other Arab states in endorsing a peace initiative by Saudi Arabia's Crown Prince Abdullah that called for full Israeli withdrawal from Arab territories occupied in the 1967 war in return for normal relations in the context of a comprehensive agreement. Syria has also cooperated with the United States regarding intelligence about al Qaeda, including receiving terrorist suspects from the United States, through third party nations, for more vigorous interrogation, a process known as "extraordinary rendition."[19] Bashar al-Asad frequently calls and visits President Hosni Mubarak in Egypt, King Abdullah ibn Abd al-Aziz of Saudi Arabia, and King Abdullah ibn Hussein of Jordan to consult and coordinate policy on a variety of Middle East issues. All three of these countries and their leaders are close allies of the United States.

Pope John Paul II visited Damascus in 2001, and President Bashar returned the visit to the Vatican in 2002, also attending the pope's funeral in 2005. British Prime Minister Tony Blair met with Bashar in Damascus in 2002, and, again, Bashar made a return visit shortly thereafter to Britain to meet with Blair as well as Queen Elizabeth II.[20] In 2004, the so-called Middle East "quartet" (the United States, Russia, the European Union, and the United Nations), entrusted with the implementation of the "road map" to peace, held a meeting in Dublin, Ireland, to discuss the modalities of an Israeli withdrawal from the Gaza Strip. Various proposals were discussed during a two-day meeting of EU foreign ministers and their counterparts from Algeria, Egypt, Israel, Jordan, Lebanon, Morocco, the Palestinian Authority, Turkey, Tunisia, and Syria.[21] Iyad Allawi, Iraq's interim prime minister at the time, visited Damascus and Beirut in 2004 to improve relations and garner more widespread support within the Arab community for the interim government. In Damascus, Allawi stated that "it is clear that our visit here is the beginning of a bright chapter in relations between our two brotherly peoples. We are opening a new page with Syria."[22] A number of economic accords were signed between the two countries during the visit as well as pledges to cooperate regarding the infiltration of anticoalition militants into Iraq, and this posture has continued, as it is now in the interest of Damascus to see Iraq stabilize.[23] In mid-2005, representatives of more than eighty countries, including U.S. secretary of state Condoleezza Rice and UN secretary general Kofi Annan, met in Brussels for a conference on Iraq in an attempt to increase international support for the newly formed regime in Baghdad. Representatives from Syria (as well as Iran) attended the conference, showing that for most of the world, Damascus is not an outlaw regime.

Syria is not a pariah state by any means, and it is certainly not an Iraq, despite attempts by anti-Syrian interests to link Syria to Iraq and to tie Bashar al-Asad to the likes of Saddam Hussein or Iranian President Mahmoud Ahmadinejad. This illusion is total fabrication for the purpose of promoting misguided foreign policy agendas. The vast majority of countries, including some of America's closest allies, engage Syria at a number of different levels and hold fast to the opinion that Syria is not a rogue state. Are they all wrong?

Syria has WMD—most likely chemical and biological weapons.[24] It supports groups that are deemed terrorist by the United States, such as Hamas and Hezbollah. Syria did, indeed, outstay its welcome in Lebanon and bungled the political process there, particularly with its clumsy intervention in August 2004 to extend pro-Syrian Lebanese president Emile Lahoud's term in office by three years. In addition, it created the environment in which the Hariri assassination occurred. Syria is not a free, open, and pluralistic society; political repression and human rights violations still exist in the country. But Syria is in a dangerous neighborhood virtually surrounded by what it perceives to be, and largely are, real threats. This threat was especially acute following the

Hariri assassination as there were a number of countries and groups openly advocating a change of regime in Damascus. In such circumstances, the Syrian regime, perhaps understandably, cracked down on domestic opposition elements. The regime typically overreacted and jailed some individuals who in no way, shape, or form should be imprisoned, but in such a threatening environment, Damascus chose to err on the side of caution. However, there have been political and economic improvements overall, even if they are occurring at a slower pace than many expected. Many expectations were very unrealistic to begin with given the corrupt, inefficient, broken-down system Bashar inherited. Even the pro-democracy opposition to the regime has often recognized that for the time being, the best hope for reform in Syria lies with Bashar al-Asad.[25]

Washington's view of Syria requires a more nuanced understanding. There are a number of close allies of the United States who currently meet some or all of the criteria for rogue states or repressive regimes, such as Pakistan (many Arabs would include Israel as well), but they are not classified as such because they are aligned with U.S. interests (although the early second-term Bush administration has made an effort strongly to encourage these regimes to implement democratic reform). Application of the "rogue" or "repressive" label enables the U.S. government to use sanctions or the threat of sanctions (or even military action) to batter into submission states whose agendas conflict with those of the United States and to compel them to behave in ways more compatible with U.S. interests. Since January 2005, the Bush administration has ratcheted upward the pressure on Damascus and has sought a change of regime in all but name.

History has shown that Syria's internal policies are often elastic, changing with the external and internal threats to the regime and societal stability. It is not a surprise that Decree 50 (2001), restricting press freedoms, was promulgated only eleven days after September 11 and in the same year that hard-line right-wing elements came to power in both Israel and the United States. When the pressure is perceived to be less, as it was during most of the 1990s and during Bashar's first year in power, the regime is more inclined to undertake political and economic reform. As Andrew Tabler of the Beirut *Daily Star* wrote with regard to the U.S. stance toward Syria,

> The primary casualty in this contest of wills could very well be the Syrian people. Their widely expressed hopes for greater consensus building and economic reform could easily fall victim to an American failing to deal effectively and realistically with the symptoms or origins of terror-

ism in the region, a Syrian state that is unlikely to reform under the barrel of a gun, and opponents of the Syrian regime to whom spleen venting takes priority over constructive criticism.[26]

Terrorism and Lebanon

Terrorist activity has long been associated with Syria, less because of direct involvement in terrorist actions than because of Syria's support for what Washington considers terrorist organizations, such as Hezbollah, Hamas, Palestinian Islamic Jihad, and some Kurdish groups such as the Kurdistan Workers' Party (PKK), which has targeted Turkey, a U.S. friend and NATO ally.[27] Many believe that Syria was behind the 1983 bombings of the U.S. embassy in Beirut, which killed over 90 people, and the U.S. marine barracks, which claimed 241 American lives. In terms of direct involvement in terrorist activity, the last reported incident concerning Syria was an abortive attempt to place a bomb on an El Al airliner in London in 1986 (the so-called Hindawi affair), after which the United States withdrew its ambassador to Syria for a year.

There are those who believe that Syria has been wrongfully kept on the state-sponsored terrorism list and that the list is being used by Washington as a bargaining chip for concessions on the Arab-Israeli front. Others, however, do not see a distinction between direct and indirect action; that is, support for terrorist groups such as Hamas and Hezbollah is reason enough to keep Syria on the terrorism list and, indeed, to take more concerted action against the regime.

The former posture was challenged in Lebanon after the assassination of Hariri. The United States, Europe, and most of the Arab world were united in calling on Syria to withdraw its 14,000–16,000 troops from Lebanon. This development was Bashar al-Asad's severest test, and it gave ample ammunition to those who want to contain Syria if not to generate regime change. Although Bashar had reduced Syria's troop presence in Lebanon by over 50 percent since he came to power, he had to succumb fully to regional and international pressure and implement a complete withdrawal, including Syrian intelligence agents. However, with several bombings and assassinations that have targeted anti-Syrian Lebanese figures after the withdrawal, there remains suspicion that all of the intelligence agents have not been removed, and the West worries that Damascus has tried to run things in Lebanon by "remote control" through its remaining allies in the country. Even though an anti-Syrian coalition won the majority of seats in the Lebanese parliament in elections in May and June 2005, it was not enough to remove Lahoud from the presidency, and the pro-Syrian, Shiite Hezbollah won large blocs of seats, so Syria's influence on its neighbor to the west remains significant. Regardless, Syria's isolation, resulting from its bungled policies in Lebanon and Iraq, has made it much more vulnerable than in past years. Since the Bush doctrine identifies repressive states as breeding grounds for terrorism, Syria has fallen into the crosshairs of American efforts to transform the Middle East.

After the September 11 attacks, President Bashar "condemned the terrorist attacks that targeted innocent civilians and vital centers in the United States." In a radio broadcast, he also called for "international cooperation to eradicate all forms of terrorism and guarantee the protection of basic human rights, notably the right of humans to live in security and peace wherever they are."[28] Syrian propaganda began to compare the U.S. war on Islamic extremism with its own struggles against the Muslim Brethren in the 1980s. According to many reports, Syria cooperated with the United States in investigating al Qaeda and persons associated with it. Syrian assistance to the United States included providing information gained from an interrogation of a key figure in the September 11 plot, Muhammad Haydar Zammar, who was extradited from Morocco to Syria.[29] Bashar told reporters that Syria had provided information to the United States on a planned al Qaeda operation targeting U.S. personnel.[30] U.S. assistant secretary of state William Burns informed a congressional panel that "the cooperation the Syrians have provided in their own self-interest on Al Qaeda has saved American lives."[31]

Syria does not deny claims of support for Hezbollah, Hamas, and Islamic Jihad, saying that such operations constitute legitimate resistance and not terrorism; indeed, Damascus often views Israeli activities vis-à-vis the Palestinians and its actions in Lebanon as terrorism. At the Arab League summit meeting in Beirut in 2002, Bashar explained that "there is a difference between terrorism and resistance . . . the difference between one who has a right and the other who usurps this right."[32]

President Bush said in a speech in 2002 that "Syria has spoken out against Al Qaeda. We expect it to act against Hamas and Hezbollah as well."[33] In another speech a few months later, the president asserted that "Syria must choose the right side in the war on terror by closing terrorist camps and expelling terrorist organizations."[34] These statements were used by congressional supporters of the Syrian Accountability Act to persuade President Bush to sign the legislation, which he finally did in December 2003.[35] While not disputing the accusations leveled at Damascus, members of the Bush administration, particularly State Department officials, had testified against passage of the act. They believed that at such a critical phase in the Middle East, it would reduce the administration's flexibility to pursue various policy options in Iraq as well as on the Arab-Israeli front. By 2005, however, a more belligerent attitude had been adopted toward Damascus as the Bush administration explored ways to stiffen and expand the sanctions against Syria.

U.S. relations with Syria are complex and have been guided primarily by opposing groups who believe that the United States should remain engaged with Damascus or who feel that Washington should place more pressure on Syria, possibly to generate regime change. Former secretary of state Henry Kissinger famously stated in the 1970s that there could be no war in the Middle East without Egypt and no peace without Syria. Yet there have been a number of powerful voices, much more prevalent in the Bush administration, who have written off the Asads, thereby condemning Syria and advocating a more aggressive policy of confrontation with Damascus. It is therefore little wonder that Damascus, more often than not, prefers to err on the side of caution against anticipated and potential adversaries, thus exacerbating its repressive, "Bonapartist" tendencies at home in lieu of political and economic reform.

Syria is a charter member of the original State Department list of states that sponsor terrorism, as articulated in the 1979 Export Administration Act passed by Congress.[36] But unlike the other six members of what became the officially sanctioned and oft-mentioned State Department list of state sponsors of terrorism (North Korea, Iraq, Iran, Cuba, Libya, and the Sudan), Syria was generally spared official opprobrium from successive U.S. administrations throughout the 1980s, 1990s, and into the first years of the presidency of George W. Bush, and it was (and continues to be) the only country on the list that has diplomatic representation in Washington at the ambassadorial level. In 1985, President Reagan delivered a speech in which he named Iran, Libya, Cuba, North Korea, and Nicaragua as "outlaw states" that were subverting U.S. interests.[37] The Clinton administration assiduously avoided grouping Syria publicly with the usual suspects of state sponsors of terrorism; indeed, Anthony Lake, Clinton's national security adviser, wrote a seminal essay in *Foreign Affairs* in 1994 outlining the threat to global security from what he termed the "backlash states." Syria was nowhere to be found in the article; only North Korea, Libya, Iran, and Iraq were named.[38] Syria has also been subject to less stringent terms and application of antiterrorism legislation throughout the 1990s in comparison to other countries on the State Department list.[39]

Syria narrowly avoided inclusion in the Iran-Libya Sanctions Act in 1996 that expanded restrictions on U.S. interaction with both of those countries.

U.S. sanctions against Syria were applied nonetheless pursuant to the Anti-Terrorism and Arms Export Act of 1989, including bans on economic aid (including U.S. support in international forums for multilateral economic assistance) and military sales and limits on the sale of dual-use items. But these sanctions allowed at least a modicum of private economic and cultural interaction as well as leaving the door open to diplomacy. The sanctions studiously did not cut U.S.-Syrian ties anywhere nearly as deeply as these acts and their supplements did in the cases of Libya, Iran, Iraq (before the 2003 war), and North Korea. At times the doors of diplomacy between Washington and Damascus were wide open, as evidenced by over twenty trips to Syria made by U.S. secretary of state Warren Christopher during the height of the peace process in the first four years of the Clinton administration. In fact, Clinton was the first sitting president since Nixon to visit Syria, arriving in Damascus in 1994 to energize the peace process. He definitely believed that Syria was the key to a comprehensive Arab-Israeli peace. Echoing the view of many in the Clinton administration, Lake wrote, "A decisive Syrian-Israeli agreement would allow Jordan and Lebanon to resolve their differences with Israel in short order. An Israeli-Syrian peace would thus shore up the agreement between Israel and the PLO and greatly advance U.S. efforts to widen the circle of peacemakers, bolster the network of Middle East moderation, and construct a bastion against backlash states."[40]

The prevailing decision by the Clinton team regarding Syria was to engage Damascus rather than actively contain it through economic sanctions or military pressure. This decision made a great deal of sense considering the fact that Syria joined the U.S.-led UN coalition to liberate Kuwait in the 1991 Gulf War and played a key role in convening the Madrid peace process later that year.

The Anti-Syria Lobby

However, in the mid-1990s, there was an influential chorus that began to make its voice heard categorically denouncing Syria as a partner in peace. Essentially, Syria's involvement in the process, according to this version, was fraudulent, and the U.S. policy of engaging Damascus was misguided, if not dangerous, to both U.S. and Israeli interests. A seminal representation of this emerging viewpoint was a six-page report prepared in 1996 by the Jerusalem-based Institute for Advanced Strategic and Political Studies entitled, "A Clean Break: A New Strategy for Securing the Realm."[41] As the report states, it was compiled from discussions among the "Study Group on a New Israeli Strategy toward 2000," consisting of, among others, Richard Perle, Douglas Feith, David

Wurmser, and Meyrav Wurmser (David Wurmser's Israeli-born wife). All of these people have or had important positions either in the Bush administration itself or entities that are closely aligned to various elements in the administration. Perle has been called a godfather of the neoconservative movement as it has been applied in the Bush White House, and he was an adviser to the Department of Defense who sat on the Defense Policy Board. Feith was undersecretary of defense for policy and was one of the main proponents of the war in Iraq. David Wurmser, a neoconservative scholar with close ties to the Israeli right, was appointed in 2003 to join the national security team of Vice President Dick Cheney, led by his then national security adviser, Lewis "Scooter" Libby. Meyrav Wurmser headed the Middle East studies section at the Hudson Institute, a conservative think tank in Washington, D.C.

The report was constructed for Likud Party leader Benjamin Netanyahu in the immediate aftermath of his election victory as Israeli prime minister in 1996. It offered recommendations regarding Middle East policy and even had passages in bold print marked "TEXT" to highlight suggestions for a "possible speech" by the new Israeli premier. In many ways, this report became a blueprint for the Bush administration's foreign policy toward the Middle East. Along with Iraq, a primary target in the estimation of the authors was Syria. The implementation of Bush's Middle East policy appears to have followed many of the recommendations made in this report.

The report contends that "efforts to salvage Israel's socialist institutions—which include pursuing supranational over national sovereignty and pursuing a peace process that embraces the slogan, 'New Middle East'—undermine the legitimacy of the nation and lead Israel into strategic paralysis and the previous government's [that of Yitzhak Rabin and Shimon Peres] 'peace process.'" The authors of the report suggest that Syria "challenges Israel on Lebanese soil," and calls on Israel to seize the strategic initiative by engaging Hezbollah, Syria, and Iran as "the principal agents of aggression in Lebanon" in the following manner: strike at Syria's drug money and counterfeiting infrastructure in Lebanon; establish the precedent that Syrian territory "is not immune from attacks emanating from Lebanon by Israeli proxy forces"; and strike at Syrian military targets in Lebanon "and should that prove insufficient, strik[e] at select targets in Syria proper."[42]

The report suggests that

Israel can shape its strategic environment, in cooperation with Turkey and Jordan, by weakening, containing, and even rolling back Syria. This effort can focus on removing Saddam Hussein from power in Iraq—an important Israeli strategic objective in its own right—as a means of foiling Syria's regional ambitions. . . .

Most important, it is understandable that Israel has an interest [in] supporting diplomatically, militarily and operationally Turkey's and Jordan's actions against Syria, such as securing tribal alliances with Arab tribes that cross into Syrian territory and are hostile to the Syrian ruling elite.[43]

In 2000, a pro-Israeli (specifically, pro-Likud) research group called the Middle East Forum, along with the United States Committee for a Free Lebanon (USCFL), released a study entitled, "Ending Syria's Occupation of Lebanon: The U.S. Role."[44] The report was officially the work of the Lebanon Study Group, cochaired by Daniel Pipes, the president of Middle East Forum, and Ziad Abdelnour, an expatriate investment banker from Lebanon who established the USCFL in 1997. The USCFL describes itself as a "nonprofit, nonsectarian think tank" that wants to get rid of "dictatorships, radical ideologies, existential conflicts, border disagreements, political violence, and weapons of mass destruction" from the Middle East. These are all laudable goals. Largely reflecting the program of Lebanese Christian groups, it advocated removing Syrian troops and deleterious influences from Lebanon, and has been a remorseless critic of both Hafiz and Bashar al-Asad. The 2000 report explicitly called for the use of military force to eliminate weapons of mass destruction from Syria and end its "occupation" of Lebanon. Lebanon occupies a strategically vital corner of the world, and "preserving Lebanon's free Christian community" is "the cornerstone for safeguarding the country's special freedoms that uplift all its communities."[45]

Among the signers of the document were Richard Perle; David Wurmser; Douglas Feith; Michael Ledeen from the American Enterprise Institute, who has been a leading voice of neoconservative foreign policy toward the Middle East; Elliott Abrams, who is in charge of Middle East policy on the National Security Council; Frank Gaffney, a former aid to Perle in the Reagan administration who now heads the Center for Security Policy; the late former UN ambassador Jeane Kirkpatrick; and David Steinmann, chairman of the Jewish Institute for National Security Affairs. All except Kirkpatrick have played key roles in and outside of the Bush administration in the development of its Middle East policy, including, of course, the war in Iraq. While most observers agree that it was time for Syria to get out of Lebanon, its presence in the country was something of a lightning rod for those who advocated a more aggressive policy against Damascus. It provided a merger of interests between Lebanese Christian émigré groups and pro-Israeli groups. As the Turks and others have learned, one of the optimum ways an interest group or country can advance its objectives in Washington is to attach itself to the pro-Israeli lobby on issues of mutual concern—in this case, the weakening or replacement of the regime in Syria.[46]

These anti-Syrian and, indeed, anti-Asad reports and claims are more often than not analysis by assertion. They fail fully to consider the strategic position from the viewpoint of Damascus at a particular time and tend to lay all wrongs at the feet of Hafiz and Bashar al-Asad. One glaring example is the focus on the bombing of the marine barracks in Beirut in October 1983. This outrage comes up repeatedly in reports and congressional testimony by anti-Syrian organizations, scholars, and pundits as a prime example of how Syria is not a friend of the United States. It is astonishing that when mentioning the marine barracks attack carried out by groups aligned with Syria, critics almost always fail to mention that it was the Israeli invasion of Lebanon in June 1982 that precipitated the chaos that soon enveloped the country, creating the conditions in which such tragic events could occur. The invasion became an Israeli albatross. It was Israel's disastrous decision to stay on in southern Lebanon that radicalized the Lebanese Shiite community and created fertile ground for the rise of Hezbollah—all of this after the Shiites initially welcomed the Israeli invasion to expel the despised Palestine Liberation Organization military units. Although well intentioned at first, the presence of a U.S.-led multinational force combined with exclusionary cold war American diplomacy to exacerbate a deteriorating situation.

To say that Syria was responsible for the mess that became Lebanon in ensuing years is confusing current myopic policy intent with reality, playing upon most people's ignorance of history to advance an agenda. Indeed, the George H. W. Bush administration, as an unofficial quid pro quo for Syria's participation in the 1991 Gulf War coalition, is widely believed to have given Damascus the green light to consolidate its position in Lebanon in 1990–1991, leaving the 1989 al-Taif agreement, which effectively ended the Lebanese civil war, to be interpreted and implemented by Syria, thus leading to the 1991 Brotherhood Agreement between Damascus and Beirut that cemented the relationship between the two countries.

Did Syria stay in Lebanon too long? Yes. Did it take political and economic advantage of its position there? Absolutely. As one critical but fairly accurate assessment of the Syrian role in Lebanon characterized the situation:

[It is a] creeping Anschluss to absorb a country no pan-Syrian or pan-Arab nationalist has ever really accepted as a stand-alone entity. Another, equally important, reason [for Syria's continued presence in Lebanon] is the craven corruption of much of the Lebanese political class, who interlock as clients with the Syrian nomenklatura in their shared pillage of what should be a much more vibrant economy. Far from withdrawing, Damascus reconsecrated the pre-war sectarian system in a way designed to highlight its own role as indispensable arbiter and bulwark against a relapse into conflict. It cultivated political clients, including warlords and rival forces within each community, using lucrative patronage and divide-and-rule tactics to prevent the emergence of a cross-confessional national force.[47]

Since Syria first sent troops into Lebanon as an Arab League–mandated action at the beginning of the Lebanese civil war in 1975–1976, it played more of a stabilizing role there than the obverse. Syrian influence, when weighed against the alternative, was an ameliorating one.

Syria, at least publicly, did not express interest in annexing Lebanon, although Amin Gemayel, the former Lebanese president, disagreed: "Syria consider[ed] its presence here not as something temporary, not as a foreign occupation, but as something natural. They [thought] that Lebanon [was] a part of Syria."[48] As one Lebanese journalist said, "They gave us security, but what a price we've paid for this security. They took our money, they took our democracy."[49] Despite popular perception, however, Syria's stabilizing role in the aftermath of the destructive civil war actually better enabled the Lebanese to increase their independence from Damascus. Bashar al-Asad understood this fact, and he realized over the years that Syria would not remain in Lebanon in perpetuity. In fact, a "background note" on Syria from the State Department in 2004, commenting on the 1991 "treaty of brotherhood, cooperation, and coordination" between Syria and Lebanon, said that "the treaty provides the most explicit recognition to date by the Syrian Government of Lebanon's independence and sovereignty"—quite a different view from the supporters of the Syrian Accountability Act and others who saw the treaty as additional proof that Lebanon was falling further into the bosom of Syria.[50] Despite what was publicized most of the time, there were those in and outside of Lebanon who were not so eager to see the Syrians leave or to support the 2003 Syrian Accountability Act. As former CIA Middle East analyst Martha Kessler noted in 2004, "Lebanon has really never healed since its civil war. It still has a huge Palestinian community that is deeply disenchanted and disenfranchised. The stability of Lebanon is a big unknown should Syria withdraw."⁵¹ This comment seems somewhat prophetic in light of the conflict that flared up between Hezbollah in southern Lebanon and Israel in the summer of 2006 after Hezbollah's capture of two Israeli soldiers. One suspects that this conflict might not have occurred had Syrian troops still been stationed in Lebanon.

In addition, both Syria's participation in the 1991 Gulf War coalition as well as its direct involvement in the Madrid peace process tend to be glossed over or trivialized by anti-Syrian organizations when, in fact, they were vitally important to U.S. interests and helped reshape the regional balance of power that for about a decade came very close to establishing the paradigm for a comprehensive Arab-Israeli peace. The fact that both the Madrid and Oslo processes failed to achieve their ultimate objectives does not diminish and certainly does not negate Syria's contribution. Hafiz al-Asad was indeed serious about peace with Israel, and by most accounts, the two sides traversed about 80 percent of the distance toward peace as a result of intense negotiations in 1995–1996 and in late 1999–early 2000. Concrete issues were discussed regarding timing for withdrawals, security arrangements, and normalizing relations. The issue of Israeli withdrawal from the Golan Heights to the 1967 line complicated negotiations, but depending upon with whom one talks, the late president Yitzhak Rabin indicated that he was prepared to withdraw to the 1967 line. Regarding the 1999–2000 Syrian-Israeli discussions, one only has to read President Clinton's autobiography—as well as U.S. lead negotiator Dennis Ross's *The Missing Peace*—to learn that it was not the Syrians alone who were to blame for the breakdown but also the Israelis.⁵² The fact that Lieutenant General Moshe Yaalon, the Israeli army chief of staff, commented in 2004 that Israel would be prepared to give up the Golan Heights in return for peace with Syria suggests that Syria is not the dire threat to Israel and the region as a whole as it has been portrayed. Also in 2004, Yaalon gave an interview in which he indicated that if a peace agreement with Syria were reached in which the Golan were given up, the Israel Defense Forces would still be able to defend Israel.⁵³ These ideas reemerged during and after the summer 2006 conflict with Hezbollah, as many Israelis began to see that Syria could have a mollifying influence on the Lebanese Shiite Islamist party if it were brought back to the negotiating table regarding a return of the Golan Heights.

With Hafiz al-Asad it was always the strategic situation internally and externally at a particular time, rather than a tightly articulated ideology, that dictated his foreign policy direction. To him, groups such as Hezbollah, Hamas, and the Palestinian Islamic Jihad were always the opposite side of the coin to the peace process, to be delicately utilized as leverage against Israel in order to exact necessary concessions. They were also functional elements of his asymmetrical military posture vis-à-vis Israel—after several wars, he knew that he could not fight Israel directly, a situation made more desperate with the end of the cold war, termination of Soviet largesse, and further deterioration of Syria's economy and armed forces. These alignments and realignments, part of a strategic chess game, were very much part and parcel of who Hafiz al-Asad was, and he tended to be good at such gambits given Syria's relative weakness. Bashar is very similar in this, and in 2006, he was also trying to deal with no less a strategic threat, although whether or not he will be as adept as his father in playing this game remains to be seen. Early in Bashar's tenure in power, he still had much to learn, but then again, his father did not become known as the "lion of Damascus" overnight. So far Bashar has confounded the critics. One does not remain president of Syria for seven years without some gravitas, cleverness, and strength. He has skillfully maneuvered out of the government those "old guard" elements that got in his way, directed the nationalistic response against U.S. and UN pressure toward support for his regime, and begun to build up his quiver with arrows of leverage in the form of Hamas, Hezbollah, and Syria's relationship with Iran.

Syria *has* been targeted. Many Bush administration hawks were hoping that the war in Iraq might provoke turmoil in Syria sufficient to overthrow the regime, something they were also hoping for in Iran. The administration was also concerned that the U.S. debacle in Lebanon not be repeated, that is, that Syria not be allowed to play a destabilizing role in Iraq. This heightened belligerency toward Syria became especially noticeable as the United States shifted its strategic modus operandi in the post–September 11 era to that of preventive war as articulated in the Bush doctrine. Indeed, it is a strategy that advocates when necessary a preventive war though preemption. Al Qaeda's use of the failed-state environment of Afghanistan to build up its terrorist network convinced policymakers that the United States could no longer wait for a threat to become manifest. It was now compelled to deal with countries that facilitated terrorist activities before the actual threat emerged. Syria was identified as one of—or close to being one of—these types of states.

The Bush administration's focus more on Iraq than on an Arab-Israeli peace tended to diminish Syria's utility in the eyes of many in the administration already suspicious of Syrian motives in the 1990s. But it was also important to keep a line open to Syria because it could still play an important role in the containment of Iraq, especially after it gained a seat on the UN Security Council. In addition, relations with Syria might help to restrain Hezbollah and possibly to limit Iranian influence in the region through the

Syrian connection. Thus one could still hear positive comments on Syria emanating from administration figures, usually in the State Department. For instance, in response to a query about why he included a visit to Syria in his tour of the Middle East in 2001, Secretary of State Colin Powell stated, "Syria is an important nation in the region . . . and so I thought it was very, very appropriate for me as part of this quick trip through the Middle East . . . to stop in Syria for a few hours."[54] Some of these voices were heard again in the midst of the 2006 Israeli-Hezbollah conflict, as it became clear that Syria remains a country that requires attention and cannot be summarily ignored (at least this is Bashar's hope).[55]

I believe that Syria's growing opposition to U.S. military preparations against Iraq in late 2002 and early 2003, despite voting for UN Security Council Resolution 1441 in November 2002, provided grist for the mill for those who had already adopted an anti-Syrian posture. Subsequent accusations of support for elements fighting against U.S. forces in Iraq provided the ultimate ammunition against any rapprochement with Syria. In 2005, the *Washington Post* discussed the spread of WMD, including a specifically named Syrian company: "With the naming of a Syrian facility, Damascus, which is suspected of providing cover for insurgents in Iraq and targeting political foes in Lebanon, could take the place once reserved for Iraq alongside North Korea and Iran as members of what Bush referred to as an 'axis of evil.'"[56] The transition was complete, and the Kissinger admonition regarding Syria no longer applied in foreign policymaking circles in Washington.

Conclusion

"[Hafiz al-]Assad's only hope of surviving both internally and externally was through a systemic policy of instilling terror in his own population, as well as spreading it in the population of neighbor states."[57] While exaggerated to some extent to make a point, this line of thought has also been applied to Bashar. But it may be too early to declare whether or not he is a true reformer or a Bonapartist interested only in regime maintenance. Given its international standing when compared to countries such as North Korea or Libya, or its "repressive" level when compared to countries such as Turkmenistan or Burma, Syria does not sink to that level—it displays nowhere near the abhorrent behavior of these and other countries or of Iraq before the war.

The United States needs to give Bashar a chance. He is probably the only person in Syria who has the necessary legitimacy to implement reform and pursue peace with Israel. Syria is no Libya, a country that habitually acted outside of the norms of commonly acceptable international behavior; therefore a more positive relationship with Syria could be tremendously advantageous to the United States, especially with regard to the global war against terrorism.

Syria is almost as sectarian as Lebanon, and if the center should precipitously fall with Bashar's overthrow or political incapacitation, the country could devolve into violent strife. What would emerge after the dust settles could very well be a polity that is Islamist and capable of making common cause with like-minded elements in Iraq and Lebanon. That would certainly not be in anyone's interest. Given this context, the United States and its European friends could maintain some pressure on Syria, but it should be mixed with the carrots of economic aid, lifting sanctions, and engagement in the peace process.

The UN investigation into the Hariri assassination was an albatross for the Syrian regime into 2006. On October 21, 2005, the UN report compiled by German diplomat Detlev Mehlis was submitted to the UN Security Council.[58] In the report, Syria was implicated in and found at least indirectly responsible for the murder. The original draft of the report outlined a trail of names that led directly into the heart of the Syrian regime, particularly to Asef al-Shawkat, Bashar's head of intelligence and brother-in-law, and Maher al-Asad, his younger brother, who is a member of the Baath Party's central committee and head of the republican guard. The UN Security Council, however, could not agree on concerted action by the end of the year, particularly with Russia and China hesitant to accede to U.S. demands that UN sanctions against Syria seriously be considered. The term of the UN investigation was then extended into 2006, with a new UN representative issuing a preliminary report in June 2006 that was decidedly less accusatory toward Syria than the Mehlis version.

Bashar al-Asad in 2006 was a more confident leader and more securely in power than at any other time in his presidency—some may say that he is, in fact, overconfident. This confidence may explain any Syrian involvement in the premeditated Hamas and Hezbollah capture of Israeli soldiers in July 2006, although Iran's hand is more likely the stronger one, with Damascus playing more the role of a conduit. The forceful Israeli response against Hamas in the Gaza Strip and Hezbollah in Lebanon threatened to include Damascus, especially as Syria is much easier to punish than Iran.

During my visit with President al-Asad on July 25, 2006, in the midst of the Lebanese crisis, it was clear to me that the Syrian leader wanted a return of the Golan Heights. He hoped that the resolution to the crisis in Lebanon might involve Syria, thus dealing himself back into the diplomatic game. The discussion and negotiations surrounding the passage of UN Security Council Resolution 1701, which established a very tenuous cessation of hostilities between Hezbollah and Israel, did not, however, include Syria. Israel did not even attack Syria during the conflagration, confining itself to bombing the transportation routes between Syria and Lebanon so as to prevent Syria from rearming Hezbollah. However, Syria again became an active topic of discussion in Washington, as important groups and figures advocated reopening a dialogue with Damascus. Similar debates occurred in Israel. So at least in a virtual sense, Syria temporarily returned from marginalization. Emblematic was Bashar's response to my question about President Bush's expletive regarding Syria that was caught on tape in an offhand discussion over lunch with British Prime Minister Tony Blair during the G-8 summit in July, at the outset of the Lebanese crisis. I expected a somewhat caustic response, but Bashar said that it was actually a positive thing; at least the president of the United States was *thinking* about Syria instead of ignoring it.[59] While coupling Syria to Iran in Washington circles had become commonplace by 2006, Bashar probably sees it as a positive development. The more influence he is perceived as having, the better his strategic position will be vis-à-vis Israel, Lebanon, and other regional issues.

Bashar is no longer the inexperienced, untested young ruler, but he has to be careful that he does not overstep his bounds. He has made mistakes, but he has also shrewdly and cleverly answered his critics and doubters to survive the onslaught of the past few years and consolidate his position. Will Bashar utilize this newfound confidence and security to outline a bold vision of the future and implement the type of systemic reform Syria needs? Will he engage in cogent or reckless foreign policy ventures in an attempt to improve his country's regional position? Bashar seems to have steered Syria on a path that will lead it out of its regional and international isolation. If this continues, perhaps reform will commence in earnest along with an improvement in U.S.-Syrian and even Israeli-Syrian relations. What Syria does not need is just another version of the dictatorial, stultifying rule of Bashar's father.

Notes

1. *New York Times* (April 15, 2003). Afterwards, it was open season on Syria. In June 2003, Undersecretary of State John Bolton placed Syria on a "second tier axis of evil" along with Cuba and Libya. Syria was termed by administration figures as a member of the "junior varsity of evil," the "ladies auxiliary of the axis of evil," and an "axis of evil aspirant." Quoted in Ross Leonard Fisher, "There's Something about Syria: U.S. Foreign Policy toward Syria during the Clinton and George W. Bush Administrations, *1994–2004*," unpublished Ph.D. thesis, University of Otago (Dunedin, New Zealand, 2004), 122–123.

2. White House, "State of the Union Address" (February 2, 2005), www. white house.gov/news/releases/2005/02/20050202-11.html.

3. Interview with President Bashar al-Asad, Damascus, June 1, 2004; also see David W. Lesch, *The New Lion of Damascus: Bashar al-Asad and Modern Syria* (New Haven, 2005), 117.

4. Interview with Imad Moustapha, Washington, D.C., July 17, 2004; Lesch, *New Lion of Damascus*, 117.

5. Interview with Farouk al-Sharaa, Damascus, June 3, 2004; Lesch, *New Lion of Damascus*, 117–118. Al-Sharaa became vice president in a cabinet shuffle in February 2006. Former Syrian ambassador to the United States Walid Mouallem became the new foreign minister.

6. Interview with Asma al-Asad, Damascus, Syria, June 3, 2004.

7. Committee to Protect Journalists, "Middle East and North Africa. Attacks on the Press 2003: Syria" (New York, 2003), www.cpj.org/attacks03/mideast03/syria.html.

8. Economist Intelligence Unit, *Syria: Country Report* (London, February 2006).

9. *Syria Comment* (August 11, 2004), www.syriacomment.com.

10. United Nations Human Rights Committee, "International Covenant on Civil and Political Rights: Consideration of Reports Submitted by States Parties under Article 40 of the Covenant; Second Periodic Report of States Parties Due in 1984— Syrian Arab Republic" (Geneva, January 19, 2000), www.hri.ca/fortherecord2001/documentation/tbodies/ccpr-c-syr-2000-2.htm.

11. Ibid.

12. Interview with President Bashar al-Asad, Damascus, May 26, 2004.

13. Ibid.

14. *Jordan Times* (August 30, 2004).

15. Ibid.

16. Transparency International, "Corruption Perceptions Index 2006" (Berlin, 2006), www.transparency.org/news_room/in_focus/2006/cpi_2006__1/cpi_table.

17. Human Rights Watch, "World Report 2002" (New York, 2003).

18. Bashar's critics contend that this campaign was as much an attempt to clear the path for his succession by removing potential adversaries on charges of corruption as it was a vehicle to stamp out unsavory business practices.

19. *Washington Post* (June 26, 2005).

20. In fact, many of Europe's leaders paid a visit to al-Asad. Even Jose Maria Aznar, the Spanish prime minister at the time and one of the few Europeans who supported the U.S. war in Iraq, expressed concerns over Washington's increasingly belligerent attitude toward Syria. Stressing his "very warm" contacts with Bashar, Aznar declared, "Syria is and will remain a friend of Spain and will not be the target of any military action." *Financial Times* (April 16, 2003).

21. *Financial Times* (May 6, 2004).

22. *Financial Times* (July 27, 2004).

23. Ibid.

24. See Anthony H. Cordesman, *Syria and Weapons of Mass Destruction* (Washington, D.C., 2000). When I asked Bashar what his reaction was to those who accused Syria of having WMD, he stated, "That's a very simple question. If we want to have it, we are not going to use it against Turkey, Iran, Iraq, or Lebanon—it would be against Israel, this is the only war we have. But how can we use them practically? If we want to use it to kill Israelis, how many Palestinians are we going to kill as well? So, practically, we cannot use them, while Israel can kill only Arabs. You cannot use them. Besides, the most successful experience against Israel was Hezbollah [guerilla warfare]. WMD is not to be used—it is a political deterrent. Maybe not everything you announce in politics . . . but I mean, generally, sometimes you have things you have and sometimes you announce things you don't have—for political purposes. You may have or you don't have." Interview with Bashar al-Asad, Damascus, May 31, 2004; Lesch, *New Lion of Damascus*, 255.

25. For instance, see comments by Aktham Naisse, head of the Committees for the Defense of Democratic Liberties and Human Rights, in a Reuters report of August 26, 2004. Naisse, who has been in and out of jail over the past few years, stated that "there is a reform current within the regime that is working, albeit slowly, and we must encourage it. I now see that only the regime has the ability to implement this reform and we have to bet on this." See www.alertnet.org/thenews/newsdesk/NU548121.htm.

26. Andrew J. Tabler, "Bush's Small Carrot and Big Stick with Syria," *Daily Star* (Beirut) (May 25, 2004).

27. However, in 1998, Syria agreed to expel PKK members (especially PKK leader Abdullah Ocalan) in response to Turkish political and military pressure—the so-called Adana Accord—and the State Department believes that Syria has "generally upheld its agreement with Ankara not to support the Kurdish PKK." Congressional Research Service, "Syria: U.S. Relations and Bilateral Issues," 9.

28. Quoted in Lesch, *New Lion of Damascus*, 101.

29. Ibid.

30. See in particular James Risen and Tim Weiner, "C.I.A. Is Said to Have Sought Help from Syria," *New York Times* (October 30, 2001). A high-level U.S. official informed me that the article was "right on the mark."

31. Congressional Research Service, "Syria: U.S. Relations and Bilateral Issues," 9.

32. Quoted in Christopher Hemmer, "Syria under Bashar al-Asad," in Barry R. Schneider and Jerrold M. Post (eds.), *Know Thy Enemy: Profiles of Adversary Leaders and Their Strategic Cultures* (2003, 2nd ed.), www.au.af.mil/au/awc/awcgate/cpc-pubs/know_thy_enemy/, 234–235.

33. White House, "President to Send Secretary Powell to Middle East" (April 4, 2002), www.whitehouse.gov/news/releases/2002/04/text/20020404-1.html.

34. White House, "President Bush Calls for New Palestinian Leadership" (June 24, 2002), www.whitehouse.gov/news/releases/2002/06/20020624-3.html.

35. Officially entitled the Syria Accountability and Lebanese Sovereignty Restoration Act of 2003, it was passed by the House of Representatives in October 2003 by a

vote of 398-4. It cleared the Senate in November 2003 by a vote of 89-4, and President Bush signed it into law on December 12, 2003. The act directs the president to block the export to Syria of items on the U.S. Munitions List or Commerce Control List of dual-use items. In addition, it requires the president to impose at least two of the following sanctions on Syria: prohibit export of U.S. products (other than food or medicine); prohibit U.S. businesses from investing or operating in Syria; restrict the movement of Syrian officials in Washington, D.C., and New York; prohibit aircraft of any Syrian carrier from using U.S. airspace or take-off from or landing in the United States; reduce U.S. diplomatic presence in Syria; and block property transactions in which the government of Syria has an interest or is subject to U.S. jurisdiction. In May 2004, Bush activated the first and fourth sanctions, both of which are mostly symbolic, considering that there were no Syrian carriers in the U.S. to begin with and that trade between the two countries was minimal, less than $300 million in exports and less than $200 million in imports in 2002.

36. This listing was in combination with the 1976 Export Arms Control Act. The Export Administration Act "sought to limit the military capability of a foreign state to sponsor international terrorism." Some of the exports subject to national security controls are dual-use items that can be used for military as well as nonmilitary purposes. There is also the Foreign Assistance Act, which prohibits U.S. financial aid to any country designated by the State Department as a state sponsor of terrorism.

37. U.S. State Department, "Address by President Reagan before the American Bar Association," *Current Policy*, DCCXXI (July 8, 1985).

38. Anthony Lake, "Confronting Backlash States," *Foreign Affairs*, LXXIII (1994), 45–55.

39. For instance, the 1996 Anti-Terrorism Act allowed financial dealings in Syria as long as the transactions were not related to (or potentially related to) acts of terrorism.

40. Anthony Lake, *Conceptualizing U.S. Strategy in the Middle East* (Washington, D.C., 1994).

41. Richard Perle and others, "A Clean Break: A New Strategy for Securing the Realm" (Jerusalem, June 1996), www.iasps.org/strat1.htm. It is also not a surprise that an anti-Syrian chorus started to rise at this time because of the general breakdown of the Madrid and Oslo processes after the election of Benjamin Netanyahu in May 1996, which itself was helped by the Hamas and Islamic Jihad suicide bombings in Israel the preceding February and March, followed by interim Prime Minister Shimon Peres's "Grapes of Wrath" military action in Lebanon in April. This was a proxy blow against Syria, which houses political offices of both Islamic Jihad and Hamas in Damascus. Syria's failure to condemn the bombings explicitly greatly angered Tel Aviv.

42. Ibid.

43. Ibid.

44. Lebanon Study Group, "Ending Syria's Occupation of Lebanon: The U.S. Role" (Philadelphia, May 2000), www.meforum.org/research/lsg.php.

45. Ibid.

46. In fact, until 2006, evolving Israeli-Turkish military cooperation over the past decade was seen in Damascus as a pincer movement designed to isolate and pressure Syria.

47. David Gardner, "Last Fling of the Party People," *Financial Times* (February 5–6, 2005).

48. Megan K. Stack, "Deep Roots Hold Syrian Influence in Lebanon," *Los Angeles Times* (February 20, 2005).

49. Ibid.

50. See www.state.gov/r/pa/ei/bgn/3580pf.htm, 10.

51. AP report, *San Antonio Express-News* (October 27, 2004).

52. Dennis Ross, *The Missing Peace: The Inside Story of the Fight for Middle East Peace* (New York, August 9, 2004).

53. Zeev Schiff, "Yaalon Challenges the Politicians," *Haaretz* (August 16, 2004). Schiff writes, "When Syrian President Bashar Assad reiterated in January [2004] that he was willing to resume negotiations with Israel, Foreign Minister Silvan Shalom approached Prime Minister Ariel Sharon and recommended not rejecting Assad's proposal. Sharon's response was: Is the price clear to you? He wants the Golan Heights and I am not willing. The IDF agreed with Shalom. So did Chief of Staff Moshe Yaalon, as did head of Military Intelligence Aharon Zeevi-Farkash. Both of them doubted Assad's offer was serious. They knew the Iranians were pressuring him not to hold talks with Israel. But the IDF top brass believed that if it became clear Assad meant what he said, that would be good. And if the whole thing was only a gimmick to remove American pressure, well, it would be good to reveal the gimmick for what it was. The IDF holds the opinion—also found in the recently published memoirs of former U.S. President Bill Clinton and of U.S. special Middle East envoy Dennis Ross—that Israel is at fault for the failure of the talks with the Syrians at Shepherdstown, West Virginia, in January 2000, and that at the time it would have been possible to reach an agreement with Hafez Assad, the father of the current president."

54. Appearance on *Face the Nation*, February 11, 2001, as quoted in Fisher, *There's Something about Syria*, 95.

55. See, for instance, my op-ed in the *Washington Post*, "Try Talking to Syria" (July 27, 2006).

56. *Washington Post* (June 27, 2005).

57. U.S. House of Representatives, Committee on International Relations, "Syria: Implications for U.S. Security and Regional Stability," hearing before the Subcommittee on the Middle East and Central Asia, 108 Cong. 1 sess. (Washington, D.C., September 16, 2003).

58. *New York Times* (October 22, 2005).

59. Author interview with President Bashar al-Asad, Damascus, Syria, July 25, 2006.

twelve
Tunisia's "Sweet Little" Regime

Clement Henry

Tunisia is neither aggressive nor is it up to North Korean standards of internal repression. Yet, in thinking about internally repressive regimes, the term "rogue," often used for externally aggressive regimes, is useful because it connotes a regime that has run amok like a male rogue elephant. The principal characteristic of such a regime is that it deviates from the values and beliefs of the community that it purports to rule—so much so that some may perceive its leader to be irrational or mentally ill. But unlike the elephant "of a savage destructive disposition" that is "driven away from the herd," the regime stays on to control and possibly to corrupt the state.[1] Such, at least, is the sad political situation of Tunisia today under the rule of President Zine El Abidine Ben Ali. It is not so much the quantity of repression per se that would define this as a rogue regime, or a very highly repressive one, as it is the extent to which its practices deviate from the expectations of the local and the broader community.

From this perspective—viewing the political leadership of such regimes as deviating from applicable social norms—it follows that regimes like those of Ben Ali are vulnerable from within. It is not so much the quantity as the irrational nature of the repression that delegitimates them. Unable to control public opinion and retain a semblance of legitimacy, they may become vulnerable to combinations of internal and international pressures for change.

The Ben Ali regime is one of a number of dictatorships in the Arab region coddled by the United States.[2] It is at least as repressive as the others—Egypt,

Jordan, Morocco, Saudi Arabia, and the little principalities of the Gulf Cooperation Council—and it certainly deviates the most from its society's legitimate expectations. Ben Ali was initially welcomed as Tunisia's savior when,
as prime minister, he had President Habib Bourguiba constitutionally
removed from office by persuading physicians to certify that he was no
longer physically fit to serve. The "historic change" of November 7, 1987,
promised steady progress toward democracy, and the new regime efficiently
carried out a structural adjustment program initiated in 1986 to meet a foreign exchange crisis. The troubles began in 1991, after the regime, having lib-
erated Islamist opponents of the Bourguiba regime, not only refused to recognize their Nahda Party but also determined to eliminate them and
intimidate anybody else who might defend them. At the height of the repression in 1991–1992, the Ben Ali regime was probably as tough as most of the
others included in this volume if repression is to be measured by the number of political prisoners per capita, quantitative or qualitative indexes of
torture, deaths in jail, or other measures of individual suffering. This chapter presents body counts and other measures of political repression and tries
to compare them with those of other regimes, but such measures require
further interpretation.

It is argued here that substantive deviation from social expectations may
leverage up the body counts in any fair reckoning of the extent of repression
that one is asked to evaluate. Crudely speaking, one tortured Tunisian may
count for more on a relative or "normalized" scale of repression than several
victims of another country in which torture is more habitual and the regime
has less of a political community of values to violate and less of a state tradition or rule of law to undermine.

The idea of deviating from political traditions, however, also has its pitfalls
because the values and beliefs of a political community are always in flux.
International fashions also change: Bourguiba's despotic developmentalism
looked good to academics, foundations, and nongovernmental organizations
(NGOs) in the 1960s, but similar Ben Ali rhetoric no longer works the same
magic in the twenty-first century. Pinning down the latter's "deviation" from
Tunisia's political traditions requires considerable elaboration and, unfortunately, runs against the grain of the best recent political study of the country,
that of Camau and Geisser.[3]

Tunisia became a police state in the 1990s, with big and visible increases in
the police force as well in arbitrary practices of neighborhood sweeps, arrests,
torture, and detention. Estimates of the number of police vary from 80,000 to

150,000, from double to almost four times the force of the mid-1980s. Even the lower number that circulates among foreign observers in Tunisia suggests that with one agent for every 110–115 Tunisians, the country has more than twice as many police officers per capita as Britain, France, or Germany.[4] The former head of Tunisian security recalls having about twenty wire taps at his disposal for Tunisian suspects in 1983 (aside from the dozens reserved for foreign embassies) compared to about 5,000 in 2004.[5]

Body Counts

The State Department's 2005 report on Tunisia's human rights practices stated that "the government's human rights record remained poor, and the government persisted in committing serious abuses," including torture and abuse of prisoners and detainees, arbitrary arrest and detention, police impunity, lengthy pretrial and incommunicado detention, infringement of citizens' privacy rights, restrictions on freedom of speech and the press, and restrictions on freedom of assembly and association. The report describes in some detail the torture techniques of Ben Ali's police:

> The forms of torture and other abuse included: electric shock; submersion of the head in water; beatings with hands, sticks, and police batons; suspension, sometimes manacled, from cell doors and rods resulting in loss of consciousness; and cigarette burns. According to AI [Amnesty International], police and prison officials used sexual assault and threats of sexual assault against the wives of Islamist prisoners to extract information, to intimidate, and to punish.[6]

While asserting that there had been some improvement in prison conditions in the late 1990s, the report noted that

> prison conditions ranged from spartan to poor, and generally did not meet international standards. Foreign diplomatic observers who visited prisons described the conditions as "horrible." Overcrowding and limited medical care posed a significant threat to prisoners' health. Sources reported that 40 to 50 prisoners were typically confined to a single 194 square foot cell, and up to 140 prisoners shared a 323 square foot cell. Current and former prisoners reported that inmates were forced to share a single water and toilet facility with more than 100 cellmates, creating serious sanitation problems.[7]

Political prisoners were often singled out for especially harsh treatment. Some leaders of Nahda, the banned Islamist party, have been in jail since 1991 and in solitary confinement for protracted periods. Strong circumstantial evidence existed that some were being killed in prison. The State Department report noted a recent death: "On June 17 [2005], Moncef Ben Ahmed Ouahichi, a Jendouba resident, died of a cerebral hemorrhage at La Rabta Hospital in Tunis. This followed his arrest June 10 and his release the next day, at which time he was unconscious and bearing bruises."[8] Torture or inadequate medical care also resulted in three reports of deaths in prison in 2002 and of early releases of prisoners at death's door.[9]

Little reliable quantitative information about political prisoners is available. A credible article on prison conditions claims that Tunisia had 253 prisoners per 100,000 inhabitants in 2002—which would make a total of roughly 25,000 prisoners for this country of 10 million.[10] But how many of them were political prisoners? In *Report 2001*, covering the events of 2000, Amnesty International claimed there were "up to 1,000" political prisoners but subsequently reformulated it to "hundreds," including "many . . . held for more than a decade," even after "scores" were released on November 3, 2004.[11] Human Rights Watch put the number at 500 in 2004 and then raised it to "more than 500" in a detailed exposé of the abysmal situation of 10 of some 40 or more political leaders from the Nahda party and others who had been held in virtual isolation since 1992.[12] The International Association for the Support of Political Prisoners counted 542 political prisoners by name in 2004 and indicated that there were probably many more, but President Ben Ali subsequently released substantial numbers of them in 2005, and at least 75 of the 1,600 he pardoned in February 2006 were also recognized to be political prisoners.[13] Human Rights Watch estimated, however, that over 300 political prisoners remained in jail in 2006 after these releases.[14] No independent body, not even the International Red Cross, has had the opportunity to visit Tunisia's prisons since 1991, much less to perform a census.

If 300 is roughly the correct number of political prisoners, they account for only 1 percent of the country's prison population, or 3 per 100,000 Tunisian inhabitants. By this conservative measure, Tunisia was still more or less holding its own with Egypt, Kuwait, and Morocco, and seemed slightly more repressive than Syria, estimated in 2004 to be holding only 200 Syrian political prisoners out of a population almost twice as large.[15]

The quality of the treatment of prisoners has improved since 1991–1992, when the big crackdown on the Nahda party occurred and thousands were arrested. At that time many prisoners, on their eventual release, described treatment that clearly amounted to torture, including routine beatings by prison guards and even by senior staff and prison wardens, and the shackling of some prisoners hand and foot much of the day. Prisoners with health problems were often denied medication or proper care, and infestations and skin diseases were rampant due to poor hygienic conditions. Inmates were subject to extremes of weather without adequate clothing and bedding. Hygiene was substandard and overcrowding so severe that cellmates had no choice but to sleep in shifts. On family-visit days, guards routinely humiliated and mistreated the inmates' relatives.[16]

In response to bad publicity in 2002 about prison conditions deteriorating again after some improvement in the late 1990s, Ben Ali delegated the head of his handpicked High Committee for Human Rights and Basic Liberties (Comité Supérieur des Droits de l'Homme et des Libertés Fondamentales) to investigate the situation.[17] Although the resulting report was not published, Ben Ali promised to carry out some of its recommendations, including better sanitation and "extending breakfast to the entirety of the prison population."[18] He did not address the issue of political prisoners, especially leaders arbitrarily sentenced by military courts in 1992. Close to 100 of the 265 Nahda activists sentenced in mid-1992 for attempting to overthrow the government remained in custody in 2006, although the alleged "plot" was seen at the time as just another excuse to lock up Ben Ali's political opponents. Apparently, many of the leaders were kept for years under solitary confinement. As Human Rights Watch had concluded earlier, "Tunisia's policy of targeting specific prisoners for long-term segregation from the rest of the prison population, whether in solitary or in small-group confinement, stands in stark contrast to the claim that its prisons comply with international standards."[19]

Other Indicators of Political Repression

As the State Department noted in 2004, "Security forces physically abused, intimidated, and harassed citizens who voiced public criticism of the Government."[20] One of them was Abderrahmane Tlili, head of one of Tunisia's six officially recognized opposition parties represented in parliament and the son of a distinguished Tunisian trade unionist. Plainclothes hooligans from the police beat him up very badly in the street outside his mother's home after he threatened to expose the Ben Ali family with compromising documents.

Then, after the official police rescued him and took him to the hospital, others ransacked his home for the documents.[21]

Another victim is Mokhtar Yahyaoui, a leading Tunisian judge dismissed from his post for criticizing the manipulation of Tunisian justice by the Ben Ali regime. Tunisia's version of Haiti's Tontons Macoutes assaulted him for organizing defense lawyers on behalf of political prisoners. His nephew, who had produced an online political opposition magazine, TUNeZINE, died at the age of thirty-six of a heart attack shortly after being released from two years in prison.[22]

Women were not exempt from attacks by plainclothes hooligans. Sihem Bensedrine, a journalist and political activist who resigned from the leadership of one of Ben Ali's make-believe opposition parties, suffered various police attacks and smears on her reputation, including fake pornographic videos. Human rights lawyer Radhia Nasraoui, who went on a hunger strike to get her (secular leftist) husband released from jail, also suffered numerous indignities, and her children were deprived of passports. Journalists and lawyers were special targets, and their children, like Judge Yahyaoui's daughter, might be slapped around as a further warning to unrepentant opponents. Hooligans from the police even grabbed the mobile telephone of Hélène Flautre, the EU parliament's president of its Human Rights Commission, and prevented her from having a private dinner conversation with the wife of a political prisoner in May 2006 by sitting down at their table in a hotel dining room.[23]

Moncef Marzouki tried in 1994 to run against Ben Ali for the presidency, and two days after the elections, he was jailed for almost four months. He then continued to teach and practice medicine in Tunisia but sent his family to safety in France while he spent time in and out of jail, working for various human rights causes. Deprived of his livelihood in Tunisia, he, too, finally moved to France in 2001 to work and teach at a Paris hospital. Many independent journalists, beginning with Kamel Labidi, have also been obliged to leave the country in order to pursue their profession. Journalist Taoufik Ben Brik's passport was confiscated; in response, he went on a hunger strike that gained him international attention and protection.

The state of the public media is deplorable. "If in certain countries like Algeria, Bosnia, or even Turkey, one kills journalists standing up, in others, like Tunisia, one participates in a slow death of the profession, by asphyxiation," a group of Tunisian journalists wrote to the International Federation of Journalists in 1995. The press became so "asphyxiated," in fact, that in 1997 the World Association of Newspapers expelled the Tunisian Association of

Newspaper Directors—a tool of the Ben Ali regime—for its inattention to the deterioration of press freedom in the country.[24]

Although some magazines and newspapers are ostensibly privately owned, they operate under stringent regulation and self-censorship. *Es-Sabah* lost any remaining shreds of autonomy in 2000 when its owner-publisher left the country, ostensibly for family reasons, and Abdellatif Fourati, its leading journalist, was dismissed. *La Presse*, which is privately owned but which had never displayed the independence of *Es-Sabah*, was indistinguishable from the official government press.[25] *Haqa'iq/Réalités*, a bilingual weekly, briefly lost its publicity revenues from government advertisements after publishing a controversial investigative report on prison conditions.[26] It then published the government's version of what happened to Hédi Yahmed, the unfortunate young author of the report, who departed shortly thereafter to France to pursue his professional career.[27] The government also refused permission for Al-Jazeera to set up an office in Tunis, despite a request by the president of the Tunisian Union of Journalists. In fact the Union, after expressing concerns about freedom of the press, was denied permission to hold its congress in 2006.

Tunisia's low newspaper circulation may be seen as another indicator of the regime's repressiveness because people are free not to buy papers, which suffer from a lack of real news content. Figure 12-1 shows that interest peaked in the 1980s and early 1990s, when there was some give in the political system, but then it declined, reaching levels in 2000 and 2001 similar to those of 1970, when Tunisia was a much poorer and less literate society. Figure 12-1 also compares Tunisia with America's other important allies in the Arab region as well as with Syria and Iran. Tunisia and Syria run neck-and-neck for the lowest newspaper circulations.

Tunisia's handling of the Internet is another sad story. One of the first southern Mediterranean states to gain full connectivity to the Internet (1991), it was among the last to extend it to the public. When, in 1997, President Ben Ali finally decided that Tunisia needed to catch up, he still managed to keep control of the public's access to news and even to personal correspondence. The law defining the service providers required them "to assure continual surveillance of the content of servers exploited by the service provider so as not to permit dissemination of information which is contrary to public order and morality," as if they were running a cinema or theater.[28] Consequently, few dared to respond to official tenders. Ben Ali's daughter and a close friend of the family run the only two service providers that offer connections to the public. People are encouraged to set up their e-mail accounts with the service providers rather than with Hotmail or Yahoo

Figure 12-1. Newspaper Circulation, 1970–2001[a]

Readership per 1,000 population

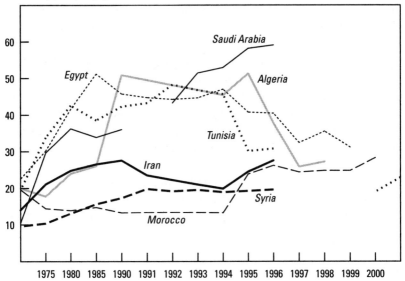

Source: World Bank, *World Development Indicators*, CD-ROM edition (Washington, D.C., April 2004).

a. Countries are listed in the order of their most recent newspaper count. The World Bank stopped publishing these data after the 2004 World Development Indicators; otherwise, Algeria would probably be upgraded ahead of Egypt and Morocco. I counted the circulation claimed by thirty-five Algerian newspapers in 2002 to reach 1,492,000, or close to 50 readers per 1,000 inhabitants, approaching the level reached in 1990 when political reformers governed the country.

because the latter are periodically shut down, although it is common knowledge that the official service providers also offer full access to Tunisia's Internet police, which has been strengthened in recent years. Telephone and Internet charges have been reduced to encourage people to use their home connections, where they can be easily monitored. As the Tunisian League of Human Rights (Ligue Tunisienne des Droits de l'Homme [LTDH]) reported in May 2004, "the e-mail, particularly of political or human rights activists, can be intercepted and mailboxes shut down by pirating passwords." One journalist was thrown into prison for four months for sending an e-mail from an Internet café.[29]

Tunisian opposition sites and newspapers are blocked, as are many foreign journals and newspapers like *Le Monde* and other potentially subversive resources. Tunisia's "publinets" (Internet cafés) are so restricted by spy software in the computers and so infested with plainclothes police that demand for their services may be decreasing rather than increasing, although most of Tunisia's 700,000 users depend on them rather than on more expensive connections at home. In any event, the number of these publicly sponsored enterprises dropped from 340 to 260 in 2002, mainly as a result of police sweeps in June and July directed against publinets that did not fully comply with regulations.[30] There were 305 publinets in 2005, serving as a "low-tech point of control" because the cafe owners were "required by the state to monitor customer access to prevent access to 'banned' content."[31] At least three groups of young Internet surfers were caught, imprisoned, and in some cases tortured in 2002 before being subjected to trials and long prison sentences.[32] Released in 2005, the Zarzis group remains deprived of educational opportunities and under virtual house arrest.

The development of the police state in Tunisia, moreover, has not been confined to niche specializations like Internet surveillance. With a fourfold numerical increase since 1987, police are more visible on the streets. They specialize in repressing NGOs as well as political dissidents.

A final indicator of repressiveness, much more difficult to quantify, concerns the degree of political pluralism that a regime tolerates. How autonomous are the NGOs and in what domains are they allowed to operate? Tunisia has thousands of them, but only a dozen or so are truly independent, not government satellites encouraged by the regime as a "civil society" counterweight to opposition Islamists.[33] The Islamists are in exile, jail, or, in the cases of those released in 2005 and 2006, under virtual house arrest—suffering "social death," as Hibou describes their condition.[34] The regime has, however, encouraged a semblance of political pluralism by legalizing a few "opposition" parties and even allocating to them a small percentage of seats in parliament that they could not otherwise win against the state party juggernaut, the Democratic Constitutional Rally (Rassemblement Constitutionnel Démocratique [RCD]).

Although handpicked for their loyalty, opposition leaders have sometimes been in trouble for trying to do their job. Tlili, mentioned above, is one example. Another was Mohamed Mouada, the head of the largest opposition party. He was arrested in 1996 and sentenced to eleven years on charges of providing intelligence to a foreign power; though he was released after a few months, he remained under constant surveillance. Mouada was arrested again in 2001 after criticizing the president and again was released after a few months.

The regime has not succeeded, however, in totally abolishing political activism. Human rights organizations exist, though they operate with great difficulty. One tactic used to neutralize the Tunisian League of Human Rights was to pack its meetings with an influx of RCD activists. Another was to encourage "moderates" to desert the "extremists," whom the regime could not control. This tactic virtually paralyzed the LTDH in 1994, when it fell victim to internal power struggles that removed activists like Marzouki from office. Other organizations operate illegally and are consequently vulnerable. However, Tunisian human rights activists enjoy significant support from international NGOs and occasional backing from France and even the United States. Therefore the regime must weigh its sense of security against the political costs of incremental losses of international support.

In May 2006, the regime seemed to be panicking. First the police broke into the office of the head of the Tunisian Bar Association and attacked lawyers protesting a new law that threatened the profession's independence. On May 11, security forces detained the head of the newly formed Syndicate of Journalists for holding a secret meeting. A week later, the police even prevented the family members of a deceased human rights activist from entering the headquarters of the Tunisian League for Human Rights to attend a memorial ceremony in his honor. Then the police detained the Swiss representative of Amnesty International, who was attending a meeting of the Tunisian section, and asked him to leave the country on May 21. A week later, in the presence of foreign guest observers, including Flautre, police physically blocked LTDH delegates from holding their congress.[35]

Fortunately for the opposition, Tunisia is too close to France for its suffering to be ignored totally. Online and in France, various opposition groups publicly engage in exile politics and support Tunisian human rights. The ruling party insulates the masses from the small elite of human rights activists at home, however, and the only serious threat to the regime would be if internal dissidents within the ruling apparatus were to join forces with those activists.

Deviating from Tunisian Traditions?

In terms of repression indicators, the Ben Ali regime holds its own against other regimes in the Arab region that routinely torture political suspects and keep some of their opponents under lock and key. As noted earlier, its ratio of political prisoners per 100,000 population roughly matches that of Egypt, Kuwait, and Morocco, and even exceeds Syria's. Its press is among the dullest and most conformist in the region. This dismal human rights record is further darkened by the degree to which the Ben Ali regime has deviated from the country's established norms. Serious observers argue, however, that the Ben Ali regime did not significantly deviate from Bourguiba's norms.

In 1956, Bourguiba became prime minister of independent Tunisia and proceeded with the full support of his Neo-Destour Party, which in turn controlled an elected national assembly, to establish a presidential regime. He then reorganized the party to ensure his personal authority. In 1974 he had the Tunisian constitution amended to award him a life-long presidency.

Like Ben Ali, Bourguiba murdered or physically intimidated his opponents, even as far back as 1937 when his Neo-Destour Party battled and outflanked the old Destour forces of Abdelaziz Thaalbi. When a split occurred in 1955 between Bourguiba, who favored independence in cooperation with France, and his erstwhile collaborator and party organizer, Salah Ben Youssef, who preferred a more radical pan-Arab approach, the result was virtual civil war. The new Tunisian government, with French military assistance, cracked down on the Youssefists in the early months of independence, and captured Youssefists suffered miserable fates in Tunisian jails unless they were shot on the spot or hanged in a public square. The estimated 900 deaths in 1955–1956 were double those of Tunisians killed or executed in their independence struggle against France (1934–1954). One of Bourguiba's "enforcers" supervised the execution of Salah Ben Youssef in a Frankfurt hotel room in 1961. Apparently, too, trade union leader Ahmed Tlili and former planning minister Ahmed Ben Salah were subsequently targeted.[36]

Bourguiba's regime was torturing students returning from the Middle East as early as 1963 to preserve Tunisians from infectious Arab ideologies such as Baathism. Then in 1968, it was the turn of homegrown leftists. The state security court convicted 130 students and young graduates, although many had apparently already suffered "torture with unheard of cruelty" so as "to terrorize them out of any desire for contestation."[37] The treatment may have been extended to hundreds of students arrested in the early 1970s. Then in the 1980s, it was the turn of the Islamists. Ever more senile, Bourguiba called back his "enforcer" to be assistant director of the ruling party and demanded capital punishment for Rashid Ghannouchi, the Islamist leader, and others among the scores of Islamists on trial.

Instead of deviating from Bourguiba's legacy, Ben Ali could be viewed as rectifying it and preventing the excessive punishments Bourguiba sought when, as prime minister in 1987, Ben Ali conspired with party director Hédi Baccouche and others to retire the old man from office. As president in 1988, he released the hundred or so Islamists whom Bourguiba had jailed. He also intended to curb some of Bourguiba's other excesses. Close associates of Ben Ali insisted at the time, for instance, that the president had no desire to emulate Bourguiba's personality cult. Rather, he advocated freedom of the press and other measures of political liberalization in 1988. The public media were deplorable in Bourguiba's final years: the daily television news opened with archives of Bourguiba delivering speeches in the 1950s and 1960s before showing a few current scenes of a doddering old man being adulated by his courtiers.

By the early 1990s, however, Ben Ali was practicing the full Bourguiba, cult and all. The presidency grew at the expense of the ministries, the council of ministers, and the prime minister, for the youthful-looking president, computer at hand, took active control of the administration. Instead of breaking with the one-party system, he encouraged the ruling party to grow even more, from roughly 1 million members in 1986 to 2 million in 1997, fleshing out some of the older leadership with new cadres.[38] The party continued as it had during much of Bourguiba's reign to be an appendage of government administration, with hierarchical controls extending in parallel with the ministry of the interior down to the local level. It did not serve as a recruitment channel for political leadership since ministers tended to be recruited for their technocratic organizational abilities and then parachuted into party command posts rather than the reverse. In Bourguiba's time, ministers tended to have had more of a political background in the party, trade union, or student union than those recruited after 1987.[39] But Bourguiba's party, too, had been largely transformed into an administrative apparatus by 1958, two years after independence.[40] The exercise of personal power, moreover, tended to transform the political elite into insecure individual courtiers seeking the presidential monarch's favor. In this sense, little has changed between the Bourguiba and the Ben Ali periods.

By engineering constitutional change in 2002 to permit him to keep holding office, Ben Ali even seemed to be competing with Bourguiba's legacy of a life-long presidency.[41] Indeed, if it is true that Ben Ali has cancer and is grooming his wife to succeed him, he may outdo Bourguiba's excesses.[42] Ben Ali's cult of personality is an even greater deviation from Tunisian traditions because he is no Bourguiba; when history repeats, the second time has to be a farce. What most Tunisians could accept of their founding father, they can hardly accept of an upstart ex-military intelligence officer with limited political experience. Ben Ali lacks Bourguiba's historical legitimacy.

The Ben Ali regime's economic corruption, moreover, has exceeded all Bourguibian boundaries. True, Bourguiba built palaces—although not removing all of his neighbors for security reasons as Ben Ali did in extending the perimeters of his Carthage palace. True, some of Bourguiba's wife's family and friends may have made commercial mistakes. One of them, for instance, was chairman of the Union of International Banks, which had become an insolvent state enterprise by 1986 when he was fired and imprisoned—at about the time Bourguiba divorced his wife.[43] These stories pale, however, against the lurid tales of the corruption of the "seven families" surrounding Ben Ali. Some reports even suggest that Ben Ali has lost control of the battle among those family clans.[44]

Undermining the State

The question of how deviant the Tunisian regime may be should not be decided by comparisons between Ben Ali and Bourguiba in his later years but rather by how much each deviated from Tunisian political traditions. Both leaders insisted on a state of law but proceeded to undermine it.

The state building of the precolonial and colonial periods may have been incomplete, but Tunisia's state tradition is at least as strong as Morocco's or Egypt's and arguably stronger, given the degree to which a protracted nationalist struggle steeped Tunisia's elites in the colonizer's political culture. Bourguiba built upon this legacy in his golden years of political pedagogy (1955–1965). After his first heart attack in 1965, a politically debilitating succession crisis ensued that lasted over two decades. The critical turning point came in 1971–1972, when Bourguiba—had he not been a megalomaniac—might have accepted reforms within the ruling party that would have institutionalized pluralistic competition. Instead, he purged the liberals with the help of organized labor, got himself elected president for life (boasting in the process about himself being a miracle that happens only once in a millennium), and then suppressed the major trade union.

Ben Ali's autocracy is a logical continuation of Bourguiba's. But Ben Ali's deviations from the rule of law are excessive for several reasons. International public opinion is no longer as tolerant of developmental despots as it was in the 1960s. Echoes of disapproval in turn influence elite public opinion inside Tunisia, leading to greater disaffection, just as opposition from within receives more support abroad than in Bourguiba's day. The Tunisian middle classes have vastly expanded from a core of fewer than 5,000 university-educated professionals in 1965, and they are in constant contact with Europe, as are the lower classes.[45] Tunisia also enjoys a rich legacy of nongovernmental organizations and political infrastructure, social capital that is currently wasting away under centralized party command.

The costs to the state budget of developmental dictatorship are greater than they used to be. On the positive side, prudent economic policies have kept inflation in check while spurring growth and substantially reducing, although not eliminating, poverty. The state banks, however, have huge port-folios of nonperforming loans that stubbornly persist despite vast sums spent each year to clean them up.[46] Many of the loans are to the regime's wealthy retainers. Corruption, too, deters private investment. Tunisia is extremely competent in getting more than its share of aid from the EU, but its ability to attract foreign direct investment is limited by business perceptions of a vora-cious local mafia. Consequently, unable to attract enough investment, Tunisia takes on more debt in the race to grow fast enough to keep unemployment under control. Although debt service has not reached the level that obliged a major economic stabilization agreement with the International Monetary Fund in 1986, the need for continued growth may keep nudging up Tunisia's debt level ratios. In 2005, the value of the short- and long-term external debt amounted to 79 percent of gross national income, higher than any other country's in the Middle East and North Africa (including Turkey) except for Syria and Lebanon.[47]

Support from the United States and the World Bank helps Tunisia stay afloat. The World Bank promised loans worth at least $200–$300 million annually for the period from July 2004 to June 2008 if Tunisia pursued struc-tural reform or $100 million if reforms stalled. Tunisia managed to obtain a loan to develop its Internet capabilities in preparation for the World Summit on the Information Society that it hosted in 2005 (on behalf of the United Nations and the International Telecommunications Union) to discuss man-agement of the Internet. It gained this privilege after being praised by the Internet Corporation for Assigned Names and Numbers for democratizing the local Internet![48] No new loans from the World Bank were forthcoming in 2006 and 2007, however, except $66.8 million toward a Tunis sewage project.[49]

If corruption has not yet, as in the nineteenth century, undermined Tunisian state finances, the police and the judiciary do seem to be unraveling. Torturing prisoners has become routine. While at a Geneva hospital in 2001, a former minister of the interior narrowly escaped arrest for the torture of a former Tunisian victim then residing in Switzerland.[50] In the opposition press, one also reads that the police are incapable of doing routine duties because they are so caught up in political surveillance and other tasks. There is a dan-ger, in fact, that the police may displace the ruling party as the focus of control, as happened to the Baath Party in Iraq. Within the party there are echoes of disturbances at the local level, such as the arrest in 1998 of a Central Com-mittee member who was mayor of Kasserine (in the relatively neglected south-western part of the country) and had criticized government policy.[51]

The most spectacular sign of state breakdown occurred in 2001, when Tunis civil circuit chief judge Moktar Yahyahoui wrote a letter to the president denouncing the total absence of independence of the Tunisian judiciary. The correspondent for *Le Monde* went so far as to write of "Ben Ali's lost battle," now that the true state of the regime's foundations lay revealed.[52] Indeed, the human rights opposition seems bolder of late, sensing a weakening of authority. Even the cowed and quiescent press showed some signs of life in 2004, when a number of journalists from *La Presse* and *Essahafa* wrote an open letter to the prime minister and other government officials complaining of "a return in force of the policy of censorship and of pressure on their writings" and of their newspapers' editorial practices.[53] The investigative activities of independent Tunisian journalists during the October 2004 elections also indicated a growing impatience with fake competition.

These presidential and parliamentary elections did little to strengthen the regime. As in previous presidential elections, Ben Ali had token opposition and won 94.8 percent of the vote (with a participation rate of 74 percent of the eligible voters). Independent journalists observed that the president's campaign virtually monopolized the media, receiving 77 percent of the minutes accorded by the broadcasting media and 92 percent of the surface of the written press. Two of Ben Ali's presidential contenders, moreover, expressed their support for the incumbent president and were permitted prime time, whereas afternoon prayers interrupted the third opponent's broadcast. Little time or space remained for any of the parliamentary candidates, and most time was allocated to those of the ruling RCD. Although the opposition did manage to be heard, "in several cases the MDS [Mouvement Démocratique Socialiste, the largest of the opposition parties] and independent candidates announced their support for President Ben Ali instead of presenting their own programs."[54]

Another source of embarrassment for the regime was the World Summit on the Information Society. How could a regime so unfriendly to the free flow of information be an appropriate host to such a gathering? The International Freedom of Expression Exchange (IFEX)—an international consortium of NGOs such as Article 19 (named after Article 19 in the Universal Declaration of Human Rights), the International Federation of Journalists, and Reporters Sans Frontières—wrote an open letter to UN secretary general Kofi Annan urging the United Nations and member states to change the venue of the world summit unless minimal rights could be guaranteed, including those of local as well as international media.[55] From January 14 to 19, 2005, when the IFEX fact-finding mission was in Tunisia, the authorities unblocked some websites, but further monitoring demonstrated systematic filtering based on an American software program. A careful study published on the eve of the summit showed that the government blocked not only the obviously political sites such as Kalima, an online opposition newspaper, but virtually all "anonymizer" sites from which Tunisians could engage in undetected surfing.[56]

Indeed, the human rights situation deteriorated in 2006. In a six-part series about Tunisia's "political mafia," one Tunisian wrote that "Tunisia has turned back to the German Gestapo of Hitler's era. Criminal networks have been formed to shut off all publicity or information because they are aware of the danger that weapons of confrontation represent: they have banned the press, have restructured it and organized it, forbidden any publicity from opposition elements, and repressed all free thought, reflection, and political activities."[57]

The series of articles observed "signs pointing to the collapse" of the regime but expressed little confidence in Tunisia's divided and impotent opposition parties. One sign of the regime's vulnerability, more reminiscent of the Soviet Union than Nazi Germany, was instructions given to the national soccer team training in Switzerland not to talk to the foreign press. Of greater political import, but expressing the same closed mentality, the authorities sabotaged a seminar of international NGOs in September 2006. It was meant to prepare the International Conference on Employment and the Right to Work in the Euro-Mediterranean Region to be held in Berlin in 2007. The European and Arab delegates arrived to discover that there were no longer any hotel reservations, despite arrangements made by the Friedrich Ebert Stiftung, a German foundation that had earlier worked with Tunisia on an EU-sponsored project to develop trade unions. Even the Amilcar Hotel, owned by the Tunisian General Union of Labor, was closed to the delegates despite available space. Evidently the authorities had taken umbrage at the presence of leading Tunisian human rights activists protected by the Europeans.[58]

Policy Implications

Tunisia, a well-known development model in the 1950s and 1960s, could again become a modern showcase, albeit not on its present course of mixing bogus privatization and cosmetic reform with the standard practices of a police state. For policymakers interested in democratizing the Arab and Muslim world, Tunisia deserves serious attention because it offers the best prospects for success: a relatively large middle class, social capital, political infrastructure, prudent economic management, and relatively efficient administration.[59] Although it is still in practice a one-party state, grassroots party organizations could take on new life if the rule of law came to be respected. It remains a relatively powerful state, although corruption and a brutal disrespect for human rights are corroding its strength.

There is little that the United States alone can do to halt the deterioration, but the European Union is also committed to human rights and democratic reform through partnership agreements with its southern neighbors. The two must work together despite their differences; indeed, a common European commitment to better governance in Tunisia would also serve to strengthen its own union. Whether or not Tunisia is the most egregious violator of human rights in the region, it is the most promising target for reform. Not only do its internal social and economic conditions augur well for democracy, but with fewer economic or strategic rents than its neighbors, the country is less able to derail a common approach by the outside powers. Combined EU-U.S. efforts could also help to heal the divisions within the Atlantic alliance over other countries such as Iraq, where the stakes are higher.

There are some signs that the European Union may be reevaluating its relationship with Tunisia. Shortly after Flautre's mission, the European Parliament passed a resolution regretting that "the situation as regards freedoms and human rights in Tunisia is still a cause for concern" and calling for Tunisia to cooperate with the EU and the United Nations on a number of fronts, including agreeing to a visit by the UN special rapporteur on the independence of judges and lawyers. Noting that Tunisia held the presidency of the Euro-Mediterranean Parliamentary Assembly, the European Parliament also called for "better cooperation" between the assembly and the Tunisian presidency "in terms of respecting human rights."[60] Although the parliament has little power over the EU executive, much less its constituent states, the countries that have some influence on Tunisia, such as France, Germany, and Italy, may use the resolution to put more pressure on Tunisia and to encourage the parliament's human rights committee to continue its fine work. The United States, too, could be more responsive to the EU parliament's concerns and also to those expressed by its own State Department human rights section.

Working together, Europe and the United States could attempt to persuade Ben Ali that his place in history lies in presiding over a genuinely competitive succession process when his term expires in 2009. Meanwhile, the Europeans and Americans should continue to support those few genuinely autonomous

NGOs that continue to defy dictatorial and arbitrary rule.[61] Since the EU currently enjoys greater moral authority than the United States in the region, it should be especially persistent in defending the human rights movement within Tunisia, as its moral authority may serve to curb some of the excesses of the police. Awareness of strong outside support may in turn further embolden the domestic opposition.

Tunisia could regain the moral high ground that it occupied during its first ten years of independence under a healthy Bourguiba, but this time under leadership constrained by stronger institutions and the rule of law. It could again become a model for development and political change in Africa and in the Arab world were the current regime to be exposed to gentle but focused and sustained international pressure.

Unfortunately, the United States sends the wrong signal by stationing a regional bureau of the Middle East Partnership Initiative in the country. Although any liberation of Tunisia is likely to be accompanied by a torrent of anti-American political rhetoric, a new dialogue with aspiring Tunisian democrats (including the Islamists) could also offer both parties an opportunity to recover their positive political traditions. If the United States were ready to face up to a Middle East with fewer friendly repressive allies, Tunisian civil society (and Tunisian officials embarrassed by the excesses of the police state) could positively respond to the U.S. commitment to freedom and democracy.

Notes

1. *The Compact Edition of the Oxford English Dictionary*, II (Oxford, 1971), 2566.

2. An alternate meaning for "rogue" is "one who is of a mischievous disposition," as in William Shakespeare's "Ah, you sweet little Rogue" in *Henry IV* (1597), or as another dramatist wrote in 1672, "It's a pretty little rogue; she is my mistress." Ibid.

3. Michel Camau and Vincent Geisser, *Le syndrome autoritaire: Politique en Tunisie de Bourguiba à Ben Ali* (Paris, 2003), 18.

4. Ibid., 204–205.

5. Ahmed Bennour, personal communication, Paris, July 16, 2004. Bennour also observed that the budget for the Ministry of the Interior had increased from 170 million Tunisian dinars in 1984 to about 660 million in 2004.

6. U.S. State Department, "Tunisia," in *2005 Country Reports on Human Rights Practices* (Washington, D.C., March 8, 2006), www.state.gov/g/drl/rls/hrrpt/2005/61700.htm.

7. Ibid.

8. Ibid.

9. Human Rights Watch, "Tunisia," in *World Report 2003* (New York, 2003), www. hrw.org/wr2k3/mideast8.html.

10 . Hédi Yahmed, "Hal yejib islah es-sujoun fi Tunis?" ("Do Tunisia's Prisons Need to Be Reformed?"), *Haqa'iq/Réalités* (Washington, D.C., December 12, 2002), cited by U.S. State Department, "Tunisia," in *2003 Country Reports on Human Rights Practices* (February 25, 2004), www.state.gov/g/drl/rls/hrrpt/2003/27939.htm. See also Sami Ben Gharbia, "Tunisian Prison Map" (2006), kitab.nl/tunisianprisonersmap; "La carte des prisons tunisiennes," *Tunisnews* (October 4, 2006), www.tunisnews.net/5octobre 06f.htm. Both Tunisian sources cite "Le système carcéral en chiffres," *Le Monde diplomatique* (June 2003), 25, www.monde-diplomatique.fr/2003/06/A/10218. Tunisia came fourth, after the United States, Russia, and South Africa, but ahead of China and Israel, in the number of prisoners per 100,000 inhabitants.

11. Amnesty International, "Tunisia: Releases of Scores of Political Prisoners Is a Positive Step" (London, November 4, 2004), web.amnesty.org/library/Index/ENG MDE300092004?open&of=ENG-TUN; "Amnesty International Report 2001: Tunisia" (New York, 2001), web.amnesty.org/web/ar2001.nsf/webmepcountries/TUNISIA? OpenDocument.

12. On the eve of Ben Ali's visit to Washington, Human Rights Watch stated, "Most of Tunisia's 500 political prisoners are suspected Islamists who were convicted after unfair trials on nonviolent charges such as membership in a political organization outlawed by the government." Human Rights Watch, "Tunisia: Long-Term Solitary Confinement of Political Prisoners," Report XVI (July 2004), 4, hrw.org/reports/2004/tunisia0704/.

13. For the figures from the International Association for the Support of Political Prisoners, see State Department, "Tunisia," *2005 Country Reports*. See also Chris Heffelfinger, "Jailed Extremists Pardoned in Tunisia," *Terrorism Focus*, III (Washington, D.C., February 28, 2006), jamestown.org/terrorism/news/article.php?articleid=2369914.

14. Human Rights Watch, "Tunisia: Free Jailed Website Moderator" (March 17, 2006), hrw.org/english/docs/2006/03/16/tunisi13005.htm.

15. Amnesty International's 2005 annual report estimated Egypt's political prisoners to be in the thousands, for a population seven times Tunisia's; Kuwait's 29 known political prisoners for a population well under one-tenth of Tunisia's gives a slightly higher ratio. See "Amnesty International Report 2005" (New York, 2005), web.amnesty. org/report2005/index-eng. With triple Tunisia's population, Morocco had prosecuted some 1,500 of the 3,000 suspects arrested after the Casablanca bombings of May 2003. Amnesty reports that substantial numbers of them were imprisoned, again filling the jails after earlier releases of most of Morocco's thousands of political activists jailed in the 1960s and 1970s. See Amnesty International, "Annual Report 2006" (New York, 2006), web.amnesty.org/report2006/mar-summary-eng. For Syrian figures, see Joshua Landis, "Is Syria Holding Fewer Political Prisoners than

Any Other Major Middle Eastern Country?" (August 11, 2004), faculty-staff.ou.edu/ L/Joshua.M.Landis-1/syriablog/2004/08/is-syria-holding-fewer-political.htm. Not included in the Syrian count are perhaps 200 Lebanese and numerous Palestinian and Jordanian prisoners.

16. Human Rights Watch, "Tunisia: Long-Term Solitary Confinement," 10.

17. The concerned functionary, Zakaria Ben Mustapha, a former minister and mayor of Tunis, had made an earlier investigation in 1995, when prisons were probably at their worst, and reported that they fully met international standards. See Human Rights Watch, "Tunisia: Long-Term Solitary Confinement," 13, citing "La situation dans les prisons répond aux 'normes' internationales, selon une commission d'enquête," Agence France-Presse (August 15, 1995).

18. "Prisons: Des mesures immédiates," *Haqa'iq/Réalités* (February 20, 2003), www.realites.com.tn.

19. Human Rights Watch, "Tunisia: Long-Term Solitary Confinement," 35.

20. State Department, "Tunisia," in *2003 Country Reports.*

21. Abdelqahhar, "Limogeague et aggression d'Abderrahmane Tlili: La fin d'une entente mafieuse," *L'Audace,* CIII (September 2003), web.archive.org/web/ 20030925155018/http://www.laudace.fr/#6. According to this account, Tlili's original crime was to have been overheard on a tapped phone conversation promising one of his mistresses that she would become Tunisia's "first lady." Other accounts say he had asked Ben Ali for a government of national union and for *alternance.* Ben Ali dismissed him from his position as head of the Civil Aviation Authority, one of a succession of parastatal management positions he had occupied since the 1980s. Rather than quietly accepting political disgrace, Tlili retaliated by threatening to reveal documents implicating Ben Ali's family in various schemes. This article in *L'Audace* estimates that Tlili stole an amount equivalent to one-fifth of Tunisia's national debt ($12.6 billion at the end of 2002) over the years.He was tried for generating projects for friends worth about $4 million and for having foreign bank accounts and real estate. In April 2004, he was sentenced to nine years in jail and fined 52 million dinars.

22. TUNeZINE (www.tunezine.com) stopped publishing on March 14, 2006, but its website points to other opposition press sources online, notably www.reveil tunisien.org and www.tunisnews.net.

23. Hélène Flautre, "Compte-rendu de la visite d'Hélène Flautre en Tunisie des 26–27 mai 2006" (May 29, 2006), www.flautre.net/spip.php?article241.

24. Hamed Ibrahimi, "Une presse asphyxiée, des journalistes harcelés," *Le Monde diplomatique* (February 1997), 4–5; Kamel Labidi, "How Tunisia Slid off Its Progressive Course," *Christian Science Monitor* (August 18, 1997).

25. Its long-retired editor revisited *La Presse* in 1998. He told me that some of his former associates were complaining to him, some of them in tears, about being professionally humiliated by some of the newer recruits. Personal interview, Tunis, July 1998.

26. Yahmed, "Hal yejib islah es-sujoun fi Tunis?"

27. "'L'affaire Hédi Yahmed.' Les points sur les 'i,'" *Haqa'iq/Réalités* (January 9, 2003), www.realites.com.tn. For Yahmed's version, see "The Article That Forced Hedi Yahmed to Flee His Country," *RAP21 Newsletter*, XVI (January 5, 2003), www.rap21. org/article1153.html?var_recherche=Hedi+Yahmed. Both articles are cited by Human Rights Watch, "Tunisia: Long-Term Solitary," 15–16.

28. *La Presse* (April 20, 1997), 3.

29. "Médias sous surveillance: Rapport de la LTDH-Tunisie Mai 2004," final section transcribed in *L'Audace*, CXII (June 2004), 24. The report also observes that neighboring Algeria has 1.3 Internet cafés per 10,000 inhabitants compared to Tunisia's 0.3.

30. States Department, "Tunisia," in *2003 Country Reports*; Human Rights Watch, "Tunisia 2002."

31. OpenNet Initiative, "Internet Filtering in Tunisia 2005" (November 2005), 7, www.opennetinitiative.net/studies/tunisia/ONI_Tunisia_Country_Study.pdf.

32. Six youths and a minor were arrested in Zarzis in late 2002 on grounds of "forming a band with the object of preparing armed strikes [*attentats*]." They claimed simply to be surfing the net for information about the political situation in the Middle East. Jailed and originally condemned to sentences ranging from nineteen to twenty-six years in jail, they gained slight reductions, down to an average of thirteen years on a prison farm, on appeal in July 2004. Florence Beaugé, "Six jeunes internautes devant la cour d'appel de Tunis," *Le Monde* (July 6, 2004), 3; José Garçon, "Six internautes tunisiens dans la toile de Ben Ali," *Libération* (July 7, 2004), cited in *L'Audace*, CXIII-CXIV (July–August 2004); International League of Human Rights, "Tunisie: Condamnation des 'internautes de Zarzis' à de lourdes peines au terme d'un procès entaché d'irrégularités" (July 7, 2004), www.fidh.org/article.php3?id_article=1558.

33. By one count, Tunisia had 7,500 NGOs in 2001–2002, or 53.6 organizations per 100,000 inhabitants, one of the higher densities in the Arab world. See Salim Nasr, "Arab Civil Societies and Public Governance Reforms: An Analytic Framework and Overview," paper presented at the United Nations Development Programme Conference on Good Governance for Development in the Arab Countries (Dead Sea, Jordan, February 6–7, 2005),www.arabgov-initiative.org/publications/civilsociety/arab-civil society.pdf.

34. Béatrice Hibou, "Domination and Control in Tunisia: Economic Levers for the Exercise of Authoritarian Power," *Review of African Political Economy*, CVIII (June 2006), 188–189.

35. Flautre, "Compte-rendu de la visite"; Arabic Network for Human Rights Information, "Tunisia: A Hysterical Escalation of Repression" (May 23, 2006), www.hrinfo. net/en/reports/2006/pr0523.shtml.

36. Souhayr Belhassen, "Les legs bourguibiens de la répression," in Michel Camau and Vincent Geisser (eds.), *Habib Bourguiba: La trace et l'héritage* (Paris, 2004), 392.

On the treatment of Youssefists in 1955–1956, see pages 395–396. Belhassen is a veteran journalist and vice president of the LTDH.

37. Ibid., 397.

38. Camau and Geisser, *Le syndrome autoritaire*, 181, 217–218.

39. Ibid., 194–195.

40. Clement Henry Moore, *Tunisia since Independence: The Dynamics of One-Party Rule* (Berkeley, 1965), 113–114.

41. The constitutional amendment passed in May 2002 abolished the term limit and extended the eligibility of candidates to seventy-five years of age.

42. For a summary of recent speculation, see "Comment Zine El-Abidine Ben Ali a été dépossédé du pouvoir," *Libération* (August 14, 2003), cited by Tamurth.net (September 7, 2003), ww.tamurth.net/article.php3?id_article=390.

43. For an analysis of the Union of International Banks, see Clement M. Henry, *The Mediterranean Debt Crescent* (Gainesville, 1996), 181–183.

44. When a French banker's yacht stolen in Corsica in May 2006 reappeared in Sidi Bou Said, with Ben Ali's wife's nephew Imad Trabelsi at the helm, the online journal reveiltunis.org interpreted the event as one more illustration of the president's family troubles. See "La famille de Ben Ali en eaux troubles," *Reveil Tunisien* (June 14, 2006), www.reveiltunisien.org/article.php3?id_article=2218. For a background discussion of the Trabelsi family's excesses before the yacht scandal, see Hamime, "La mafia politique tunisienne enlisée dans les affaires juteuses," *Reveil Tunisien* (April 12, 2006), www.reveiltunisien.org/article.php3?id_article=2149.

45. Camau and Geisser, *Le syndrome autoritaire*, 163.

46. Despite three World Bank Economic Competitiveness Adjustment Loans (ECAL) designed to clean up the banking system, nonperforming loans constituted 24 percent of the country's loan portfolio in 2004, up from 22 percent in 2000. See World Bank, *World Development Indicators 2006* (Washington, D.C., 2006). A fourth ECAL, already promised in the World Bank's 2004 Country Assistance Strategy, went into effect in 2005. The 2004 Country Assistance Strategy called for nonperforming loans to be reduced to below 17 percent by 2008. See World Bank Group, "Memorandum of the President of the International Bank for Reconstruction and Development to the Executive Directors on a Country Assistance Strategy for the Republic of Tunisia," Report 28791-TUN (June 3, 2004), 39.

47. World Bank, *World Development Indicators 2006* (Washington, D.C., 2006).

48. Reporters Sans Frontiéres, "Internet under Surveillance 2004: Tunisia" (2004), www.rsf.org/article.php3?id_article=10768.

49. World Bank, "Tunisia: World Bank Supports Wastewater Treatment Services" (July 6, 2006), web.worldbank.org/WBSITE/EXTERNAL/NEWS/0,,contentMDK: 20984909~pagePK:34370~piPK:34424~theSitePK:4607,00.html.

50. With the help of Track Impunity Always (TRIAL), a Swiss human rights NGO, the victim attempted to have former interior minister Abdallah Kallel prosecuted in

the Swiss court system. Because Kallel fled, this prosecution was no longer possible, but the Tunisian residing in Switzerland then attempted to mount a civil lawsuit against him. See Fati Mansour, "Les audaces juridiques d'un réfugié décidé à faire payer ses bourreaux tunisiens: Une victime traîne l'etat tunisien devant un tribunal suisse," *Le Temps* (Geneva) (October 20, 2004), cited in *L'Audace*, CXVIII (December 2004), 12–13. On June 9, 2005, TRIAL, supporting the principle of Swiss jurisdiction in this matter, announced that the hearing was held in the absence of the Tunisian government defendant and that the Court of First Instance would issue a verdict. See TRIAL, "La plainte contre l'ancien ministre de l'interieur Abdallah Kallel va de l'avant" (Geneva, June 9, 2005), www.tunisnews.net/9juin05.htm.

51. Camau and Geisser, *Le syndrome autoritaire*, 360.

52. Florence Beaugé, "Le combat perdu du président Ben Ali," *Le Monde* (July 21, 2001).

53. Reporters without Borders, "Tunisia—2005 Annual Report" (Paris, 2006), www.rsf.org/article.php3?id_article=13314.

54. These figures come from a study conducted by thirteen independent Tunisian journalists, including Abdellatif Fourati, Sihem Bensedrine, and Souhayr Belhassen, that was sponsored by International Media Support, the Center for Media Policy and Development, the LTDH, the Tunisian Association for Women Democrats, and the National Council for Liberties in Tunisia. See "Monitoring the Coverage of the October 2004 Legislative and Presidential Elections in Tunisia" (November 2004), www.i-m-s.dk/media/pdf/Monitoring%20the%20coverage.pdf. See also Larbi Chouikha, "L'Opposition à Ben Ali et les elections de 2004," in *L'Année du Maghreb 2004* (Paris, 2006), 361–373.

55. IFEX Tunisia Monitoring Group, "Tunisia: Freedom of Expression under Siege" (February 2005), www.ifex.org/en/content/view/full/64665/.

56. OpenNet Initiative, "Internet Filtering in Tunisia in 2005," 10, 14, 16.

57. Hamime, "Tunisie: La mafia politique et les signes annonciateurs de la chute," part III, *Reveil Tunisien* (March 1, 2006), www.reveiltunisien.org/article.php3?id_article=2101. Author's translation.

58. Vanya Walker-Leigh, "Tunisia under Fire for Ban on NGO Meet," Inter Press Service (September 18, 2006), ipsnews.net/news.asp?idnews=34757. See also Omar Mestiri, "La Benalie 'terre d'accueil et d'ouverture,'" *Kalima*, XLV (September 3, 2006).

59. As Mokhtar Trifi, the current president of the LTDH, recently suggested. See Anne Applebaum, "A Good Place to Have Aided Democracy," *Washington Post* (February 13, 2007), A21.

60. European Parliament, "European Parliament Resolution on Tunisia," P6-TA-2006-0269 (Strasbourg, June 15, 2006), www.europarl.europa.eu/sides/getDoc.do?Type=TA&Reference=P6-TA-2006-0269&language=EN. An earlier version of the resolution considered "that the implementation of all these reforms must be treated as a priority of the EU-Tunisia partnership and must constitute a fundamental element in the development of relations between the European Union and Tunisia; considers, in

that regard, that if Tunisia does not act in accordance with this agenda, the Council and the Commission will have to take appropriate action in the context of the Association Agreement." See European Parliament, "European Parliament Resolution on Tunisia," B6-0355/2006 (Strasbourg, June 12, 2006), www.europarl.europa.eu/sides/getDoc.do?objRefId=120192&language=EN.

61. See the two concluding paragraphs of David L. Mack, "Democracy in Muslim Countries: The Tunisian Case," *National Strategy Forum Review*, IV (Summer 2005), www.nationalstrategy.com/Summer.2005.final.pdf.

Contributors

MARGARITA M. BALMACEDA is associate professor at the John C. Whitehead School of Diplomacy and International Relations, Seton Hall University, and an associate of the Davis Center for Russian Studies at Harvard University and the Harvard Ukrainian Research Institute. She was coeditor of *Independent Belarus* (2002), and editor of *On the Edge: The Ukrainian-Central European-Russian Security Triangle* (2000). Balmaceda was a Fulbright lecturer at the Belarusian State University in Minsk, where she taught courses on international relations and energy security.

MARY CAPRIOLI is assistant professor of political science at the University of Minnesota, Duluth. She has published numerous articles on rogue states and other subjects in the *Journal of Conflict Resolution, International Studies Quarterly*, and *Journal of Peace Research*.

PRISCILLA A. CLAPP, recently retired from a thirty-year career in the U.S. diplomatic service, serves as vice president for governmental affairs with Safe Ports, LLC, a company building integrated security systems in major international ports and maritime supply chains. During her career with the U.S. State Department and Foreign Service, Clapp served as chief of mission at the U.S. embassy in Burma (1999–2002), deputy chief of mission at the U.S. embassy in South Africa (1993–1996), principal deputy assistant secretary of state for refugee programs (1989–1993), political counselor in the U.S. embassy in

Moscow (1986–1988), and chief of political-military affairs in the U.S. embassy in Japan (1981–1985). Her books include *Managing an Alliance: The Politics of U.S.-Japanese Relations*, with I. M. Destler and others (1976), *Bureaucratic Politics and Foreign Policy*, with Morton Halperin (1974, 2006); and *U.S.-Japanese Relations in the 1970's*, with Morton Halperin (1974).

YI FENG is dean and the Luther Lee Chair of Government at the School of Politics and Economics, Claremont Graduate University. He wrote *Democracy, Governance and Economic Performance: Theory and Evidence* (2003) and edited *China's Financial Market Reform: Progress, Problems and Prospects* (2000). He is editor of *International Interactions*.

GREGORY GLEASON teaches international relations and administration at the University of New Mexico. He is the author of *Markets and Politics in Central Asia* (2003), *Central Asian States: Discovering Independence* (1996), and *Federalism and Nationalism: The Struggle for Republican Rights in the USSR* (1991).

JOHN R. HEILBRUNN is assistant professor at the Colorado School of Mines. He is a research associate of the Centre d'Etude d'Afrique Noire at the University of Bordeaux. He is the author of *Markets, Profits and Power: The Politics of Business in Benin and Togo* (1996).

CLEMENT HENRY is professor of government and Middle East studies at the University of Texas at Austin. His most recent books are *The Politics of Islamic Finance* (2004), coedited with Rodney Wilson, and *Globalization and the Politics of Development in the Middle East* (2001), coauthored with Robert Springborg. He wrote *The Mediterranean Debt Crescent: Money and Power in Algeria, Egypt, Morocco, Tunisia, and Turkey* (1996), and coauthored or coedited *Oil in the New World Order* (1995) and *Maghreb et Maitrise Technologique* (1995).

DAVID W. LESCH is professor of Middle East history in the department of history and director of the Middle East concentration in the International Studies Program at Trinity University, San Antonio, Texas. Among his publications are *The New Lion of Damascus: Bashar al-Asad and Modern Syria* (2005); *The Middle East since 1945*, volumes 14 and 15 of the *History in Dispute* series (2003); *1979: The Year That Shaped the Modern Middle East* (2001); *The Middle East and the United States: A Historical and Political*

Reassessment (editor, 1996, 1999, 2003, 2006); and *Syria and the United States: Eisenhower's Cold War in the Middle East* (1992).

MARCUS NOLAND is a senior fellow at the Institute for International Economics, Washington, D.C., and an associate of the International Food Policy Research Institute. He was senior economist at the Council of Economic Advisers in the Executive Office of the President of the United States, and has held research or teaching positions at Johns Hopkins University, the University of Southern California, Tokyo University, Saitama University, the University of Ghana, the Korea Development Institute, and the East-West Center. With numerous publications to his credit, Noland's most recent books are *Famine in North Korea: Markets, Aid, and Reform*, with Stephan Haggard (2007); *Korea after Kim Jong-il* (2004); *Industrial Policy in an Era of Globalization: Lessons from Asia*, with Howard Pack (2003); *No More Bashing: Building a New Japan-United States Economic Relationship*, with C. Fred Bergsten and Takatoshi Ito (2001), and *Avoiding the Apocalypse: The Future of the Two Koreas* (2000).

MARTHA BRILL OLCOTT is senior associate at the Carnegie Endowment for International Peace and co-director of the Carnegie Moscow Center Project on Ethnicity and Politics in the former Soviet Union. Olcott specializes in the problems of transitions in Central Asia and the Caucasus as well as the security challenges in the Caspian region more generally. Olcott served on the faculty of Colgate University from 1974 to 2002. She was for five years director of the Central Asian American Enterprise Fund. Prior to her work at the Carnegie Endowment, Olcott served as a special consultant to former secretary of state Lawrence Eagleburger. She is the author and coauthor of many books, including *Central Asia's Second Chance* (2005) and *Getting It Wrong: Regional Cooperation and the Commonwealth of Independent States* (2000).

SAUMIK PAUL is currently pursuing his Ph.D. in economics at the Claremont Graduate University. In addition, he serves as an extended-term consultant for the World Bank.

ROBERT I. ROTBERG is president of the World Peace Foundation and director of the Program on Intrastate Conflict and Conflict Resolution at the Kennedy School of Government, Harvard University. He was professor of political science and history, MIT; academic vice president, Tufts University; and president, Lafayette College. He is the author and editor of numerous books and articles on U.S. foreign policy, Africa, Asia, and the Caribbean, most recently *Building a New Afghanistan* (2007), *A Leadership for Peace: How Edwin Ginn Tried to Change the World* (2007), *Battling Terrorism in the Horn of Africa* (2005), *Crafting the New Nigeria: Confronting the Challenges* (2004), *When States Fail: Causes and Consequences* (2004), *State Failure and State Weakness in a Time of Terror* (2003), *Ending Autocracy, Enabling Democracy: The Tribulations of Southern Africa 1960–2000* (2002), *Peacekeeping and Peace Enforcement in Africa: Methods of Conflict Prevention* (2001), and *Truth v. Justice: The Morality of Truth Commissions* (2000).

PETER F. TRUMBORE is assistant professor of political science at Oakland University in Rochester, Michigan. He has published articles about rogue states and other subjects in *International Studies Quarterly*, the *Journal of Peace Research*, *Irish Studies in International Affairs*, the *European Journal of International Relations*, and the *Journal of Conflict Resolution*.

Index

Surnames starting with "al" or "al-" are alphabetized by the following part of the name.